THE CONCISE
BRITISH FLORA
IN COLOUR

BY W. KEBLE MARTIN

*"O all ye green things upon the earth, bless ye the Lord.
Praise him and magnify him for ever."*

W. KEBLE MARTIN, MA, DSc, FLS

THE CONCISE
BRITISH FLORA
IN COLOUR

with nomenclature edited and revised by Douglas H. Kent

and Foreword by
H.R.H. The Prince Philip, Duke of Edinburgh
KG, PC, KT, GMBE, FRS

EBURY PRESS
AND MICHAEL JOSEPH

First published May 1965
Second Impression (with revisions) June 1965
Third Impression September 1965
Fourth Impression November 1965
Fifth Impression April 1967
Second (revised) edition 1969
Second Impression December 1969
Third Impression June 1971
Fourth Impression October 1972
Third edition 1974
Second Impression 1976
Third Impression 1978
© George Rainbird Ltd 1965, 1969

ISBN 0 7181 1417 5

This book was designed and produced by
GEORGE RAINBIRD LIMITED

36 Park Street, London WIY 4DE

and was printed in Hong Kong

Foreword

I am delighted that Mr Keble Martin's beautiful paintings and drawings of British wild flowers have, at long last, been published.

It represents a life's work and has taken nearly sixty years to complete. Although there are many books of this kind, few of them cover virtually all the British Wild Flowers with such accuracy in the compass of one colourful volume.

The dedicated and painstaking skill which has gone into each plate in order to ensure complete accuracy in colour and detail will, I am sure, make this book invaluable to both amateur and professional botanists. I hope it will also stimulate new interests and bring delight to many thousands of readers.

Contents

Preface to the First Edition

In recent years many illustrated works on the British flora have issued from the press. It may appear at first sight to be superfluous to publish another. But there seem to be good reasons for this. The present work is on a somewhat different scale, comprising as it does some 1480 figures mostly in colour, drawn with all the care of which the draughtsman was capable, over a period of about sixty years. It is an attempt to attain scientific accuracy without losing the attractive appearance of the flowers. Although this work has been such a long while in preparation, an effort has always been made to keep it in touch with changing ideas through contact with leading botanists of each period. The drawings however are in a form in which their sequence could not be altered. With small exceptions this follows that of the National Herbarium at the British Museum, and *The London Catalogue of British Plants*, XIth Edition.

A further reason for desiring publication is that a number of experts have helped by selecting and identifying specimens for these drawings, thus ensuring suitable and accurate material for the purpose. In addition some three hundred of the specimens drawn were sent by a wide circle of botanists. Valuable help, as acknowledged below, has been given in the preparation of the short text, especially in bringing the nomenclature into accord with the Rules of the International Botanical Congress. The production of this work has therefore been very much a combined effort, and it is only fair to all these botanists that the result should be published.

Every figure of these plates was drawn direct from nature. The drawings were first made in the form of pen outlines on small separate sheets. On each sheet the name of the species was recorded, with the date, the place from which the specimen came, and the name of the sender, if any, or of the referee who named it. These sheets form four octavo loose-leaf volumes. We hope they may ultimately be made accessible for reference at the British Museum (Natural History Dept.) by the kindness of the Keeper of Botany.

In building up the plates the draughtsman's aim has been to show an average fragment, with its essential features, and to give each a place in the sun without crowding. He has tried where possible to show white or pale coloured flowers against green foliage, as in the hedge-row, though this was not always possible. These aims involved much patience in rearranging and redrawing. During the years there have always been gaps on the plates, because the necessary specimens could not be obtained. Some of these gaps have waited for twenty or even twenty-five years before being filled. The author's own visits to distant botanical spots have of necessity been rather few and brief. Owing to the pressure of the author's parochial work the specimens received by post sometimes perished. Some species difficult to obtain had to be sent in two or more seasons, but, owing to great kindness and much forbearance shown by correspondents, the gaps were all filled at last.

It was the desire to know the food plants of Lepidoptera that first promoted the effort to identify the plants required. Then the author was studying for his degree in the Botany School at Oxford, under Professor S. H. Vines and Mr A. W. Church. It was Mr Church who specially urged his students to draw whatever they saw under the microscope and started them in the habit of drawing. The desire to help others in recognizing the plants around them led to the idea of this present work. In this the text is short, mentioning for the most part features that cannot be shown effectively in the figures.

It is an amateur work, which was from the beginning treated as a secondary interest and a recreation. For after further training at a Theological College the author was plunged at his own request in the Church work of large industrial parishes, which was happy work, but it left little time indeed for botany. Progress with these drawings was therefore slow and mostly confined to an annual holiday; and yet before 1918 work on the present lines was well under way.

For a few years, from 1921 to 1926, the author was in a small parish, and his work for a neighbouring housing estate had not yet begun. He had more time for this work, and several plates were redrawn. From 1949 he no longer held a benefice. And it happened that in five successive years as a Public Preacher he was in charge of some parish for more than six months in the winter, but had more interrupted engagements in the summer, and several other plates were redrawn.

We should like to make two suggestions about gathering flowers: first that it should be done sparingly, and secondly that collectors should be fully courteous to the owner of enclosed land.

We have tried to take care of the flowers, and only to gather rare species very sparingly or not at all. Often we have hidden them with foliage from less scrupulous fingers. And when leading walks or expeditions of field clubs, we have tried to persuade others to do the same. Unfortunately there was sometimes one in the party, who thought it his special privilege to pick the only specimen seen or even to come back afterwards and do so! It really is important that we should preserve rare and interesting flowers for future generations.

Real botanists understand this. Gathering the flower prevents the casting of seed. Even for drawing these figures we have sometimes been content with two florets from a good spike with an upper and a lower leaf. We have walked miles in mountain mist and rain to restore a small rare plant to its own niche.

We commend botanizing as a means of healthy recreation for young and old. It is an interest that takes us out to the beautiful places of the earth. And if we really know the wild flowers around us at home, the plants almost speak to us of their struggles to grow. This interest stays with us to the end of our pilgrimage. It is not exactly an armchair study. To fulfil it properly we need good boots, a compass and a companion, and must face the thorns and steep places, the dense clouds and sharp mountain thunderstorms or the tides and island crossings. But we take no undue risks. It is good fun and healthy.

We said that valuable help had been given in editing the short text. Mr Douglas Kent, formerly Editor of the *Proceedings of the Botanical Society of the British Isles*, has kindly helped much with it, making many adjustments, especially to the nomenclature, and adding a list of authorities for the names. The brief descriptions are indebted to the earlier Floras. The first pages were written before the publication of the Flora by Messrs Clapham, Tutin and Warburg; but the whole is now doubtless indebted in greater or less degree to this latter work. We gratefully acknowledge the debt, and commend that work to all who wish to make a more serious study of the British Flora. We have followed Mr H. W. Pugsley's

Prodromus of the British Hieracia and his *Revision of Euphrasiae*, both of them published in the *Journal of the Linnean Society*, and also Dr C. E. Hubbard's *Grasses*.

We are much indebted to the Keeper of Botany and his staff at the British Museum (Natural History) and also to the Director and the Herbarium staff at the Royal Botanic Gardens at Kew. In both we have had valuable advice accompanied by the selection of suitable material from the National Herbaria for drawing. This has been especially the case in the choice of Sedges and Grasses, but in other groups also.

In drawing the figures we have had helpful advice or determination of specimens from those who have specialized in several groups. This was often coupled with the posting of fresh specimens as follows: *Fumaria*, H. W. Pugsley, who also personally conducted us around Cornwall in search of these; *Cruciferae* and many other groups, Dr G. C. Druce; *Rubus*, Wm. Watson, who himself wrote the notes for the text on those figured; the Rose plate was redrawn after kind criticism of N. Y. Sandwith; *Sorbus*, A. J. Wilmott; *Mentha*, R. Graham; *Salix*, R. D. Meikle; *Potamogeton*, Dr G. Taylor; *Cyperaceae*, E. Nelmes and A. W. Stelfox; *Gramineae*, Dr C. E. Hubbard. All these gave valuable help and we are much indebted to them. For other drawings we acknowledge with gratitude that many botanists past and present kindly helped by sending fresh specimens, carefully determined and posted for this work. They are too numerous to name here. Their names are on the separate drawings referred to above.

We wish further to acknowledge our debt to Dr W. S. Bristowe (of Spider fame, President of the Ray Society) for earlier research into the possibility of publication. We are extremely grateful to His Royal Highness the Duke of Edinburgh for his active interest and to Squadron-Leader David Checketts for introducing the project to Mr George Rainbird and his colleagues.

After these acknowledgements we hope that the plates may have a chance of speaking for themselves. The author is very conscious of their limitations.

Preface to the Second Edition

The past three years have been a period of considerable botanical study and experiment, and we are indebted to Mr Douglas H. Kent for adapting the text of this work to current botanical opinion, especially regarding closely related forms and subspecies, and in some cases, regarding nomenclature. In the text he has also described a number of additional established alien species. Mr Kent was formerly Editor of the *Proceedings of the Botanical Society of the British Isles*, and now, although busy in other ways, he has devoted much time and interest to making this *Concise British Flora* a standard work both for professionals and amateurs.

W. Keble Martin
Broadymead, Woodbury 1969

Glossary

achene A small dry indehiscent fruit, strictly of one free carpel.
acicle A very slender prickle or stoutish bristle.
acuminate Having a gradually diminishing point.
acute Sharply pointed but not drawn out.
alternate Arranged successively on opposite sides of a stem.
amplexicaul Clasping the stem with their base.
angle(d) (s) The meeting of two planes to form an edge.
annual A plant completing its life cycle from germination to death within one year.
anther The terminal portion of a stamen containing the pollen grains.
apex The growing point of a stem; the tip of an organ.
apiculate Furnished with a small broad point at the apex.
appressed Lying flat along the whole length of an organ.
arcuate Bent like a bow.
aril The exterior covering of the seed in certain plants, e.g. *Taxus baccata*, developed from the stalk or base of the ovule.
aristate Awned.
attenuate Gradually tapering to a point.
auricles Small ear-like appendages at the base of a leaf.
awn A bristle-like part.
axil The upper angle formed by the union of the stem and the leaf.
axillary Growing in an axil.
axis The central part of a plant, around which the organs are developed.

beak A pointed projection.
beard Awn.
biconvex Having a more or less rounded surface on both sides.
biennial A plant requiring two years to complete its life cycle, growing in the first year, and flowering and fruiting in the second.
bifid Divided halfway down into two parts.
bipinnate When the divisions of a pinnate leaf are themselves pinnate.
biserrate Doubly serrate.
blunt Ending in a rounded form, neither tapering to a point, nor truncate.
bract(s) Modified leaves intermediate between the calyx and the normal leaves.
bracteate Having bracts.
bracteoles Minute bracts.
bulb An underground organ which is really a modified plant bud with fleshy scales, yielding stem and roots.
bulbils Small bulbs or tubers usually arising in the axils of the leaves or amongst the florets of an inflorescence, but sometimes found on the root.

calyx The outermost of the floral envelopes.
campanulate Bell-shaped.
capillary Hair-like.
capitate Growing in heads; pin-headed.
capitulum A close cluster of sessile flowers.
capsule A dry, dehiscent fruit.
carpel A modified leaf of one, or several, of which the pistil is formed.
carpophore The continuation of the stalk between the carpels.
cauline Borne on the stem, not radical.
cernuous Nodding.
ciliate Fringed with hairs.
cladode A leaf-like branch, as in *Ruscus aculeatus*.
clasping Grasping.
claw The narrow base of a petal in certain genera, e.g. *Dianthus*.
cleft Deeply cut, but not to the midrib.
commissure The faces by which two carpels adhere, particularly in *Umbelliferae*.
confluent United at some part.
connate Similar organs distinct in origin but eventually becoming united.
connivent Making contact or converging.
contiguous Adjacent to each other; making contact at the edges.
cordate Heart-shaped.
corm Bulb-like fleshy underground stem, as in *Anemone*, etc.
corolla The petals as a whole.
corona The circumference or margin of a radiated compound flower, particularly in *Compositae*.
cotyledon(s) The first leaf or leaves of the embryo.
crenate With rounded marginal teeth.
crenulate Minutely crenate.
cruciform Cross-shaped.
cryptogam A flowerless plant.
cuneate Wedge-shaped.
cuspidate Spear-shaped at the tip.
cyme A flower-cluster of a broad and flattened type, as in *Sambucus nigra*.

deciduous Dropping off; shedding its leaves in the autumn.
decumbent Lying on the ground but tending to rise at the end.
decurrent Extending downwards, as when leaves are extended beyond their insertion and run down by a wing on the stem as in *Carduus* and *Cirsium*.
deflexed Bent sharply downwards.
dehiscent Opening to shed its seeds.
deltoid Shaped like an equilateral triangle.
dentate Toothed; notched.
denticulate Minutely toothed.
depressed When flattened vertically or at the top.
dichotomous Forked, parted by pairs from top to bottom.

diffuse Widely or loosely spreading.
digitate A compound leaf divided into five leaflets, as in *Aesculus hippocastanum*.
dioecious Having the sexes on different plants.
disk The central part of a capitulum in *Compositae* as opposed to the ray florets; the expanded base of a style in *Umbelliferae*.

elliptic(al) Oval but acute at each end.
elongate Much lengthened.
emarginate Slightly notched at the edges.
entire With an even margin; not toothed or cut at the edges.
epicalyx An involucre resembling an accessory calyx, as in *Malva*.
epichile The terminal part of the labellum of an orchid when it is distinct from the basal portion.
excurrent Where the stem remains central, the other parts being regularly placed around it.
exserted Protruding.

family A group of related genera.
fascicle(d) A close cluster or bundle.
fastigiate Tapering to a point like a pyramid.
filament The stalk of an anther.
filiform Thread-like.
fimbriate With a fringed margin.
flexuose Zigzag.
floret A small flower, one of a cluster.
follicle A dry dehiscent fruit formed of one carpel opening by a ventral suture to which the seeds are attached.
fringe(d) With hair-like appendages on the margins.
frond The leaf-like part of a fern and other cryptogams.
fruit The ripe seeds and their surrounding structure.

gamopetalous Having the petals united at the edges in the form of a tube.
genus The smallest natural group containing related but distinct species.
gibbous Swollen on one side.
glabrous Smooth, devoid of hair or other clothing.
gland A wart-like structure on the surface, embedded or protruding, from any part of a plant.
glandular Having glands.
glaucous Covered with a bluish green bloom.
globose Round.
glume A small bract with a flower in the axil as in grasses.

hastate Spear-shaped.
herb Any non-woody vascular plant.
herbaceous Having the texture of leaves.

hirsute Hairy, with long, usually soft, hairs.
hispid Clothed with stiff hairs or bristles.
hooded Formed into a hood at the end.
hyaline Very thin and translucent.
hybrid A plant produced by the fertilization of one species by another.
hypochile The basal portion of the labellum in an orchid.

incumbent Resting or leaning upon.
inferior Below the ovary.
inflorescence The arrangement of the flowers on a stem or branch.
intercalary Inserted between or amongst others.
internode The space between two adjacent nodes.
involucre The whorl of bracts enclosing a number of flowers as in *Compositae* and *Umbelliferae*.
involute Having the margins rolled upwards.

keel(ed) The lower petal or petals when shaped like the keel of a boat as in *Vicia*, *Lathyrus*, etc.

labellum The lower petal of certain flowers, particularly orchids.
laciniate Jagged; deeply and irregularly divided into segments.
lanate Covered with soft, flexuous, matted hairs.
lanceolate Narrow, tapering at each end.
lateral Fixed on, or near, the side of an organ.
leaflet A subdivision of a compound leaf.
lemma The flowering glume of a grass.
lenticel Corky spots having the shape of a double-convex lens on young bark.
ligulate Strap-shaped.
ligule A small thin projection from the top of the leaf-sheath in grasses; a strap-shaped petal, e.g. in *Compositae*.
limb The border or exposed part of a calyx or corolla, as distinct from the tube or throat.
linear Slender.
linear-lanceolate Slender but tapering to a point at the tip.
lobed Said of leaves which are divided, but not into separate leaflets.
lunate Shaped like the new moon.

membranous Thin, dry and semi-transparent.
mucronate Abruptly tipped with a short, straight point.
muricate With sharp points or prickles.

nectary The honey gland of a flower.
nerve A vein or slender rib.
node A point in a stem where a leaf is borne.
notch An indentation.

ob- As a prefix means inversely or oppositely.
oblong Longer than broad.
obtuse Blunt.
ochrea Provided with a tubular membranous stipule.

opposite Growing in pairs at the same level on opposite sides of a stem.
orbicular Nearly round and flat.
oval Broadly elliptic.
ovary The vessel in which the seeds are formed.
ovate Egg-shaped.
ovate-oblong Egg-shaped, but much longer than broad.
ovoid Of a solid object which is egg-shaped in outline.

palea The inner bract or glume of a grass; the chaffy scales on the receptacle in many *Compositae*.
palmate Lobed or divided into more than three leaflets arising from a central point.
panicle A raceme with branching pedicels.
papillae Small elongated protuberances.
papillose Warty; having papillae.
pappus The tufts of hairs on achenes or fruits, particularly in *Compositae*.
pectinate Resembling the teeth of a comb.
pedicel The stalk of a single flower.
peduncle The stalk supporting either a flower or a flower-cluster.
pellucid Transparent.
peltate Shield-shaped with the stalk in the centre.
perennial A plant that lives for more than two years and usually flowers annually.
perfoliate With the leaf united round the stem, as in *Montia perfoliata*.
perianth The floral envelopes, calyx or corolla, or both.
pericarp A seed vessel, including the adhering calyx if present.
petal A flower leaf, often brightly coloured, forming part of a corolla.
petaloid Resembling a petal.
petiole A leaf-stalk.
petiolate Having a petiole.
pilose Hairy, usually with long soft hairs.
pinnate With leaflets arranged on opposite sides of a common stalk or rachis.
pinnatifid Deeply cut into segments nearly to the midrib.
pistil The female organ of a flower, consisting when complete of ovary, style and stigma.
pollinia A pollen mass composed of large numbers of cohering pollen grains.
polypetalous Having many separate petals.
pore A small aperture.
procumbent Trailing; lying loosely on the ground.
proliferous Bearing progeny as off-shoots.
prostrate Lying closely on the surface of the ground.
pruinose Covered with a whitish bloom.
pubescent Covered with fine short hairs.
pyriform Pear-shaped.

raceme An unbranched inflorescence with flowers borne on equal pedicels.
rachis The axis of an inflorescence, compound leaf or branch.
radical Growing from the root.
ray The outer part of a compound radiate flower.

receptacle The uppermost part of the stem nearing the flowers.
recurved Bent moderately backwards in a curve.
reflexed Bent abruptly backwards.
reniform Kidney-shaped.
reticulate Marked with a network of veins.
retuse Terminating in a rounded end, the centre of which is slightly indented.
revolute Rolled or curved downwards.
rhizomatous Having the character of a rhizome.
rhizome An underground, creeping stem, producing roots and leafy shoots.
rhomboid(al) Similar in shape to a diamond in a pack of playing cards.
rib(bed) A primary vein; furnished with ribs.
rosette A cluster of leaves in circular form, as in *Plantago major*.
rotate (of a corolla) Wheel-shaped, circular and flat with a short tube.
rugose Wrinkled.

saccate Pouched.
sagittate Shaped like the barbed head of an arrow.
saprophyte A plant that lives on decaying vegetable matter.
scabrid Rough.
scale A thin scarious structure, often a degenerate leaf.
scape A leafless flower-stalk rising from the root.
scarious Very thin, dry and semi-transparent.
secund All turned to one side.
segment A division into which a plant organ, e.g. a leaf, may be cleft.
sepal A leaf of the calyx, the outer whorl of the perianth.
septate Divided into partitions.
serrate Toothed like a saw.
sessile Without a stalk.
setae Bristles.
sinuate Having a deep wavy outline.
sinuous Undulating.
sinus A depression between two teeth.
spadix A succulent spike with a fleshy axis, as in *Arum maculatum*.
spathe A large bract enclosing a flower cluster, usually a spadix.
spathulate Spatula-shaped.
spike An inflorescence in which the flowers are sessile round an axis.
spikelet A small spike; the inflorescence of grasses.
spine A thorn.
spur A slender projection from the base of a perianth segment, or of a corolla, as in *Aquilegia vulgaris*.
stamen One of the male reproductive organs of a plant.
staminodes Infertile, often reduced, stamens.
standard The large, often erect, posterior petal of a corolla in *Papilionaceae*.
stellate Star-shaped.
stigma The part of the pistil or style which receives the pollen.
stipule A leaf-like appendage usually at the base of the petiole.
stipulate Having stipules on it.

stolon A creeping stem which roots at intervals.
stoloniferous Having stolons.
striate(ions) Marked with slender streaks or furrows.
strict Narrow, upright and very straight.
style The space between the ovary and the stigma.
sub- Under or below.
subulate Awl-shaped.
succulent Juicy.

teeth Small marginal lobes.
terete Long and round, without ridges or grooves.
terminal Borne at the top of the stem.
testa The outer coat of the seed.
tomentose Densely pubescent, with woolly entangled hairs.
trifid Three-cleft but not to the base.
trifoliate Having three leaflets.

trigonous Of a solid body, three-angled, with plane faces.
triquetrous Triangular and acutely angled.
truncate As though abruptly cut off at the end.
tube The united parts of a corolla or calyx.
tuber A thickened part of an underground stem or root of one year's duration.
tubercle A small spherical or ovoid swelling.

umbel A type of inflorescence in which equal pedicels proceed from a common centre.
umbellate Having partial or secondary umbels.
unarmed Without spines or prickles.
undulate Wavy.
unisexual Of one sex only.

valvate When parts of a flower bud meet but do not overlap.
valve One of the pieces into which a capsule naturally separates at maturity.
vascular Furnished with vessels.
vernal Appearing in spring.
villous Covered with shaggy hairs.
viscid Clammy or sticky.
vitta(e) The aromatic oil tubes of the pericarp in many species of *Umbelliferae*.
viviparous Producing young plants instead of flowers.

whorl(ed) A ring of leaves or flowers around a stem at the same level as each other.
wing(ed) The lateral petals in the flowers of *Fumariaceae* and *Papilionaceae*; the flat membranous appendages of some seeds.

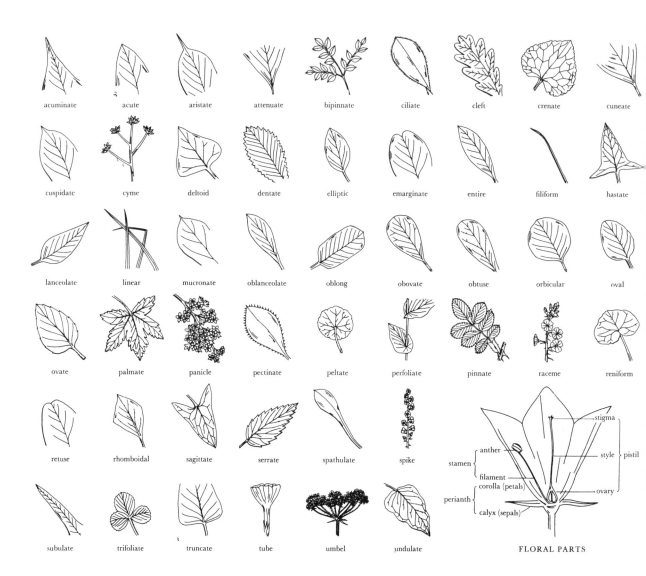

acuminate · acute · aristate · attenuate · bipinnate · ciliate · cleft · crenate · cuneate

cuspidate · cyme · deltoid · dentate · elliptic · emarginate · entire · filiform · hastate

lanceolate · linear · mucronate · oblanceolate · oblong · obovate · obtuse · orbicular · oval

ovate · palmate · panicle · pectinate · peltate · perfoliate · pinnate · raceme · reniform

retuse · rhomboidal · sagittate · serrate · spathulate · spike · stigma · style · pistil · stamen · anther · filament · corolla (petals) · ovary · perianth · calyx (sepals)

subulate · trifoliate · truncate · tube · umbel · undulate · FLORAL PARTS

Abbreviations

ABBREVIATIONS OF AUTHORS' NAMES FOR THE PLANT SPECIES

No dates are given for living authors

Aellen–P. Aellen
Airy Shaw–H. K. Airy Shaw
Ait.–W. Aiton, 1731–1793
Ait.f.–W. T. Aiton, 1766–1849
All.–C. Allioni, 1725–1804
Allman–G. J. Allman, 1812–1898
Anderss.–N. J. Andersson, 1821–1880
Andreas–C. H. Andreas
Andrz.–A. L. Andrzejowski, 1784–1868
Arcangeli–G. Arcangeli, 1840–1921
Ard.–P. Arduino, 1728–1805
Arn.–G. A. W. Arnott, 1799–1868
Arrondeau–E. T. Arrondeau, d. 1882
Aschers.–P. F. A. Ascherson, 1834–1913
Ashe–W. W. Ashe, 1872–1932
auct.–auctor, auctores; author(s)

Bab.–C. C. Babington, 1808–1895
Backh.–J. Backhouse, 1825–1890
C. Bailey–C. Bailey, 1838–1924
Bak.–E. G. Baker, 1864–1949
H. G. Bak.–H. G. Baker
J. G. Bak.–J. G. Baker, 1834–1920
Balb.–G. B. Balbis, 1765–1831
P. W. Ball–P. W. Ball
Bartal.–B. Bartalini, 1746–1822
Bast.–T. Bastard, 1784–1846
Baumg.–J. C. G. Baumgarten, 1765–1843
Beauv.–A. M. F. J. Palisot de Beauvois, 1752–1820
Bechst.–J. M. Bechstein, 1757–1822
Beck–G. Ritter Beck von Mannagetta und Larchenau, 1856–1931
W. Becker–W. Becker, 1874–1928
Beeby–W. H. Beeby, 1849–1910
Béguinot–A. Béguinot, 1875–1940
Bellardi–C. A. L. Bellardi, 1741–1826
A. Benn.–A. Bennett, 1843–1929
Benth.–G. Bentham, 1800–1884
Bernh.–J. J. Bernhardi, 1774–1850
Bertol.–A. Bertoloni, 1775–1869
Bess.–W. S. J. G. von Besser, 1784–1842
Betcke–E. F. Betcke, 1815–1865
Bicknell–C. Bicknell, 1842–1918
Bieb.–F. A. Marschall von Bieberstein, 1768–1826
Bigel.–J. Bigelow, 1787–1879
Biv.–A. de Bivona-Bernardi, 1774–1837
Blanche–E. Blanche, 1824–1908
Bluff–M. J. Bluff, 1805–1837
Boenn.–C. M. F. von Boenninghausen, 1785–1864
Boiss.–P.-E. Boissier, 1810–1885
Bonnier–G. E. M. Bonnier, 1853–1922
Boott–F. Boott, 1792–1863
Bor.–A. Boreau, 1803–1875
Borbás–V. von Borbás, 1844–1905
Borkh.–M. B. Borkhausen, 1760–1806
Börner–C. Börner
Borrer–W. Borrer, 1781–1862
R. Br.–R. Brown, 1773–1858
M. E. Bradshaw–M. E. Bradshaw
A. Braun–A. Braun, 1805–1877
Bréb.–L. A. de Brébisson, 1798–1872
Britton–N. L. Britton, 1859–1934
Brodesson–E. Brodesson, fl. 1906–1912
Bromf.–W. A. Bromfield, 1801–1851
Brot.–F. da Avellar Brotero, 1744–1828
Brummitt–R. K. Brummitt
Bub.–P. Bubani, 1806–1888
Buchen.–F. G. P. Buchenau, 1831–1906

Bunge–A. von Bunge, 1830–1890
Burgsd.–F. A. L. von Burgsdorf, 1747–1802
Burm.f.–N. L. Burman, 1734–1793
Burnat–E. Burnat, 1828–1920
Buser–R. Buser, 1857–1931
Butcher–R. W. Butcher

Caruel–T. Caruel, 1830–1898
Casp.–J. X. R. Caspary, 1818–1887
Cass.–A. H. G. de Cassini, 1781–1832
Cav.–A. J. Cavinilles, 1745–1804
Cavara–F. Cavara, 1857–1929
Celak.–L. J. Celakovsky, 1834–1902
Chaix–D. Chaix, 1730–1799
Cham.–A. L. von Chamisso, 1781–1838
Chatel.–J. J. Chatelain, 1736–1822
Chaub.–L. A. Chaubard, 1785–1854
Chazelles–M. de Chazelles, fl. 1790
Chevall.–F. F. Chevallier, 1796–1840
Chouard–P. Chouard
Clairv.–J. P. de Clairville, 1742–1830
Clapham–A. R. Clapham
Clarion–J. Clarion, 1780–1856
Clavaud–A. Clavaud, 1828–1890
Colem.–W. H. Coleman, 1816–1863
Compton–R. H. Compton
C. D. K. Cook–C. D. K. Cook
D. E. Coombe–D. E. Coombe
Corb.– L. Corbière, 1850–1941
Coult.–J. M. Coulter, 1851–1928
Court.–R. J. Courtois, 1806–1835
Coutinho–A. X. P. Coutinho, 1851–1939
Coville–F. V. Coville, 1867–1937
Crantz–H. J. N. von Crantz, 1722–1799
Crép.–F. Crépin, 1830–1903
Cronq.–A. Cronquist
Cunn.–A. Cunningham, 1791–1839
Curt.–W. Curtis, 1746–1799
Custer–J. L. Custer, 1755–1828

Dahl–O. C. Dahl, 1862–1940
Dahlst.–A. G. A. Dahlstedt, 1856–1934
Dandy–J. E. Dandy
Davey–F. H. Davey, 1868–1915
Davies–H. Davies, 1739–1821
DC.–A. P. de Candolle, 1778–1841
Del.–A. R. Delile, 1778–1850
Delarb.–A. Delarbre, 1724–1814
Déségl.–P. A. Déséglise, 1823–1883
Desf.–R. L. Desfontaines, 1750–1833
Desv.–A. N. Desvaux, 1784–1856
Dickson–J. Dickson, 1738–1822
Dippel–L. Dippel, 1827–1914
Don–D. Don, 1799–1841
G. Don–G. Don, 1798–1856
Donn–J. Donn, 1758–1813
Dougl.–D. Douglas, 1798–1834
Drej.–S. T. N. Drejer, 1813–1842
Druce–G. C. Druce, 1850–1932
Duby–J. E. Duby, 1798–1885
Duchesne–A. N. Duchesne, 1747–1827
Dumort.–B. C. J. Dumortier, 1797–1878
Durieu–M. C. Durieu de Maisonneuve, 1796–1878
Duroi–J. P. Duroi, 1741–1785
Dyer–W. T. Thiselton Dyer, 1843–1928

Edmondst.–T. Edmondston, 1825–1846
Ehrh.–J. F. Ehrhart, 1742–1795
Ehrend.–F. Ehrendorfer
Ell.–S. Elliot, 1771–1830

Fenzl–E. Fenzl, 1808–1879
Fernald–M. L. Fernald, 1873–1950
Fieb.–F. X. Fieber, 1807–1872
Fiori–A. Fiori, 1865–1950
Fisch.–F. E. L. von Fischer, 1782–1854
Foggitt–W. Foggitt, 1835–1917
Forsk.–P. Forskål, 1732–1763
E. Forst.–E. Forster, 1765–1849
G. Forst.–J. G. A. Forster, 1754–1794
J. R. Forst.–J. R. Forster, 1729–1798
T. F. Forst.–T. F. Forster, 1761–1825
Fouc.–J. Foucaud, 1847–1904
P. Fourn.–P. Fournier, 1877–1964
Fourr.–P. J. Fourreau, 1844–1871
Fr.–E. M. Fries, 1794–1878
Franch.–A. R. Franchet, 1834–1900
Fritsch–K. Fritsch, 1864–1934

Gaertn.–J. Gaertner, 1732–1791
Garcke–F. A. Garcke, 1819–1904
Gaudich.–C. Gaudichaud-Beaupré, 1789–1854
Gaudin–J. F. A. T. G. P. Gaudin, 1766–1833
Gay–J. E. Gay, 1786–1864
Gilib.–J. E. Gilibert, 1741–1814
Gilmour–J. S. L. Gilmour
Girard–F. de Girard, fl. 1842
Gled.–J. G. Gleditsch, 1714–1786
C. C. Gmel.–C. C. Gmelin, 1762–1837
S. G. Gmel.–S. G. Gmelin, 1744–1774
Godfery–M. J. Godfery, d. 1945
Godr.–D. A. Godron, 1807–1880
Good.–S. Goodenough, 1743–1827
Gouan–A. Gouan, 1733–1821
Graebner–K. O. R. P. P. Graebner, 1871–1933
R. A. Graham–R. A. Graham, 1915–1958
Gray–S. F. Gray, 1766–1836
A. Gray–A. Gray, 1810–1888
Gregory–Mrs. E. S. Gregory, 1840–1932
Gremli–A. Gremli, 1833–1899
Gren.–J. C. M. Grenier, 1808–1875
Grimm–J. F. K. Grimm, 1737–1821
Griseb.–A. H. R. Grisebach, 1814–1879
H. Groves–H. Groves, 1855–1912
J. Groves–J. Groves, 1858–1933
Gunn.–J. E. Gunnerus, 1718–1773
Guss.–G. Gussone, 1787–1866

Hack.–E. Hackel, 1850–1926
Hagerup–O. Hagerup, 1889–1961
Haller f.–A. von Haller, 1758–1823
Halliday–G. Halliday
F. J. Hanb.–F. J. Hanbury, 1851–1938
Hardouin–L. Hardouin, 1800–1858
Hartig–H. J. A. R. Hartig, 1839–1901
Hartm.–K. J. Hartman, 1790–1849
Harz–K. O. Harz, 1842–1906
Hassk.–J. C. Hasskarl, 1811–1894
Hausskn.–H. K. Haussknecht, 1838–1903
Hayek–A. E. von Hayek, 1871–1928
Hayne–F. G. Hayne, 1763–1832
Hedlund–T. T. Hedlund, 1861–1953
Heg.–J. J. Hegetschweiler, 1789–1839
Hegi–G. Hegi, 1876–1932
Henry–L. Henry, 1853–1913
Henslow–J. S. Henslow, 1796–1861
Hepper–F. N. Hepper
Herbert–W. Herbert, 1778–1847
F. Hermann–F. Hermann
Heynh.–G. Heynhold, fl. 1838–1850
Heywood–V. H. Heywood
Hiern–W. P. Hiern, 1839–1925

Hiit.–H. I. A. Hiitonen
Hill–J. Hill, 1716–1775
Hoffm.–G. F. Hoffmann, 1760–1826
Hoffmanns.–J. C. Hoffmannsegg, 1766–1849
Holmberg–O. R. Holmberg, 1874–1930
Honck.–G. A. Honckeny, 1724–1805
Hook.–W. J. Hooker, 1785–1865
Hook.f.–J. D. Hooker, 1817–1911
Hoppe–D. H. Hoppe, 1760–1846
Hork.–J. Horkel, 1769–1846
Hornem.–J. W. Hornemann, 1770–1841
Hose–J. Hose, d. 1800
Host–N. T. Host, 1761–1834
House–H. D. House, 1878–1949
Houtt.–Houttuyn, 1720–1798
Howard–H. W. Howard
Howell–T. J. Howell, 1842–1912
C. E. Hubbard–C. E. Hubbard
Huds.–W. Hudson, 1730–1793
Hull–J. Hull, 1761–1843
P. F. Hunt–P. F. Hunt
Hyland.–N. Hylander

Ilse–H. Ilse, 1835–1900
Ives–E. Ives, 1779–1861

Jacq.–N. J. von Jacquin, 1727–1817
Jacq.f.–J. F. von Jacquin, 1766–1839
Jalas–J. Jalas
Jansen–P. Jansen, 1882–1955
Johans.–K. K. Johansson, 1856–1928
Jord.–A. Jordan, 1814–1897
Juss.–A. L. de Jussieu, 1748–1836
Juz.–S. V. Juzepczuk, 1893–1959

Kar.–G. S. Karelin, 1801–1872
Karst.–G. K. W. H. Karsten, 1817–1908
Kenyon–W. Kenyon, fl. 1847
Ker-Gawl.–J. Gawler (né J. B. Ker), 1764–1842
Kerner–A. J. Kerner von Marilaun, 1831–1898
Kir.–I. P. Kirilow, 1821–1842
Kirschleger–F. R. Kirschleger, 1804–1869
Kit.–P. Kitaibel, 1757–1817
Kittel–M. B. Kittel, 1796–1875
Knuth–R. G. P. Knuth, 1874–1957
Koch–W. D. J. Koch, 1771–1849
K. Koch–K. (C.) H. E. Koch, 1809–1879
Koel.–G. L. Koeler, 1765–1807
Koerte–F. Koerte, 1782–1845
E. H. L. Krause–E. H. L. Krause, 1859–1942
Krecz.–V. I. Kreczetowicz, 1901–1942
Kunth–K. S. Kunth, 1788–1850
Kuntze–K. (C.) E. O. Kuntze, 1843–1907
Kütz.–F. T. Kützing, 1807–1892

L.–C. von Linné (C. Linnaeus), 1707–1778
L.f.–C. von Linné, 1741–1783
Laest.–L. L. Laestadius, 1800–1861
Lag.–M. La Gasca y Segura, 1776–1839
Lagr.-Foss.–A. R. A. Lagrèze-Fossat, 1814–1874
Laichard.–J. N. von Laicharding, 1754–1797
Lam.–J. B. A. P. de M. de Lamarck, 1744–1829
Lamotte–M. Lamotte, 1820–1883
Láng–A. F. Láng, 1795–1863
Lange–J. M. C. Lange, 1818–1898
Lapierre–J. M. Lapierre, 1754–1834
Latourr.–M. A. L. C. de Latourette, 1729–1793
Lebel– J. E. Lebel, 1801–1878
Lecoq–H. Lecoq, 1802–1871
Ledeb.–C. F. von Ledebour, 1785–1851
Leers–J. D. Leers, 1727–1774
Le Gall–N. J. M. Le Gall, 1787–1860
Lehm.–J. G. C. Lehmann, 1792–1860
Leight.–W. A. Leighton, 1805–1889
Lejeune–A. L. S. Lejeune, 1779–1858
Le Jolis–A. F. Le Jolis, 1823–1904
Less.–C. F. Lessing, 1809–1862
Léveillé–A. A. H. Léveillé, 1863–1918
Ley.–A. Ley, 1842–1911
Leyss.–F. W. von Leysser, 1731–1815
L.-Garland–L. V. L. Garland, né Lester, 1860–1944

L'Hérit.–C. L. L'Héritier de Brutelle, 1746–1800
Liebl.–F. K. Lieblein, 1744–1810
Lightf.–J. Lightfoot, 1735–1788
Liljeb.–S. Liljeblad, 1761–1815
Lindl.–J. Lindley, 1799–1865
Lindm.–C. A. M. Lindman, 1856–1928
Link–J. H. F. Link, 1767–1851
E. F. Linton–E. F. Linton, 1848–1928
Lois.–J. L. A. Loiseleur-Deslongchamps, 1774–1849
Lönnr.–E. Lönnrot, 1802–1884
Loret–H. Loret, 1810–1888
Lousley–J. E. Lousley
A. Löve–A. Löve
D. Löve–D. Löve
Lyons–L. J. C. Lyons, 1792–1874

Mabille–P. Mabille, fl. 1864–1872
Mackenzie–K. K. Mackenzie, 1877–1934
Macreight–D. C. Macreight, 1799–1868
Manton–I. Manton
Marsh.–H. Marshall, 1722–1801
E. S. Marshall–E. S. Marshall, 1858–1919
Martyn–T. Martyn, 1735–1825
Mattuschka–H. G. von Mattuschka, 1734–1779
Mauri–E. Mauri, 1791–1836
Maxim.–K. J. Maximowicz, 1827–1891
Medic.–F. K. Medicus, 1736–1808
Meerb.–N. Meerburgh, 1734–1814
Meikle–R. D. Meikle
Meissn.–C. F. Meissner, 1800–1874
Melderis–A. Melderis
Melville–R. Melville
Merát–F. V. Merát, 1780–1851
Mert.–F. K. Mertens, 1764–1831
Mey.–C. A. Meyer, 1795–1855
E. Mey.–E. H. F. Meyer, 1791–1858
Michx.–A. Michaux, 1746–1802
Michx.f.–F. A. Michaux, 1770–1855
Mikan f.–J. C. Mikan, 1769–1844
Mill.–P. Miller, 1691–1771
Moench.–C. Moench, 1744–1805
Moq.–C. H. B. A. Moquin-Tandon, 1804–1863
More–A. G. More, 1830–1895
Moss–C. E. Moss, 1872–1931
Muhl.–G. H. I. Muhlenberg, 1753–1815
Murb.–S. S. Murbeck, 1859–1946
Murr.–J. A. Murray, 1740–1791
A. Murr.–A. Murray, 1812–1878
J. Murr–J. J. Murr, 1864–1932

Naeg.–O. Naegeli, 1871–1938
Neck.–N. J. von Necker, 1729–1793
Nees–C. G. D. Nees von Esenbeck, 1776–1858
Neves–J. de Barros Neves
Nevski–S. A. Nevski, 1908–1938
Newbould–W. W. Newbould, 1819–1886
Neygenf.–F. W. Neygenfind, fl. 1821
Nied.–F. J. Niedenzu, 1857–1937
Nordb.–G. Nordborg
Nutt.–T. Nuttall, 1786–1859
Nyman–C. F. Nyman, 1820–1893

Oborny–A. Oborny, 1840–1925
Ockendon–D. J. Ockendon
Oeder–G. C. von Oeder, 1728–1791
Opiz–P. M. Opiz, 1787–1858
Ostenf.–C. H. Ostenfeld, 1873–1931

Pall.–P. S. Pallas, 1741–1811
Palla–E. Palla, 1864–1922
Panz.–G. W. F. Panzer, 1755–1829
Paol.–G. Paoletti, 1865–1941
Parl.–F. Parlatore, 1816–1877
Parnell–R. Parnell, 1810–1882
Pedersen–A. Pedersen
Pennell–F. W. Pennell, 1886–1952
Pers.–C. H. Persoon, 1762–1836
Peter–G. A. Peter, 1853–1937
Petermann–W. L. Petermann, 1806–1855
Petrak–F. Petrak
Pilg.–R. K. F. Pilger, 1876–1953

Piré–L. A. H. J. Piré, 1827–1887
Planch.–J. E. Planchon, 1823–1888
Podp.–J. Podpera, 1878–1954
Poggenb.–J. F. Poggenburg, 1840–1893
Pohl–R. W. Pohl
Poir.–J. L. M. Poiret, 1755–1834
Polatschek–A. Polatschek
Poll.–J. A. Pollich, 1740–1780
Porter–T. C. Porter, 1822–1901
Pourr.–P. A. Pourret de Figeac, 1754–1818
Prantl–K. A. E. Prantl, 1849–1893
C. Presl–C. (K.) B. Presl, 1794–1852
J. Presl–J. S. Presl, 1791–1849
Pritchard–N. M. Pritchard
M. C. F. Proctor–M. C. F. Proctor
Pugsl.–H. W. Pugsley, 1868–1947
Pursh–F. T. Pursh, 1774–1820

Rabenh.–G. L. Rabenhorst, 1806–1881
Raf.–C. S. Rafinesque-Schmaltz, 1783–1840
Rafn–C. G. Rafn, 1769–1808
Raunk.–C. Raunkiaer, 1860–1938
Räusch.–E. A. Räuschel, fl. 1772–1797
Rech.f.–K. H. Rechinger
Regel–E. A. von Regel, 1815–1892
Rehd.–A. Rehder, 1863–1949
Rehm.–A. Rehman, 1840–1917
Reichard–J. J. Reichard, 1743–1782
Reichb.–H. G. L. Reichenbach, 1793–1879
Reichb.f.–H. G. Reichenbach, 1823–1889
Req.–E. Requien, 1788–1851
Retz.–A. J. Retzius, 1742–1821
Reut.–G. F. Reuter, 1805–1872
Rich.–L. C. M. Richard, 1754–1821
Riddelsd.–H. J. Riddelsdell, 1866–1941
Ridley–H. N. Ridley, 1855–1956
Robson–E. Robson, 1763–1813
Rochel–A. Rochel, 1770–1847
Roem.–J. J. Roemer, 1763–1819
Roffey–J. Roffey, 1860–1927
Ronn.–K. Ronniger, 1871–1954
Rostk.–F. W. G. Rostkovius, 1770–1848
Rostrup–F. G. E. Rostrup, 1831–1907
Roth–A. W. Roth, 1757–1834
Rothm.–W. Rothmaler, 1908–1962
Rouy–G. C. C. Rouy, 1851–1924
Royle–J. F. Royle, 1799–1858
Rupr.–F. J. Ruprecht, 1814–1870
Ruthe–J. F. Ruthe, 1788–1859
Ryd.–P. A. Rydberg, 1860–1931

St Amans–J. F. B. St Amans, 1748–1831
St John–H. St John
Salisb.–R. A. Salisbury, né Markham, 1761–1829
Salmon–C. E. Salmon, 1872–1930
Samp.–G. A. da Silva Ferreira Sampaio, 1865–1937
Sauter–A. E. Sauter, 1800–1881
Savi–G. Savi, 1769–1844
Savigny–M. J. C. L. de Savigny, 1777–1851
Savouré–H. S. Savouré, 1861–1921
Schau.–J. C. Schauer, 1813–1848
Scheele–G. H. A. Scheele, 1808–1864
Scherb.–J. Scherbius, 1769–1813
Schiffn.–V. F. Schiffner, 1862–1944
Schinz–H. Schinz, 1858–1941
Schischk.–B. K. Schischkin, 1886–1963
Schkuhr–C. Schkuhr, 1741–1811
Schlecht.–D. F. L. von Schlechtendal, 1794–1866
Schleich.–J. C. Schleicher, 1768–1834
Schleid.–M. J. Schleiden, 1804–1881
Schmidt–F. W. Schmidt, 1764–1796
F. Schmidt–F. Schmidt, 1832–1908
C. K. Schneid.–C. K. Schneider, 1876–1951
Schönh.–F. C. H. Schönheit, 1789–1870
Schönl.–S. Schönland, 1860–1940
Schott–H. W. Schott, 1794–1865
Schousb.–P. K. A. Schousboe, 1766–1832
Schrad.–H. A. Schrader, 1767–1836
Schrank–F. von Paula von Schrank, 1747–1835
Schreb.–J. C. D. von Schreber, 1739–1810
Schult.–J. A. Schultes, 1773–1831

.. H. Schultz–C. H. Schultz, 1805–1867
. W. Schultz–F. W. Schultz, 1804–1876
.. F. Schultz–K. F. Schultz, 1765–1837
). E. Schulz–O. E. Schulz, 1874–1936
.. Schulz–R. Schulz, 1873–1926
.chumach.–H. C. F. Schumacher, 1757–1830
.chur–P. J. F. Schur, 1799–1878
.chwarz–O. Schwarz
.chweigg.–A. F. Schweigger, 1783–1821
.chwein.–G. A. Schweinfurth, 1836–1925
.cop.–G. A. Scopoli, 1723–1788
.eb.–A. Sebastioni, 1782–1821
.. D. Sell–P. D. Sell
.enn.–Frère Sennen (E. M. Grenier-Blanc), 1861–1937
.ibth.–J. Sibthorp, 1758–1796
.ieb.–P. F. von Siebold, 1796–1866
.ilva–A. R. Pinto da Silva
.immons–H. G. Simmons, 1866–1943
.ims–J. Sims, 1749–1831
.m.–J. E. Smith, 1759–1828
.. E. Sm.–G. E. Smith, 1804–1881
.. Sm.–H. Smith
.mall–J. K. Small, 1869–1938
.obol.–G. F. Sobolevski, 1741–1807
.obrinho–L. G. Sobrinho
.oland.–D. C. Solander, 1736–1782
.oó–R. de Soó
.oy.-Will.–H. F. Soyer-Willemet, 1791–1867
.pach–E. Spach, 1801–1879
.preng.–C. (K.) P. J. Sprengel, 1766–1833
.tapf–O. Stapf, 1857–1933
.tearn–W. T. Stearn
.tefánsson–S. Stefánsson, 1863–1921
.teph.–F. Stephani, 1842–1927
.. Stephenson–T. Stephenson, 1855–1948
.. A. Stephenson–T. A. Stephenson, 1898–1961
.terneck–J. von Sterneck, fl. 1864–1901
.terner–K. R. Sterner, 1891–1956
.terns–E. E. Sterns, 1846–1926

Stev.–C. von Steven, 1781–1863
Stokes–J. Stokes, 1755–1831
Suksd.–W. N. Suksdorf, 1850–1932
Summerhayes–V. S. Summerhayes
Sutton–C. Sutton, 1756–1846
Sw.–O. Swartz, 1760–1818
Syme–J. T. I. B. Syme, né Boswell, 1822–1888

Tausch–I. F. Tausch, 1793–1848
Ten.–M. Tenore, 1780–1861
Thell.–A. Thellung, 1881–1928
C. Thomas–C. Thomas
Thuill.–J. L. Thuillier, 1757–1822
Timm–J. C. Timm, 1734–1805
Torr.–J. Torrey, 1796–1873
Tourlet–E. H. Tourlet, 1843–1907
Towns.–F. Townsend, 1822–1905
Tratt.–L. Trattinick, 1764–1849
Trin.–K. B. von Trinius, 1778–1844
Turcz.–N. Turczaninow, 1796–1864
D. Turner–D. Turner, 1775–1858
Turra–A. Turra, 1730–1796
Turrill–W. B. Turrill, 1890–1961
Tutin–T. G. Tutin

Ucria–B. Ucria, 1739–1796
Ulbr.–E. Ulbrich, 1879–1952

Vaarama–A. Vaarama
Vahl–M. H. Vahl, 1749–1804
Valentine–D. H. Valentine
Van Hall–H. C. Van Hall, 1801–1874
Vermeul.–P. Vermeulen
Vest–L. C. von Vest, 1776–1840
Vierh.–F. Vierhapper, 1876–1932
Vig.–A. L. G. Viguier, 1790–1867
Vill.–D. Villar(s), 1745–1814
Viv.–D. Viviani, 1772–1840

Wachter–W. H. Wachter, 1882–1946
Wahlb.–P. F. Wahlberg, 1800–1877
Wahlenb.–G. G. Wahlenberg, 1780–1851
Waldst.–F. A. Graf von Waldstein-Wartemberg, 1759–1823
Wall.–N. Wallich, 1786–1854
Wallr.–K. F. W. Wallroth, 1792–1857
Walp.–W. G. Walpers, 1816–1853
Walters–S. M. Walters
E. F. Warb.–E. F. Warburg, 1908–1966
H. C. Wats.–H. C. Watson, 1804–1881
W. C. R. Wats.–W. C. R. Watson, 1885–1954
Weatherby–C. A. Weatherby, 1875–1949
Webb–P. B. Webb, 1793–1854
D. A. Webb–D. A. Webb
Weber–F. Weber, 1781–1823
Weig.–C. E. von Weigel, 1748–1831
Weihe–K. E. A. Weihe, 1779–1834
C. West–C. West
Weston–R. Weston, 1773–1806
Wettst.–R. Ritter von Wettstein, 1863–1931
W. Wettst.–W. von Wettstein
L. C. Wheeler–L. C. Wheeler
F. B. White–F. B. W. White, 1842–1894
Wibel–A. W. E. C. Wibel, 1775–1814
Willd.–C. (K.) L. Willdenow, 1765–1812
Willk.–H. M. Willkomm, 1821–1895
Wilmott–A. J. Wilmott, 1888–1950
Wimm.–C. F. H. Wimmer, 1803–1868
Wirtg.–P. Wirtgen, 1806–1870
With.–W. Withering, 1741–1799
Wolf–J. Wolf, 1765–1824
Wolfg.–J. F. Wolfgang, 1776–1859
Wulf.–F. X. von Wulfen, 1728–1805

D. P. Young–D. P. Young

Zahn–K. H. Zahn, 1865–1940
Ziz–J. B. Ziz, 1779–1829
Zucc.–J. G. Zuccarini, 1797–1848

ABBREVIATIONS USED IN THE TEXT

agg.–aggregate
flo.–flower(s)
fr.–fruit(s)

inflo.–inflorescence
o–absent
subsp.–subspecies

var.–variety
*–not native, alien

Plate I

❄ indicates plant is illustrated

RANUNCULACEAE

Clematis vitalba L. **Traveller's Joy, Old Man's Beard.** ¶Stems rope-like, climbing by twisted leaf stalks; flo. greenish; fr. feathery. Mostly on calcareous and alluvial soils in S. England, rarer and mainly introduced in N. Flo. July. ❄.

Thalictrum alpinum L. **Alpine Meadow Rue.** ¶Small, wiry, 3–8 in.; flo. purplish, drooping; stamens pendulous. On wet mountain turf and rocks, N. Wales and Yorkshire northward. Flo. July. ❄.

Thalictrum minus L. agg. ¶Closely related forms; leaflets variable, their length not much exceeding breadth; stamens drooping. Flo. June–Aug.
Subsp. *minus.* **Cliff Meadow Rue.** *T. montanum* Wallr. *T. collinum* auct. ¶Shortly creeping or not; branching above the middle; leaflets medium. On limestone sea cliffs, mountain rocks and chalk, local. ❄.
Subsp. *arenarium* (Butcher) Clapham. **Sand Meadow Rue.** *T. dunense* auct. ¶Stolons widely creeping; stem short, branched and leafy to base. On coastal sand dunes, from S. Wales and Norfolk northwards. ❄.
Subsp. *majus* (Crantz) Rouy & Fouc. **Greater Meadow Rue.** *T. kochii* Fr. ¶Stem 2–4 ft branching from about the middle; leaflets large. On shady rocks and riversides, sometimes creeping on soft soils, Wales, N. England and Scotland. ❄.

Thalictrum flavum L. **Common Meadow Rue.** ¶Stems 2–4 ft stout, subsimple; leaflets oblong; flo. crowded; stamens erect. In damp meadows, ditches and stream sides. Flo. June–July. ❄.

Pulsatilla vulgaris Mill. **Pasque Flower.** *Anemone pulsatilla* L. ¶Stem 4–10 in.; leaves finely divided, hairy; flo. violet, silky outside; fr. feathery. On calcareous slopes, S. and E. England. Flo. April–May. ❄.

Anemone nemorosa L. **Wood Anemone.** ¶Rootstock horizontal; stem 6 in.; sepals petaloid, white, rarely lilac (var. *purpurea* DC. ❄) or pale blue (var. *caerulea* DC. ❄). Common in woods except on acid soils. Flo. March–April. ❄.

Anemone ranunculoides L. **Yellow Wood Anemone.** ¶Similar in habit to *A. nemorosa*; leaves deeply divided, very shortly stalked; sepals petaloid, golden yellow, solitary, or in pairs. Garden escape. Occasionally naturalized in woods and plantations. Flo. April–May.

Anemone apennina L. **Blue Anemone.** ¶Similar in habit to *A. nemorosa* but with a tuberous, blackish, elongated rhizome; stem leaves in whorls of 3, glabrous above pubescent below; flo. solitary, with 8–15 narrow, bright blue, rarely white, perianth segments. Garden escape. Occasionally naturalized in woods and plantations. Flo. April–May.

Adonis annua L. **Pheasant's Eye.** ¶Annual. Stem 8–15 in.; leaves finely divided; flo. scarlet; achenes with straight beak. In corn-fields, S. and E. England, rarely naturalized. Flo. May–Sept. ❄.

Myosurus minimus L. **Mouse-Tail.** ¶Annual, 2–6 in.; leaves basal, linear; flo. greenish; sepals with spur; carpels many, spiked. Damp arable fields in England, rare. Flo. April–June. ❄.

CLEMATIS
VITALBA.

THALICTRUM
MAJUS.

GREATER
MEADOW
RUE.

THALICTRUM
ALPINUM.

THALICTRUM
MINUS.

VAR.
CAERULEA.

VAR. PURPUREA.

THALICTRUM
ARENARIUM

ADONIS
ANNUA.
PHEASANT
EYE

THALICTRUM
FLAVUM
COMMON
MEADOW RUE.

ANEMONE
NEMOROSA.
WOOD ANEMONE.

MYOSURUS
MINIMUS

PULSATILLA
VULGARIS.

Plate 2   ❃ indicates plant is illustrated

RANUNCULACEAE (*continued*)

Ranunculus circinatus Sibth. **Circular-leaved Crowfoot.** ¶Leaves all submerged, segments short, in one plane, wheel like. In canals, ponds and slow streams, mainly lowland. Flo. June–Aug. ❃.

Ranunculus fluitans Lam. **River Crowfoot.** ¶Stems long and stout; submerged leaves 3–10 in.; flo. large, petals 5–8; stamens shorter than achenes. In rather rapid streams. Flo. June–Aug. ❃.

Ranunculus trichophyllus Chaix. **Dark Hair Crowfoot.** ¶Leaves all submerged, segments short, dark, rigid; petals narrow; achenes hairy, crowded. In ponds and slow streams, England and S. Scotland. Flo. June. ❃.

Ranunculus aquatilis L. **Water Crowfoot.** *R. heterophyllus* Weber. ¶Floating leaf segments wedge shaped or variously cut. Submerged leaves not rigid; peduncles short; stamens exceeding achenes. ❃.

Ranunculus peltatus Schrank. ¶Floating leaves with rounded segments; submerged leaves rather stiff; peduncles long and tapering; flo. large. Ponds and slow streams, common. ❃.
Var. *floribundus* (Bab.) Druce. ¶Petals not contiguous; peduncles short and slender. Now regarded as a mere habitat form and unworthy of varietal status. ❃.

Ranunculus penicillatus (Dumort.) Bab.
Var. *penicillatus*. *R. pseudofluitans* (Syme) Newbould ex J. G. Bak. & Foggitt. *R. peltatus* Schrank subsp. *pseudofluitans* (Syme) C. D. K. Cook. ¶Floating leaves alternate; submerged leaves long, tassel-like, much branched; flo. large. Fast-flowing streams in E. and S. England, the Midlands, Wales and Ireland. Flo. May–June.
Var. *calcareus* (Butcher) C. D. K. Cook. *R. calcareus* Butcher. ¶Similar to var. *penicillatus* but floating leaves absent; submerged leaves shorter and very much branched with up to 150 ultimate segments. Chiefly in calcareous streams in S.E. England and the Midlands. Flo. May–June. ❃.
Var. *vertumnus* C. D. K. Cook. *R. sphaerospermus* auct. angl., non Boiss. & Blanche. ¶Entire leaves absent; divided leaves globose to reniform in outline; shorter than mature internodes; segments rigid, much branched. Canals, ditches and slow streams in S. England and the Midlands. Flo. May–June. ❃.

Ranunculus baudotii Godr. **Seaside Crowfoot.** ¶Floating leaves cut into 3 subequal segments; submerged leaves rigid; stamens shorter than head of many achenes. Brackish water near sea. ❃.
Var. *confusus* (Godr.) Syme. ¶Is more slender with longer stamens. Now regarded as a mere habitat form and unworthy of varietal status. ❃.

Ranunculus tripartitus DC. **Little Three-lobed Crowfoot.** ¶Stems very slender; floating leaves small, with obovate or lobed segments; submerged leaves very fine or absent (f. *lutarius* ❃†); flo. minute, petals 3 mm.; achenes few, 3–5. In shallow pools, S. and W. England and Wales. Flo. May.

Ranunculus omiophyllus Ten. **Moorland Crowfoot.** *R. lenormandii* F. W. Schultz. ¶With floating leaves only, divided half-way into 3 rounded, crenate segments; petals 5–6 mm. In moorland pools, mostly in W. and N. Flo. May–Sept. ❃.

Ranunculus hederaceus L. **Ivy-leaved Crowfoot.** ¶Leaves notched, with shallow lobes broadest at their base; petals often hardly longer than the sepals. Creeping on mud and in shallow water throughout the British Isles, though rather local. ❃.

†*Ranunculus tripartitus* f. *lutarius* is possibly referable to the hybrid *R. omiophyllus* × *tripartitus*.

SUBSPECIES
SPHÆROSPERMUS.

×4

RANUNCULUS
AQUATILIS.

R. TRIPARTITUS.

RANUNCULUS
TRICHOPHYLLUS.

× 4

R. BAUDOTII.

RANUNCULUS
CIRCINATUS.

R. TRIPARTITUS
f. LUTARIUS.

VAR. CONFUSUS.

× 5

R. FLUITANS.

R. HEDERACEUS.

× 4

SUBSP.
PSEUDO-FLUITANS.

RANUNCULUS
PELTATUS.

RANUNCULUS
OMIOPHYLLUS

R. PELTATUS.

VAR.
FLORIBUNDUS.

Plate 3   ❀ indicates plant is illustrated

RANUNCULACEAE (*continued*)

Ranunculus sceleratus L. **Celery-leaved Crowfoot.** ¶Annual, 1–2 ft; petals small, yellow; receptacle elongated; achenes many. In muddy ditches and sides of ponds. Flo. May–Sept. ❀.

Ranunculus ophioglossifolius Vill. ¶Annual, $\frac{1}{2}$–1 ft; flo. small, $\frac{1}{4}$ in., pale yellow; achenes covered with tubercles. In marshes, Gloucestershire, formerly in Jersey and Dorset, very rare. Flo. June–July. ❀.

Ranunculus flammula L. **Lesser Spearwort.**
Subsp. *flammula*. ¶Suberect, 6–18 in.; basal leaves oval. Wet places. Flo. May–Sept. ❀.
    Var. *tenuifolius* Wallr. ¶Fairly stout, arching, rooting at some nodes. ❀.
Subsp. *scoticus* (E. S. Marshall) Clapham. ¶Lower leaves without or almost without a blade. Gravelly lake margins, N. England, Scotland, Ireland. ❀.

Ranunculus reptans L. ¶Stem creeping, slender, rooting at every node; leaves linear-lanceolate; achenes with slender, curved beak. Sandy lake margins in N., very rare. Material previously referred to this species is now regarded as the hybrid *R. flammula* × *reptans*. Flo. July. ❀.

Ranunculus lingua L. **Great Spearwort.** ¶Stem 2–3 ft, hollow; leaves very large, ovate-oblong, clasping stem; flo. 1$\frac{1}{2}$–2 in. wide. In marshes, fens and ditches, local. Flo. July–Sept. ❀.

Ranunculus auricomus L. **Goldilocks.** ¶Stem 1 ft; petals often imperfect; achenes on tubercles of receptacle, downy with hooked beak. In woods and thickets. Flo. April–July. ❀.

Ranunculus acris L. **Common Meadow Buttercup.** ¶Stem 1–3 ft without stolons; leaves with middle lobe subsessile; sepals not reflexed. Abundant in meadows. Flo. April–Sept. ❀.

Ranunculus repens L. **Creeping Buttercup.** ¶Stems 1–2 ft with leafy stolons rooting at nodes; mid lobe of leaves stalked; sepals not reflexed. Cultivated land and pastures. Flo. May–Aug. ❀.

Ranunculus bulbosus L. **Bulbous Buttercup.** ¶Stem 6–18 in., base bulbous; mid lobe of leaves stalked; sepals reflexed. Abundant in dry pastures. Flo. May–July. ❀.

Ranunculus sardous Crantz. **Pale Hairy Buttercup.** ¶Annual, 6–18 in.; sepals hairy, reflexed; achenes bordered and tuberculate. On damp arable, waste and grassland on heavy soils chiefly near the sea, local. Flo. June–Sept. ❀.

Ranunculus parviflorus L. **Small-flowered Buttercup.** ¶Stems prostrate, spreading; flo. very small; achenes few, bordered and with short, hooked tubercles. In arable land and short grass. Common in S.W. ❀.

Ranunculus arvensis L. **Corn Buttercup.** ¶Annual, 6–24 in.; fr. bordered and with long curved spines. Formerly common in cornfields, particularly on calcareous soils, mostly S. England. Flo. May–July. ❀.

Ranunculus paludosus Poir. **Jersey Buttercup.** ¶Plant with tubers and stolons; stem 6–12 in., silky; leaf segments narrow; flo. large, bright yellow. In Jersey only. Flo. May.

Ranunculus ficaria L. **Lesser Celandine.** ¶Tuberous; leaves cordate; flo. glossy yellow. Common. In shady places, axillary bulbils sometimes replace the often infertile frs. Flo. March–May. ❀.

RANUNCULUS
SCELERATUS.

VAR.
TENUIFOLIUS.

RANUNCULUS
LINGUA.

SUBSP.
SCOTICUS.

RANUNCULUS
AURICOMUS.

RANUNCULUS
ACRIS.

RANUNCULUS BULBOSUS.

RANUNCULUS
REPTANS.

RANUNCULUS
FLAMMULA.

RANUNCULUS
REPENS.

RANUNCULUS
OPHIOGLOSSIFOLIUS.

RANUNCULUS
ARVENSIS.

RANUNCULUS
SARDOUS.

RANUNCULUS PARVIFLORUS.

RANUNCULUS
FICARIA

Plate 4   ✾ indicates plant is illustrated

RANUNCULACEAE (*continued*)

Caltha palustris L. **Marsh Marigold, Kingcup, Mollyblobs.**
Subsp. *palustris.* ¶Stems suberect, 1–2 ft; flo. 1¼ in. wide, bright yellow. In marshes, common. Flo. March–April. ✾.
Subsp. *minor* (Mill.) Clapham. ¶Stems decumbent or rooting; leaves often triangular; flo. few and smaller. On mountains in N. Flo. April–June.

Trollius europaeus L. **Globe Flower.** ¶Stems 1–2 ft; flo. 1 in., globular; perianth segments orbicular, pale yellow, inner (petals) with nectaries. Subalpine meadows. Flo. June–July. ✾.

Helleborus viridis L.
Subsp. *occidentalis* (Reut.) Schiffn. **Green Hellebore.** ¶Stems 1–2 ft; leaves glabrous beneath; flo. 1–1¾ in., green. In woods mostly on chalk in S. and E. England. Flo. March–April. ✾.

Helleborus foetidus L. **Stinking Hellebore.** ¶Stems 1–2 ft; flo. many, drooping, green with purple edges. In bushy places on calcareous soils in S. and W. England. Flo. Feb.–March. ✾.

*Eranthis hyemalis (L.) Salisb. **Winter Aconite.** ¶Stems 4–6 in.; sessile leaflets forming an involucre; flo. bright yellow. Not native, naturalized in plantations. Flo. Jan.–March. ✾.

Aquilegia vulgaris L. **Columbine.** ¶Perennial, 1–2 ft; spur much curved inwards; fr. ¾–1 in. Native, on shady slopes and in woods, local, chiefly on the chalk. Flo. May–July. ✾.

*Aquilegia pyrenaica DC. ¶Has spur less curved; fr. ½ in. Planted and naturalized in Caenlochan Glen, Clova Mountains, Angus.

*Consolida ambigua (L.) P. W. Ball & Heywood. **Larkspur.** *Delphinium ambiguum* L. *D. ajacis* auct. ¶Annual, 12–18 in.; fr. of 1 pubescent follicle, tapering to beak. More or less naturalized in cultivated ground. Flo. June–July. ✾.

Aconitum anglicum Stapf. **Monk's Hood.** ¶Perennial, 2–4 ft; leaves light green, more narrowly divided than in Continental forms. Shady places by streams, S.W. England and Wales. Flo. May–June. ✾.

*Aconitum napellus L. *sensu lato.* **Monk's Hood.** ¶Similar to *A. anglicum* but with darker green, less narrowly divided leaves. Garden escape. Naturalized on heaths and commons, in thickets etc. Flo. May–June.

Actaea spicata L. **Baneberry, Herb Christopher.** ¶Rhizome stout, stem 1–2 ft, herbaceous; flo. white; berry black, poisonous. In woods on limestone, Yorkshire, Lancashire and Westmorland. Flo. May. ✾.

*Paeonia mascula (L.) Mill. **Paeony.** ¶Stem 2 ft; flo. red; fr. large and downy. In rock clefts, Steepholme, Bristol Channel. Perhaps brought by monks in Middle Ages. Flo. May–June. ✾.

BERBERIDACEAE

Berberis vulgaris L. **Barberry.** ¶A spinous shrub, 4–6 ft; flo. yellow with irritable stamens. The host plant of the wheat rust. In hedges and copses. Flo. May–June. ✾.

*Mahonia aquifolium (Pursh) Nutt. **Oregon Grape.** *Berberis aquifolium* Pursh. ¶Shrub with dark green, ovate, spinose, dentate, evergreen leaflets; flo. bright yellow in clustered, suberect racemes; fr. globose, bluish black, pruinose. Commonly planted in woods and thickets, as pheasant cover, where it readily becomes naturalized. Flo. April–May.

*Epimedium alpinum L. **Barrenwort.** ¶Rhizomatous; stem 12 in.; perianth segments red and pale yellow. In subalpine woods, not native. Flo. May. ✾.

CALTHA
PALUSTRIS

MARSH
MARIGOLD

TROLLIUS
EUROPAEUS
GLOBE FLOWER

HELLEBORUS
VIRIDIS
SUBSP.
OCCIDENTALIS.

HELLEBORUS
FOETIDUS

ACONITUM
ANGLICUM.

AQUILEGIA
VULGARIS.
COLUMBINE

BERBERIS
VULGARIS.

WINTER
ACONITE
ERANTHIS
HYEMALIS.

DELPHINIUM
AMBIGUUM.

BANE
BERRY
ACTAEA SPICATA

PAEONIA
MASCULA

EPIMEDIUM
ALPINUM.

Plate 5   ❄ indicates plant is illustrated

NYMPHAEACEAE

Nuphar lutea (L.) Sm. **Yellow Water Lily.** ¶Flo. 2–3 in. wide; stigma 10–20 rayed, margin entire. In canals, ponds and slow streams, floating from a creeping root. Flo. June–Sept. ❄.

Nuphar pumila (Timm.) DC. ¶Flo. 1–1½ in. wide; stigma with 8–10 rays projecting as teeth on the margin. Mostly in small lakes in Scotland, rare elsewhere. Flo. June–Aug. ❄.

Nuphar × spennerana Gaud. *N. intermedia* Ledeb. *N. lutea × pumila.* ¶Intermediate between *N. lutea* and *N. pumila.* Stigma with 9–14 rays. Northern Britain.

Nymphaea alba L. **White Water Lily.** ¶Flo. very large; stigma with 15–20 rays. In ponds, canals and slow streams. Frequently planted for ornamental purposes. Flo. July–Aug. ❄.
Subsp. *occidentalis* Ostenf. ¶Smaller in all parts. N. Scotland, etc.

PAPAVERACEAE

Papaver rhoeas L. **Common Red Poppy.** ¶Filaments of stamens not dilated; capsule round, glabrous; stigma rays 8–12. In cornfields, etc., abundant. Flo. all the summer. ❄.

Papaver dubium L. **Long Smooth-headed Poppy.** ¶Filaments not dilated above; capsule long, glabrous; stigma rays 6–12, lobes spreading. Cornfields and waste places. Flo. June–July. ❄.

Papaver lecoqii Lamotte. ¶Very near *P. dubium*, but sap always yellow, leaves more cut and acute; stigma lobes depressed. In calcareous fields, E. England, rare.

Papaver argemone L. **Long Rough-headed Poppy.** ¶Filaments dilated above; capsule long and bristly; stigma rays 4–6. In cornfields and dry places. Flo. June–July. ❄.

Papaver hybridum L. **Round Rough-headed Poppy.** ¶Filaments dilated above; capsule round and bristly; stigma rays 4–8. In sandy fields, mostly S. and E. England. Flo. June–July. ❄.

Papaver somniferum L. **Opium Poppy.** ¶Variable; leaves lobed, glaucous; flo. large, lilac, white or pink. A weed of cultivation, especially in fens, not native. ❄.

Meconopsis cambrica (L.) Vig. **Welsh Poppy.** ¶Perennial, 1–2 ft, with yellow sap. On damp, shady rocks in S.W. England, Wales and Ireland, introduced elsewhere. Flo. June–July. ❄.

Glaucium flavum Crantz. **Yellow Horned-Poppy.** ¶Perennial, 1–3 ft; flo. yellow; pod up to 12 in. On shingly beaches. Flo. June–Oct. ❄.

Roemeria hybrida (L.) DC. **Violet Horned-Poppy.** ¶Annual, 9–18 in.; flo. violet; pod 2–3 in. Casual, not native. ❄.

Chelidonium majus L. **Greater Celandine.** ¶Perennial, 1–3 ft; flo. ¾–1 in., yellow. In banks and hedgerows near houses. Probably introduced by herbalists. Flo. May–Sept. ❄.

PAPAVER HYBRIDUM

PAPAVER
ARGEMONE.

CHELIDONIUM
MAJUS

PAPAVER
SOMNIFERUM

MECONOPSIS
CAMBRICA.

PAPAVER
RHOEAS.

PAPAVER DUBIUM

ROEMERIA
HYBRIDA

GLAUCIUM
FLAVUM.

NYMPHAEA
ALBA

NUPHAR
LUTEA

NUPHAR
PUMILA.

Plate 6   ❅ indicates plant is illustrated

FUMARIACEAE

Corydalis lutea (L.) DC. **Yellow Corydalis.** ¶Perennial, 6–12 in.; branched from root. On old walls. Flo. May–Sept. ❅.

Corydalis bulbosa (L. emend. Mill.) DC. **Purple Corydalis.** *C. solida* (L.) Sw. ¶Perennial, 6–10 in.; tuber solid; flo. purplish rose; bracts digitate. Naturalized on cultivated ground in few places. Flo. April–May.

Corydalis cava (L.) Schweigg. & Koerte. *C. bulbosa* auct. *C. tuberosa* DC. ¶Resembling *C. bulbosa* but tuber hollow; small floral leaves entire; flo. white to purple, larger than those of *C. bulbosa*; bracts ovate, entire. Naturalized in a few places. Flo. April–May.

Corydalis claviculata (L.) DC. **Climbing Corydalis.** ¶Annual, stems 1–4 ft. In heathy woods and shady slopes, especially on peaty soil. Flo. June–Sept. ❅.

In the genus *Fumaria* Mr H. W. Pugsley gave liberal help both in finding and determining specimens for this work.

Fumaria occidentalis Pugsl. ¶Flo. very large, 12–15 mm.; lower petal with broad margin; fr. 3 × 3 mm., keeled and rugose. Field borders in Cornwall only, endemic. Flo. June. ❅.

Fumaria capreolata L.
Subsp. *babingtonii* (Pugsl.) P. D. Sell. **White Fumitory.** *F. pallidiflora* Jord. ¶Peduncle long; flo. large, 10–13 mm.; lower petal with narrow margin; upper petal narrow; wings not exceeding keel; fr. 2 × 2 mm., not keeled, pedicel recurved. In hedges and field borders. Flo. June. ❅.
Var. *devoniensis* Pugsl. ¶Flo. more suffused with pink; fr. 2½ × 2½ mm.

Fumaria purpurea Pugsl. ¶Peduncle long; flo. large, 10–13 mm., reddish purple; upper petal rather broad; wings exceeding keel; pedicel less recurved. In hedges and field borders mostly in W. and N., local, endemic. Flo. June. ❅.

Fumaria martinii Clavaud. *F. paradoxa* Pugsl. ¶Peduncle much shorter than the long lax raceme; pedicel recurved in flo., straight in fr.; flo. 10–13 mm., light rose. In field borders mostly in Cornwall and Guernsey. Flo. June–Sept. ❅.

Fumaria bastardii Bor. ¶Peduncle shorter than lax raceme; flo. 9–12 mm.; upper petal narrow, without dark tip. Field borders in Ireland, Cornwall, Jersey, etc. Flo. June–Sept. ❅.

Fumaria muralis Sond. ex Koch.
Subsp. *muralis*. ¶Peduncle equalling lax few-flowered raceme; flo. 9–11 mm., upper petal apiculate, not broad. In field borders, rare.
Subsp. *boraei* (Jord.) Pugsl. **Few-flowered Fumitory.** *F. boraei* Jord. ¶Leaf segments broad and flat; raceme lax, few flowered; upper petal broad. On cultivated ground, common in West of England. Flo. May–Aug. ❅.
Subsp. *neglecta* Pugsl. ¶Raceme lax, many flowered; upper petal obtuse, not broad. Cultivated land in W. Cornwall, rare.

Fumaria densiflora DC. *F. micrantha* Lag. ¶Leaf segments linear, channelled; peduncle much shorter than the long raceme; sepals large and rounded; flo. small, 6–7 mm. In arable fields in E. England, rare or absent in W. Flo. June–Sept. ❅.

Fumaria officinalis L. **Fumitory.**
Subsp. *officinalis*. ¶Peduncle shorter than the many-flowered raceme; usually more than 20 flowered; sepals narrower than corolla; fr. truncate or retuse. In arable ground, chiefly on light soils. Flo. May–Sept. ❅.
Subsp. *wirtgenii* (Koch) Arcangeli. ¶Similar to subsp. *officinalis*, but raceme 10–20 flowered and sepals narrower. In arable ground, chiefly on chalky soils in E. and S.E. England.

Fumaria vaillantii Lois. ¶Leaves linear, flat, often glaucous; peduncle shorter than raceme; flo. small, 5–6 mm.; sepals minute. On chalky arable land, mostly in S.E. England. Flo. June–Sept. ❅.

Fumaria parviflora Lam. ¶Leaf segments small, linear, channelled, very glaucous; raceme subsessile; flo. small white, 5–6 mm.; sepals minute. On chalky arable land. Flo. June–Sept. ❅.

CRUCIFERAE

Matthiola sinuata (L.) R. Br. **Sea Stock.** ¶Herbaceous, diffuse; lower leaves sinuate, dentate. On shores and cliffs of S.W. coasts, local. Flo. May–Aug. ❅.

Matthiola incana (L.) R. Br. **Hoary Stock.** ¶Shrubby and erect; lower leaves entire. On sea cliffs in I. of Wight, etc. Flo. May–July.

Cheiranthus cheiri L. **Wallflower.** ¶Alien from Southern Europe naturalized on old walls, castles and rock cuttings.

CORYDALIS
LUTEA

CORYDALIS
CLAVICULATA

FUMARIA
CAPREOLATA

×2.

FUMARIA
OCCIDENTALIS

×2

FUMARIA
PURPUREA

FUMARIA
BORAEI

FUMARIA
MARTINII.

FUMARIA DENSIFLORA.

×2

×2

FUMARIA
BASTARDI.

×2

FUMARIA
OFFICINALIS

FUMARIA PARVIFLORA.

FUMARIA VAILLANTII

MATTHIOLA
SINUATA

Plate 7

CRUCIFERAE (continued)

Nasturtium officinale R. Br. **Water Cress.** *Rorippa nasturtium-aquaticum* (L.) Hayek. ¶Perennial, stem 2–4 ft, rooting; seeds in two series; pods about 2 × 16 mm. Common in running water. Flo. May–Oct. ✿.

Nasturtium microphyllum (Boenn.) Reichb. *N. uniseriatum* Howard & Manton. *Rorippa microphylla* (Boenn.) Hyland. ¶Similar to above but seeds in one series, pods slender, 1 × 20 mm., leaves often smaller. Flo. May–Oct.

Nasturtium microphyllum × officinale. Rorippa × sterilis Airy Shaw. ¶Fr. dwarf and deformed with few good seeds. Common.

Rorippa sylvestris (L.) Bess. **Creeping Yellow Cress.** *Nasturtium sylvestre* (L.) R. Br. ¶Rootstock creeping; stem 9–18 in.; leaves pinnate; pods linear. On river banks and wet places. Flo. June–Sept. ✿.

Rorippa islandica (Oeder ex Murray) Borbas, *Nasturtium palustre* (L.) DC. var. *pusillum* (Willd.) DC. ¶Plant prostrate; leaves with narrow and numerous lateral segments, together with a very small terminal lobe; petioles with inconspicuous wings and no auricles; pods 2–3 times as long as pedicels; sepals shorter than 1·6 mm.; flo. small, yellow. Sea coasts, very local and restricted, W. Ireland, I. of Man, Orkneys, W. mainland of Scotland. Flo. June–Sept.

Rorippa palustris (L.) Bess. **Marsh Yellow Cress.** *Nasturtium palustre* (L.) DC., non Crantz, *Rorippa islandica* auct., non (Oeder ex Murray) Borbás. ¶Root fibrous; stem 1–2 ft; leaves pinnatifid with irregularly toothed lateral segments, together with a very prominent ovate terminal lobe; petioles auricled; pods not more than *c.* 2 times as long as pedicels; sepals longer than 1·6 mm. Streamsides, marshes, damp waste ground, etc. S. Scotland southwards, common; local in Ireland. Flo. June–Sept.

Rorippa amphibia (L.) Bess. **Amphibious Yellow Cress.** *Nasturtium amphibium* (L.) R. Br. ¶Rootstock stoloniferous; stem 2–3 ft; leaves serrate or pinnate; pods short. In watery places from York southward. Flo. June–Sept. ✿.

Rorippa amphibia × palustris ¶Intermediate between the parents, with cauline leaves 2–3 times as long as broad and usually acutely serrate. A rare sterile hybrid, which occasionally occurs where the parents grow together, e.g. Thames between Hammersmith and Richmond.

Rorippa amphibia × sylvestris ¶Intermediate between the parents, with ripe pods up to 1·5 mm. broad and petals shorter than 3 mm. A fertile hybrid which often occurs where the parents grow together. Recorded from the Arun, Sussex; Thames, Oxford; frequent by the Severn in Shropshire, Worcestershire and Gloucestershire, etc.

Barbarea vulgaris R. Br. **Common Yellow Rocket, Winter Cress.** ¶Uppermost leaves undivided, toothed; flo. about 8 mm. wide; buds glabrous; pods ¾–1 in.; style 3 mm. Common in hedge banks. Flo. May–Aug. ✿.

Barbarea stricta Andrz. **Lesser Yellow Rocket.** ¶Uppermost leaves undivided, toothed; flo. 5–6 mm. wide; buds downy at top; pods appressed, ¾–1 in.; style about 1 mm. Local, Yorkshire, Surrey, etc. Flo. May–Aug. ✿.

Barbarea intermedia Bor. ¶Leaves all pinnatifid, terminal lobe oval; flo. 5–6 mm. wide; buds glabrous; pods ¾–1 in. Cultivated fields and waysides, local, not native. Flo. May–Aug.

Barbarea verna (Mill.) Aschers. **American Cress.** *B. praecox* (Sm.) R. Br. ¶Upper leaves with linear-oblong lobes; flo. about 9 mm. wide; pods about 2 in. long, rather spreading. Naturalized in waste places. Flo. May–July. ✿.

Cardaminopsis petraea (L.) Hiit. **Mountain Rock-Cress.** *Arabis petraea* (L.) Lam. ¶Stem 3–8 in.; leaves stalked spathulate, lower toothed; flo. white or tinted purple. On high mountains, N. Wales, Scotland, Tipperary, Leitrim. Flo. July. ✿.

Arabis alpina L. **Alpine Rock-Cress.** ¶Stem leaves clasping with rounded basal lobes, 3–6 teeth each side and clothed with stellate hairs; flo. white, 2 sepals saccate. In the mountains of Skye. Flo. July–Aug. ✿.

Arabis caucasica Willd. **Garden Arabis.** *A. albida* Stev. ex Jacq. f. ¶Stem leaves with about 2 teeth each side, and basal lobes pointed; flo. rather larger than above. Garden walls. Flo. March–May.

Arabis stricta Huds. **Bristol Rock-Cress.** *A. scabra* All. ¶Perennial; stems erect, purple, 5–10 in.; leaves forming dense rosette, toothed, hispid; pod 2 in. long. On cliffs of R. Avon, Bristol. Flo. March–May. ✿.

Arabis hirsuta (L.) Scop. **Hairy Rock-Cress.** ¶Stem erect, leafy; rosette leaves stalked, hispid, subentire; pods 1–1½ in., stalked; stem leaves slightly clasping stem; seeds winged. Common on limestone rocks and walls. Flo. June–Aug. ✿.

Arabis brownii Jord. **Fringed Rock-Cress.** *A. ciliata* auct. ¶Like above but with stem leaves subglabrous or ciliate, with round base not clasping stem; seeds not winged. Sand dunes, W. Ireland. Flo. July–Aug.

Arabis turrita L. **Tower Rock-Cress.** ¶Rosette leaves elliptical, stalked; stem leaves narrow, base cordate clasping stem, stellate hairy; flo. yellowish; pods 3–4½ in., recurved. On walls at Cambridge, formerly at Oxford and Kinross, now very rare.

Arabis glabra (L.) Bernh. **Glabrous Tower-Cress.** *A. perfoliata* Lam., *Turritis glabra* L. ¶Stem leaves glabrous, clasping stem; flo. yellowish; pods 1½–2½ in., erect; seeds not winged. On dry banks, local, rare in W. Flo. May–July. ✿.

Cardamine amara L. **Large Bitter Cress.** Stoloniferous, 1–2 ft; leaflets tapering below; flo. white; anthers purple. On moist meadows and riversides, local. Flo. April–June. ✿.

Cardamine pratensis L. **Cuckoo Flower, Lady's Smock.** ¶Perennial, 1–2 ft, subglabrous; flo. lilac, rarely white; anthers yellow. Common in moist meadows. Flo. April–June. ✿.

Cardamine hirsuta L. **Hairy Bitter Cress.** ¶Annual, 6–12 in.; basal leaves many, sparsely hairy; stamens 4; fr. pedicels erect. Abundant in open ground. Flo. March–Sept. ✿.

Cardamine flexuosa With. **Greater Bitter Cress.** *C. sylvatica* Link. ¶Biennial, 8–18 in.; basal leaves few; stamens 6; fr. pedicels spreading. Abundant in shade and moist ground. Flo. April–Sept. ✿.

Cardamine trifolia L. ¶Basal leaves with 3 roundish leaflets; flo. white or pale pink. Alien. Flo. April–June.

WATER CRESS

RORIPPA AMPHIBIA.

RORIPPA NASTURTIUM-AQUATICUM

BARBAREA VERNA

BARBAREA VULGARIS

RORIPPA SYLVESTRIS.

RORIPPA ISLANDICA.

BARBAREA STRICTA

ARABIS STRICTA.

CARDAMINE AMARA.

CARDAMINE PRATENSIS.

CARDAMINOPSIS PETRAEA.

CARDAMINE FLEXUOSA.

ARABIS ALPINA

TURRITIS GLABRA

ARABIS HIRSUTA

CARDAMINE HIRSUTA

Plate 8   ❀ indicates plant is illustrated

CRUCIFERAE (*continued*)

Cardamine impatiens L. **Narrow-leaved Bitter Cress.** ¶Stem leaves with basal auricles like stipules; leaflets toothed; flo. small; pods spreading. On shady limestone rocks, local. Flo. May–Aug. ❀.

Cardamine bulbifera (L.) Crantz. **Coral Root.** *Dentaria bulbifera* L. ¶Root white and scaly; stem 1–2 ft with purple bulbils in axils; petals pink or lilac. In calcareous woods, very local. Flo. April–May. ❀.

Alyssum alyssoides (L.) L. **Hoary Alyssum.** *A. calycinum* L. ¶Plant 6 in., hoary with stellate hairs; flo. yellow; calyx persistent; pods rounded. Naturalized in arable land and sandy tracks. Flo. May–June.

Lobularia maritima (L.) Desv. **Sea Alyssum.** *Alyssum maritimum* (L.) Lam. ¶Plant 6–10 in., grey with forked hairs; calyx not persistent; petals white entire. On sandy ground near the sea, etc., not native. Flo. June–Sept. ❀.

Berteroa incana (L.) DC. *Alyssum incanum* L. ¶Plant 1–1½ ft, grey with stellate hairs; petals white, deeply bifid; stamen filaments toothed or winged at base. Casual in arable land.

Draba muralis L. **Wall Whitlow Grass.** ¶Stem 8–12 in.; stem leaves broadly ovate, sessile, dentate; flo. small; petals narrow, white. On limestone rocks and walls. Flo. April–May. ❀.

Draba incana L. **Hoary Whitlow Grass.** ¶Stem leafy, 2–10 in.; leaves lanceolate toothed, with stellate hairs; flo. white; pods twisted. On mountain rocks to 3000 ft. Flo. June–July. ❀.

Draba norvegica Gunn. **Rock Whitlow Grass.** *D. rupestris* R. Br. ¶Stem usually leafless, 1–3 in.; leaves mostly entire; flo. white; pods not twisted. Mountains in Scotland above 3000 ft, rare. Flo. July–Aug. ❀.

Draba aizoides L. **Yellow Whitlow Grass.** ¶Stem leafless, 2–5 in.; leaves acute, margins ciliate; flo. larger, 8 mm., bright yellow. On rocks and walls, Pennard near Swansea, doubtful native. Flo. March–May. ❀.

Erophila verna (L.) Chevall.
Subsp. *verna*. **Whitlow Grass.** ¶Stem 3–6 in.; leaves with forked hairs; pods boat shaped. On walls and dry places, mostly calcareous. Flo. March–May. ❀.
Subsp. *spathulata* (Láng) Walters. *Erophila spathulata* Láng. *E. boerhaavii* (Van Hall) Dumort. ¶With short forked hairs; pods obovoid, rounded at top; flo. smaller. Local. ❀a.
Var. *brachycarpa* (Jord.). ¶Pods orbicular; petals only 1·5 mm. ❀b.
Subsp. *praecox* (Stev.) Walters. *Erophila praecox* (Stev.) DC. ¶Leaves with long simple hairs; pod obovate. Local.

Cochlearia officinalis L. **Common Scurvy Grass.** ¶Lower leaves cordate, long stalked; pod subglobose; stems 4–10 in. On sea cliffs and shores. Flo. May–Aug. ❀.

Cochlearia pyrenaica DC. **Alpine Scurvy Grass.** *C. alpina* (Bab.) H. C. Wats. *C. officinalis* L. subsp. *alpina* (Bab.) Hook. ¶Lower leaves cordate; stem leaves triangular or ovate, lobed; pod obovate. On mountains. Flo. June–Sept.

Cochlearia micacea E. S. Marshall. ¶Pod 2–3 times as long as broad, tapering at apex; leaves small. ❀.

Cochlearia danica L. **Stalked Scurvy Grass.** ¶Lower leaves cordate; stem leaves stalked and lobed; flo. white or pinkish. On seaside cliffs and shores, also inland on railway ballast. Flo. Feb.–June. ❀.

Cochlearia scotica Druce. **Northern Scurvy Grass.** ¶Lower leaves suborbicular; stem leaves elliptical, sessile. On shores in N. Scotland. Flo. June–Sept. ❀.

Cochlearia anglica L. **English Scurvy Grass.** ¶Lower leaves ovate; upper leaves clasping stem; pods large obovoid. On muddy shores and estuaries. Flo. April–July. ❀.

Armoracia rusticana Gaertn., Mey. & Scherb. **Horse Radish.** *A. lapathifolia* Gilib. ¶Leaves oblong, 1–2 ft long and 4 in. wide; root thick and used for flavouring. Alien from E. Europe. Flo. June–Sept.

Hesperis matronalis L. **Dame's Violet.** ¶Stems 2–3 ft; leaves 2–4 in. broadly lanceolate; flo. ¾ in., white or lilac. Alien, in plantations on waste ground, by waysides, river banks, etc. Flo. May–July. ❀.

Arabidopsis thaliana (L.) Heynh. **Thale Cress.** *Sisymbrium thalianum* (L.) Gay. ¶Annual; stem slender, 6–9 in.; flo. white. Common on dry banks and wall tops and in cultivated fields. Flo. April–May. ❀.

Sisybrium officinale (L.) Scop. **Hedge Mustard.** ¶Stem 1–2 ft, stiff and erect; pods hairy, appressed; flo. yellow. Common on hedge banks and waste land. Flo. June–Aug. ❀.
Var. *leiocarpum* DC. has glabrous pods.

Sisymbrium altissimum L. *S. pannonicum* Jacq. ¶Lower leaves with many triangular lobes, upper sessile with pairs of linear lobes; pods long, thin, spreading; peduncle 6–9 mm. Alien, naturalized in many waste places. Flo. May–Oct.

Sisymbrium orientale L. *S. columnae* Jacq. ¶Hispid; leaves petiolate, lobes few, 2–3 pairs; upper leaves hastate with oblong terminal lobe; pods long and thick; pedicel 3–4 mm. In waste places. Flo. May–Oct.

Sisymbrium irio L. **London Rocket.** ¶Glabrous, 1–2 ft; lower leaves many, with oblong lobes; upper leaves with hastate terminal lobe. In waste places, rare. Called London Rocket since it appeared in quantity after the fire of 1666. Flo. May–Oct.

Sisymbrium loeselii L. ¶Differs from *S. irio* in its bright yellow petals being about twice as long as sepals and in its young pods not overtopping the open flo. Waste places. Flo. June–Oct.

Descurainia sophia (L.) Webb ex Prantl. **Flixweed.** *Sisymbrium sophia* L. ¶Stem 1–3 ft, branched above, slightly downy; leaves finely divided; flo. small, pale yellow. In waste places. Flo. June–Aug. ❀.

Alliaria petiolata (Bieb.) Cavara & Grande. **Garlic Mustard.** *Sisymbrium alliaria* (L.) Scop. ¶Stem 2–3 ft; leaves broad, cordate or reniform, garlic scented; flo. white. Abundant in hedge banks. Flo. April–June. ❀.

COCHLEARIA
DANICA.

COCHLEARIA
OFFICINALIS.

a

EROPHILA
SPATHULATA

b.

EROPHILA
VERNA.

COCHLEARIA
SCOTICA.

DRABA
AIZOIDES.

ARDAMINE
IPATIENS.

CARDAMINE
BULBIFERA.

COCHLEARIA
ANGLICA.

DRABA
NORVEGICA

COCHLEARIA
MICACIA

DRABA
INCANA

LOBULARIA
MARITIMA.

ALLIARIA
PETIOLATA

SISYMBRIUM
OFFICINALE.

ARABIDOPSIS
THALIANA.

SISYMBRIUM
IRIO.
LONDON
ROCKET.

DESCURAINIA SOPHIA.

DRABA MURALIS.

HESPERIS
MATRONALIS.

Plate 9   �֍ indicates plant is illustrated

CRUCIFERAE (continued)

Erysimum cheiranthoides L. **Treacle Mustard.** ¶Stem 1–2 ft with a few forked hairs; leaves lanceolate; flo. yellow, often in a neat ring. In cultivated lowland fields, local. Flo. June–Sept. �֍.

*Conringia orientalis (L.) Dumort. *Erysimum orientale* (L.) R. Br. ¶Stem 1–2 ft; leaves glaucous, oval, cordate, clasping the stem; flo. yellowish white. Introduced in cultivated land. Flo. May–July.

*Camelina sativa (L.) Crantz. **Gold of Pleasure.** ¶Stem 2–3 ft; leaves oblong-lanceolate, with pointed auricles; flo. small, yellow; pods obovate, 6–9 mm. In arable fields, not native.

Subularia aquatica L. **Awlwort.** ¶Root of many white fibres; stem 1–3 in.; leaves all radical, subulate; pods ⅛ in. oblong. Margins of alpine lakes, N. Wales, N. England, Scotland. Flo. June–Aug. ✖.

Brassica oleracea L. **Wild Cabbage.** ¶Biennial, 1–2 ft; leaves very broad, glaucous; flo. in long spike and large. On sea cliffs in England and Wales. Flo. May–Aug. ✖.

*Brassica napus L. **Rape, Swede.** ¶Root spindle shaped; leaves glaucous; flo. yellow: Rape, grown for fodder. Root more tuberous; leaves glaucous; flo. pale orange: Swede. Flo. May–Aug.

*Brassica rapa L. **Turnip.** *B. campestris* L. ¶Root tuberous; leaves bright green; flo. overtopping the buds, bright yellow. Arable fields and river banks. Flo. May–Aug. ✖.

Brassica nigra (L.) Koch. **Black Mustard.** *Sinapis nigra* L. ¶Pods 4 angled, glabrous, appressed; beak short, narrow, seedless, valve 1 nerved. On riversides, cliffs and banks. Common near S.W. coasts. Flo. June–Aug. ✖.

Rhynchosinapis monensis (L.) Dandy. **Isle of Man Cabbage.** *Brassicella monensis* (L.) O. E. Schulz. ¶Mostly decumbent, glabrous; leaves radical, pinnatifid; pods spreading; beak 1–3 seeded valves 3 nerved. On shores of N.W. coasts. Flo. May–June. ✖.

Rhynchosinapis cheiranthos (Vill.) Dandy. **Wallflower Cabbage.** *Brassicella erucastrum* auct. ¶Stem erect, branched, leafy, hispid below; leaves lobed, hispid beneath. On W. coasts and the Channel Islands. Flo. June–Aug. ✖.

Rhynchosinapis wrightii (O. E. Schulz) Dandy. **Lundy Cabbage.** *Brassicella wrightii* O. E. Schulz. ¶Like *R. cheiranthos* but more robust, erect 1½–3 ft, stem clothed with deflexed hairs; leaves very hairy; pods thicker, hairy with about 40 seeds; flo. larger, 2·5 cm across. On Lundy Island, N. Devon only and endemic there. The sole host of 2 endemic beetles. Named after Dr Elliston Wright who observed the differences, and sent the plant to Prof. Schulz (*Journal of Bot.*, Nov. 1936)

Sinapis arvensis L. **Charlock.** *Brassica arvensis* (L.) Rabenh., non L. *B. kaber* (DC.) L. C. Wheeler. ¶Hispid; pods spreading and longer than the conical beak; valves usually 3 nerved; seeds dark. Abundant in arable land. Flo. May–July. ✖.

*Sinapis alba L. **White Mustard.** *Brassica hirta* Moench, *B. alba* (L.) Rabenh. ¶Hispid with reflexed hairs; pods short, about 3 seeded, equalling the wide sword-like beak; seeds pale. On arable land, alien. Flo. June–Aug. ✖.

*Hirschfeldia incana (L.) Lagr.-Foss. **Hoary Mustard.** *Brassica adpressa* Boiss. ¶Hoary plant; pods very short, appressed with short 1-seeded beak; uppermost leaves narrow, entire, often sub glabrous. Introduced in Sussex, Kent, Middlesex, Norfolk, Jersey and Alderney, etc. Flo. June–Sept.

Diplotaxis tenuifolia (L.) DC. **Wall Rocket.** ¶Stem leafy, branched 1–2 ft; leaves glaucous, segments long and narrow; flo. long pedicelled. On walls, waste places, railway yards, etc. Flo. July–Sept. ✖.

ERYSIMUM
CHEIRANTHOIDES.

BRASSICA OLERACEA.

BRASSICA RAPA
TURNIP.

RHYNCHOSINAPIS
CHEIRANTHOS

RHYNCHOSINAPIS
MONENSIS.

SINAPIS
ARVENSIS.
CHARLOCK.

SUBULARIA AQUATICA.

BRASSICA
NIGRA.
BLACK MUSTARD

SINAPIS
ALBA
WHITE
MUSTARD

DIPLOTAXIS TENUIFOLIA.

Plate 10

❋ indicates plant is illustrated

CRUCIFERAE (*continued*)

Diplotaxis muralis (L.) DC. **Annual Wall Rocket, Sand Rocket.** ¶Stem 6–15 in., simple or branched at base; leaves often mostly basal, lobed; flo. short stalked. Waste land and railway ballast. Flo. Aug.–Sept. ❋.

❋Diplotaxis erucoides (L.) DC. **White Rocket.** ¶Stem tall; leaf lobes toothed, terminal lobe large; flo. white or lilac. Introduced, weed of cultivated land, S. England. Flo. May–Sept.

Capsella bursa-pastoris (L.) Medic. **Shepherd's Purse.** ¶Basal leaves forming rosette; stem leaves amplexicaul; pods triangular or obcordate. A very common weed, but variable. Flo. all the year. ❋.

❋Capsella rubella Reut. ¶Similar to *C. bursa-pastoris* but with smaller flo., the petals scarcely exceeding the sepals; flo. buds red; apical notch of pod shallow. On waste ground in Sussex, Surrey, Bucks., etc., introduced. Flo. March–Sept.

❋Coronopus didymus (L.) Sm. **Swine Cress.** *Senebiera didyma* (L.) Pers. ¶Prostrate, foetid; petals minute or 0; pods stalked, small, of 2 rounded lobes. On bare waste ground mostly in S. and S.W. England, introduced. Flo. June–Sept. ❋.

Lepidium latifolium L. **Dittander.** ¶Stems 3 ft, branched; leaves large, basal lobed, upper oblong; flo. many; pods elliptical. In salt marshes, mostly in E. England, adventive on canal and river banks, in gravel pits, etc., in the London area. Flo. July–Aug. ❋.

Lepidium ruderale L. **Narrow-leaved Pepperwort.** ¶Stem ½–1 ft; leaves mostly pinnate; petals usually 0; pods oval or nearly round, deeply notched. On waste land, especially near E. coast. Flo. May–July. ❋.

❋Lepidium sativum L. **Garden Cress.** ¶Stem 1 ft; lower leaves pinnatifid, upper entire, linear, not clasping the stem; pod deeply notched; narrowly winged above. A garden escape. Flo. June–Sept.

Lepidium campestre (L.) R. Br. **Field Pepperwort.** ¶Stem ½–1 ft, branched at top; upper leaves clasping stem, soft and hairy; anthers yellow; pod papillose; style short. On dry banks. Flo. May–Aug. ❋.

Lepidium heterophyllum Benth. var. *canescens* Godr. **Downy Pepperwort.** *L. smithii* Hook. ¶Perennial; stems many, branched mostly from below or from base; stamens with violet anthers; pod nearly smooth; style longer than notch. On light soils and dry banks. Flo. May–Aug. ❋.

Var. *alatostylum* (Towns.) Thell. ¶Has the pod without a notch, wings continued to style.

❋Cardaria draba (L.) Desv. **Hoary Cress.** *Lepidium draba* L. ¶Stoloniferous; stem 1–2 ft, branched above; leaves oblong, sagittate, clasping the stem; pod cordate, tapering above. On arable land, not native. Flo. May–June. ❋.

Thlaspi arvense L. **Field Penny Cress.** ¶Glabrous annual, 1 ft or more; leaves clasping; pods very large, ½–¾ in., nearly round, broadly winged and notched. On cultivated land. Flo. May–Aug. ❋.

Thlaspi perfoliatum L. **Perfoliate Penny Cress.** ¶Annual, 3–8 in.; stem leaves deeply cordate; pods smaller; style short. On limestone fields, Worcestershire, Gloucestershire, Oxfordshire, Wiltshire, adventive on railway tracks elsewhere, rare. Flo. April–May. ❋.

Thlaspi alpestre L. **Alpine Penny Cress.** ¶Erect, 6–12 in.; stem leaves narrow, cordate; flo. white or pink; anthers often purple; style longer. On rocks and mountains, Somerset and N. Wales to Forfar. Flo. May–Aug. ❋.

❋Thlaspi alliaceum L. ¶Annual, 6–18 in. or more; stem hairy below; stem leaves with auricles; flo. white; fr. winged, with apical notch; whole plant smelling strongly of garlic. On cultivated land in S. England, introduced. Flo. April–June.

Iberis amara L. **Candytuft.** ¶Erect, 6–12 in.; leaves lanceolate, mostly lobed; flo. pink or white with outer petals larger; pods winged and notched. In chalky fields, mostly in S. England, local. Flo. July–Aug. ❋.

Teesdalia nudicaulis (L.) R. Br. **Shepherd's Cress.** ¶Stems 2–4 in.; leaves mainly radical with broad terminal lobe; flo. white, 2 outer petals longer; stamens 6 with minute white basal scale. On sand and gravel, often on acid soils. Flo. April–June. ❋.

Hornungia petraea (L.) Reichb. *Hutchinsia petraea* (L.) R. Br. ¶Stem 2–4 in., branched; leaves pinnate, lobes small; petals small, equal; pods elliptical. On limestone rocks and dunes in the W., local. Flo. March–May. ❋.

Isatis tinctoria L. **Woad.** ¶Stems 2–4 ft, branched; radical leaves oblong, crenate; stem leaves with basal lobes; flo. yellow; fr. pendulous. On chalk and clay especially near Tewkesbury, Gloucestershire. A prehistoric introduction. Flo. June–Sept. ❋.

CAPSELLA
BURSA-PASTORIS.

CORONOPUS
DIDYMUS.

CARDARIA
DRABA.

LEPIDIUM
RUDERALE.

LOTAXIS
MURALIS

CORONOPUS
SQUAMATUS.

LEPIDIUM
LATIFOLIUM.

THLASPI PERFOLIATUM.

LEPIDIUM
HETEROPHYLLUM.

THLASPI
PESTRE.

THLASPI
ARVENSE.

LEPIDIUM
CAMPESTRE.

IBERIS
AMARA.

ISATIS TINCTORIA.

TEESDALIA
NUDICAULIS.

HORNUNGIA PETRAEA

Plate 11　　　　　❀ indicates plant is illustrated

CRUCIFERAE (continued)

Crambe maritima L. **Sea Kale.** ¶Stem 1–3 ft; leaves broad and fleshy; flo. white; pods spherical or oval. On shingle and sea cliffs. This was first cultivated and introduced to Covent Garden by Mr Curtis in 1795 from the S. Devonshire coast, where it was plentiful, but it is now in consequence very rare. Flo. June–Aug. ❀.

Cakile maritima Scop. **Sea Rocket.** ¶Branches 1–2 ft; leaves mostly with oblong lobes; flo. lilac or white; pod of 1 or of 2 unequal cells. On sea sand and shingle. Flo. June–Aug. ❀.

Raphanus raphanistrum L.
Subsp. *raphanistrum.* **Wild Radish.** ¶Annual, 1–2 ft; leaf segments few; flo. pale yellow, golden, white, lilac or rarely, violet; pod slightly constricted; between 4 and 8 seeds. Arable land. Flo. May–Sept. ❀.
Subsp. *maritimus* (Sm.) Thell. **Sea Radish.** *Raphanistrum maritimus* Sm. ¶Biennial, very hispid; leaf segments many, often overlapping; pod deeply constricted; seeds 2–3. Sandy sea-shores and cliffs, local. Flo. June–Aug. ❀.

*Raphanus sativus L. **Radish.** ¶Root tuberous; stem often tall; pod inflated, scarcely constricted. An escape from cultivation, origin unknown. Flo. June–Sept. ❀.

RESEDACEAE

*Reseda alba L. ¶Stems erect, glabrous; leaves pinnate; petals 5–6, all trifid, white; stigmas usually 4. In waste places, introduced (but this is not the scented *R. odorata* of gardens). Flo. June–Aug.

Reseda lutea L. **Wild Mignonette.** ¶Leaves pinnate; petals 6, the lower entire, the lateral 2 cleft; stigmas 3. Mostly on chalky soil in England but frequently adventive by railways. Flo. June–Aug. ❀.

Reseda luteola L. **Dyer's Rocket, Weld.** ¶Stem erect, 2–3 ft; leaves oblong, entire; petals 5, 2 lower entire, lateral 3 cleft. On stony or calcareous soil, common. Flo. June–Aug. ❀.

CISTACEAE

Tuberaria guttata (L.) Fourr. **Spotted Rockrose.** *Helianthemum guttatum.* (L.) Mill.
Subsp. *guttata.* ¶Erect herbaceous annual, stellate hairy; upper leaves oblong with stipules, much narrower than the lower; bracts absent; petals yellow with red spot. On dry cliffs, rare, Channel Islands. Flo. June–Sept. ❀.
Subsp. *breweri* (Planch.) E. F. Warb. *Helianthemum breweri* Planch. ¶Similar to subsp. *guttata* but branched from base; upper leaves with stipules, scarcely narrower than the lower; bracts present. Rocky places near the sea, rare, W. and N. Wales and W. Ireland.

Helianthemum canum (L.) Baumg. **Hoary Rockrose.**
Subsp. *canum.* ¶Shrubby, dwarf; leaves hairy, green or greyish above

and hoary beneath, without stipules; flo. usually 2–5, yellow ½ in. wide. Limestone rocks, rare, S. Wales to Westmorland, an isolated colonies in W. Ireland. Flo. May–July. ❀.
Subsp. *levigatum* M. C. F. Proctor. ¶Similar to subsp. *canum* but ver prostrate; leaves small, dark green, glabrous or subglabrous above flo. usually 1–3, yellow, with short inflo. Upper Teesdale.

Helianthemum nummularium (L.) Mill. **Common Rockrose.** *H chamaecistus* Mill. ¶Shrubby, diffuse; leaves with stipules, whit beneath; 2 outer sepals small; flo. yellow, ¾ in. On dry and ca careous soils, common. Flo. June–Sept. ❀.

Helianthemum apenninum (L.) Mill. **White Rockrose.** *H. polifoliu* Mill. ¶Shrubby, hoary; leaves grey above and beneath, wit stipules, margin revolute; flo. white. On sea cliffs, Somerset an S. Devonshire, local. Flo. May–July. ❀.

Helianthemum apenninum × nummularium = H. × sulphureum Willd. ¶Wit sulphur-yellow flo. sometimes occurs where the parents gro together.

POLYGALACEAE

Polygala vulgaris L. **Common Milkwort.** ¶Leaves lanceolate, lowe small; flo. blue (or white or pink); calyx wing as broad as fr., it lateral veins looping up with central vein. Fairly common o rough pastures and banks, especially on chalky soils. Flo. May Sept. ❀.

Polygala oxyptera Reichb. ¶Stems prostrate; leaves narrow lanceolat flo. pink or white; calyx wing narrower than fr. On sandy shore and stony hills, local. This is now regarded as a form of *P. vulgar*i Flo. May–Aug. ❀.

Polygala serpyllifolia Hose. **Heath Milkwort.** *P. seryllacea* Weihe ¶Flower stem branched above; leaves all small elliptical; fl deep blue-purple; calyx wing as wide as fruit, its veins loopin up. Common, especially on heaths and peaty moors. Fl May–Aug. ❀.

Polygala calcarea F. W. Schultz. **Chalk Milkwort.** ¶Lower leav large, obovate; flo. purer blue; calyx wing longer than fr., vei slightly rejoining or not. On chalk downs in S. and E. Englan Flo. May–July. ❀.

Polygala amara L. ¶Plant small, erect; lower leaves large, obovat flo. blue; calyx wings narrower than fr., its veins free. On ca careous rocks, W. Yorkshire and Durham, rare. Flo. June–Aug. ❀

Polygala austriaca Crantz. ¶Similar to above, plant more slende lower leaves large, obovate; flo. small bluish lilac, white or pin calyx wings ½ width of fr., and scarcely branched. On calcareou downs in Kent and formerly in Surrey, very rare. Flo. June–Au ❀.

RAPHANUS
MARITIMUS

RAPHANUS
RAPHANISTRUM

SEA ROCKET
CAKILE
MARITIMA

×2

FRUIT OF
RAPHANUS
SATIVUS.

SEA KALE
CRAMBE
MARITIMA.

POLYGALA OXYPTERA.

TUBERARIA
GUTTATA.

RESEDA
LUTEOLA.

POLYGALA
SERPYLLIFOLIA

×2

RESEDA
LUTEA.

POLYGALA
VULGARIS

POLYGALA
CALCAREA.

HELIANTHEMUM
APENNINUM.

ROCKROSE
HELIANTHEMUM
CHAMAECISTUS.

POLYGALA
AMARA.

HELIANTHEMUM
CANUM.

POLYGALA AUSTRIACA.

Plate 12

✽ indicates plant is illustrated

VIOLACEAE

(a) Leaves enlarging after flowering.

Viola palustris L. **Bog Violet.**
Subsp. *palustris*. ¶Stems white and creeping; leaves orbicular-reniform; flo. lilac, rarely white, with dark veins; spur short. In wet boggy places, especially on peat, widespread in Britain. Flo. April–July. ✽.
Subsp. *juressii* (Neves) Coutinho. *Viola epipsila* auct. angl. *V. juressii* Link ex Neves. ¶Leaves often with hairy petioles and more toothed than subsp. *palustris*; flo. larger; spur longer. In similar habitats to subsp. *palustris*. Mainly confined to S. England and Wales.

Viola odorata L. **Sweet Violet.** ¶Plant with stolons; leaves cordate; petioles and peduncles with deflexed hairs; stipules glandular; flo. fragrant, blue-purple, April. ✽. 'a'.
Var. *dumetorum* (Jord.) Rouy & Fouc. ¶Flo. white with violet spur; lateral petals bearded. Common in S.W. England. ✽. 'c'.
Var. *praecox* Gregory. ¶Summer leaves pointed; flo. small, blackish purple. Flo. early Jan.–March. ✽. 'b'.
Var. *subcarnea* (Jord.) Parl. ¶Flo. all pink. ✽. 'd'.
Var. *imberbis* (Leight.) Henslow. ¶Flo. white with violet spur; lateral petals beardless.

Viola × permixta Jord. (*V. hirta × odorata*). ¶Variable, flo. paler. ✽. 'x'.

Viola hirta L. **Hairy Violet.** ¶Plant without stolons; leaves triangular-cordate, hairy; flo. from rosette.
Subsp. *hirta*. ¶Leaves large, elongate; flo. large; spur hooked. On pastures and banks, mostly on calcareous soil. Flo. April. ✽.
Subsp. *calcarea* (Bab.) E. F. Warb. ¶Leaves shorter; flo. smaller, petals narrow; spur short and straight. Growing with subsp. *hirta* and intermediates. ✽.

(b) Leaves not enlarging after flowering.

Viola rupestris Schmidt. **Teesdale Violet.** ¶Small pubescent plants; leaves roundly cordate; flo. on short branches; spur short; capsule downy. On calcareous rocks and turf above Teesdale. Flo. May–June. ✽.

Viola reichenbachiana Jord. ex Bor. **Woodland Violet.** *V. sylvestris* auct. ¶Branched from the base; flo. lilac; spur long, red-purple; appendages of calyx small. In woodland glades and banks of lanes. Flo. April–May. ✽.

Viola reichenbachiana × riviniana. ¶Intermediate between the two parents, sometimes occurs where they grow together.

Viola riviniana Reichb. **Common Violet.**
Subsp. *riviniana*. ¶Branched freely from base; leaves cordate ovate; flo. blue-purple; spur broad, furrowed and pale. Common in woodland borders and hedge banks. Flo. April–June. ✽.
Var. *diversa* Gregory. ¶Plant dwarf and floriferous; petals and spurs variable in colouring. In upland pastures.
Subsp. *minor* (Gregory) Valentine. ¶Dwarf plant; leaves very small and often purple beneath; spurs yellow. In upland or moorland grass. ✽.

Viola canina L. **Dog Violet.**
Subsp. *canina*. ¶Branched from base; leaves cordate, prolonged; flo. almost pure blue; spur yellow. On heaths and sand dunes. Flo. April–June. ✽.
Subsp. *montana* (L.) Hartm. ¶Bushy plants with underground stems; leaves thin triangular; flo. pale blue; spur slender, green. In fens, Cambridgeshire and Huntingdonshire. Flo. April–June. ✽.

Viola × militaris Savouré (*V. canina × lactea*). ¶Intermediate betwee the two parents, sometimes occurs where they grow together.

Viola canina × riviniana. ¶Variable, but usually intermediate betwee the two parents, sometimes occurs where they grow together.

Viola × ritschliana W. Becker (*V. canina × stagnina*). ¶Occurs rarel where the two parents grow together.

Viola lactea Sm. **Pale Heath Violet.** ¶Upper leaves tapering at bot ends; stipules larger with green teeth; petals pale, subacute. O heaths in S. and S.W. England. Flo. May–June. ✽.

Viola lactea × riviniana. ¶Intermediate between the two parents sometimes occurs where they grow together.

Viola stagnina Kit. **Fen Violet.** ¶Plant with underground stems leaves triangular; petals very pale, round; spur yellowish, ben downwards. Fens and limy marshes, E. England and Ireland. ✽

Melanium Section. **Pansies.**

The British Pansies have sometimes been treated as belonging t several micro-species. Mr R. D. Meikle of the Kew Herbarium ha kindly advised us to reduce them to the following arrangement.

Viola arvensis Murr. **Field Pansy** (including many named forms) ¶Annual plants with petals shorter than sepals. Very variable with leaves lanceolate and hairy or finely pubescent or broadl oval and glabrous. The mid lobe of stipules may be rather broa and foliaceous or narrow and lanceolate. Widely spread in arabl land especially cornfields. Flo. April–Oct. ✽.
The form with oval, glabrous leaves was figured as var. *obtusifolia* ✽.

Viola tricolor L. **Tricolor Pansy** (including many named forms).
Subsp. *tricolor*. ¶Annual plants (except forma *lepida*); petals longe than sepals, often highly coloured; variable, with leaves ovate o oblong lanceolate; the mid lobe of stipules may be broad an crenate or narrow entire. In cornfields and other cultivated land Flo. April–Sept. ✽.
Forma *lepida* Jord. ¶With shoots rising from twiggy undergroun stems. 'A form with perennial habit induced by environment. R.D.M. ✽.
V. arvensis × tricolor (including *V. variata* Jord.). ¶'A very common variable and widespread hybrid.' R.D.M.
Subsp. *curtisii* (E. Forst.) Syme. **Seaside Pansy.** *V. curtisii* E. Forst ¶Perennial; underground stems rising 6 in. or more with slende branches at surface; flo. yellow; spur slender, exceeding smal calyx appendages. Sand dunes on the W. coast and elsewhere. ✽ 'The hybrid *V. arvensis* subsp. *curtisii × tricolor* arises freely and ha purple flowers.' R.D.M.

Viola lutea Huds. **Mountain Pansy.** ¶Perennial; stems slender rising singly a few inches from underground rhizomes; leaf stipule with linear-lanceolate mid lobe; flo. large, $1–1\frac{1}{4}$ in., yellow o purple; spur long and slender. In mountain pastures, often o limestone. Flo. June–Aug. ✽.

Viola lutea × tricolor. ¶Intermediate between the two parents, some times occurs where they grow together.

Viola kitaibeliana Schult. **Dwarf Pansy.** *V. nana* (DC.) Godr ¶Plant small in all its parts; flo. very small, pale, with short entir calyx appendages. On sand in Channel Islands, Scilly Isles an W. Cornwall. Flo. April–July. The small figure is labelle *V. nana*. ✽.

VIOLA
ODORATA

V.
ODORATA

VIOLA
REICHENBACHIANA
(=SYLVESTRIS)

VIOLA PALUSTRIS.

V. ODORATA
× 3

VIOLA
HIRTA

VIOLA
LACTEA

V. HIRTA
VAR.
CALCAREA.

VAR. MINOR

VIOLA
STAGNINA

VIOLA
RIVINIANA

SUBSP.
MONTANA

VIOLA
CANINA

VIOLA
CANINA

VIOLA
ARVENSIS

VIOLA RUPESTRIS.

SUBSP
CURTISII.

VIOLA
TRICOLOR

VAR.
LEPIDA.

VIOLA
LUTEA.

VAR.
OBTUSIFOLIA

VIOLA
NANA

Plate 13   ❊ indicates plant is illustrated

FRANKENIACEAE

Frankenia laevis L. **Sea Heath.** ¶Stems prostrate, wiry; leaves small, oblong, heath-like, margins strongly revolute; flo. pink. On sand and gravel, S. and E. coasts. Flo. July–Aug. ❊.

CARYOPHYLLACEAE

Dianthus armeria L. **Deptford Pink.** ¶Stem 12–18 in., erect; leaves green, tapering; flo. clustered, crimson; calyx bracts acuminate, as long as calyx. On sandy soils, local and scarce. Flo. July–Aug. ❊.

Dianthus deltoides L. **Maiden Pink.** ¶Perennial, barren shoots green; flo. stems erect, slender; leaves lanceolate; calyx bracts ovate, near ½ length of calyx; petals pink with dark spot. On dry banks and hilly pastures, local. Flo. June–Sept. ❊.

Dianthus gratianopolitanus Vill. **Cheddar Pink.** *D. caesius* Sm. ¶Leaves on barren shoots linear-lanceolate, glaucous, rather blunt, edges rough; calyx bracts roundly ovate, ¼ length of calyx; flo. pink with shallow teeth. On limestone cliffs at Cheddar. Flo. June–July. ❊.

Dianthus plumarius L. **Wild Pink.** ¶Leaves on barren shoots linear, glaucous, very acute, with rough edges; calyx bracts ¼ length of calyx; petals cut nearly to the middle, fragrant. On old walls. The origin of the garden pink. Flo. June–Aug. ❊.

Dianthus caryophyllus L. **Wild Carnation.** ¶Leaves long, linear, glaucous with smooth edges; calyx bracts ¼ length of calyx; petal teeth shallow; very fragrant. The origin of the garden carnation, naturalized on old walls. Flo. July–Aug. ❊.

Dianthus barbatus L. **Sweet William.** ¶Stem 1–2 ft, erect; basal leaves in a rosette; stem leaves broadly lanceolate; flo. short stalked in dense cymes; petals bearded, dark purple to pink, streaked with white. Garden escape, sometimes naturalized in chalky railway cuttings, etc. Flo. July–Aug.

Petrorhagia nanteuilii (Burnat) P. W. Ball & Heywood. *Kohlrauschia prolifera* auct. *Dianthus prolifer* auct. ¶Annual, erect, 6–18 in.; flo. clustered within inflated oval bracts; leaves linear; petals small, rose coloured, notched. On sand and gravel in S. England, rare. Flo. June–Oct. ❊.

Saponaria officinalis L. **Soapwort.** ¶Perennial, stoloniferous; stems 1–3 ft; leaves ovate; calyx cylindrical not angular. On banks of streams and rivers, S.W. England and Wales (elsewhere introduced). Flo. Aug.–Oct. ❊.

Vaccaria pyramidata Medic. *Saponaria vaccaria* L. ¶Annual; stem 1–2 ft; leaves oblong; calyx inflated, 5 angled. Not native. Flo. June–July. ❊.

Cucubalus baccifer L. ¶Plant long, climbing over bushes; leaves oval; calyx teeth broad and open; petals long, narrow, bifid, greenish white; fr. a black berry. In copses and bushy sea cliffs, very rare, perhaps introduced by migratory birds. Flo. July–Sept.

Silene vulgaris (Moench) Garcke. **Bladder Campion.** *S. cucubalus* Wibel.
Subsp. *vulgaris*. ¶Perennial, erect, 12–18 in.; branched above; bracts small, scarious; calyx inflated; petals white, rarely with a corona. On pastures and waste ground. Flo. May–Aug. ❊.
Subsp. *maritima* (With.) Á. & D. Löve. **Sea Campion.** *Silene maritima* With. ¶Plant decumbent; bracts leaf-like; flo. mostly solitary; petals broad, with a corona. On sea cliffs and shingle, common; rare by alpine streams. Flo. June–Aug. ❊.
*Subsp. *macrocarpa* Turrill. ¶Plant slightly smaller than subsp. *vulgaris* with long stolons; leaves longer and narrower; petals pink or greenish. Introduced, but long naturalized on Plymouth Hoe, S. Devonshire. Flo. June–Aug.

Silene conica L. **Striated Catchfly.** ¶Annual, erect, 3–12 in.; calyx with many veins, conical in fr.; flo. pink. On sandy fields, mostly near E. and S. coasts, local. Flo. May–June. ❊.

Silene gallica L. **Small Catchfly.** *S. anglica* L. ¶Annual, erect, 12–18 in.; leaves hairy; calyx viscid; petals slightly cloven, dull white or pink. On sandy and gravelly fields. Flo. June–Oct. ❊.
Var. *quinquevulnera* (L.) Mert. and Koch. ¶Petals white with dark blotch. In Channel Islands and casual in S. England. ❊.

Silene acaulis (L.) Jacq. **Moss Campion.** ¶Stems densely matted; leaves small, linear; flo. stalks short, solitary. On high mountain rocks from N. Wales northwards. Flo. July–Aug. ❊.

Silene otites (L.) Wibel. **Spanish Catchfly.** ¶Stems erect, 1–2 ft, viscid below; leaves mostly radical; flo. small, yellowish, whorled. On sandy fields, Norfolk, Suffolk, Cambridgeshire. Flo. June–July. ❊.

Silene nutans L. **Nodding** or **Nottingham Catchfly.** ¶Stem 1–2 ft, viscid above; flo. drooping. Flo. May–July. Cf. *Watsonia*, II, 80–90. ❊.
Var. *salmoniana* Hepper. ¶Slender with narrow leaves; flo. yellowish; capsule 11–14 mm. on stalk (carpophore) 3–4·5 mm. On chalk in S.E. England, local.
Var. *smithiana* Moss. ¶Stronger plant; leaves broader; petals white; capsule 8–10 mm., carpophore 2–2·5 mm. On cliffs, local, E. Devonshire, E. Kent, Nottinghamshire, N. Wales, E. Scotland.

Silene italica (L.) Pers. **Italian Catchfly.** ¶Stem 1–2 ft, hairy and viscid; flo. on opposite branches, suberect, yellowish white above; carpophore as long as capsule. Plant resembling *S. nutans*. In quarries, Kent, etc., rare, introduced from S. Europe. Flo. June–July.

FRANKENIA
LAEVIS.

×2

KOHLRAUSCHIA
PROLIFERA.

*DIANTHUS
PLUMARIUS.

SAPONARIA
OFFICINALIS.

DIANTHUS
DELTOIDES

* DIANTHUS
CARYOPHYLLUS.

*VACCARIA PYRAMIDATA.

DIANTHUS
CAESIUS.
= D.GRATIANOPOLITANUS.

DIANTHUS
ARMERIA.

VAR. QUINQUE-
-VULNERA.

SILENE
NUTANS.

SILENE. CONICA.

SILENE.
OTITES.

SILENE
VULGARIS.

SILENE GALLICA.

SILENE ACAULIS.

SILENE MARITIMA.

Plate 14

CARYOPHYLLACEAE (continued)

Silene noctiflora L. **Night-flowering Catchfly.** *Melandrium noctiflorum* (L.) Fr. ¶Stem 1 ft, hairy and viscid; calyx 10 veined; flo. fragrant at night, pale pink above; styles 3. Cultivated land, S. and E. England. Flo. July–Aug. ✤.

Silene alba (Mill.) E. H. L. Krause. **White Campion.** *Lychnis alba* Mill. *Melandrium album* (Mill.) Garcke. ¶Flo. dioecious, white; fertile calyx ¾–1 in., teeth linear-lanceolate; styles 5; capsule teeth erect. Common. Flo. May–Sept. ✤.

Silene dioica (L.) Clairv. **Red Campion.** *Lychnis dioica* L., *Melandrium dioicum* (L.) Coss. & Germ.
Subsp. *dioica*. ¶Flo. dioecious, deep pink, rarely white; fertile calyx ½ in., teeth triangular; styles 5; capsule teeth revolute. Common in woods, etc. Flo. mostly May–June. ✤.
Subsp. *zetlandica*. (Compton) Clapham. ¶Similar to subsp. *dioica* but stem much stouter and densely hairy; basal leaves slender stalked; stem leaves narrower and pubescent on both surfaces; flo. larger. Orkney and Shetland.
Hybrids of *S. alba* and *S. dioica* are fairly common.

Lychnis flos-cuculi L. **Ragged Robin.** ¶Upper leaves narrow, glabrous; petals with 4 spreading segments, rose; coronal scales narrow. In marshes, wet meadows and fens, common. Flo. May–June. ✤.

Lychnis viscaria L. **Red Catchfly.** *Viscaria vulgaris* Bernh. ¶Stem 1 ft, very sticky at nodes; petals broad, slightly notched and with coronal scales. On rocks, N. Wales and Scotland, very local. Flo. June–July. ✤.

Lychnis alpina L. **Alpine Campion.** *Viscaria alpina* (L.) G. Don. ¶Rootstock branches ending in rosettes or flo. stems 3–8 in.; flo. clustered, dull rose, petals bifid. Alpine moors to 3000 ft, Cumberland and Clova Mountains. Flo. June–July. ✤.

Agrostemma githago L. **Corn Cockle.** *Lychnis githago* (L.) Scop. ¶Stem 1–2 ft; leaves linear; flo. large, solitary, purple, without corona; calyx leafy. In cornfields, becoming very rare. Flo. June–Aug. ✤.

Holosteum umbellatum L. **Umbellate Chickweed.** ¶Stem 2–6 in., viscid above; flo. umbellate, white or pale pink; sepals with broad scarious tips. On old walls, E. England, almost extinct. Flo. April–May. ✤.

Cerastium diffusum Pers. **Dark Green Chickweed.** *C. atrovirens* Bab., *C. tetrandrum* Curt. ¶Branched from base, 4–8 in. bracts, leafy; sepals 4 (or 5) scarious, margin narrow; petals notched, veins branched. In sand, mostly near the sea. Flo. April–Oct. ✤.

Cerastium pumilum Curt. **Dwarf Chickweed.** ¶Stem 1–3 in.; lower leaves obovate stalked; sepals and small upper bracts with scarious margins; petals slightly notched, veins branched; fr. drooping, later erect. Calcareous banks mostly in S. England. Flo. April–May. ✤.

Cerastium semidecandrum L. **Scarious Chickweed.** ¶Upper half of bracts and tips of sepals broadly scarious; petals very slightly notched, veins simple. Common on dry soils. Flo. April–May. ✤.

Cerastium glomeratum Thuill. **Clustered Mouse-ear.** *C. vicosu* auct. ¶Stem glandular; bracts green, very hairy; flo. cluste dense; tips of sepals acute and hairy. Very common in field Flo. April–Sept. ✤.

Cerastium brachypetalum Pers. ¶Bracts herbaceous, petals and filamen ciliate, inflo. lax. Stems covered with spreading-ascending hair Railway cutting near Sharnbrook, Bedfordshire. First found 194 Flo. May.

Cerastium fontanum Baumg.
Subsp. *triviale* (Murb.) Jalas. **Common Mouse-ear.** *C. holosteoid* Fr., *C. vulgatum* auct. ¶Stems and lanceolate leaves hairy; fl larger, not clustered; tips of sepals glabrous. Common in field larger flowered on mountains. Flo. April–Sept. ✤.
Subsp. *scoticum* Jalas & Sell. ¶Similar to subsp. *triviale*, but with longe petals, larger seeds bearing large tubercles and basal part of sepa prominently keeled. Scottish mountains, chiefly in Clova region

Cerastium alpinum L. **Alpine Mouse-ear.**
Subsp. *alpinum*. ¶Plant greyish green, with soft long hairs and some times almost glandular hairs; leaves broadly ovate; bracts wit scarious margins; seeds small with acute tubercles. On mountain N. Wales, N. England and Scotland. Flo. June–Aug. ✤.
Subsp. *lanatum* (Lam.) Aschers. & Graebner. ¶Similar to subsp alpinum, but whole plant lanate; glandular hairs absent. O mountains, Scotland.

Cerastium arcticum Lange. **Arctic Mouse-ear.**
Subsp. *arcticum*. *Cerastium edmondstonii* auct., non (H. C. Wats. Murb. & Ostenf. ¶Leaves elliptic, yellowish green, margin sparsely ciliate, otherwise glabrous to slightly pubescent; bract without scarious margins; seeds large, tubercles obtuse. O mountains, N. Wales and Scotland. Flo. June–Aug. ✤.
Subsp. *edmondstonii* (H. C. Wats.) Á. & D. Löve, *C. nigrescen* Edmondst. ex H. C. Wats. ¶Plant dwarf, compact, densel tufted, purplish and glandular; leaves shorter, roundish an darker green. Serpentine rocks, Shetland.

Cerastium arvense L. **Field Mouse-ear.** ¶Stems prostrate; leave narrow, downy; petals twice as long as sepals. On calcareou and sandy soils, local. Flo. April–Aug. ✤.

*Cerastium tomentosum L. **Snow-in-Summer.** ¶Perennial; similar t *C. arvense* but whole plant covered with dense silvery-white hairs petals white, twice as long as sepals. Garden escape, naturalize in fields, on banks, etc. Flo. May–Sept.

Cerastium cerastoides (L.) Britton. *Stellaria cerastoides* L. ¶Stem prostrate, rooting, with alternate hairy line; pedicels slender terminal. By high mountain rills, Cumberland and Scotland Flo. July–Aug. ✤.

Moenchia erecta (L.) Gaertn., Mey. & Scherb. **Upright Moenchia** *Cerastium quaternellum* Fenzl. ¶Glaucous 2–4 in.; sepals with broad white margins; petals 4 entire. On bare sandy and gravelly places in England. Flo. April–June. ✤.

SILENE
ALBA.

EVENING
CAMPION.

SILENE
DIOICA
RED
CAMPION.

LYCHNIS
FLOS-CUCULI
RAGGED ROBIN

LYCHNIS
VISCARIA

LYCHNIS ALPINA.

SILENE
NOCTIFLORA.

CERASTIUM
HOLOSTIOIDES.
a   b

AGROSTEMMA
GITHAGO
CORN COCKLE.

CERASTIUM
CERASTOIDES.

CERASTIUM
ARVENSE.

C. ALPINUM.

CERASTIUM
GLOMERATUM.

C.PUMILUM.

CERASTIUM
DIFFUSUM.

CERASTIUM
SEMIDECANDRUM

CERASTIUM
ARCTICUM.

HOLOSTEUM
UMBELLATUM

MOENCHIA
ERECTA.

Plate 15   ✼ indicates plant is illustrated

CARYOPHYLLACEAE (*continued*)

Myosoton aquaticum (L.) Moench. **Great Chickweed.** *Stellaria aquatica* (L.) Scop. ¶Stems long, soft and trailing; leaves subsessile; styles 5; capsule with 5 bifid valves. In wet places and streamsides. Flo. June–Aug. ✼.

Stellaria nemorum L. **Wood Stitchwort.**
Subsp. *nemorum*. ¶Leaves mostly long stalked; bracts decreasing gradually in size at each branching of inflo.; styles 3; capsule with 6 valves; margins of seeds with row of rounded tubercles. In wet shady places, N. Devonshire and Midlands to Scotland. Flo. May–Aug. ✼.
Subsp. *glochidisperma* Murb. ¶Similar to subsp. *nemorum* but bracts decreasing abruptly in size after first branching of inflo.; margins of seeds with long cylindrical papillae. In wet shady places, Wales and Monmouthshire. Flo. May–Aug.

Stellaria media (L.) Vill. **Chickweed.** ¶Stems annual with single line of hairs; sepals hairy; stamens 5; petals 5, rarely 0; anthers red. Abundant in cultivated land. Flo. all the year. ✼.

Stellaria pallida (Dumort.) Piré. *S. apetala* auct. ¶Stems procumbent, slender; leaves small, yellowish green; sepals small, 3 mm.; petals 0 or minute; stamens 3; anthers grey; seeds small and pale. In dunes, sandy places and pine woods. Flo. March–May.

Stellaria neglecta Weihe. **Greater Chickweed.** ¶Stems 1–3 ft with single hairy line; leaves broadly ovate, acuminate; pedicels and sepals usually hairy; stamens 10. In hedge banks. Flo. April–Aug. ✼.
Var. *elizabethae* (F. W. Schultz) Béguinot, *S. umbrosa* Opiz. ¶Pedicels and sepals glabrous; pedicels straight in fr., deflexed at base, later erect; fr. more sharply tubercled. Locally common in S.W. ✼.

Stellaria holostea L. **Greater Stitchwort.** ¶Perennial; angles of stems and leaf margins rough, scabrid; leaves widest below the middle; veins of sepals hardly visible, scarious margin narrow. Very common in hedges and sides of thickets. Flo. April–June. ✼.

Stellaria palustris Retz. **Marsh Stitchwort.** *S. glauca* With. ¶Angles of stem and leaf margins smooth; leaves glaucous, tapering from base; sepals 3 nerved, scarious margin wide; stamens red. In marshes and fens, local. Flo. May–July. ✼.

Stellaria graminea L. **Lesser Stitchwort.** ¶Stems 1–3 ft, diffuse; leaves bright green, margins smooth, ciliate below; bracts scarious, ciliate; sepals 3 nerved. Very common in grass. Flo. May–Oct. ✼.

Stellaria alsine Grimm. **Bog Stitchwort.** *S. uliginosa* Murr. ¶Stems 6–18 in., glaucous, diffuse; flo. branches short; lobes of adjacent petals near together. Common in boggy places. Flo. May–July. ✼.

Minuartia verna (L.) Hiern. **Vernal Sandwort.** *Arenaria verna* L. ¶Leafy shoots tufted; leaves linear, acute; sepals 3 veined; flo. stems few flowered; petals longer than sepals; seeds papillose. On calcareous rocks and moors in W. and N. Flo. June–Sept. ✼.
Var. *gerardii* (Willd.) Hiern. ¶Dwarf plant; leaves blunt, appressed Kynance Cove, Cornwall. ✼.

Minuartia recurva (All.) Schinz & Thell. *Arenaria recurva* All. ¶Small perennial, densely caespitose; stems woody; leaves recurved awl shaped; sepals 5–7, veined; flo. stems few flowered; petals white, twice as long as sepals; seeds smooth. Discovered on mountains in Cork and Kerry, Ireland in 1964. Flo. June–Sept.

Minuartia rubella (Wahlenb.) Hiern. **Mountain Sandwort.** *Arenaria rubella* (Wahlenb.) Sm. ¶Stems tufted, 2–4 in.; flo. branches mostly 1 flowered; leaves linear, blunt, 3 veined. On high Scottish mountains, very rare. Flo. July–Aug. ✼.

Minuartia stricta (Sw.) Hiern. *Arenaria uliginosa* Schleich. ex DC. ¶Small perennial tufts; leaves filiform, veinless; flo. stalks long 1–2 in. erect, filiform. In Teesdale only, a plant of Arctic Circle Flo. June–July.

Minuartia hybrida (Vill.) Schischk. **Fine-leaved Sandwort.** *Arenaria tenuifolia* L. ¶Stem annual, 4–6 in., much forked, glabrous, or glandular above; stamens 10. On sandy or chalky soils and walls mostly in E. England. Flo. May–June. ✼.

Moehringia trinervia (L.) Clairv. **Three-veined Sandwort.** *Arenaria trinervia* L. ¶Stems diffuse, 8–12 in.; leaves broadly ovate, acute, 3–5 veined; seeds with an appendage. Common in shady places. Flo. May–July. ✼.

Arenaria serpyllifolia L. **Thyme-leaved Sandwort.** ¶Erect, rigid pubescent; leaves and sepals ovate, acute; capsule 2·5 mm. wide. On dry places, cliffs and walls. Flo. June–Aug. ✼.

Arenaria leptoclados (Reichb.) Guss. **Slender Sandwort.** ¶Erect, very slender; leaves narrower; inflo. longer; sepals lanceolate; capsule only 1·5 mm. wide. Now regarded by some botanists as a subspecies of *A. serpyllifolia*, in which case the name used is *A serpyllifolia* L. subsp. *leptoclados* (Reichb.) Nyman. Common on dry soil and walls. Flo. June–Aug. ✼.

Arenaria cilata L.
Subsp. *hibernica* Ostenf. & Dahl. **Irish Sandwort.** ¶Small and prostrate; branches ascending 2–3 in.; leaves obovate, blunt, ciliate; petals exceeding 3 ribbed sepals. Ben Bulben, Co. Sligo. Flo. May–Aug. ✼.

Arenaria norvegica Gunn. **Arctic Sandwort.**
Subsp. *norvegica*. ¶Stems short; leaves obovate, blunt; sepals faintly 3 ribbed; capsule not constricted at top; teeth suberect. In stony places, Argyll, Sutherland, Hebrides and Shetlands. Flo. July–Aug. ✼.
Subsp. *anglica* Halliday. ¶Leaves lanceolate, acute; capsule constricted at the top, teeth revolute. On high calcareous rocks, W. Yorkshire. Flo. May–Sept. ✼.

MYOSOTON
AQUATICUM.

STELLARIA MEDIA.

STELLARIA
NEGLECTA.

STELLARIA
NEGLECTA
VAR ELIZABETHAE.

STELLARIA
HOLOSTEA.

STELLARIA
PALUSTRIS

STELLARIA
NEMORUM.

STELLARIA
GRAMINEA.

×6

STELLARIA
ALSINE

MINUARTIA
RUBELLA

ARENARIA CILIATA

MOEHRINGIA
TRINERVIA.

VAR GERARDI

MINUARTIA
HYBRIDA.

MINUARTIA VERNA.

ARENARIA
ANGLICA

ARENARIA NORVEGICA.

ARENARIA
SERPYLLIFOLIA.

ARENARIA
LEPTOCLADOS

Plate 16 ✾ indicates plant is illustrated

CARYOPHYLLACEAE (*continued*)

Honkenya peploides (L.) Ehrh. **Sea Purslane.** *Arenaria peploides* L. ¶Stolons creeping; leaves fleshy, margins membranous; flo. often dioecious; capsule globose. On sandy and pebbly seashores. Flo. May–Sept. ✾.

Minuartia sedoides (L.) Hiern. **Mossy Cyphel.** *Arenaria sedoides* (L.) F. J. Hanb., *Cherleria sedoides* L. ¶Stems in dense cushions; leaves linear; flo. solitary; petals usually o, or minute. On Scottish mountains, local. Flo. June–Aug. ✾.

Sagina maritima Don. **Sea Pearlwort.** ¶Prostrate or erect; leaves blunt or apiculate; sepals suberect in fr.; petals 4 minute or o. On seaside cliffs and rocks. Flo. May–Sept. ✾.

Sagina apetala Ard.
Subsp. *apetala*. **Ciliate Pearlwort.** *S. ciliata* Fr. ¶Very slender stems all flowering; outer sepals pointed, all appressed in fr., tips patent; petals minute or o. Locally common in dry places, etc. Flo. May–Sept. ✾. The plants are apt to be glandular on dry heaths (*S. filicaulis* Jord.)
Subsp. *erecta* (Hornem.) F. Hermann. **Annual Pearlwort.** *S. apetala* auct. ¶Stems suberect, all flowering; leaves tapering, mucronate; sepals spreading in fr.; petals very minute. Locally common in bare places. Flo. May–Aug. ✾.

Sagina procumbens L. **Common Pearlwort.** ¶Branches spreading, prostrate from a central rosette; sepals blunt, spreading in fr.; pedicel top recurved in unripe fr. Common. Flo. May–Oct. ✾.

Sagina × normaniana Lagerh. **Scottish Pearlwort.** *S. procumbens × saginoides, S. scotica* (Druce) Druce. ¶Like the above but with fr. obviously smaller, 2·5 × 2 mm., about equal to sepals; stems more slender; rosette leaves longer. In wet turf on mountains in Scotland. Flo. July–Sept. ✾.

Sagina saginoides (L.) Karst. **Mountain Pearlwort.** *S. linnei* C. Presl. ¶Branches spreading from central rosette; petals 5, rounded, nearly equal to sepals; fr. large, 3·5–4 × 2·5 mm., exceeding appressed sepals. On mountains in Scotland. Flo. June–Aug. ✾.

Sagina intermedia Fenzl. **Alpine Pearlwort.** *S. nivalis* auct., *S. caespitosa* auct. ¶Small, densely tufted; petals 5; fruiting sepals suberect; pedicels short and straight. On mountain tops in Scotland, rare. Flo. June–Aug. ✾.

Sagina subulata (Sw.) C. Presl. **Heath Pearlwort.** ¶Stems tufted, glandular; leaves tapering, ciliate and hair pointed; petals 5; pedicels long and glandular. On dry heaths, local. Flo. June–Aug. ✾.

Sagina nodosa (L.) Fenzl. **Knotted Pearlwort.** ¶Leafy to top of stem, with many bundles of leaf buds in axils; petals large; fr. pedicels straight. In wet sandy places. Flo. July–Sept. ✾.

Spergula arvensis L. **Corn Spurrey.** *S. vulgaris* Boenn. ¶Plant scarcely viscid; seeds covered with club-shaped papillae. Common in sandy cornfields. Flo. June–Aug. ✾.
Var. *sativa* (Boenn.) Mert. & Koch. ¶Plant very viscid; seeds nearly smooth, with a narrow wing; leaves often grey-green.

*Spergula morisonii Bor. *S. vernalis* auct. *S. pentandra* auct. non L. ¶Stems stiffly erect; leaves not furrowed beneath; seeds with a broad wing. On sandy cultivated ground, Sussex. First found in 1943.

Spergularia rubra (L.) J. & C. Presl. **Red Spurrey.** ¶Leaves flat; stipules silvery, torn; seeds tubercled, the margin thick, not winged. Common on gravelly and sandy soils. Flo. May–Oct. ✾.

Spergularia bocconii (Scheele) Aschers. & Graebn. *S. campestris* auct. non Aschers. ¶Plant covered with minute glands; branches dichotomous, bearing many small, short-stalked flo.; petals shorter than sepals; stipules broad. On dry sandy and rocky places on S.W. coasts and Essex, rare. Flo. May–Sept. ✾.

Spergularia marina (L.) Griseb. **Sea Spurrey.** *S. salina* J. & C. Presl. ¶Branches spreading or prostrate; leaves flat above, rounded beneath; bracts often leafy; calyx longer than petals, shorter than pedicels, a few of the seeds winged. Salt marshes by the sea. Flo. June–Aug. ✾.

Spergularia media (L.) C. Presl. **Perennial Sea Spurrey.** *S. marginata* Kittel. ¶Plant larger, subglabrous; upper bracts small; petals often exceeding calyx, pale pink; capsule almost twice length of calyx; seeds all winged. On muddy salt marshes. Flo. June–Sept. ✾.

Spergularia rupicola Lebel ex Le Jolis. **Rock Spurrey.** ¶Plant glandular; leaves short and fascicled; stipules acute, capsule not much exceeding calyx; seeds pear shaped, not winged. Sea cliffs and rocks. Flo. June–Sept. ✾.

Polycarpon tetraphyllum (L.) L. **Four-leaved Allseed.** ¶Leaves obovate, some opposite, some in whorls of 4; sepals hooded; petals minute, white. On sea cliffs in Scilly Isles, Cornwall, Devonshire, Dorset, and common in Channel Isles. Flo. June–July. ✾.

PORTULACACEAE

*Montia sibirica (L.) Howell. *Claytonia sibirica* L. *C. alsinoides* Sims. ¶Succulent, 6–10 in.; stem leaves opposite but separate; flo. pink. Alien from N. America, spreading along streams, in damp woods, etc. Flo. May–July. ✾.

*Montia perfoliata (Willd.) Howell. *Claytonia perfoliata* Don ex Willd. ¶6–10 in.; stem leaves opposite and united; flo. smaller, white. Naturalized in cultivated ground. Flo. May–July. ✾.

Montia fontana L. **Water Blinks.** ¶All forms grow in trickles of water or in very wet places on acid soil, and of smaller size on pastures. Flo. May–Oct. ✾.
Subsp. *fontana*. ¶Seeds smooth and shining. In northern counties only.
Subsp. *chondrosperma* (Fenzl) Walters. ¶Seeds dull, with rather coarse tubercles. Widely distributed.
Subsp. *amporitana* Senn. Subsp. *intermedia* (Beeby) Walters. ¶Seeds smaller, less than 1 mm., finely tuberculate with high tubercles. Widely distributed.
Subsp. *variabilis* Walters. ¶Seeds more or less smooth, but not so shining as in subsp. *fontana*.

CHERLERIA SEDOIDES.

SAGINA PROCUMBENS.

HONKENYA PEPLOIDES.

SAGINA INTERMEDIA.

SAGINA CILIATA.

SAGINA APETALA.

SAGINA NORMANIANA.

MONTIA FONTANA.

AGINA UBULATA.

×2½

SAGINA SAGINOIDES.

SAGINA MARITIMA.

MONTIA PERFOLIATA.

×10

POLYCARPON TETRAPHYLLUM.

MONTIA SIBIRICA.

SAGINA NODOSA.

SPERGULA ARVENSIS.

SPERGULARIA BOCCONII.

SPERGULARIA MARINA.

SPERGULARIA MEDIA.

SPERGULARIA RUBRA.

SPERGULARIA RUPICOLA

Plate 17

�# indicates plant is illustrated

TAMARICACEAE

* *Tamarix gallica* L. **Tamarisk.** ¶Shrub, 5–10 ft; branches slender; leaves minute, glaucous; flo. buds globose; stamens inserted in depressions of the disk. On sandy shores in S. England, planted. Flo. July–Sept.

* *Tamarix anglica* Webb. ¶Very similar to above; leaves greener; flo. buds ovoid; stamens inserted on sharp elevations of the disk. Sandy shores, S. and E. England. Flo. July–Sept. ✿.

ELATINACEAE

Elatine hexandra (Lapierre) DC. **Waterwort.** ¶Plants matted, submerged; flo. stalked; petals 3; stamens 6; seeds nearly straight. In edges of lakes and reservoirs. Flo. July–Sept. ✿.

Elatine hydropiper L. ¶Similar to *E. hexandra*, but leaf stalked; flo. sessile; petals 4; stamens 8; seeds curved. In edges of lakes and pools, rare. Flo. July–Aug. ✿.

HYPERICACEAE

Hypericum androsaemum L. Tutsan. ¶Small shrub, 1–3 ft; slightly aromatic; flo. ¾ in.; leaves ovate, obtuse; stamens in 5 bundles; styles shorter than stamens; berry red, globose, becoming bluish black when ripe, indehiscent. In damp woods, hedgerows and shady ditches, mostly in W. Flo. June–Aug. ✿.

* *Hypericum inodorum* Mill. *H. elatum* Ait. ¶Similar to *H. androsaemum*, 1½–4 ft; leaves slightly smaller, strongly aromatic when bruised; flo. ½ in.; styles longer than stamens; berry dehiscent. Garden escape, naturalized in hedgerows and thickets particularly in S.W. England. Flo. June–Sept.

* *Hypericum hircinum* L. ¶Similar to *H. androsaenum* and *H. elatum*; stems quadrangular; leaves emitting a strong goat-like odour when bruised; flo. ½ in.; styles longer than stamens; berry dehiscent. Garden escape, naturalized in woods and thickets, rare. Flo. May–Sept.

* *Hypericum calycinum* L. **Rose of Sharon.** ¶Stems many, creeping, ascending 18 in.; flo. 2–3 in. wide. From S.E. Europe, extensively naturalized in woods and wastes. Flo. July–Sept. ✿.

Hypericum perforatum L. **Perforate St John's Wort.** ¶Stem 2 ribbed; leaves elliptic, with many pellucid dots; sepals lanceolate, acute. Common, especially on calcareous soils. Flo. June–Sept. ✿.

Hypericum maculatum Crantz. *H. quadrangulum* auct. *H. dubium* Leers. Subsp. *maculatum.* ¶Plant slender with few branches, usually at an angle of 30° from 4 ribbed stem; leaves oval; pellucid dots few or absent; densely reticulate; sepals ovate, obtuse; petals entire with glands on surface in forms of dots. In moist places chiefly in Scotland. Flo. July–Sept.

Subsp. *obtusiusculum* (Tourlet) Hayek. ¶Plant stouter with ma▯ branches, usually at an angle of 50° from 4 ribbed stem; leav▯ oval, with pellucid dots; sparsely reticulate; petals sometim▯ crenate with glands on surface in form of streaks or lines. ▯ damp woods, hedge banks, etc., widespread, but local. Fl▯ July–Sept. ✿.

Hypericum × *desetangsii* Lamotte (*H. maculatum* subsp. *obtusiusculum* ▯ *perforatum*). ¶Stem upright with 2 very prominent and 2 fai▯ raised lines; leaves ovate-oblong, with or without large pelluc▯ glandular dots. Sometimes occurs where the two parents gro▯ together.

Hypericum tetrapterum Fr. **Square-stalked St John's Wort.** ▯ *quadrangulum* L., *H. quadratum* Stokes. ¶Stem 4 winged; leav▯ oval with pellucid veins and small dots; flo. ⅜ in.; sepals lance▯ late, acute. In bogs and streamsides, common. Flo. July–Aug. ✿

Hypericum undulatum Schousb. ex Willd. **Wavy St John's Wor▯** ¶Stem 2 ribbed; leaves ovate with wavy edges and pelluc▯ dots and veins; sepals ovate, acute; petals partly red outsid▯ In bogs, Devonshire and Cornwall, and S. Wales. Flo. Jul▯ Aug. ✿.

Hypericum canadense L. ¶Stem erect, 3–6 in., 4 angled, reddis▯ leaves narrow, oblong; flo. ¼ in.; capsule dark red. In bogs a▯ damp fields, W. Ireland, only.

Hypericum humifusum L. **Creeping St John's Wort.** ¶Stems slend▯ prostrate, 2 ribbed; flo. few, ⅜ in.; sepals unequal. On grave▯ banks and heaths, common. Flo. June–Sept. ✿.

Hypericum linarifolium Vahl. **Narrow-leaved St John's Wor▯** ¶Stems erect, nearly round; leaves narrow, obtuse, marg▯ revolute; sepals acute with black glandular teeth. On roc▯ S. Devon, Wales and Channel Islands, rare. ✿.

Hypericum pulchrum L. **Beautiful St John's Wort.** ¶Stems ere▯ round; leaves short, cordate, obtuse, with pellucid dots; bu▯ red; blunt sepals and petals edged with black glands. On d▯ banks, fairly common. Flo. June–Aug. ✿.
Forma *procumbens* Rostrup. ¶Plant prostrate on sea cliffs a▯ mountains.

Hypericum hirsutum L. **Hairy St John's Wort.** ¶Stem 2 ft, roun▯ pubescent; leaves ovate, striate, with pellucid glands; flo. pal▯ sepals with black glands. In woodland borders. Flo. July–Aug. ✿

Hypericum montanum L. **Mountain St John's Wort.** ¶Stem roun▯ leaves, bracts and sepals with marginal black glands; infl▯ dense; petals pale yellow. On calcareous soils, local. Flo. Jul▯ Aug. ✿.

Hypericum elodes L. **Bog St John's Wort.** ¶Plant softly tomentos▯ stems creeping or floating; leaves suborbicular; flo. few; pet▯ erect. In spongy bogs, common. Flo. July–Aug. ✿.

HYPERICUM
CALYCINUM.

H. ANDROSAEMUM.

HYPERICUM
MONTANUM.

TAMARIX
ANGLICA.

HYPERICUM
TETRAPTERUM.

H. MONTANUM

HYPERICUM PULCHRUM.

HYPERICUM
UNDULATUM.

HYPERICUM
PERFORATUM.

ATINE
XANDRA

HYDROPIPER.

HYPERICUM
LINARIFOLIUM.

HYPERICUM
HIRSUTUM.

HYPERICUM HUMIFUSUM.

HYPERICUM
MACULATUM

HYPERICUM
ELODES.

Plate 18 ✿ indicates plant is illustrated

MALVACEAE

Althaea officinalis L. **Marsh Mallow.** ¶Stout, erect, 2–3 ft, velvety pubescent throughout; flo. clustered; epicalyx bracts 6–9, narrow; sepals ovate, acuminate. Marshes near sea. Flo. Aug–Sept. ✿.

Althaea hirsuta L. **Hispid Marsh Mallow.** ¶Slender, hispid, spreading 6–18 in.; flo. solitary; epicalyx narrow; sepals long, setaceous. W. Kent and Somerset, rare, doubtful native. Flo. July–Aug. ✿.

Lavatera arborea L. **Tree Mallow.** ¶Stem 3–8 ft, stout, woody, pubescent; epicalyx bracts 3, connate, larger than calyx; fr. wrinkled. On sea cliffs and rocks. Flo. July–Sept. ✿.

Lavatera cretica L. **Lesser Tree Mallow.** *L. sylvestris* Brot. ¶Smaller plant, herbaceous, with stellate hairs; epicalyx shorter than calyx; fr. smooth. Plant like *Malva sylvestris*. W. Cornwall, Scilly Isles. Flo. June. ✿.

Malva moschata L. **Musk Mallow.** ¶Erect, 2 ft; stem leaves cut to narrow segments; flo. pink; fr. stalks erect; calyx enlarged; carpels hispid. On dry banks. Flo. July–Aug. ✿.
Var. *heterophylla* Lej. & Court. ¶Lower leaves entire, upper cut into about 3 broad segments. Flo. often more autumnal. ✿.

Malva sylvestris L. **Common Mallow.** ¶Leaves 2–3 in. wide, lobes folded, triangular; flo. rose-purple; fr. spreading; carpels reticulate, usually glabrous. Common. Flo. June–Sept. ✿.

Malva neglecta Wallr. **Dwarf Mallow.** *M. rotundifolia* auct. non L. ¶Prostrate, pubescent; leaves $\frac{1}{2}$–$1\frac{1}{2}$ in. wide; flo. $\frac{3}{4}$ in., pale; epicalyx shorter than calyx; carpels pubescent, smooth. Common in S. England. Flo. June–Sept. ✿.

Malva pusilla Sm. **Small Mallow.** ¶Epicalyx equalling deltoid calyx lobes; flo. $\frac{1}{4}$ in. wide; carpels netted, rugose, margined meeting with a toothed edge. Introduced. Flo. June–Sept. ✿.

Malva parviflora L. ¶Flo. $\frac{1}{4}$ in. wide; petal claws glabrous; calyx lobes broadly ovate, enlarged in fr.; carpels pubescent, edge winged and wavy. A rare alien. Flo. June–Sept.

Malva verticillata L. ¶Plant erect, 2–$2\frac{1}{2}$ ft; flo. $\frac{3}{4}$ in. wide; carpels smooth, angles square; sepals enlarged in fr. Naturalized in a few places. Flo. July–Sept.

TILIACEAE

Tilia platyphyllos Scop. **Broad-leaved Lime.** ¶Twigs and under sides of leaves downy; flo. few, pendulous; fr. with prominent ribs. Woods by rivers Wye, Teme and Severn, elsewhere planted. Flo. June. ✿.

Tilia × vulgaris Hayne. **Common Lime.** *T. europaea* auct. *T. cordata × platyphyllos.* ¶Leaves green and glabrous beneath except hairs at axils of veins; flo. pendulous; fr. downy, slightly ribbed. In plantations, not native. Flo. July.

Tilia cordata Mill. **Small-leaved Lime.** ¶Twigs glabrous; leaves small, glaucous beneath with hairs at axils of veins; flo. erect; fr. thin walled, slightly angular. In woods and on cliffs, especially on limestone. Flo. July. ✿.

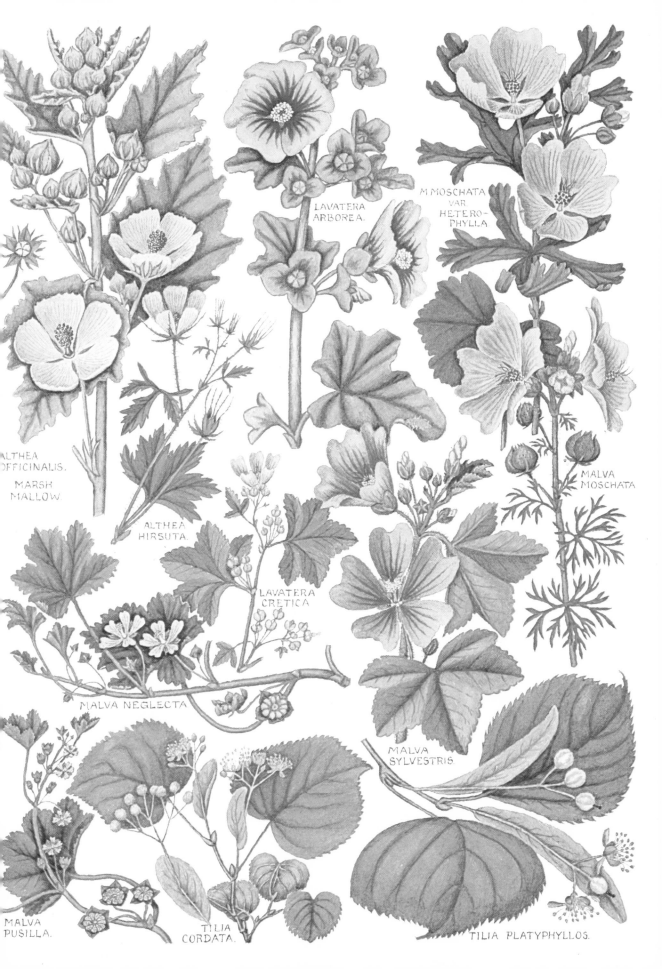

ALTHEA
OFFICINALIS.
MARSH
MALLOW.

ALTHEA
HIRSUTA.

LAVATERA
ARBOREA.

M. MOSCHATA
VAR.
HETERO-
PHYLLA.

MALVA
MOSCHATA

LAVATERA
CRETICA.

MALVA NEGLECTA

MALVA
SYLVESTRIS.

MALVA
PUSILLA.

TILIA
CORDATA.

TILIA PLATYPHYLLOS.

Plate 19   ✿ indicates plant is illustrated

LINACEAE

Radiola linoides Roth. **Allseed.** *R. millegrana* Sm. ¶Very small annual, 1–2 in.; repeatedly forked; flo. minute; sepals 3 cleft. In bare sandy places, sometimes with *Anagallis minima*. Flo. July–Aug. ✿.

Linum catharticum L. **White Flax.** ¶Annual, stem slender, 2–6 in.; leaves opposite, elliptic; petals white, suberect. On dry banks and basic soils, common. Flo. June–Aug. ✿.
Var. *dunense* Druce. ¶Very small, about 1 in. long, quite prostrate. Dunes. ✿.

Linum perenne Mill. **Blue Flax.**
Subsp. *anglicum* Ockendon, *L. anglicum* Mill. ¶Perennial, 1–2 ft; leaves alternate, linear; flo. blue; sepals obovate, glabrous, less than ½ length of fr. On chalk and limestone. Flo. June. ✿.

Linum bienne Mill. **Pale Flax.** *L. angustifolium* Huds. ¶Perennial, 1–1½ ft; leaves linear; flo. very pale mauve; sepals ovate, ciliate, more than ½ length of fr. On dry banks, S. and S.W. England. ✿.

GERANIACEAE

Geranium sanguiuneum L. **Blood-red Geranium.** ¶Stems diffuse, 1–2 ft; flo. solitary, 1½ in. wide, crimson; peduncle long. On dry rocks and sea cliffs, local. Flo. July–Aug. ✿.
Var. *lancastrense* (With.) Druce. ¶Stems procumbent; flo, pale pink. N. Lancashire coast.

Geranium macrorrhizum L. ¶Plant aromatic; stems erect, hairy, ½–1 ft; leaves smooth, 5 lobed; flo. in pairs on short peduncles; petals pink or red. Garden escape. Naturalized on walls and banks, chiefly in S.W. England. Flo. May–Aug.

Geranium versicolor L. **Streaked Cranesbill.** *G. striatum* L. ¶Stems erect, hairy, 1–2 ft; peduncle 2 flowered; petals emarginate, pale with purple veins. Shady places in S. and W., especially Cornwall. ✿.

Geranium endressii Gay. ¶Alien, similar to above, but petals more rounded, deep pink without darker veins. Garden escape. Naturalized on banks, in fields, etc. Flo. May–June.

Geranium endressii × versicolor. ¶Similar to above but petals pink with dark veins. Garden escape. Naturalized in fields, on banks, etc. Sometimes more frequent than either of the parents. Flo. May–June.

Geranium nodosum L. ¶Erect, glabrous, 1–2 ft; stem leaves with 3–5 large ovate, acute lobes; flo. pale rose-purple. Garden escape, sometimes confused with *G. endressii*. Flo. May–Sept.

Geranium phaeum L. **Dusky Cranesbill.** ¶Stems erect, 1–2 ft; flo. ¾ in., blackish purple, petals wavy; sepals awned. In plantations and waste places, not native. Flo. May–Aug. ✿.

Geranium sylvaticum L. **Wood Cranesbill.** ¶Erect, 1–3 ft; stem leaves sessile; flo. ¾ in., reddish purple; filaments fiiform; fr. erect. In N. England and Scotland. Flo. June–July. ✿.

Geranium pratense L. **Meadow Cranesbill.** ¶Erect, 2–4 ft; leave nearly all petiolate; flo. 1¼ in., blue-purple; fr. reflexed; filament wide at base. In meadows and banks. Flo. June–Sept. ✿.

Geranium platypetalum Fisch. & Mey. *G. ibericum* auct., non L. ¶Stems erect, 1–2 ft; leaves roundish, heart shaped, long stalked deeply 5–7 lobed; woolly; flo. 1–1½ in. in pairs, or more, in ope panicles; petals bluish violet to purple; calyx rough. Garde escape. Established on waste ground, in fields, etc. Flo. May–Aug

Geranium pyrenaicum Burm. f. **Pyrenean Cranesbill.** *G. perenne* Huds ¶Stems 2 ft, diffuse, downy; flo. ½ in., red-purple; petals deepl notched; carpels smooth. Roadsides and fields, S. and E. England Flo. June–Aug. ✿.

Geranium molle L. **Soft Cranesbill.** ¶Prostrate, softly pubescent flo. ½ in.; petals deeply notched; carpels wrinkled. Very commo on cultivated and waste land. Flo. April–Sept. ✿.

Geranium pusillum L. **Small-flowered Cranesbill.** ¶Flo. ¼ in. lilac; petals notched; carpels smooth, keeled, hairs appressed On cultivated fields and light soils. Flo. June–Sept. ✿.

Geranium rotundifolium L. **Round-leaved Cranesbill.** ¶Leave round, lobes less deep; petals entire, flesh-pink; carpels keele with spreading hairs. On cliffs, walls and banks, local. Flo June–July. ✿.

Geranium dissectum L. **Cut-leaved Cranesbill.** ¶Leaves deeply cut; peduncles short; petals bifid, red-purple; carpels smooth hairs erect. Common in hedge banks and arable land. Flo May–Aug. ✿.

Geranium columbinum L. **Dove's-foot Cranesbill.** ¶Stems long spreading; leaf segments narrow; sepals awned; petals rounded pale rose. On dry, mainly calcareous soils. Flo. June–July. ✿.

Geranium lucidum L. **Shining Cranesbill.** ¶Stems red; leaves roun and glossy, lobes shallow; petals rounded, pink. On shady banks common on acid soils. Flo. May–Aug. ✿.

Geranium robertianum L. **Herb Robert.**
Subsp. *robertianum.* ¶Stems erect, rather hairy; petals spreading anthers reddish; carpels wrinkled, downy. Common every where on banks. Flo. April–Oct. ✿.
Subsp. *maritimum* (Bab.) H. G. Bak. ¶Stem prostrate, succulent red; leaves and flo. smaller; carpels glabrous. On shingle beaches
Subsp. *celticum* Ostenf. ¶Stems reddish on nodes and petiole bases flo. pale; fr. hairy, large. Limestone rocks, S. Wales and Galway

Geranium purpureum Vill. **Lesser Herb Robert.**
Subsp. *purpureum.* ¶Plant upright; leaf segments narrow; stamen yellow; carpels much wrinkled, glabrous; fr. hairy or glabrou with closely set ridges. Sea cliffs, rocky places, etc., sometime inland, Channel Islands, S. England, S. Wales and Ireland. Flo May–Sept. ✿.
Subsp. *forsteri* (Wilmott) H. G. Bak. ¶Plant prostrate; petioles o rosette leaves very short; fr. hairy or glabrous, often occurring together; ridges less apparent. Stabilized shingle beaches Guernsey, Hampshire and Sussex.

LINUM BIENNE.

NUM ANGLICUM

RADIOLA
LINOIDES

GERANIUM
SYLVATICUM

GERANIUM
PRATENSE.

GERANIUM
VERSICOLOR

GERANIUM
SANGUINEUM.

LINUM CATH-
ARTICUM.

GERANIUM
PHÆUM

GERANIUM MOLLE.

GERANIUM MOLLE.
x 5.

ERANIUM
RPUREUM

GERANIUM
ROTUNDIFOLIUM.

GERANIUM
PUSILLUM.

HERB
ROBERT.

GERANIUM
PYRENAICUM

ERANIUM
LUCIDUM.

GERANIUM ROBERTIANUM.

GERANIUM COLUMBINUM.

GERANIUM
DISSECTUM.

Plate 20   ✳ indicates plant is illustrated

GERANIACEAE (continued)

Erodium cicutarium (L.) L'Hérit. **Common Storksbill.**
Subsp. *cicutarium*. ¶Leaves pinnate, leaflets cut to narrow segments; peduncles 6–9 flowered; petals rose, usually unspotted; filaments gradually enlarged at base. On light land and coast dunes. Flo. June–Sept. ✳.
Var. *pimpinellifolium* Cav. ¶Two upper petals with dark spot. ✳.
Subsp. *dunense* Andreas. **Dune Storksbill.** *E. lebeli* Jord. ¶Stem short, stout, prostrate, very glandular, sticky; leaflet segments broader; peduncles 3–5 flowered; petals pale; filaments gradually enlarged at base; pit on carpel conspicuous. On coastal sand dunes. ✳.
Subsp. *bipinnatum* (Willd.) Tourlet, *E. glutinosum* Dumort. ¶Plant very glandular, sticky; branches more slender, prostrate; peduncles 2–4 flowered; petals pale; filaments suddenly enlarged or dentate below; carpels with small pit at top. Sand dunes on coast, scarce.

Erodium moschatum (L.) L'Hérit. **Musky Storksbill.** ¶Leaves large, pinnate, leaflets ovate, coarsely toothed, smelling of musk; base of filament toothed. Seaside W. England, Ireland, introduced inland. Flo. June–Aug. ✳.

Erodium maritimum (L.) L'Hérit. **Sea Storksbill.** ¶Branches prostrate; leaves small, oval, toothed or lobed, not pinnate; petals pale, often absent. On sea cliffs and exposed places inland. Flo. May–Sept. ✳.

OXALIDACEAE

Oxalis acetosella L. **Wood Sorrel.** ¶Leaves radical from creeping rhizome; scape 1 flowered; petals white or rarely rose; capsule ovoid, 5 angled. In woods, common. Flo. April–May. ✳.

*Oxalis corniculata L. **Yellow Sorrel.** ¶Stems prostrate, pubescent; trifoliate leaves with small stipules; flo. 1–7 together; pedicels reflexed in fr.; capsule oblong, hairy, erect. Chiefly in S. England, naturalized. Flo. June–Sept. ✳.

*Oxalis europaea Jord. **Upright Yellow Sorrel.** *O. stricta* auct. ¶Stolons slender; stem erect, subglabrous; leaves purple tinted; stipules 0; flo. yellow, 2–6 together; fr. pedicel straight; capsule oblong. A garden weed, mostly in S.E. England.

*Oxalis articulata Savigny. *O. floribunda* Lehm. ¶Root tuberous; leaves radical; flo. many, ¾ in., rose-purple. Garden weed.

*Oxalis corymbosa DC. ¶Similar to *O. articulata* but with larger leaflets and flowers; leaflets with minute red dots on the margins; flo. purplish pink. Garden weed, common in London area.

*Oxalis latifolia Kunth. ¶Similar to *O. corymbosa* but leaves glabrous without red dots on margins. Introduced. Weed of cultivated ground in Devon and Cornwall. Flo. May–Sept.

*Oxalis tetraphylla Cav. ¶Leaflets 4; peduncles pubescent; flo. rose-red, similar in size to *O. corymbosa*. Naturalized in fields in Jersey. Flo. May–Sept.

*Oxalis pes-caprae L. **Bermuda Buttercup.** *O. cernua* Thunb. ¶Leaves many, springing from buried bulb; peduncles bearing flo. in umbels; flo. large, bright yellow. Frequent weed in bulb fields in the Scilly Isles, less frequent in Cornwall and Channel Islands. Flo. March–June.

*Oxalis incarnata L. ¶Similar to *O. acetosella* from which it differs in its slender, erect, bulbil-bearing stems. Garden escape, naturalized on walls and banks chiefly in S.W. England. Flo. May–July.

BALSAMINACEAE

Impatiens noli-tangere L. **Wild Balsam, Touch-me-not.** ¶Plant succulent, 1–2 ft; nodes swollen; flo. yellow, 1–3 together; spur tapering, point recurved. By streams, Lake District, N. Wales introduced elsewhere. Flo. July–Sept. ✳.

*Impatiens capensis Meerb. **Orange Balsam.** *I. fulva* Nutt., *I. biflora* Walt. ¶Leaves ovate with shallow teeth; flo. orange; spur tapering, reflexed at tip. N. American plant, naturalized on river banks, mostly in S. and Midlands. Flo. June–Aug. ✳.

*Impatiens parviflora DC. **Small Yellow Balsam.** ¶Stem 6–18 in. leaves ovate with many acute teeth; flo. 3–10 on peduncle, pale yellow; spur nearly straight. Naturalized in woods and waste except in S.W. From Siberia. Flo. July–Sept.

*Impatiens glandulifera Royle. **Indian Balsam.** *I. roylei* Walp. ¶Stem stout, 4–6 ft; leaves opposite, teeth many, acute; flo. large, rose and pink; spur inflated, with short reflexed point. Spreading beside rivers, rarely on waste ground. Flo. July–Sept. ✳

AQUIFOLIACEAE

Ilex aquifolium L. **Holly.** ¶Small tree 10–40 ft; flo. white, sub dioecious; berries red, poisonous. Common in woods and hedge. Flo. April–May. ✳.

CELASTRACEAE

Euonymus europaeus L. **Spindle.** ¶Shrub 5–15 ft; flo. small, greenish fr. beautiful, lobed and pink, with seeds enclosed in an orange aril (an aftergrowth from seed stalk). The plant harbours the 'Black Army' aphis. In copses and hedges, common in S. England extending to S. Scotland and Ireland. Flo. June–July. ✳.

RHAMNACEAE

Rhamnus catharticus L. **Buckthorn.** ¶Shrub 5–10 ft; branches opposite, ending in thorns; flo. 4 partite, dioecious. On calcareous soil, chiefly in mid and S.E. England. Flo. May–July. ✳.

Frangula alnus Mill. **Berry-bearing Alder.** *Rhamnus frangula* L. ¶Branches alternate, without thorns; flo. white, 5 partite, perfect fr. black when ripe. On peaty heaths and damp hedgerows. Flo. May–Sept. ✳.

ACERACEAE

*Acer pseudoplatanus L. **Sycamore.** ¶Tree 40–60 ft; flo. dense pendulous; stamens twice as long as petals; juice not milky Common everywhere, an ancient introduction. Flo. April–June ✳ (fruit only).

*Acer platanoides L. **Norway Maple.** ¶Tree 40–60 ft; leaves shining on both surfaces; juice milky; flo. in erect corymbs. Introduce but readily regenerating. Flo. April–May.

Acer campestre L. **Common Maple.** ¶Small tree, 10–20 ft; flo. erect stamens equalling petals; wings of fr. nearly in one line. Hedge rows from Yorkshire southward; introduced elsewhere. Flo. May–June. ✳.

ERODIUM DUNENSE.

ERODIUM MARITIMUM

×2

ERODIUM MOSCHATUM

ERODIUM CICUTARIUM

×2

VAR. PIMPINELLIFOLIUM

OXALIS CORNICULATA.

WOOD SORREL

OXALIS ACETOSELLA

ILEX AQUIFOLIUM

IMPATIENS NOLI-TANGERE.

IMPATIENS GLANDULIFERA.

IMPATIENS CAPENSIS

RHAMNUS CATHARTICUS.

EUONYMUS EUROPAEUS.

ACER PSEUDO-PLATANUS

ACER CAMPESTRE.

FRANGULA ALNUS

Plate 21

PAPILIONACEAE

Lupinus nootkatensis Donn ex Sims. **Lupin.** ¶Stems stout, herbaceous, subsimple, 1–2 ft; leaf petioles long; flo. blue. On river shingle, abundant in mid Scotland and Orkneys. Not native, from N.W. America. Flo. July–Aug.

Lupinus arboreus Sims. **Tree Lupin.** ¶A woody shrub with many spreading branches; petioles short; flo. yellow. Locally naturalized and spreading, not native. Flo. June–Sept.

Genista anglica L. **Petty Whin.** ¶Stems 1–2 ft, woody, diffuse, spinous; leaves ovate, glabrous; flo. yellow. On damp heaths, up to 2000 ft, England and Scotland. Flo. May–June. ❀.

Genista pilosa L. **Hairy Greenweed.** ¶Stems ½–1 ft, woody, without spines; leaves ovate, silky beneath; flo. pubescent, yellow; pod downy. W. Cornwall, W. Wales, Sussex, rare. Flo. May–Sept. ❀.

Genista tinctoria L. **Dyer's Greenweed.** ¶Stems 1–2 ft suberect, striate; leaves oblong-lanceolate; flo. and pods glabrous. On rough grassy places, S. England to S. Scotland. Flo. July–Sept. ❀.
Var. *humifusa* L. (Dickson) Druce, non L. ¶Branches prostrate, hairy; pods hairy. W. Cornwall.

Ulex europaeus L. **Common Gorse, Furze.** ¶Stems 2–6 ft; spines furrowed and straight; flo. bracts ovate, about 4 × 2 mm.; calyx hairs spreading; flo. yellow. Abundant on heaths. Flo. March–May. ❀.

Ulex europaeus × gallii. ¶Very variable, but usually intermediate between the two parents, and probably common where they grow together.

Ulex gallii Planch. **Dwarf** or **Summer Gorse.** ¶Stems 1–3 ft; spines strong, slightly furrowed, often curved; bracts minute; calyx hairs appressed; flo. golden. On heaths and moors, common in W. England, Wales and S. Ireland. Flo. July–Oct. ❀.

Ulex minor Roth. **Small Furze.** *U. nanus* T. F. Forst. ¶Stems 1–3 ft; spines weak and slender; flo. bracts minute; flo. pale yellow and small. On heaths, Dorset to Sussex, Norfolk and Nottinghamshire. Flo. July–Oct. ❀.

Sarothamnus scoparius (L.) Wimm. ex Koch. **Broom.** *Cytisus scoparius* (L.) Link.

Subsp. *scoparius.* ¶Erect shrub, 1–6 ft; branches angular, green, leaflets 1–3, silky; flo. large, bright yellow, sometimes blotched with red. On heaths. Widely distributed. Flo. May–June. ❀.

Subsp. *maritimus* (Rouy) Ulbr. Subsp. *prostratus* (C. Bailey) Tutin ¶Stems prostrate; twigs and leaves densely silky. On sea cliffs, W. Cornwall. Pembroke, Lundy Island, Channel Islands and W. Cork.

Spartium junceum L. ¶A shrub similar to *Sarothamnus scoparius* but with terete stems and linear-lanceolate leaves. Naturalized on railway banks, etc., in S. England.

Ononis repens L. **Restharrow.** *O. arvensis* auct. ¶Stem rhizomatous, procumbent, hairy all round, usually without spines; pod shorter than calyx. Common on coasts and calcareous soils inland. Flo. June–Sept. ❀.
Var. *horrida* Lange. ¶Plant spinous. ❀.

Ononis repens × spinosa. ¶Very variable, but often intermediate between the two parents, and probably common where they grow together.

Ononis spinosa L. **Prickly Restharrow.** *O. campestris* Koch & Ziz. ¶Stem erect with two lines of hairs, usually spinous; pod decidedly longer than calyx. On rough pastures in England except S.W. Flo. June–Sept. ❀.

Ononis reclinata L. **Small Restharrow.** ¶Annual; stem 2–3 in., viscid; fr. pedicels reflexed. In turf on sea cliffs, rare, S. Devon, S. Wales, Channel Islands. Flo. June–July. ❀.

Medicago sativa L. **Lucerne.** ¶Erect 1–2 ft, bushy; leaflets 1 in.; flo. purple; pod ¼ in. wide, with 2–3 turns. From S.E. Europe, cultivated, locally naturalized. Flo. April–Aug. ❀.

Medicago × varia Martyn = *M. falcata × sativa. M. silvestris* Fr. ¶Variable; pod forming 1 ring; flo. yellow to green. ❀.

Medicago falcata L. **Yellow Medick, Sickle Medick.** ¶Usually procumbent; flo. ½ in., yellow; pod sickle shaped, downy. On dry sand and gravel, Norfolk, Suffolk, Cambridgeshire, etc. Flo. June–July. ❀.

Medicago lupulina L. **Black Medick.** ¶Procumbent; flo. ⅛ in., yellow, in small oval spikes; pods very small, netted circular, becoming black. In pastures, etc., very common. Flo. May–Aug. ❀.

GENISTA
PILOSA.

ULEX
GALLII.

GENISTA
ANGLICA.

ULEX EUROPAEUS
× 4

GENISTA
TINCTORIA

ONONIS RECLINATA

SAROTHAMNUS
SCOPARIUS.

ONONIS
SPINOSA.

ULEX
EUROPAEUS

VAR HORRIDA.

ULEX
MINOR.

MEDICAGO SATIVA

ONONIS REPENS.

TRIFOLIUM
ORNITHOPODIOIDES

MEDICAGO
FALCATA

MEDICAGO
VARIA

MEDICAGO LUPULINA.

Plate 22   ❀ indicates plant is illustrated

PAPILIONACEAE (continued)

Medicago polymorpha L. **Fimbriate Medick.** *M. denticulata* Willd., *M. hispida* Gaertn. ¶Stem prostrate; stipules laciniate; flo. yellow, 1–5 on peduncle; pods netted, coiled, with spines usually long. On S. and E. coasts, introduced inland. Flo. May–Aug. ❀.

Medicago arabica (L.) Huds. **Spotted Medick.** *M. maculata* Sibth. ¶Leaflets usually with dark spot; stipules toothed; pods with 3–5 coils and curved spines. In pastures, mostly in E. and S. counties. Flo. May–Aug. ❀.

Medicago minima (L.) Bartal. **Small Medick.** ¶Prostrate, downy; leaves small; stipules subentire; peduncles very short; pods coiled and spinous. Sandy places in S.E. and E. England, introduced elsewhere, rare. Flo. May–July. ❀.

Melilotus altissima Thuill. **Yellow Melilot.** *M. officinalis* (Lam.) Hayne. ¶Stems erect, 2–3 ft; leaflets oblong, ¾ in.; petals all equal; pods acute, hairy. In fields and roadsides, S. England to S.E. Scotland. Flo. June–Aug. ❀.

*Melilotus officinalis (L.) Pall. **Ribbed Melilot.** *M. arvensis* Wallr. ¶Similar to *M. altissima*, but wing petals and standard longer than keel, pale yellowish; pods mucronate, ribbed. Common on cultivated and waste land, not native. Flo. July–Sept. ❀.

*Melilotus alba Medic. **White Melilot.** ¶More slender, 2–3 ft; flo. white; standard petal longer than keel or wing; pod netted. On cultivated waste land, not native. Flo. June–Aug. ❀.

*Melilotus indica (L.) All. **Small Melilot.** *M. parviflora* Desf. ¶Plant small in all its parts; flo. small, pale yellow; standard longer than other petals; pods globular, netted. In waste places. Flo. July–Sept.

Trifolium ornithopodioides L. **Fenugreek.** *Trigonella ornithopodioides* (L.) DC. ¶Prostrate, glabrous; leaves trifoliate; flo. pink and white, 1–3 on peduncle; pod twice length of calyx. On sandy heaths mostly near the sea, local. Flo. June–Aug. ❀ on plate 21.

Trifolium subterraneum L. **Subterranean Clover.** ¶Stems prostrate, hairy; leaflets obcordate; flo. few, pale; sterile calyces adapted as anchors to bury pods. On dry pastures, mostly S. England. Flo. May–June. ❀.

Trifolium pratense L. **Red Clover.** ¶Leaves often white blotched; heads subsessile between leaves with broad stipules; flo. pale rose. In pastures, abundant. Flo. May–Sept. ❀.

Trifolium medium L. **Zigzag Clover.** ¶Leaflets longer; stipules linear, green, tapering; heads peduncled from opposite leaves; flo. deeper colour. In pastures, especially on clay soils. Flo. June–Sept. ❀.

Trifolium ochroleucon Huds. **Cream-coloured Clover.** ¶Pubescent; leaflets obovate; stipules tips subulate; flo. cream coloured; calyx tube ribbed, teeth subulate, lowest longest. On gravel and clay in E. counties, local. Flo. June–Aug. ❀.

Trifolium squamosum L. **Teasel-headed Clover.** *T. maritimum* Huds. ¶Leaf stipules long, tapering; heads shortly peduncled, pink; calyx teeth small in flo. becoming enlarged, foliaceous, spinescent, lowest longest, 3 veined. By the sea, S. and E. England, S. Wales. Flo. June–Aug. ❀.

*Trifolium incarnatum L. **Crimson Clover.** ¶Stem with spreading hairs; leaflets obovate; calyx very hairy; flo. deep crimson. A fodder crop, persisting on roadsides, not native. Flo. June–Aug. ❀.

Trifolium molinerii Balb. ex Hornem. **Large Lizard Clover.** ¶Stem with appressed hairs; leaflets obcordate; flo. pinkish white; calyx spreading in fruit. In short grass on Lizard Head, Cornwall, and Jersey, native. Flo. June–July. ❀.

*Trifolium stellatum L. **Starry-headed Clover.** ¶Stems short; leaves and ovate stipules softly hairy; heads globose, stalked; flo. small cream; calyx enlarged in fr., spreading, star-like. On shingle at Shoreham, Sussex, naturalized from S. Europe.

Trifolium arvense L. **Hare's-foot Clover.** ¶Stems ascending, hairy; leaflets narrow; heads oblong, stalked; flo. small, white, immersed in long, pink hairs of calyx. Sandy places. Flo. July–Sept. ❀.

Trifolium bocconei Savi. ¶Erect, 2–4 in.; heads ovate, terminal, often in pairs; stipules and calyx teeth subulate; flo. small, whitish. Lizard Head, Cornwall, and Jersey. Flo. July. ❀.

Trifolium striatum L. **Soft Clover.** ¶Leaflets silky with straight veins; stipules broad, striate; heads sessile; calyx ventricose, ribbed; flo. rose-pink. Sandy fields, often by sea. Flo. June. ❀.

Trifolium scabrum L. **Rough Clover.** ¶Procumbent; leaflets pubescent, veins curved; heads sessile; flo. white; calyx tube cylindrical, teeth spreading in fr. On dry sandy places, mostly near the sea. Flo. May–July. ❀.

Trifolium glomeratum L. **Flat-headed Clover.** ¶Leaves glabrous; heads axillary, semi-globose; flo. rose-pink; calyx teeth very acute, reflexed. On sand and gravel near S. and E. coasts. Flo. June. ❀.

Trifolium suffocatum L. **Suffocated Clover.** ¶Stems short, nearly buried in sand; leaf petioles long; flo. heads sessile, often confluent; calyx teeth recurved. In sand on S. and E. coasts, local and rare. Flo. July–Aug. ❀.

Trifolium strictum L. **Upright Clover.** ¶Erect, 2–6 in.; leaflets narrow, toothed; stipules broad; heads globose, peduncled; flo. pink; calyx ribbed. Lizard Head, Cornwall, and Jersey. Flo. June. ❀.

*Trifolium hybridum L. **Alsike Clover.** ¶Plant large, spreading, up to 3 ft; leaflets toothed; heads peduncled, ¾ in. wide; flo. pink and white, drooping over fr. A survival from cultivation, naturalized on roadsides. Flo. June–Aug. ❀.

Trifolium repens L. **White** or **Dutch Clover.** ¶Closely creeping and rooting; leaf petioles long; heads long stalked; petals white or rosy, persistent, drooping over the fr. Flo. May–Oct. ❀.

Trifolium occidentale D. E. Coombe. ¶Similar to *T. repens* from which it differs in its shorter stems, dark green, smaller leaflets without blotchy markings, fewer lateral veins, fewer-flowered heads and creamy white (never pinkish) flo. Dry warm rocks, pastures and sand dunes near the sea, Scilly Isles, W. Cornwall, and Channel Islands. Flo. March–June.

MEDICAGO ARABICA

MEDICAGO POLYMORPHA.

MEDICAGO MINIMA.

TRIFOLIUM SUBTERRANIUM.

×2

TRIFOLIUM PRATENSE

TRIFOLIUM MEDIUM.

TRIFOLIUM HYBRIDUM. ALSIKE.

MELILOTUS ALTISSIMA

M. OFFICINALIS.

MELILOTUS ALBA.

TRIFOLIUM REPENS.

T. PRATENSE ×8

T. ARVENSE

TRIFOLIUM SUFFOCATUM.

TRIFOLIUM SQUAMOSUM

TRIFOLIUM GLOMERATUM.

TRIFOLIUM OCHROLEUCON.

TRIFOLIUM STRICTUM

TRIFOLIUM BOCCONEI.

TRIFOLIUM STRIATUM.

TRIFOLIUM SCABRUM

T. INCARNATUM →

TRIFOLIUM MOLINERII.

Plate 23   ❈ indicates plant is illustrated

PAPILIONACEAE (*continued*)

Trifolium fragiferum L. **Strawberry-headed Clover.** ¶Creeping and rooting; leaves and heads long stalked; flo. pink; calyx of 2 lips, upper lip enlarging and covering fr. On stiff soils, mostly S. and E. England. Flo. July–Aug. ❈.

* *Trifolium resupinatum* L. **Reversed Clover.** ¶Slender, 4–9 in.; leaflets narrow, obovate; flo. small, pink, upside down; calyx inflated, woolly. Waste places and docksides, not native. Flo. July.

Trifolium aureum Poll. **Large Hop Trefoil.** *T. agrarium* auct. ¶Mid leaflet sessile; flo up to 50 in head, bright yellow; style as long as pod. Naturalized in fields and roadsides, frequent in Scotland. ❈.

Trifolium campestre Schreb. **Hop Trefoil.** *T. procumbens* auct. ¶Mid leaflet stalked; flo. yellow, up to 40 in head, standard deflexed; style shorter than pod. In pastures, common. Flo. June–Aug. ❈.

Trifolium dubium Sibth. **Lesser Yellow Trefoil.** *T. minus* Sm. ¶Mid leaflet stalked; flo. yellow, up to 12 in head; standard folded over pod; style shorter than pod. Pastures and banks, common. Flo. June–Aug. ❈.

Trifolium micranthum Viv. **Least Yellow Trefoil.** *T. filiforme* L. ¶Very slender; mid leaflet sessile; flo. 2–6, yellow; standard narrow and deeply notched; peduncle filiform. Sandy soil, chiefly S. England and Wales. Flo. June–July. ❈.

Anthyllis vulneraria L. **Kidney Vetch.** ¶Stem and pinnate leaves silky; flo. usually yellow; heads in pairs; calyx woolly; pod small, 1 seeded. On calcareous and sandy soils and sea cliffs. Flo. June–Aug. ❈.
Var. *coccinea* L. ¶Small, with dark red flowers. Seaside. ❈.

Lotus corniculatus L. **Bird's-foot Trefoil.** ¶Decumbent; stipules ovate like leaflets; flo. bright yellow, 5–8 in head; calyx tee erect, appressed in bud. Common everywhere. Flo. June–Aug. ❈

Lotus tenuis Waldst. & Kit. ex Willd. **Narrow-leaved Bird's-fo Trefoil.** ¶Stems ascending, long and slender; leaflets and stipul linear; flo. 3–4 in head; calyx teeth erect. Stiff soils, absent or ra in N. Flo. June–Sept. ❈.

Lotus uliginosus Schkuhr. **Marsh Bird's-foot Trefoil.** *L. majus* auc *L. pedunculatus* auct., non Cav. ¶Stoloniferous and tall; leaflets an stipules larger, ovate; flo. 6–10 in head; calyx teeth spreading bud. Wet meadows and bogs, common. Flo. July–Sept. ❈ When branching in peat, less tall; leaflets smaller; standard pet very red backed and red veined. ❈.

Lotus hispidus Desf. ex DC. **Hairy Bird's-foot Trefoil.** ¶Plant sma hairy throughout; flo. 2–4 together; standard petal narrow; po short and broad. On sea cliffs, Cornwall to Hampshire, Pembrok shire and S. Ireland. Flo. July–Aug. ❈.

Lotus angustissimus L. **Long-fruited Bird's-foot.** ¶Prostrat peduncles short; flo. 1–2, yellow (fading green); standard wid pod narrow, 1 in. long. Near the sea, Cornwall to Kent an Channel Islands, introduced inland. Flo. July–Aug. ❈.

* *Tetragonolobus maritimus* (L.) Roth. *Lotus siliquosus* L. ¶Leaflets peduncles exceeding leaves; flo. orange, 1 in. long; pod winge Naturalized chiefly in Thames area (native as near as Pas d Calais).

Oxytropis halleri Bunge. *O. uralensis* auct. ¶Leaves 2–3 in., pinnat leaflets acute; flo. pale mauve; pod abruptly pointed. Rocks up t 2000 ft in Scotland, local. Flo. June–July. ❈.

Oxytropis campestris (L.) DC. ¶Leaves 6 in., leaflets blunt; flo. yellow touched with mauve; pod tapering. On rocks, 2000 ft in Perth shire and Angus, very rare. Flo. June–July. ❈.

TRIFOLIUM DUBIUM

RIFOLIUM ICRANTHUM.

TRIFOLIUM CAMPESTRE.

TRIFOLIUM AUREUM.

TRIFOLIUM FRAGIFERUM

ANTHYLLIS VULNERARIA

VAR. COCCINEA

LOTUS PEDUNCULATUS.

LOTUS TORNICULATUS.

L. HISPIDUS X 10

LOTUS ANGUSTISSIMUS.

OXYTROPIS CAMPESTRIS.

LOTUS TENUIS.

LOTUS HISPIDUS.

OXYTROPIS HALLERI.

Plate 24   ✿ indicates plant is illustrated

PAPILIONACEAE (*continued*)

Astragalus danicus Retz. **Purple Milk-vetch.** ¶Erect, 2–6 in., pubescent; leaves pinnate; stipules connate; flo. erect; purple pods erect. Calcareous soils, Gloucestershire, Wiltshire and Chilterns to E. Scotland. Flo. June. ✿

Astragalus alpinus L. **Alpine Milk-vetch.** ¶Prostrate, slender, elongate; leaf stipules free; flo. horizontal, whitish, purple tipped; pods pendulous. Rocks 2500 ft, Highlands of Scotland, rare. Flo. July. ✿

Astragalus glycyphyllos L. **Wild Liquorice, Milk-vetch.** ¶Stems stout, spreading 2–3 ft; leaflets large; flo. greenish white; pods large and curved. On calcareous soils, local. Flo. June–Sept. ✿

Ornithopus perpusillus L. **Least Bird's-foot.** ¶Stems slender; leaves pinnate; peduncle with leaf at top; flo. white, veined red, small; pod knotted. On sand and gravel, rare in N. Flo. May–July. ✿

Ornithopus pinnatus (Mill.) Druce. *O. ebracteatus* Brot. ¶Stems slender; leaflets fewer, 3–4 pairs; peduncle without leaf at apex; flo. slightly larger, 6–8 mm., yellow. Scilly Isles and Channel Islands. Flo. July–Aug. ✿

*Coronilla varia L. **Crown Vetch.** ¶Spreading plant, 1–2 ft; leaves pinnate, leaflets oblong; peduncles long; flo. many, white and purplish; calyx teeth small; pod slender. Alien. Flo. June.

Hippocrepis comosa L. **Horseshoe Vetch.** ¶Slender, spreading, sub-glabrous plant; leaves pinnate; peduncles long; flo. yellow, deflexed; pod of crescent-shaped joints. Calcareous hills. Flo. May–Aug. ✿

Onobrychis viciifolia Scop. **Sainfoin.** *O. sativa* Lam. ¶Erect, 1–2 f leaves long and pinnate; peduncle long; flo. in conical racem pink with darker veins; pod 1 seeded. Possibly native on the chal introduced on other soils. Flo. June–Aug. ✿

Vicia hirsuta (L.) Gray. **Hairy Tare.** ¶Slender, 1–2 ft; leaflets narrow 6–9 pairs; tendrils branched; peduncles ¾ in.; flo. small, pa mauve; pod hairy, 2 seeded. Common. Flo. May–Aug. ✿

Vicia tetrasperma (L.) Schreb. **Smooth Tare.** ¶Leaflets 4–6 pair obtuse; peduncle 1–2 flowered; pod glabrous, 4 seeded. In grass places and borders of thickets. Flo. May–Aug. ✿

Vicia tenuissima (Bieb.) Schinz & Thell. **Slender Tare.** *V. graci* Lois., non Soland. ¶Leaflets 3–4 pairs, linear, acute; peduncle 1– flowered; flo. ¼ in.; pod 5–8 seeded. In grassy places and arab fields in S. England, local. Flo. June–Aug. ✿

Vicia cracca L. **Tufted Vetch.** ¶Climbing, 2–6 ft; tendrils branched stipules semi-sagittate; calyx gibbous; leaves sometimes silky. I hedges and thickets. Flo. June–Aug. ✿

Vicia orobus DC. **Wood Bitter Vetch.** ¶Erect, stout, 1–2 ft; tendri o; leaflets hairy; peduncle short; flo. white and purplish. In rock woods, local. Flo. May–June. ✿

Vicia sylvatica L. **Wood Vetch.** ¶Climbing, 2–6 ft; tendrils branched lower stipules lunate, toothed. In rocky woods and sea cliffs, loca Flo. June–Sept. ✿

Vicia sepium L. **Bush Vetch.** ¶Climbing, 1–3 ft; flo. head sessile stipules semi-sagittate; pod glabrous. In hedges and grassy borde of thickets, very common. Flo. April–Oct. ✿

ASTRAGALUS
DANICUS.

ASTRAGALUS
GLYCYPHYLLOS.

VICIA
HIRSUTA
TARE.

VICIA
TETRASPERMA

VICIA
TENUISSIMA

TRAGALUS ALPINUS.

ORNITHOPUS
PERPUSILLUS.

ORNITHOPUS
PINNATUS.

ONOBRYCHIS
VICIIFOLIA.

VICIA   OROBUS.

VICIA
CRACCA.

HIPPOCREPIS
COMOSA.

WOOD
VETCH

VICIA SYLVATICA.

VICIA
SEPIUM

Plate 25 ✿ indicates plant is illustrated

PAPILIONACEAE (*continued*)

Vicia lutea L. **Yellow Vetch.** ¶Prostrate, tufted, 6–18 in.; flo. solitary; pod hairy; stipules triangular. On sea coasts, introduced inland, rare. Flo. June–Aug. ✿.

* *Vicia sativa* L. **Common Vetch.** ¶Stout, 6–18 in.; flo. ¾ in., usually in pairs; pod erect 2–3 in. Naturalized in cultivated ground and roadsides. Flo. May–July. ✿.

Vicia angustifolia L. **Narrow-leaved Vetch.** ¶Fairly stout; leaflets narrowly oblong; flo. ½–¾ in., often 2 together; calyx gibbous; pods 1½–2 in., spreading, bursting the calyx. On dry banks, meadows and grassy waste places. Flo. May–Sept. ✿.
Var. *bobartii* (E. Forst.) Koch. ¶Plant more slender; leaflets linear; flo. solitary; pod 1–1½ in., not bursting the calyx. A common form in S. and S.W. England, but many plants are intermediate.

Vicia lathyroides L. **Spring Vetch.** ¶Slender, pubescent, 3–8 in.; flo. solitary, ¼–⅓ in., calyx not gibbous at base, funnel shaped; leaflets obtuse, mucronate, ⅕–⅓ in., pods ½–1 in. In gravelly and sandy places, local. Flo. April–June. ✿.

Vicia bithynica L. **Bithynian Vetch.** ¶Perennial, 1–2 ft; leaflets ovate or linear; pod reticulate, hairy. In bushy places and sea cliffs, local. Flo. July–Aug. ✿.

Lathyrus aphaca (L.) L. **Yellow Vetchling.** ¶Stipules very large, leaf-like; leaflets 0; peduncle usually 1, sometimes 2 flowered. In dry calcareous sandy fields, mostly in S. England. Flo. May–Aug. ✿.

Lathyrus nissolia L. **Grass Vetchling.** ¶Stipules minute; petioles linear, leaf-like. In bushy and grassy places, local. Flo. May–June. ✿.

* *Lathyrus hirsutus* L. **Hairy Vetchling.** ¶1–2 ft; peduncle 2 flowered; leaflets 1 pair, linear-lanceolate; flower pale blue and crimson. In cultivated ground, Essex and Surrey, etc., not native. Flo. June–July.

Lathyrus pratensis L. **Yellow Meadow Vetchling.** ¶Stem angul 2–3 ft, not winged; leaflets 1 pair. Common in hedges and fie borders. Flo. June–Sept. ✿.

* *Lathyrus tuberosus* L. **Tuberous Vetchling.** ¶Stem angled; leafle obovate; peduncle 2–5 flowered; roots tuberous. In fields abo Fyfield, Essex, and elsewhere, not native. Flo. June–Aug. ✿.

Lathyrus sylvestris L. **Wild Pea.** ¶Stem 3–6 ft, winged; leaflets larg sword-like; stipules large, semi-sagittate. In woods and especia on wet sea cliffs. Flo. June–Aug. ✿.

* *Lathyrus latifolius* L. **Everlasting Pea.** ¶Leaflets large, ellipti glaucous; flo. 1 in.; stipules broad. On railway banks, etc., n native.

Lathyrus palustris L. **Marsh Pea.** ¶Stem winged, 2–3 ft; leaflets 2– pairs, lanceolate, with tendrils. In fens and boggy meadows, rar Flo. June–Aug. ✿.

Lathyrus maritimus (L.) Fr. **Sea Pea.** *L. japonicus* Bigel.
Subsp. *maritimus.* ¶Stem angular; leaflets 2–3 pairs, oval; stipul large, ovate, hastate. On shingle sea beaches, local and rare, and E. England and S. Wales. Flo. June–Aug. ✿.
Subsp. *acutifolius* (Bab.) Pedersen. ¶Stem slender, stragglin leaflets elliptical-lanceolate. On shingle sea beaches, very rar Shetland.

Lathyrus montanus Bernh. **Bitter Vetch.** *L. macrorrhizus* Wimm., *Orob tuberosus* L. ¶Stem winged; leaflets 2–3 pairs; peduncle 2– flowered; stipules semi-sagittate. In woods and thickets, wid spread but absent from much of E. England. Flo. May–Aug. ✿

Lathyrus niger (L.) Bernh. **Black Bitter Vetch.** *Orobus niger* ¶Stem branched, not winged; leaflets 3–6 pairs; peduncle mar flowered; stipules linear subulate. In rocky woods in Scotlan nearly extinct.

VICIA
LATHYROIDES

VICIA
SATIVA.

VICIA
BITHYNICA.

VICIA
ANGUSTIFOLIA

VICIA
LUTEA

LATHYRUS
APHACA

LATHYRUS
SYLVESTRIS.

LATHYRUS
NISSOLIA

LATHYRUS
TUBEROSUS

LATHYRUS
PRATENSIS.

MARSH
PEA

LATHYRUS
MONTANUS.

LATHYRUS
PALUSTRIS.

LATHYRUS
JAPONICUS.

SEA PEA.

Plate 26

ROSACEAE

Prunus laurocerasus L. **Cherry Laurel.** ¶Small tree; leaves evergreen, obovate-acuminate, dark green, very glossy; flo. many in erect racemes; petals white; fr. ovoid, purple-black. Planted in woods and copses where it sometimes regenerates. Flo. April–June.

Prunus mahaleb L. ¶Small tree; leaves orbicular to broad-ovate, rounded or subcordate at base, pubescent on midrib beneath, otherwise glabrous; flo. fragrant, in 6–10-flowered racemes; petals white; fr. ovoid, black. Planted in woods and copses where it sometimes regenerates. Flo. April–May.

Prunus serotina Ehrh. **Rum Cherry.** ¶Small tree, similar to *P. padus*, but with cylindrical slender racemes; flo. smaller on shorter peduncles; petals white; fr. ovoid, black; calyx persistent. Planted in woods and gardens where it sometimes regenerates; also bird-sown into other habitats. Flo. April–June.

Prunus spinosa L. **Blackthorn, Sloe.** ¶Shrub with many stout thorns; twigs black; leaves appearing after flo. Common in scrub, open woods and hedges. Flo. March–April. ❀.

Prunus domestica L. **Wild Plum.**
Subsp. *domestica*. ¶Large shrub or small tree without thorns; leaves large; petals greenish in bud; fr. oblong. Frequent in hedges, often near houses, not native. Flo. March–May. ❀.
Subsp. *insititia* (L.) C. K. Schneid. **Bullace.** *P. insititia* L. ¶Shrub with few or no thorns; twigs brown, pubescent; leaves appearing with the flowers; fr. globose. Frequent in hedges. Flo. March–May. ❀.

Prunus avium (L.) L. **Gean, Wild Cherry.** ¶Small tree; leaves acuminate; flo. umbellate; calyx tube constricted; petals obovate; fr. red. Common in woods and hedges. Flo. April–May. ❀.

Prunus cerasus L. **Sour Cherry.** ¶Shrub with suckers; flo. umbellate; calyx crenate, tube not constricted; petals orbicular; fr. red, sour. In hedges in many places. Not native. Flo. April–May. ❀.

Prunus padus L. **Bird Cherry.** ¶Small tree; leaves acuminate; flo. smaller, in long often drooping raceme; fr. black, bitter. In woods, N. England and Scotland, introduced elsewhere. Flo. May. ❀.

Spiraea salicifolia L. ¶Shrub 4 ft; leaves simple, willow-like; flo. pink, in a dense panicle, planted and occasionally naturalized. Flo. July–Aug.

Filipendula ulmaria (L.) Maxim. **Meadow Sweet.** *Spiraea ulmaria* L. ¶Herb 2–4 ft; leaves large, pinnate, usually white beneath; flo. cream. Common on wet meadows, ditches and riversides. Flo. June–Aug. ❀.

Filipendula vulgaris Moench. **Dropwort.** *F. hexapetala* Gilib., *Spiraea filipendula* L. ¶Herb 1 ft; leaves mostly radical; leaflets many, narrow, much cut; petals often 6, red outside. In chalk and limestone pastures. Flo. May–July. ❀.

Sanguisorba officinalis L. **Great Burnet.** ¶1½–3 ft, branched; flo. heads ovoid-oblong, crimson; stamens hardly exserted; fr. smooth, 4 winged. In damp meadows, local. Flo. June–Sept. ❀.

Sanguisorba minor Scop.
Subsp. *minor*. **Salad Burnet, Lesser Burnet.** *Poterium sanguisorba* L. ¶1–1½ ft; stem leaves few; heads globose; lower flo. male; stamens long exserted; fr. finely reticulate, with 4 even ridges. On dry calcareous pastures, railway banks, etc. Flo. May–Aug. ❀.
Subsp. *muricata* (Gremli) Brig. *Poterium polygamum* Waldst. & Kit. *P. muricatum* Spach. ¶Larger than subsp. *minor*, 1½–2½ ft; stem leaves several with narrow leaflets; heads often ovoid; fr. coarsely rugose with 4 irregular ridges. Naturalized in borders of fields, etc. Flo. May–Aug.

Acaena anserinifolia (J. R. & G. Forst.) Druce. ¶Fr. with 4 long barbed spines. Brought in sheep's wool from Australia and naturalized in some places. Flo. June–Aug.

Agrimonia eupatoria L. **Common Agrimony.** ¶Fr. deeply groove throughout, lower spines spreading. Common on roadsides ar waste ground. Flo. June–Aug. ❀.

Agrimonia procera Wallr. **Scented Agrimony.** *A. odorata* auc ¶Leaves stouter, glandular scented; fr. slightly grooved, low spines deflexed. Waste places on heavy soils, less common. Fl June–Aug.

Aremonia agrimonoides (L.) DC. *Agrimonia agrimonoides* L. ¶Diffe from *Agrimonia eupatoria* in having flo. in few-flowered cymes, an receptacles without spines. Naturalized in woods in Scotland.

Aphanes arvensis L. **Parsley Piert.** *Alchemilla arvensis* (L.) Sco ¶Lobes of stipules triangular, ovate, as long as broad; fr. sepa open. Common on bare soil in dry places. Flo. April–Oct. ❀.

Aphanes microcarpa (Boiss. & Reut.) Rothm. ¶Lobes of stipules twi as broad; fr. sepals closed. Common, especially on aci soils. Flo. April–Oct.

Alchemilla alpina L. **Alpine Lady's Mantle.** ¶Leaflets all separat white and silky beneath. Common on mountain pastures and roc crevices, N. England and Scotland. Flo. June–Aug. ❀.

Alchemilla conjuncta Bab. ¶Leaflets connate at base, white and silk beneath. On rocks in Glen Clova and Arran, introduced elsewher Flo. June–July. ❀.

Alchemilla glaucescens Wallr. *A. minor* auct. ¶Stems and petioles wit dense silky hairs; leaves hairy, basal sinus closed. On limestone Yorkshire, Ross, Sutherland and Leitrim. Flo. June–Sept.

Alchemilla filicaulis Buser.
Subsp. *filicaulis*. ¶Similar to above, but upper stem and pedice glabrous; leaves less hairy, stipules purplish. In mountain pasture Flo. June–Sept.
Subsp. *vestita* (Buser) M. E. Bradshaw. *Alchemilla vestita* (Buser Raunk. ¶Stems and petioles with spreading hairs; leaves hairy basal sinus open; stipules purplish. Fairly common in natura pastures. Flo. June–Sept. ❀.

Alchemilla subcrenata Buser. ¶Similar to *A. filicaulis* but stipule brownish not purplish; leaves undulate with broad lobes an coarse broad teeth. Grassland, Upper Teesdale and Weardal Flo. June–Sept.

Alchemilla minima Walters. ¶Plant small; leaves very small, hairy o folds and on veins beneath, basal sinus open; stipules brown. O limestone, Ingleborough, Yorkshire. Flo. June–Sept.

Alchemilla monticola Opiz. *A. pastoralis* Buser. ¶Plant medium; ster and petioles with spreading hairs; pedicels glabrous; leave orbicular, densely hairy on both surfaces, basal sinus closec Pastures in Upper Teesdale and Weardale, introduced elsewher Flo. June–Sept.

Alchemilla acutiloba Opiz. ¶Lower stem with spreading hairs, glabrou above; leaf lobes with straight sides. In Upper Teesdale. Flo June–Sept.

Alchemilla xanthochlora Rothm. ¶Plant large; stem and petioles wit spreading hairs; pedicels and upper sides of leaves glabrous, lobe not overlapping. Fairly common. Flo. June–Sept.

Alchemilla glomerulans Buser. ¶Stem and petioles with appressed hairs leaves hairy, lobes overlapping. On wet mountain rocks, Teesdal and mid Scotland northwards. Flo. June–Sept.

Alchemilla glabra Neygenf. *A. alpestris* auct. ¶Plant often large lowest nodes of stem with appressed hairs, glabrous above; lea lobes rather straight sided, with middle teeth on each side larger Meadows, open woods, mountains, chiefly in the N. Flo. June– Sept. ❀.

Alchemilla wichurae (Buser) Stefánsson. *A. acutidens* auct. ¶Plant small stems somewhat more hairy than in *A. glabra*; leaves orbicular i outline, basal sinus closed or nearly so. Grassland on basic soils Yorkshire to Sutherland. Flo. June–Sept.

BLACKTHORN.

PRUNUS SPINOSA

PRUNUS INSITITIA.

P. DOMESTICA.

PRUNUS CERASUS.

PRUNUS PADUS.

PRUNUS AVIUM.

× 10
FILIPENDULA ULMARIA.

FILIPENDULA ULMARIA.

SANGUISORBA OFFICINALIS.

POTERIUM SANGUISORBA.

ALCHEMILLA VESTITA.

APHANES ARVENSIS.

ALCHEMILLA GLABRA.

ALCHEMILLA ALPINA.

AGRIMONIA EUPATORIA.

ALCHEMILLA CONJUNCTA

FILIPENDULA VULGARIS.

Plate 27   ❀ indicates plant is illustrated

ROSACEAE (*continued*)

Alchemilla mollis (Buser) Rothm. ¶Plant robust, very hairy; leaves shallowly lobed, epicalyx equalling the calyx. Garden escape. Naturalized in grassy places. Flo. June–Sept.

Alchemilla tyttantha Juz. *A. multiflora* Buser ex Rothm. ¶Plant robust; leaves hairy on both surfaces; stem with downward directed spreading hairs; flo. small, glabrous. Garden escape. Well naturalized in S. Scotland. Flo. June–Sept.

Sibbaldia procumbens L. *Potentilla sibbaldii* Haller f. ¶Stem woody, depressed; petals small, inconspicuous, yellow; leaves bluish green. On mountain-tops and rocks chiefly in N. Scotland. Flo. July. ❀.

Potentilla palustris (L.) Scop. **Marsh Cinquefoil.** *Comarum palustre* L. ¶Stems 18 in., from creeping base; leaflets oblong; flo. red-purple. In fens, marshy meadows and wet moorlands. Flo. June–July. ❀.

Potentilla fruticosa L. **Shrubby Cinquefoil.** ¶Shrub, 3 ft, silky; flo. yellow, partly one sexual. Very local, Teesdale, Lake District and W. Ireland. Flo. June–July. ❀.

Potentilla sterilis (L.) Garcke. **Barren Strawberry.** *P. fragariastrum* Pers. ¶Leaflets 3, silky beneath; flo. white; receptacle hairy. Common on heaths, banks and woodland borders. Flo. Feb.–May. ❀.

Potentilla rupestris L. **Rock Cinquefoil.** ¶Stems 1–2 ft, erect; leaves large and pinnate; flo. ¾–1 in., white. On rocks in Radnorshire and Montgomeryshire, rare. Flo. May–June. ❀.

Potentilla anserina L. **Silverweed.** ¶Stoloniferous; leaves pinnate, soft and very silky; flo. solitary. Common in waste ground, roadsides and damp pastures. Flo. July–Aug. ❀.

Potentilla argentea L. **Hoary Cinquefoil.** ¶Stems decumbent, woody; leaflets 5, slender, digitate, white beneath. On dry sandy grassland, local. Flo. June–July. ❀.

Potentilla recta L. **Upright Cinquefoil.** ¶Stems erect, stout, 1–2 ft; leaves long petioled; leaflets 5, large, oblong; flo. 1 in. wide, yellow. A garden escape. Flo. June–July.

Potentilla norvegica L. ¶Stems 12–18 in., branched above; leaflets 3; sepals hairy; petals small. Introduced in many places. F June–Oct. ❀.

Potentilla intermedia L. ¶Stem ascending; lower leaflets 5 obova upper 3 oblong; petals yellow; achenes rugose. Introduced fro Europe. Flo. June–Sept.

Potentilla tabernaemontani Aschers. **Spring Cinquefoil.** *P. ver* auct. ¶Stem prostrate, rooting, branched below middle; leafl ½ in.; flo. ½ in., rather pale yellow; achenes smooth. On d calcareous rocks and grass, local. Flo. April–June. ❀.

Potentilla crantzii (Crantz) G. Beck ex Fritsch. **Alpine Cinquefo** *P. alpestris* auct. ¶Stem ascending, branched above midd leaflets 1 in.; flo. 1 in. achenes smooth; petals bright yello sometimes with an orange spot. On mountain rocks, local, fro N. Wales northwards. Flo. June–July. ❀.

Potentilla erecta (L.) Räusch. **Common Tormentil.** *P. torment* Stokes. ¶Rootstock sub-tuberous; stem slender, supported other growth; cauline leaves sessile; radical leaves vernal onl petals 4. Abundant on heaths, moors and mountains, especia on acid soils. Flo. June–Sept. ❀.

Potentilla anglica Laichard. **Procumbent Cinquefoil.** *P. procumbe* Sibth. ¶Stems decumbent, rooting in autumn; radical leav persistent; cauline leaves cuneate, with ¼ in. petiole; flo. ¾ i petals 5 or 4. On heaths, banks and wood borders, mostly basic soil. Flo. June–Sept. ❀.

Potentilla reptans L. **Creeping Cinquefoil.** ¶Stem long, creepin rooting, unbranched; leaflets mostly obovate, cauline simila petals 5. On hedge banks, waste and cultivated land, on bas soil. Flo. June–Sept. ❀.

Fragaria vesca L. **Wild Strawberry.** ¶Runners long and slende lateral leaflets sessile; receptacle covered by projecting achen Common on grassy banks and wood borders, especially calcareous soil. Flo. April–July. ❀.

Fragaria moschata Duchesne. **Hautbois Strawberry.** *F. elat* Ehrh. ¶Runners few or none; lateral leaflets shortly stalked; fl 1 in.; receptacle bare at base. Not native.

Fragaria × *ananassa* Duchesne. **Garden Strawberry.** *F. chiloen.* auct. ¶Fruiting receptacle covered by achenes embedded in f flo. 1½ in. Not native.

POTENTILLA STERILIS.
X 7.

P. STERILIS.

POTENTILLA
TABERNAEMONTANI.

POTENTILLA
CRANTZII.

P. NORVEGICA.

POTENTILLA
ARGENTEA.

POTENTILLA
ERECTA

POTENTILLA
ANGLICA.

POTENTILLA REPTANS.

POTENTILLA
RUPESTRIS.

FRAGARIA
VESCA.

POTENTILLA
PALUSTRIS.

POTENTILLA
FRUTICOSA

SIBBALDIA
PROCUMBENS

POTENTILLA
ANSERINA.

Plate 28   ❀ indicates plant is illustrated

ROSACEAE (*continued*)

There are nearly 400 species of *Rubus* in this country, and the distribution of these both in this country and on the Continent is becoming better known. A valuable handbook on this genus by the late Mr Wm. Watson has been published. But in some cases accurate determination of specimens requires the experience of those who have made a special study of the genus. It is not our intention in this present work to figure or to describe more than about a dozen samples of leading groups, in order to illustrate the kind of gradation that is found throughout the genus.

Although the desired handbook has been published, this should not invalidate our small contribution to an understanding of the genus, because in drawing the figures here shown we had valuable help from the late Mr Wm. Watson himself. He selected and posted most of the samples illustrated, and he has very kindly written the following descriptions of the selected species. He is, however, not responsible for the specimen figured as *R. caesius*, and he points out that the specimen was a hybrid. The clothing of the stems is an essential feature in determining the species, and unfortunately the finer details of this clothing are on the borderline of visibility, and are not easily figured or reproduced.

Even in the few species chosen it will be observed that in the sub-genus *Eubatus* there is a gradation. We start with the *Suberecti*, which have no stalked glands or pricklets. Indeed, the first sample has the panicle almost unarmed. Then we come to a gradual increase of prickles, which are sometimes all equal or confined to the angles of the stem. And the series continues through an increase of stalked glands, acicles and pricklets to forms which have them all very numerous, unequal and distributed all over the stem. And the last sample of this sub-genus differs also in having only 3 leaflets to each leaf instead of 5–7.

The samples chosen for illustration are not always the same as those given in edition 1 of the British Flora by Messrs Clapham, Tutin and Warburg. Of those which are different *R. sulcatus* is near to *R. nessensis*, op. cit., p. 466. *R. silvaticus* is near to *R. pyramidalis*, p. 469. *R. euryanthemus* is near to *R. pallidus*, p. 477.

Sub-genus CYLACTIS

1. *Rubus saxatilis* L. ¶On wet limestone. Fr. red. ❀ on plate 29.

Sub-genus CHAMAEMORUS

2. *Rubus chamaemorus* L. **Cloud Berry.** ¶On elevated moors. ultimately amber. ❀ on plate 29.

Sub-genus IDAEOBATUS

3. *Rubus idaeus* L. **Raspberry.** ¶In woods and heaths. Fr. felte red or amber. ❀.

Sub-genus EUBATUS. Fruit black.

x Leaves 3–5 nate, or 3–7 nate. Groups 4–11.
(*a*) Stem without stalked glands or pricklets. 4–7.

Section *Suberecti*

4. *Rubus sulcatus* Vest ex Tratt. ¶Stem tall, erect, furrowed; ro creeping; panicle almost unarmed. ❀.

Section *Sylvatici*

5. *Rubus carpinifolius* Weihe & Nees. ¶Stem arching with stro yellow prickles; panicle racemose in the upper part; sepa patent under the fruit. ❀.
6. *Rubus silvaticus* Weihe & Nees. ¶Prickles small; leaflets narrow. ❀

Section *Discolores*

7. *Rubus ulmifolius* Schott. *R. discolor* auct. ¶Leaves closely whi felted beneath; leaflets convex, usually narrow. Stame equalling the styles. ❀.
(*b*) Stem with stalked glands, acicles and pricklets. 8–11.
(1) Stem prickles subequal, seated on the angles. 8–9.

Section *Vestiti*

8. *Rubus vestitus* Weihe & Nees. ¶Densely hairy all over; prickl long, slender, straight, violet-purple; terminal leaflet roune short pointed and evenly toothed. ❀.

Section *Radulae*

9. *Rubus radula* Weihe ex Boenn. ¶Petals pink, rather sma prickles long and mostly straight; terminal leaflet ova gradually acuminate, white felted beneath. ❀.
(2) Stem prickles unequal, not confined to the angles of t stem; stalked glands and acicles numerous, some rath long and gland tipped. 10–11.

Section *Apiculati*

10. *Rubus euryanthemus* W. C. R. Wats. ¶Petals white, narrow. ❀.

RUBUS
RADULA. (RADULAE)

RUBUS
EURVANTHEMUS.

RUBUS
VESTITUS
(VESTITI)

RUBUS
CARPINIFOLIUS.
(SILVATICI)

RUBUS
SILVATICUS.

RUBUS
SULCATUS.

(DISCOLORES)
RUBUS
ULMIFOLIUS.

(SUBERECTI)

(PALLIDI)

UBUS
RAEUS.

Plate 29

ROSACEAE (*continued*)

Section *Hystrices*

11. *Rubus dasyphyllus* Rogers. ¶Petal pink; leaves thick, soft beneath, principal teeth turned outwards; stalked glands very long. ❀. xx Leaves all ternate. Groups 12–13.

Section *Glandulosi*

12. *Rubus bellardii* Weihe & Nees. ¶Petals white; leaflets sub-equal, regular, elliptical, evenly toothed. ❀.

Sub-genus GLAUCOBATUS

13. *Rubus caesius* L. ¶On wet or calcareous soils. Fr. black, pruinose. The figure represents a hybrid. ❀.

Numbers 7, 8, 11, 13 desiderate or tolerate a loamy, clayey or calcareous soil, the others are more narrowly restricted to soils that are siliceous or peaty or rich in humus.

Rubus saxatilis L. See text opposite plate 28.

Rubus chamaemorus L. See text opposite plate 28.

Dryas octopetala L. ¶Pedicel and calyx glandular; petals often 8 style feathery persistent. On basic rocks, local, N. Wales, Teesdal N. Scotland and Ireland. Flo. June–July. ❀.

Geum urbanum L. **Herb Bennet, Wood Avens.** ¶Flo. erect, yellow head of achenes sessile; style persistent as a hooked awn. Commo in woods, hedges and shady lanes. Flo. June–Sept. ❀.

Geum rivale L. **Water Avens.** ¶Flo. nodding, red; head of achen stalked; style persistent as a hooked awn. On wet rocks ar shady banks, mainly in N. and N.W. Britain, local elsewher Flo. May–Sept. ❀.

Geum rivale × *urbanum* occurs occasionally. ❀.

RUBUS
CAESIUS.

RUBUS   (HYSTRICES)
DASYPHYLLUS.

RUBUS BELLARDII.   (GLANDULOSI)

RUBUS
SAXATILIS

G. RIVALE × URBANUM.

RUBUS
CHAMAEMORUS

GEUM RIVALE.

DRYAS
OCTOPETALA.

GEUM
URBANUM

Plate 30

ROSACEAE (continued)

Rosa pimpinellifolia L. **Burnet Rose.** *R. spinosissima* auct. ¶Stem creeping, with many small straight prickles; leaflets 3–5 pairs; fr. purple. On sand dunes, cliffs and heaths, particularly near the sea. Flo. May–July. ❀.

*Rosa rugosa Thunb. ¶Stem very prickly and rough; leaflets 2–4 pairs, elliptic; dark green and rugose above, felted below; flo. large, deep pink to white; fr. large, red; sepals erect, persistent. Commonly planted for hedging and occurring in woods, thickets on heaths and waste ground as a bird-sown introduction. Flo. June–Aug.

Rosa arvensis Huds. **Trailing Rose.** ¶Stem trailing, purplish; flo. white; fr. small; styles united in an exserted column. Common in S. and W., rare in the N. and introduced in Scotland. Flo. June–July. ❀.

Rosa stylosa Desv. **Long-styled Rose.** ¶Stem stout, erect; pedicels long, hispid; disk conical; styles united in an exserted column. On basic soils chiefly in S. England and S. Ireland, locally common. Flo. June–July. ❀.

Rosa canina L. **Dog Rose.** *R. systyla* Bast. ¶Pedicels 1–2 cm., sub-glabrous; sepals falling early; stigmas conical, narrower than disk. Common. Flo. June–July. ❀.

Rosa dumalis Bechst. **Short-pedicelled Rose.** *R. coriifolia* Fr. *R. afzeliana* auct. *R. glauca* Vill. ex Lois., non Pourr. ¶Pedicels short, 1 cm., hidden in bracts; sepals persistent; stigmas flat, concealing disk. Common in N. England and Scotland, very rare in S. England. Flo. June–July. ❀.

Rosa obtusifolia Desv. ¶Leaves roundly ovate, pubescent or glandular beneath; pedicels short; sepals short, lobes broad. In England, except the N.W., local. Flo. June–July. ❀.

Rosa tomentosa Sm. **Downy Rose.** ¶Leaves pubescent, often dense so; pedicels up to 2 cm., glandular; sepals constricted at bas flo. 4 cm., pink; disk large, 4–6 times orifice. In hedges, et mainly on chalk. Flo. June–July. ❀.

Rosa sherardii Davies. **Northern Downy Rose.** *R. omissa* Dése ¶Leaves rather glaucous; pedicels ½–1½ cm.; sepals short, sligh constricted, persistent; flo. often deep pink; styles villous; di 3–3½ times orifice. Frequent in N. Britain, rare in S. Flo. Jun July.

Rosa villosa L. **Soft-leaved Rose.** *R. mollis* Sm. ¶Prickles straig and slender; leaflets roundly oval, tomentose; sepals erect, pe sistent; pedicels short, hispid; fr. globose, hispid; flo. deep pin Rather common in N. Britain, local in W. Midlands and Wal and introduced in S. England. Flo. June–July. ❀.

Rosa rubiginosa L. **Sweet Briar.** *R. eglanteria* auct. ¶Leaflets round oval, very glandular below and scented; pedicels short, glandula hispid; fr. hispid; sepals persistent; flo. usually deep pink. Most on calcareous soils. Flo. June–July. ❀.

Rose micrantha Borrer ex Sm. **Lesser Sweet Briar.** ¶Stems archin leaflets ovate, glandular beneath; pedicels long, hispid; sepa falling early; flo. pink; styles glabrous. Common in England ar Wales, rare in Scotland and Ireland. Flo. June–July. ❀.

Rosa agrestis Savi. **Narrow-leaved Sweet Briar.** *R. sepium* Thuil non Lam. ¶Stems arching; leaflets narrow, tapering to bas pedicels smooth; styles subglabrous; fr. smooth; sepals fallin early. Mostly on calcareous soils, very local. Flo. June–July. ❀

Rosa elliptica Tausch. *R. inodora* auct. ¶Similar to *R. agrestis*, b stems erect; leaflets obovate, tapering below only; styles hair sepals more persistent. Very rare, Somerset to Huntingdonshire

ROSA
PIMPINELLIFOLIA
BURNET ROSE

ROSA TOMENTOSA

ROSA
VILLOSA.

ROSA
MICRANTHA.

SWEET BRIAR
ROSA RUBIGINOSA.

ROSA AGRESTIS.

ROSA
OBTUSIFOLIA.

ROSA
SHERARDII.

ROSA DUMALIS.

DOG
ROSE
ROSA
CANINA.

ROSA
STYLOSA.

ROSA
ARVENSIS.

Plate 31   ❋ indicates plant is illustrated

ROSACEAE (*continued*)

Sorbus aucuparia L. **Rowan, Mountain Ash.** *Pyrus aucuparia* (L.) Ehrh. ¶Leaves pinnate, all leaflets separate; flo. many, smaller than in other species. In woods and scrub, etc. on light soils, native in the W. and N., probably introduced, though readily regenerating elsewhere. Flo. May–June. ❋.

Sorbus pseudofennica E. F. Warb. ¶Small tree; leaves ovate-oblong, but some with free basal leaflets. Arran. Flo. May–June.

Sorbus intermedia agg. ¶Leaves elliptic with rounded ascending lobes, felted beneath; veins 7–11 pairs.
  S. arranensis Hedlund. ¶Leaves lobed at base about ½ way to midrib; greyish felted beneath; veins 7–9 pairs; fr. ovoid. Arran. Flo. May–June. ❋.
  S. leyana Wilmott. ¶Leaves broader, cuneate at base; basal lobe nearly ½ way to midrib; petals and fr. a little larger than in previous species. Breconshire. Flo. May–June.
  S. minima (A. Ley) Hedlund. **Least White Beam.** *Pyrus minima* A. Ley. ¶Leaves elliptic, twice as long as broad, base lobed about ¼ way to midrib; petals 4 mm.; fr. small, 6–8 mm., subglobose. Limestone crags, Breconshire. Flo. May–June. ❋.
  S. intermedia (Ehrh.) Pers. *Pyrus intermedia* Ehrh. ¶Leaves elliptic, lobed at base ¼–⅓ way to midrib, yellowish felted beneath; fr. very oblong. Planted, but freely regenerating. Flo. May.
  S. anglica Hedlund. **Cheddar White Beam.** *S. mougeotii* Soy.-Will. & Godr. var. *anglica* (Hedlund) C. E. Salmon. ¶Leaves broadly ovate, about 1½ times as long as broad; lobed⅛–¼ way to midrib, greyish felted beneath; fr. subglobose, with few lenticels. On limestone rocks, Devon to Shropshire and Wales, also in Kerry. Flo. May.

Sorbus aria agg. ¶Leaves ovate or obovate, toothed or slightly lobed, white felted beneath; veins 7–14 pairs.
  S. aria (L.) Crantz. *Pyrus aria* (L.) Ehrh. ¶Leaves oval, usually curved to base; veins 10–14 pairs; fr. longer than broad, scarlet; lenticels small. In calcareous woods, S. England, though frequently planted elsewhere. Flo. May–June. ❋.
  S. × thuringiaca (Ilse) Fritsch. (*S. aria × aucuparia*). ¶Leaves oblong, sometimes with 1–3 pairs of free leaflets at base; serrate; green and glabrous above, greyish-green felted beneath; veins 10–12 pairs; fr. subglobose, scarlet; lenticels few, inconspicuous. Sometimes found where the parents grow together, also occurs as a planted tree. Flo. May–June.
  S. × vagensis **Wilmott.** (*S. aria × torminalis*). ¶Tree, with wide crown and spreading branches; leaves ovate, deeply lobed, with acuminate lobes finely, and sometimes doubly, serrate, teeth small, yellowish green above, greenish-grey felted beneath; fr. brownish, longer than broad. In woods on limestone, Wye Valley. Flo. May–June.
  S. leptophylla E. F. Warb. ¶Shrub, similar to *S. aria* but leaves yellow or dark green above; teeth curved on outer margins; veins *c.* 11 pairs. On limestone rocks, Breconshire. Flo. May.
  S. wilmottiana E. F. Warb. ¶Shrub or small tree, similar to *S. aria* but leaves bright green above, teeth curved on outer margins; veins *c.* 8–9 pairs; fr. crimson. In woods on limestone, Cheddar Gorge. Flo. May–June.
  S. eminens E. F. Warb. ¶Shrub or small tree similar to *S. aria* but leaves bright green above, teeth symmetrical; veins *c.* 10–11 pairs. In woods on limestone, Wye Valley and Avon Gorge. Flo. May–June.
  S. hibernica E. F. Warb. **Irish White Beam.** ¶Leaves oval, shortly cuneate at the base; veins 9–11 pairs; teeth triangular, acute, turned outwards; fr. broader than long. In woods on limestone, Ireland. Flo. May.
  S. porrigentiformis E. F. Warb. *S. porrigens* Hedlund, pro parte. ¶Leaves obovate, rounded above, tapering below, 1½ times as long as broad, greyish felted beneath; veins 8–10 pairs; fr. broader than long, crimson, with few large lenticels. In woods on limestone S. Devon to Mendips, Wye Valley and Wales. Flo. May–June. ❋.
  S. lancastriensis E. F. Warb. ¶Shrub similar to *S. aria* but teeth of leaves symmetrical and pointing outwards; veins *c.* 8–10 pairs; fr. crimson with a number of large lenticels towards the base. On limestone rocks, Lancashire and Westmorland. Flo. May–June.
  S. rupicola (Syme) Hedlund. **Rock White Beam.** ¶Leaves obovate, rounded above, length nearly double the breadth, white felted beneath; veins 7–9 pairs; fr. broader than long, with many rather smaller lenticels. On limestone rocks, S. Devon to Scotland and N. and W. Ireland. Flo. May–June.
  S. vexans E. F. Warb. ¶Small tree, similar to *S. aria* but leaves obovate, with cuneate base; veins *c.* 8–10 pairs; fr. longer than broad, with few small lenticels. In rocky woods near coast Somerset and S. Devon. Flo. May.

Sorbus latifolia agg. **¶Broad-leaved White Beam.** ¶Leaves with triangular lobes; veins 7–9 pairs; fr. orange, subglobose or longer than broad. ❋.
  S. bristoliensis Wilmott. ¶Leaves obovate; anthers pink; fr. longer than broad, bright orange, with small lenticels. In rocky wood on limestone, Avon Gorge. Flo. May–June.
  S. subcuneata Wilmott. ¶Leaves elliptic, tapered at the base white felted beneath; anthers cream; fr. subglobose, brownish orange. In open oakwoods, Somerset and Devon. Flo. May–June.
  S. devoniensis E. F. Warb. ¶Leaves ovate, round at base, with shallow triangular lobes; greyish-green felted beneath; fr. subglobose. In woods, Devon, E. Cornwall and Ireland. Flo. May–June.

Sorbus torminalis (L.) Crantz. **Wild Service Tree.** *Pyrus torminalis* (L.) Ehrh. ¶Leaves oval, deeply lobed, green beneath; fr. elongated, brown. In woods on clay and limestone in England. Flo. May–June. ❋.

Pyrus pyraster Burgsd. **Pear.** *P. communis* auct. ¶Flo. on very short rachis; petals broad, very concave, white; fr. 2–4 cm., sometime tapered into stalk. Throughout England, not common. Flo. April–May. ❋.

Pyrus cordata Desv. **Lesser Pear.** ¶Leaves rather small, round subglabrous; flo. on longer rachis, smaller; petals narrow obovate, pink; fr. very small, 1–2 cm., obovoid or round. In hedges near Plymouth, very rare. Flo. April–May. ❋.

Malus sylvestris Mill. **Crab Apple.** *Pyrus malus* L. ¶Small tree; flo. in an umbel; styles united below. In woods. Flo. May. ❋.

Malus domestica Borkh. **Cultivated Apple.** *Malus sylvestris* Mill subsp. *mitis* (Wallr.) Mansf. *Pyrus malus* L. var. *mitis* Wallr ¶Similar to *M. sylvestris* but young twigs tomentose, glabrous later; buds hairy; leaves obtuse, pubescent beneath; pedicels calyx, etc., woolly; fr. largish, sometimes sweet. Naturalized in hedges, woods, etc. Flo. May.

Mespilus germanica L. **Medlar.** ¶Small thorny tree; stalks pubescent leaves large; sepals persistent, linear. Naturalized in hedges mostly in England. Flo. May–June.

Crataegus laevigata (Poir.) DC. **Two-styled Hawthorn.** *C. oxyacanthoides* Thuill. ¶Leaf lobes broader than long, without axillary hairs beneath; styles 2. In woods on heavy soils, S. and E. England, the Midlands, Wales and Ireland; rare in N. and introduced in Scotland. Flo. May–June. ❋.

Crataegus × media Bechst. (*C. laevigata × monogyna*). ¶Hybrids, intermediate between the two species are common where the parent plants grow together.

Crataegus monogyna Jacq. **Common Hawthorn.** ¶Leaf lobes longer than broad, very variable, with hairs in axils beneath, style 1 Common in hedges, etc., though often planted. Flo. May–June. ❋.

Cotoneaster integerrimus Medic. ¶Leaves 1 in. or more, rounded at base; petals erect, pink. On rocks, Great Orme's Head, Caernarvon. Flo. April–June. ❋.

SORBUS
ARRANENSIS.

SORBUS
PORRIGENTI-
-FORMIS

SORBUS
AUCUPARIA.

SORBUS
MINIMA

SORBUS
LATIFOLIA.

SORBUS
ARIA.

SORBUS
TORMINALIS.

MALUS SYLVESTRIS

PYRUS
COMMUNIS

PYRUS
CORDATA

CRATAEGUS
MONOGYNA

CRATAEGUS OXYACANTHOIDES

COTONEASTER
INTEGERRIMA.

Plate 32   ✿ indicates plant is illustrated

ROSACEAE (continued)

Cotoneaster microphyllus Wall. ex Lindl. ¶Leaves ½ in. or less, obovate; petals white and spreading. Introduced from India. Bird-sown from gardens and naturalized on banks, in chalk pits, etc. Flo. May–June.

Cotoneaster simonsii Bak. ¶Leaves ½ in. or more, green and glabrous above, sparsely pubescent beneath, cuneate at base; petals erect, pink. Bird-sown from gardens and naturalized on cliffs, heaths, etc. Flo. May–July.

Cotoneaster horizontalis Decne. ¶Similar to *C. simonsii*, but procumbent with horizontal spreading stems; leaves small, dark green, glabrous above. Bird-sown from gardens and naturalized on cliffs, old walls, in chalk pits, etc. May–July.

SAXIFRAGACEAE

Saxifraga oppositifolia L. **Purple Saxifrage.** ¶Stems many, prostrate; leaves many, opposite; flo. rose-purple, solitary. On mountain rocks, mostly in N. Britain. Flo. April–June. ✿.

Saxifraga nivalis L. **Clustered Alpine Saxifrage.** ¶Leaves in basal rosette, broadly obovate; stem naked; flo. in a close head. On higher mountain rocks, mostly in Scotland, rare. Flo. July–Aug. ✿.

Saxifraga stellaris L. **Starry Saxifrage.** ¶Stems with small rosettes of subsessile leaves; sepals reflexed. Common on wet mountain rocks and streamsides. Flo. June–July. ✿.

Saxifraga hirculus L. **Yellow Bog Saxifrage.** ¶Erect, leafy, with prostrate basal branches; lower leaves petiolate; flo. yellow, ovary free. On wet moorland grass, N. England, Scotland and Ireland, rare. ✿.

Saxifraga aizoides L. **Yellow Mountain Saxifrage.** ¶Prostrate with ascending branches; leaves sessile; flo. several, yellow, ovary partly inferior. Common on wet mountain rocks, Wales to N. Scotland and in Ireland. Flo. June–Aug. ✿.

Saxifraga umbrosa L. ¶Leaves oval with obtuse teeth, terminal tooth shorter and broader; petiole shorter than blade, very ciliate. Yorkshire, introduced before 1800.

Saxifraga spathularis Brot. **St Patrick's Cabbage.** *S. umbrosa* auct., non L. ¶Leaves, oval, with triangular equal teeth; petiole longer than blade, sparsely ciliate. On mountain rocks in Ireland. Flo. June–Aug.

Saxifraga spathularis × *umbrosa* = *S.* × *urbium* D. A. Webb, *S. umbrosa* L. var. *crenatoserrata* Bab. **London Pride.** ¶Leaves subacute, with equal angular teeth; flo. stem less glandular, sterile. ✿.

Saxifraga hirsuta L. *S. geum* L. *S. lactiflora* Pugsl. ¶Leaves orbicular or reniform, cordate, crenate; petiole slender, much longer than blade. On rocks in S.W. Ireland. Flo. May–July. Figure is probably that of *S.* × *polita* auct. = *S. hirsuta* × *spathularis*. ✿.

Saxifraga tridactylites L. **Rue-leaved Saxifrage.** ¶Plant small, annual, glandular; leaves 3–5 lobed, upper entire. On light dry soils and wall tops. Flo. April–June. ✿.

Saxifraga granulata L. **Meadow Saxifrage, Bulbous Saxifrage.** ¶Stem with large bulbils at base; leaves cordate, with round lobes. In meadow grass, in England, except the S.W., where it is a introduction, rare in Wales. Flo. April–June. ✿.

Saxifraga cernua L. **Lesser Bulbous Saxifrage.** ¶Stem erect, with small red bulbils in axils; flo. terminal or none. On rock ledges of mountain tops, Perthshire and Argyll, very rare. Flo. July. ✿.

Saxifraga rivularis L. **Alpine Rivulet Saxifrage.** ¶Stems weak, trailing, ascending in flo.; leaves reniform, 3–7 lobed. On wet rocks on high mountains in Scotland, very rare. Flo. July–Aug. ✿.

Saxifraga cespitosa L. **Tufted Saxifrage.** ¶Plant small, compact, leaf lobes oblong, obtuse; glandular hairs short, dense. On mountain rocks, Wales and Scotland, very rare. Flo. May–July. ✿.

Saxifraga hartii D. A. Webb. ¶Similar to *S. cespitosa*, but plant looser, leaves larger and densely covered with short glandular hairs, lobes subacute; petals larger, pure white. Sea cliffs, Arranmore Island, Donegal. Flo. May–June.

Saxifraga rosacea Moench. **Irish Saxifrage.** ¶Plant rather compact, with erect barren branches, and few longer glandular hairs. On wet mountain rocks, W. Ireland, local. Flo. June–Aug. ✿.

Saxifraga hypnoides L. **Mossy Saxifrage.** ¶Barren branches long and prostrate, often with axillary tufts; leaf lobes acute, aristate. On mountain rocks, Somerset and Wales to N. Scotland, and Ireland. Flo. May–July. ✿.
Var. *platypetala* Sm. ¶Axillary leaf buds few or 0; petals broad, contiguous, flat. ✿.

Chrysosplenium oppositifolium L. **Golden Saxifrage.** ¶Upper leaves opposite; basal leaf petiole equalling blade. Common, especially on acid soils, but rare in parts of E. England and the Midlands. Flo. March–May. ✿.

Chrysosplenium alternifolium L. **Alternate-leaved Golden Saxifrage.** ¶Upper leaves alternate or only 1; basal petioles longer than blade. Often on basic soil, local, absent from extreme W. Britain. Flo. March–June. ✿.

PARNASSIACEAE

Parnassia palustris L. **Grass of Parnassus.** ¶Flo. solitary; stamens 5, and 5 staminodes, fringed with stalked glands. On wet moorlands and fixed sand dunes, absent from the S.W., and now very rare in S. England and the Midlands. Flo. July–Sept. ✿.

SAXIFRAGA OPPOSITIFOLIA.

CHRYSOSPLENIUM OPPOSITIFOLIUM

CHRYSOSPLENIUM ALTERNIFOLIUM

SAXIFRAGA RIVULARIS.

SAXIFRAGA STELLARIS

SAXIFRAGA UMBROSA.

SAXIFRAGA TRIDACTYLITES.

SAXIFRAGA NIVALIS.

SAXIFRAGA CERNUA.

SAXIFRAGA HIRSUTA.

SAXIFRAGA AIZOIDES.

SAXIFRAGA CESPITOSA.

SAXIFRAGA GRANULATA

SAXIFRAGA ROSACEA.

S. HYPNOIDES VAR. PLATYPETALA

SAXIFRAGA HYPNOIDES.

PARNASSIA PALUSTRIS.

SAXIFRAGA HIRCULUS.

Plate 33   ✽ indicates plant is illustrated

GROSSULARIACEAE

Ribes rubrum L. **Red Currant.** *R. sylvestre* (Lam.) Mert. & Koch. ¶Inflo. drooping; receptacle with a raised rim; sepals broader than long. In woods and beside streams, frequent. Flo. April–May. ✽.

Ribes spicatum Robson. **Upright Red Currant.** *R. petraeum* auct. ¶Inflo. erect; receptacle deeper, without raised rim; sepals circular. In woods on limestone, N. England to N. Scotland. ✽.

Ribes nigrum L. **Black Currant.** ¶Leaves strong smelling; flo. drooping, campanulate; fr. black. In woods and by streams, locally native. Flo. April–May. ✽.

*Ribes sanguineum Pursh. **Flowering Currant.** ¶Leaves bluntly lobed, pubescent beneath; flo. pink; fr. dark bluish black, pruinose. Garden outcast or bird-sown from gardens, naturalized by streams, etc. Flo. April–May.

Ribes alpinum L. **Alpine Currant.** ¶Flo. dioecious in erect spikes; male numerous, small; female few; fr. red. On limestone rock, mainly N. England and Wales. Flo. April–May. ✽.

Ribes uva-crispa L. **Gooseberry.** *R. grossularia* L. ¶Stems spinous at the nodes; flo. 1 or 2; fr. usually bristly. In woods and hedges, native, or bird-sown from gardens. Flo. March–April. ✽.

CRASSULACEAE

Crassula tillaea L.-Garland. **Mossy Tillaea.** *Tillaea muscosa* L. ¶Plant small and reddish with minute, crowded, oval leaves; flo. very small, axillary. On sandy soil, local, S. Devon to Norfolk. Flo. June–July. ✽.

Crassula aquatica (L.) Schönl. *Tillaea aquatica* L. ¶Leaves linear, not crowded; flo. minute, axillary. On wet mud, perhaps only casual. Flo. June–July. ✽.

Umbilicus rupestris (Salisb.) Dandy. **Pennywort.** *Cotyledon umbilicus-veneris* auct. ¶Leaves peltate; petals united in a tube; stamens 10. On rock crevices and walls, common on acid soils. Flo. June–Aug. ✽.

Rhodiola rosea L. **Roseroot.** *Sedum rosea* (L.) Scop., *S. rhodiola* DC. ¶Rootstock thick and fleshy; flo. dioecious with 4 linear petals. In rock crevices, Wales to Scotland, and Ireland. Flo. May–Aug. ✽.

Sedum telephium L. **Orpine, Livelong.** *S. purpureum* auct.
Subsp. *telephium*. ¶Leaves flat, rounded at base; flo. reddish purp rarely white. In woods. Flo. July–Sept.
Subsp. *fabaria* (Koch) Kirschleger. *Sedum fabaria* Koch. ¶Leaves tapering at base, sometimes shortly stalked. Flo. July–Sept. ✽.

*Sedum spurium Bieb. *S. stoloniferum* auct. ¶Stems procumbe creeping, forming dense mats with numerous ascending branche leaves opposite, flat, obtuse; flo. pink in flat terminal cym Garden escape. Naturalized on hedge banks, waste ground, e Flo. July–Sept.

*Sedum dasyphyllum L. **Thick-leaved Stonecrop.** ¶Stems procu bent or ascending; leaves roundly obovoid, glandular. On wa and limestone rocks. Not native. Flo. June–July. ✽.

Sedum anglicum Huds. **English Stonecrop.** ¶Prostrate with sho erect, forked flo. stems; leaves spurred. On rocks especially grani and sandy soil, abundant. Flo. June–Aug. ✽.

Sedum album L. **White Stonecrop.** ¶Prostrate, with erect muc branched flo. stems; leaves not spurred. On limestone roc Mendips and S. Devon, on walls elsewhere. Flo. June–Aug. ✽.

Sedum acre L. **Wall Pepper.** ¶Creeping, with ascending flo. ste with few short branches; leaves hot tasting. On limestone rocks a walls, railway tracks and on basic soils. Flo. June–July. ✽.

*Sedum sexangulare is similar to *S. acre*, without hot taste and wi smaller flo. Not native.

Sedum forsteranum Sm. **Rock Stonecrop.** *S. rupestre* L. pro parte.
Subsp. *forsteranum*. ¶Leaves linear, erect, tufted at ends of branche flo. stems slender, tall, usually green, sometimes glauco branched; inflo. convex in flo. Local on damp rocks and cli Devon to Wales. Flo. June–July. ✽.
Subsp. *elegans* (Lej.) E. F. Warb. *Sedum elegans* Lej. *S. rupestre* subsp. *elegans* (Lej.) Syme. ¶Similar to subsp. *forsteranum* b glaucous and usually more robust; inflo. flat-topped in flo. Loc on dry rocks and cliffs, Devon to Wales. Flo. June–July.

*Sedum reflexum L. **Reflexed Stonecrop.** ¶Leaves stout, recurve equally distributed, not tufted; flo. larger. On old walls a rockeries, common, not native. Flo. June–Aug. ✽.

Sedum villosum L. **Hairy Stonecrop.** ¶Annual, erect, glandula shortly branched; petals ovate pink. On wet mountain roc Yorkshire to N. Scotland. Flo. June–July. ✽.

*Sempervivum tectorum L. **Houseleek.** ¶Leaves in a close persiste rosette, thick, obovate, mucronate; petals red. An ancie introduction, planted on walls and roofs.

RIBES UVA-CRISPA.

RIBES SYLVESTRE.

RIBES ALPINUM.

RIBES NIGRUM.

IBES PICATUM.

SEDUM DASYPHYLLUM.

SEDUM FABARIA. ORPINE.

RASSULA TILLAEA.

CRASSULA AQUATICA.

SEDUM ANGLICUM.

SEDUM ALBUM.

SEDUM VILLOSUM.

SEDUM ACRE.

SEDUM FORSTERANUM.

SEDUM REFLEXUM.

SEDUM ROSEA.

MBILICUS UPESTRIS.

Plate 34   ❧ indicates plant is illustrated

DROSERACEAE

Drosera rotundifolia L. **Sundew.** ¶Leaves orbicular, spreading, long petioled; flo. stem from centre. Common on wet moors and peat bogs. Flo. June–Aug. ❧.

Drosera anglica Huds. **Great Sundew.** ¶Leaves 4 in., tapering into petiole; flo. stem from centre. In wet peat bogs, local. Flo. July–Aug. ❧.

Drosera × obovata Mert. & Koch. (*D. anglica × rotundifolia*). ¶Similar to *D. intermedia* but with a straight scape up to 3 times as long as the leaves. This sterile hybrid sometimes occurs where the two parents grow together.

Drosera intermedia Hayne. **Long-leaved Sundew.** *D. longifolia* auct. ¶Leaves 1½ in., obovate, tapering into petiole; flo. stem from base of rosette. On damp peaty moors, fairly common in the W. Flo. June–Aug. ❧.

SARRACENIACEAE

*Sarracenia purpurea L. **Pitcher Plant.** ¶Plant stout, up to 1 ft tall, with large erect clusters of root-leaves, splashed with green and purple; leaves tubular with a flap at the apex, the whole forming a 'pitcher', often containing water in which small insects drown; flo. purple, 1 in. wide, solitary or in few-flowered racemes, nodding on leafless stems; top of style umbrella shaped. Introduced from N. America and naturalized in bogs in Roscommon and Westmeath, Ireland. Flo. June–July.

HALORAGACEAE

Hippuris vulgaris L. **Mare's Tail.** ¶Leaves narrow, linear, whorled; submerged leaves longer, more flaccid; flo. sessile; perianth almost 0; stamen 1. Pools and slow streams. Flo. June–July. ❧.

Myriophyllum verticillatum L. **Whorled Water Milfoil.** ¶Leaves mostly 5 in a whorl, pectinate; floral bracts leaf-like, variable; lower flo. female. In ponds and slow streams, scarce. Flo. July–Aug. ❧.

Myriophyllum spicatum L. **Spiked Water Milfoil.** ¶Leaves usually 4 in a whorl; flo. spike long, erect; bracts very short; upper flo. male with red petals. Ponds and slow streams. Flo. June–July. ❧.

Myriophyllum alterniflorum DC. **Alternate-flowered Water Milfoil.** ¶Leaves 3 or 4 in a whorl; flo. spike short, drooping in bud; petals yellowish. In lakes and slow streams and peaty water. Flo. May–Aug. ❧.

CALLITRICHACEAE

Callitriche stagnalis Scop. **Mud Water Starwort.** ¶Leaves usually roundly obovate, about twice as long as broad, at least 3 veined; submerged leaves never linear; bracts usually deciduous; fr. nearly round, freely produced. In ponds, ditches, canals, on wet mud, etc., very common, and widespread, up to 3000 ft. Flo. May–Sept. ❧.

Callitriche platycarpa Kütz. *C. polymorpha* auct. ¶Leaves usually obvate or rhomboid, about 3 times as long as broad, 1 veined submerged plants; bracts usually persistent; fr. small, near round, sparsely produced; styles long, deflexed, persistent. similar habitats to *C. stagnalis*. Very common and widesprea but rarely occurring above 500 ft. Flo. May–Sept. ❧.

Callitriche obtusangula Le Gall. ¶Leaves rhomboid-spathulate, form ing rosettes; bracts persistent; fr. rather square, longer than broa the edges rounded with shallow groove; styles long, persisten In ponds, ditches, streams, etc., locally common in S. England rarer in the N. Flo. May–Sept. ❧.

Callitriche palustris L. *C. verna* auct. ¶Similar to *C. platycarpa*, but fru small, 1 mm., turgid, narrowed below in side view, edges keele converging above in end view; styles short, 2 mm., erect, soo falling off. The figure was drawn from a Devon specimen, but i is now said that all the available British material formerly referre to this species belongs to *C. platycarpa*. ❧.

Callitriche hamulata Kütz. *C. intermedia* Hoffm. ¶Leaves linear, widene and emarginate at apex; bracts deciduous; fr. small, sessile, blac about as long as broad; styles reflexed. In lakes, ditches, slo streams, etc., probably widespread. Flo. April–Sept. ❧.

'*Callitriche pedunculata*' DC. ¶A complex plant which may be co specific with *C. hamulata* or a subspecies or variety of that plan It is said to differ in being smaller, with shorter leaves, and brow (not black) fr. borne on slender peduncles. ❧.

Callitriche hermaphroditica L. *C. autumnalis* L. ¶Leaves linear ½–⅝ i long, widest at base; fr. large, 2 mm., of 4 separate winged lobe In lakes and streams, chiefly in N. Britain. Flo. May–Sept. ❧.

Callitriche truncata Guss. ¶Leaves linear, ¼ in., only slightly wider a base; fr. small, 1 mm., edges not winged. In ponds and ditches i S. half of England, rare. Flo. May–Sept. ❧.

CERATOPHYLLACEAE

Ceratophyllum demersum L. **Hornwort.** ¶Leaves once or twice forked fr. with 2 spines at the base. In ponds and dikes. Flo. July–Sept. ❧

Ceratophyllum submersum L. ¶Leaves 3 times forked; fr. without spine In ponds and dikes. Flo. July–Sept. ❧.

LYTHRACEAE

Lythrum portula (L.) D. A. Webb. **Water Purslane.** *Peplis portu* L. ¶Stems prostrate, rooting; petals often 6, small, soon falling Common on mud, especially on acid soils. Flo. June–Sept. ❧.

Lythrum salicaria L. **Purple Loosestrife.** ¶Perennial, 2–4 ft; flo ½ in., clustered; styles and stamens of variable length. On rive banks, ditches and marshes, common. Flo. June–Aug. ❧.

Lythrum hyssopifolia L. **Hyssop-leaved Loosestrife.** ¶Annua ½–1 ft; flo. ⅕ in., singly in axils. In pools that dry up, local an uncertain in appearance. Flo. June–July. ❧.

DROSERA
ROTUNDIFOLIA

DROSERA
INTERMEDIA

DROSERA
ANGLICA

LYTHRUM
HYSSOPIFOLIA

HIPPURIS
VULGARIS

PEPLIS PORTULA

C. DEMERSUM

C. PEDUNCULATA

CALLITRICHE
INTERMEDIA.

LYTHRUM
SALICARIA.

USANGULA

MYRIOPHYLLUM
VERTICILLATUM

CALLITRICHE
HERMAPHRODITICA

MYRIOPHYLLUM
ALTERNIFLORUM.

LITRICHE
GNALIS.

MYRIOPHYLLUM
SPICATUM

CALLITRICHE
PALUSTRIS.

CALLITRICHE
PLATYCARPA.

CALLITRICHE
TRUNCATA

CERATOPHYLLUM
SUBMERSUM.

Plate 35   ❀ indicates plant is illustrated

ONAGRACEAE

Epilobium angustifolium L. **Rose Bay.** *Chamaenerion angustifolium* (L.) Scop. ¶Flo. horizontal; stamens long and drooping; petals a little unequal. In woodland clearings, waste and burnt ground. Flo. July–Sept. ❀.

Epilobium hirsutum L. **Great Willow Herb.** ¶Stems 4 ft, terete, hairy; leaves sessile, hairy; stigma 4 lobed. In ditches and streamsides, common. Flo. July–Aug. ❀.

Epilobium parviflorum Schreb. **Hairy Willow Herb.** ¶Stems 1–3 ft, terete, hairy; leaves oblong, sessile, softly hairy; stigma 4 lobed. In ditches and damp ground, common. Flo. June–Aug. ❀.

Epilobium montanum L. **Broad-leaved Willow Herb.** ¶Stem slender, terete; leaves stalked, ovate, acute; stigma 4 lobed. Common in woods, hedges and cultivated ground. Flo. June–Aug. ❀.

Epilobium lanceolatum Seb. & Mauri. **Spear-leaved Willow Herb.** ¶Stem with 4 slight ridges; leaves stalked, lanceolate; stigma 4 lobed. On dry banks, in woods and rock cuttings in S. England. Flo. July–Sept. ❀.

Epilobium roseum Schreb. **Pedicelled Willow Herb.** ¶Stem with 2 raised lines; leaves stalked, tapering below; stigma entire, equalling style. On damp waste and cultivated ground. Flo. July–Aug. ❀.

*Epilobium adenocaulon Hausskn. ¶Stem 2–3 ft with 4 raised lines and glandular hairs; leaves rounded below; flo. small, pale; stigma entire, shorter than style. Introduced from N. America and spreading rapidly in woods, marshes, by streamsides, on waste ground, walls, etc. Flo. June–Sept.

Epilobium tetragonum L. **Square-stalked Willow Herb.** *E. adnatum* Griseb.
Subsp. *tetragonum.* ¶Leaves oblong, shining, sessile; stigma entire; fr. 2½–4 in., plant with small autumn rosettes. In ditches and damp lanes. Flo. July–Aug. ❀.
Subsp. *lamyi* (F. W. Schultz), Léveillé. **Scarce Willow Herb.** *Epilobium lamyi* F. W. Schultz. ¶Leaves short stalked, lanceolate, glaucous; stigma entire; capsule 2½–4 in., downy. In damp places in S. England. Flo. July–Aug. ❀.

Epilobium obscurum Schreb. **Thin-runner Willow Herb.** ¶Stem with stolons and 4 raised lines; leaves short, sessile; stigma entire; capsule 1½–2½ in. Common in ditches and wet shady places. Flo. July–Aug. ❀.

Epilobium palustre L. **Bog Willow Herb.** ¶Stem terete, with slender stolons; leaves linear-lanceolate; buds drooping; stigma entire. On peaty moorland bogs, marshes, etc., common. Flo. July–Aug. ❀.

Epilobium anagallidifolium Lam. **Alpine Willow Herb.** *E. alpinum* auct. ¶Stem 4 in., stoloniferous; leaves small, elliptical; fl. drooping. By mountain springs, N. Yorkshire northwards. Fl. July–Aug. ❀.

Epilobium alsinifolium Vill. **Chickweed Willow Herb.** ¶Stem 2–8 in. with white stolons; leaves ovate, dentate; flo. drooping. By mountain streams, Wales and N. Yorkshire northwards. Flo. July–Aug. ❀.

*Epilobium nerterioides Cunn. *E. pedunculare* auct., non Cunn. ¶Stem slender, creeping; leaves suborbicular; capsule 1½–2 in., glabrous. Introduced from New Zealand. Garden escape. Spreading by streamsides, on wet rocky places, moors, etc., chiefly in S.W. and N. England, N. Wales, Scotland and Ireland. Flo. June–July.

Ludwigia palustris (L.) Ell. ¶Stem prostrate below; flo. axillary, su sessile; stamens 4, no petals. In shallow pools, New Forest and Jersey. Flo. June. ❀.

*Oenothera biennis L. **Evening Primrose.** ¶Stem without bulbo hairs; leaves lanceolate; flo. erect, petals 1 in. Garden escape. C sand dunes and waste places. Flo. June–Sept.

*Oenothera erythrosepala Borbás. *O. lamarkiana* auct. ¶Stem with bulbous hairs; leaves broadly lanceolate; petals 2 in., buds angula Garden escape. On roadsides and waste places. Flo. June–Sep

*Oenothera stricta Ledeb. ex Link. *O. odorata* auct. ¶Stem subsimpl erect, glandular; leaves linear-lanceolate; petals 1½ in., becomin red. Garden escape. Mostly on sand dunes. Flo. June–Sept.

*Oenothera parviflora L. ¶Has inflo. drooping; flo. smaller (⅔ in. Garden escape. On waste ground, etc. Flo. June–Sept.

*Fuchsia magallenica Lam. *F. gracilis* Lindl. *F. riccartonii* auct. ¶Shru up to 6 ft; leaves toothed, oval-acuminate; flo. small, solitar pendulous; sepals bright red; petals plum-purple; stigma an stamens exserted; berry black. Cultivated for hedging purpos and naturalized in S.W. England and W. Ireland. Flo. June–Sep

Circaea lutetiana L. **Enchanter's Nightshade.** ¶Rhizomes ove wintering; plant hairy; leaf base truncate, margin slightly dentic late; bracteoles o; flo. widely spaced. Common in shade. Fl July. ❀.

Circaea alpina L. **Alpine Enchanter's Nightshade.** ¶Tubers ove wintering; plant subglabrous; leaf base cordate, margin strong dentate; flo. bracteolate, clustered when open. Very local, i shady places, Wales, N.W. England, Arran. ❀.

Circaea × intermedia Ehrh. *C. alpina × lutetiana.* ¶Intermediate in mo characters and always sterile. More widely dispersed in Wale N.W. England, Scotland and N. Ireland, in areas where *C. alpin* has long been extinct.

CHAMAENERION
ANGUSTIFOLIUM

ROSE BAY.

EPILOBIUM
HIRSUTUM.

GREAT
WILLOW HERB.

EPILOBIUM
ALSINEFOLIUM.

EPILOBIUM
ANAGALLIDIFOLIUM.

EPILOBIUM
PARVIFLORUM.

EPILOBIUM
MONTANUM.

× 4

E. LAMYI.

EPILOBIUM
PALUSTRE.

EPILOBIUM
ROSEUM.

EPILOBIUM
TETRAGONUM.

EPILOBIUM OBSCURUM.

EPILOBIUM
LANCEOLATUM.

CIRCAEA
LUTETIANA.

LUDWIGIA
PALUSTRIS.

CIRCAEA ALPINA.

Plate 36   ❀ indicates plant is illustrated

CUCURBITACEAE

Bryonia dioica Jacq. **White Bryony.** *B. cretica* L. subsp. *anglica* Tutin. ¶Climbing by tendrils; leaves 5 lobed; flo. greenish white, male with 5 stamens, female with 3 bifid stigmas; berry red. Common in S.E. and mid England. Flo. May–Aug. ❀.

UMBELLIFERAE

Hydrocotyle vulgaris L. **Marsh Pennywort.** ¶Stem creeping, rooting; leaves orbicular; flo. in small sessile whorls; fr. laterally compressed. Common in peaty bogs. Flo. July–Sept. ❀.

Eryngium maritimum L. **Sea Holly.** ¶Very glaucous; radical leaves suborbicular; bracts very broad, lobes spine pointed; flo. blue. On sandy sea-shores. Flo. July–Aug. ❀.

Eryngium campestre L. ¶Pales green; radical leaves pinnate; bracts with narrow lobes; flo. white. In grass mostly near S.W. coasts, very local and rare. Flo. July–Aug. ❀.

Astrantia major L. **Melancholy Gentleman.** ¶Radical leaves broadly lobed; bracts lanceolate; umbels simple; outer flo. male. Naturalized in a few grassy places, especially in Shropshire. ❀.

Sanicula europaea L. **Sanicle.** ¶Radical leaves roundly lobed; flo. in 2–3 partial umbels; outer male; calyx long and sharp; fr. with hooks. Woods on basic soils. Flo. May–Aug. ❀.

Physospermum cornubiense (L.) DC. *Danaa cornubiensis* (L.) Burnat. ¶Leaf segments stalked, laciniate; umbel rays and pedicels long; fr. broad. Local, in woods, Cornwall, rare in S.W. Devon and Buckinghamshire. Flo. July–Aug. ❀.

Conium maculatum L. **Hemlock.** ¶Stem 6 ft, spotted; foliage poisonous; fr. suborbicular; vittae o. In damp roadsides, hedges and riv banks, common. Flo. June–Sept. ❀.

Smyrnium olusatrum L. **Alexanders.** ¶Leaves broad and celery-lik fr. becoming black; commissure narrow. On cliffs and hed banks, particularly near the sea in S. and mid England, Wales a Ireland, introduced. Flo. April–May. ❀.

Smyrnium perfoliatum L. ¶Similar to *S. olusatrum*, but with roundi upper leaves clasping the stem. Naturalized in grassy places, rar Flo. May–June.

Bupleureum fruticosum L. ¶Evergreen shrub up to 8 ft; stems slende sometimes purplish; leaves bluish green, alternate oblon lanceolate, entire, mucronate; flo. small, greenish yellow terminal umbels; bracts and bracteoles reflexed. Garden escap Naturalized in a few localities, particularly in S. Midlands. Fl July–Aug.

Bupleurum rotundifolium L. **Thorow-wax.** ¶Stem 6–12 in.; leav elliptic, upper perfoliate; bracteoles broadly ovate. In cornfiel on basic soils, very rare. Flo. June–July. ❀.

Bupleurum baldense Turra. *B. opacum* (Ces.) Lange. *B. aristatum* auc ¶Plant 1–4 in.; bracteoles ovate, concealing the sessile flowers. C dry banks near the sea, Devon, Sussex and Channel Isles. Fl June–July. ❀.

Bupleurum tenuissimum L. ¶Annual; slender, wiry, erect, 6–12 in bracts and bracteoles subulate. On salt marshes. Flo. July–Sep ❀.

Bupleurum falcatum L. ¶Perennial; stem hollow; upper leaves a bracteoles linear-lanceolate. In hedges and waste places, in Esse Flo. July–Oct. ❀.

BRYONIA
DIOICA.

ERYNGIUM
CAMPESTRE.

ASTRANTIA
MAJOR.

PHYSOSPERMUM
CORNUBIENSE.

HYDROCOTYLE
VULGARIS.

ERYNGIUM
MARITIMUM.

SANICULA
EUROPAEA.

× 4½

HEMLOCK
CONIUM
MACULATUM.

SMYRNIUM
OLUSATRUM.

× 12

BUPLEURUM
ROTUNDIFOLIUM.

BUPLEURUM BALDENSE.

BUPLEURUM
TENUISSIMUM.

BUPLEURUM
FALCATUM.

× 3

Plate 37   ❀ indicates plant is illustrated

UMBELLIFERAE (continued)

Trinia glauca (L.) Dumort. **Honewort.** ¶Stem 3–6 in.; leaf segments linear; male umbels ½ in., female 1½. On dry limestone hills, S. Devon and N. Somerset. Flo. May–July. ❀.

Apium graveolens L. **Wild Celery.** ¶Leaves with broad segments, lower segments stalked; umbels subsessile. In wet places and ditches, mostly near the sea. Flo. June–Aug. ❀.

Apium nodiflorum (L.) Lag. **Procumbent Marsh-wort.** *Helosciadum nodiflorum* (L.) Koch. ¶Ascending from a creeping base; leaves pinnate; umbels often nearly sessile. In muddy ditches and edges of ponds, common in S. England, the Midlands and Ireland, local in Wales and N. England, rare in Scotland. Flo. July–Aug. ❀.

Apium nodiflorum × repens. ¶Intermediate between the two parents, often with a coarse stem and peduncled umbels, though the peduncles vary greatly in length. This very rare hybrid sometimes occurs in the absence of the parents.

Apium repens (Jacq.) Lag. ¶Stem entirely creeping; leaf segments broadly oval; umbels peduncled. In wet places, local, Oxford-shire, E. Yorkshire and Scotland. Flo. July–Aug. ❀.

Apium inundatum (L.) Reichb. f. **Floating Marsh-wort.** *Helo-sciadum inundatum* (L.) Koch. ¶Floating; segments of submerged leaves capillary, of upper 3 lobed; umbel rays ¼ in. In ponds and dikes, rather local. Flo. June–July. ❀.

Apium × moorei (Syme) Druce. (*A. inundatum × nodiflorum*). ¶Similar to, but larger than, *A. inundatum,* but with linear segments to lower leaves. This sterile hybrid sometimes occurs where the parents grow together.

Cicuta virosa L. **Cowbane.** ¶Stem 5 ft, hollow; leaf segments linear lanceolate; bracteoles many. In ditches and marshes, rare, exce in Ireland where it is local. Flo. July–Aug. ❀.

*Ammi majus L. ¶1–2 ft, glaucous; leaves pinnate or bipinna serrate; bracts several, pinnate; bracteoles linear; fr. oblon ovoid. On waste ground, etc., introduced, scarce. Flo. July–Se

*Petroselinum crispum (Mill.) Nyman. **Parsley.** *Carum petroselinum* (Benth. ¶Leaves deltoid, tripinnate; bracts with hyaline margi flo. yellowish. Naturalized on walls and rocks, especially limesto Flo. June–Aug.

Petroselinum segetum (L.) Koch. **Corn Parsley.** *Carum segetum* Ben ¶Leaves linear, simply pinnate, segments ovate; bracts subula flo. white, anthers purple. On grass, particularly near the se chiefly in S. England. Flo. Aug.–Sept. ❀.

Carum verticillatum (L.) Koch. **Whorled Caraway.** ¶Perennia stem solid; leaf segments capillary and whorled; bracts lanceola anthers pink. In damp acid meadows, mostly W. England to Scotland. Flo. July–Aug. ❀.

*Carum carvi L. **Common Caraway.** ¶Biennial; stem striate, hollo leaf segments linear; fruit used for flavouring. Naturalized, ratl rare. Flo. June–July. ❀.

Bunium bulbocastanum L. **Tuberous Caraway.** *Carum bulbocastan* (L.) Koch. ¶Perennial; root a black 1 in. tuber; leaf segme narrow; fr. oblong. On chalky banks and grass in Hertfordshi Buckinghamshire, Bedfordshire and Cambridgeshire, local. F June–July. ❀.

Sium latifolium L. **Water Parsnip.** ¶Stem 6 ft, hollow, groove petioles sheathing; leaf segments regularly serrate. In fens a marshes, mostly in E. England, local. Flo. July–Aug. ❀.

TRINIA
GLAUCA.

CICUTA
VIROSA.

APIUM
GRAVEOLENS

×3

CARUM
VERTICILLATUM.

CARUM
CARUI.

PETROSELINUM
SEGETUM.

BUNIUM
BULBOCASTANUM.

SIUM
LATIFOLIUM.

A. REPENS.

×3

APIUM
INUNDATUM.

APIUM NODIFLORUM.

Plate 38   ✳ indicates plant is illustrated

UMBELLIFERAE (*continued*)

Berula erecta (Huds.) Coville. **Narrow-leaved Water Parsnip.** *Sium erectum* Huds., *S. angustifolium* L. ¶Stem 1–2 ft; leaf segments 1–2 in., irregularly serrate; flo. 2 mm. In marshes and ditches. Flo. July–Sept. ✳.

Sison amomum L. **Stone Parsley.** ¶Umbels small, with few rays and few minutes flo.; plant aromatic. Hedge banks in S. England and Midlands, common on basic soils, local in Wales. Flo. July–Sept. ✳.

✳Falcaria vulgaris Bernh. ¶Leaves with long linear or strap-shaped segments, regularly serrate; flo. small, yellow. Naturalized in a few places in S. and E. England. Flo. July.

Aegopodium podagraria L. **Goutweed, Ground Elder.** ¶Stem 2 ft, hollow, with white rhizomes; leaflets broad; fr. without vittae. In waste places and as a garden weed. Flo. May–July. ✳.

Pimpinella saxifraga L. **Burnet Saxifrage.** ¶Stem subterete, rough; leaflets ovate or in linear segments; styles much shorter than petals. In grass except on acid soils. Flo. July–Aug. ✳.

Pimpinella major (L.) Huds. **Greater Burnet Saxifrage.** *P. magna.* L. ¶Stem ridged, glabrous, purple below; leaves broad, simply pinnate; styles equalling petals. In grass and road borders, mostly in E. England. Flo. June–July. ✳.

Conopodium majus (Gouan) Loret. **Pignut.** *C. denudatum* Koch., *Bunium flexuosum* Stokes. ¶Root tuberous; petioles sheathing; leaf segments and fr. narrow; styles short. In woods and shaded sides of fields. Flo. May–June. ✳.

Myrrhis odorata (L.) Scop. **Sweet Cicely.** ¶Plant 2 ft, aromatic; ma flo. on shorter rays; fr. 1 in., oblong with ridges. In grass and hed banks, N. England and S. Scotland, introduced elsewhere. Fl May–June. ✳.

Chaerophyllum temulentum L. **Chervil.** ¶Stem hairy, purple spotte swollen below nodes; leaves dark green, hairy. Common in hed banks, except in mid Wales, Scotland and Ireland where it is loc Flo. June–July. ✳.

✳Chaerophyllum aureum L. ¶Stem glabrous, swollen; leaves yellov green, glabrous above; fr. ½ in. Naturalized locally in Perthshi and elsewhere. Flo. July.

Scandix pecten-veneris L. **Shepherd's Needle.** ¶Umbels of 1–2 ra only; bracteoles ciliate; fr. with long beak, 1–2 in. In cultivate land, mostly in S. and E. England. Flo. April–July. ✳.

Anthriscus caucalis Bieb. **Bur Chervil.** *A. vulgaris* Pers., non Bernh *A. neglecta* Boiss. & Reut. ¶Stem glabrous; peduncle short; ray few; flo. minute; fr. oval, muricate. Hedges and waste place often near the sea, mostly in S. and E. England. Flo. June–July. ✳

Anthriscus sylvestris (L.) Hoffm. **Cow Parsley.** ¶Stem pubescent peduncle long; rays many; flo. 3–4 mm.; fr. oblong, smoot Common except in N. Scotland and S. Ireland. Flo. April–June ✳.

✳Anthriscus cerefolium (L.) Hoffm. **Garden Chervil.** ¶Stem pubescer above nodes; peduncles very short, pubescent; flo. 2 mm.; fr. 1 mm., smooth. Introduced from E. Europe, naturalized in som waste places. Flo. May–June.

CRULA
RECTA.

AEGOPODIUM PODAGRARIA.

CONOPODIUM
MAJUS

×2

PIMPINELLA
MAJOR.

SISON
AMOMUM.

MYRRHIS
ODORATA.

PIMPINELLA
SAXIFRAGA.

SCANDIX
PECTEN-
VENERIS.

CHAEROPHYLLUM
TEMULENTUM

FLO. BUD ×18

ANTHRISCUS CAUCALIS.

ANTHRISCUS SYLVESTRIS.

Plate 39 �֍ indicates plant is illustrated

UMBELLIFERAE (*continued*)

Seseli libanotis (L.) Koch. ¶Leaf lobes oblong; peduncle long; rays, bracts and fr. pubescent; fr. ovoid. On chalk hills, local, Sussex to Cambridgeshire. Flo. July–Aug. �֍.

Foeniculum vulgare Mill. **Fennel.** ¶Stem 3–4 ft, striate, glaucous; leaf segments long, capillary, scented. On sea cliffs from Wales and Norfolk southwards, on waste ground inland. Flo. July–Oct. �֍.

Crithmum maritimum L. **Samphire.** ¶Stem 1 ft; leaves fleshy; rays stout; fr. corky. On sea cliffs of W., S. and S.E. Flo. June–Sept. ✐.

Oenanthe fistulosa L. **Common Water Dropwort.** ¶Stem a hollow tube; leaf segments linear; blade shorter than hollow petiole. In shallow pools, dikes and marshes, mostly S. England, Midlands, S. Wales and Ireland. Flo. July–Sept. ✐.

Oenanthe pimpinelloides L. **Corky-fruited Water Dropwort.** ¶Tubers distant, obovate; stem solid; leaf blade longer than petiole; fr. cylindrical. In meadows, S. England. Flo. June–Aug. ✐.

Oenanthe silaifolia Bieb. ¶Roots thickened from base; stem hollow ribbed; rays thick in fr.; fr. constricted below. In damp meadows, S. England and Midlands, rare. Flo. June.

Oenanthe lachenalii C. C. Gmel. **Parsley Water Dropwort.** ¶Roots cylindrical; stem solid; rays slender; fr. ovoid, reddish. In salt marshes and fens. Flo. June–Sept. ✐.

Oenanthe crocata L. **Hemlock Water Dropwort.** ¶Stem 4–5 hollow, grooved; leaves with broad segments; umbels 6–8 wide. In boggy places and beds of streams, mostly in S. and Britain. Flo. June–July. ✐.

Oenanthe aquatica (L.) Poir. **Fine-leaved Water Dropwort.** *phellandrium* Lam. ¶Segments of submerged leaves capillar peduncles short; fr. 3–4 mm. In ponds, dikes and fen ditches. F June–Sept. ✐.

Oenanthe fluviatilis (Bab.) Colem. **River Water Dropwort.** ¶Se ments of submerged leaves cut into narrow lobes; peduncles sho fr. 5–6 mm. In ponds and streams, N. to Lincolnshire, local Ireland. Flo. July–Sept. ✐.

Aethusa cynapium L. **Fool's Parsley.** ¶Stem 1–2 ft, hollow, striat outer bracteoles long, deflexed; poisonous. Common in cultivat land, except in N. England and Scotland where it is local. F July–Aug. ✐.

Silaum silaus (L.) Schinz & Thell. **Pepper Saxifrage.** *Silaus flav cens* Bernh. ¶Stem 1–2 ft, solid, striate; bracteoles linear wi scarious edges; flo. yellowish. In meadows and grassy plac mostly in S. and E. England, local. Flo. June–Aug. ✐.

Meum athamanticum Jacq. **Spignel, Bald-Money.** ¶Stem hollow, 1- ft; leaves finely divided, aromatic; fr. ovoid; ridges acute. In gra on mountain meadows, local. Flo. June–July. ✐.

OENANTHE
LACHENALII

OENANTHE CROCATA.
WATER DROPWORT.

OENANTHE
FISTULOSA

SESELI
LIBANOTIS

MEUM ATHAMANTICUM.

FOENICULUM
VULGARE

AETHUSA
CYNAPIUM.

OENANTHE
PIMPINELLOIDES.

OENANTHE
FLUVIATILIS

SILAUM
SILAUS

CRITHMUM
MARITIMUM.

OENANTHE
AQUATICA.

Plate 40   ✿ indicates plant is illustrated

UMBELLIFERAE (continued)

Ligusticum scoticum L. **Lovage.** ¶Stem red below; leaf segments 1–2 in. broad; fr. ridges prominent, acute. On rocky coasts, Northumberland northwards. Flo. July. ✿.

Selinum carvifolia (L.) ¶Stem ridges prominent, acute; leaf segments lanceolate, mucronate, minutely serrate; fr. ovoid; ridges winged. In damp meadows, Cambridgeshire, formerly in Nottinghamshire and Lincolnshire. Flo. July–Oct.

Angelica sylvestris L. **Wild Angelica.** ¶Stem hollow, purple; petioles inflated, sheathing; leaf segments ovate, serrate; flo. pink and white. Common by streamsides, in damp meadows, etc. Flo. July–Sept. ✿.

* *Angelica archangelica* L. *Archangelica officinalis* Hoffm. ¶Stem hollow, green; leaf segments decurrent; flo. greenish white. Naturalized on some river banks. Flo. July–Sept.

* *Levisticum officinale* Koch. ¶Stout, strongly aromatic, perennial up to 6 ft; stems glabrous; leaves pinnate; leaflets obovate-cuneate, deeply toothed; flo. small, yellow, in terminal umbels; fr. with 10 narrowly winged ribs. Garden escape. Naturalized in wet places, thickets, etc., in Scotland. Flo. July–Aug.

Peucedanum officinale L. **Sea Hog's Fennel.** ¶Stem solid; leaf segments long, 1–3 in., narrow, linear, entire. On banks by the Thames estuary, local. Flo. July–Sept. ✿.

Peucedanum palustre (L.) Moench. **Marsh Hog's Fennel.** ¶Stem hollow; leaf segments with lanceolate lobes, finely serrate. In fens and marshes, Somerset and Sussex to S. Yorkshire. Flo. July–Sept. ✿.

* *Peucedanum ostruthium* (L.) Koch. ¶Stem hollow; leaf segments few, broad, serrate; fr. suborbicular. Naturalized in moist meadows, Wales and Yorkshire to N. Scotland, and N.E. Ireland. Flo. July–Aug.

Pastinaca sativa L. **Wild Parsnip.** ¶Stem hollow, furrowed; leaf lobes broad, ovate, lobed; flo. yellow. In grassy places mainly on calcareous soil in S. and E. England, S. Wales, Midlands and Ireland. Flo. July–Aug. ✿.

Heracleum sphondylium L. **Hogweed, Cow Parsnip.** ¶Leaf segments broadly ovate, irregularly cut, petals of outer flo. enlarged. Common everywhere. Flo. June–Sept. ✿.

Var. *angustifolium* Huds. ¶Has leaves with linear-lanceola[ ] segments.

* *Heracleum mantegazzianum* Somm. & Lev. **Giant Hogwee[ ]** ¶Differs from *H. sphondylium* in its enormous size (stems up to 10 [ ] tall, red spotted); leaves and panicles very large. Naturalized [ ] rivers, etc. Flo. June–Sept.

* *Tordylium maximum* L. ¶Stem 3–4 ft; leaves simply pinnate; lob[ ] ovate to lanceolate; fr. with thick whitish ridges. In hedge[ ] marshes and bushy slopes, Essex, formerly in Oxford, Buckingham[ ] shire, Middlesex, etc., rare, introduced. Flo. June–July.

* *Coriandrum sativum* L. **Coriander.** ¶Stem solid, 1–2 ft; lower leav[ ] pinnate; lobes ovate; upper leaves bipinnate; umbels small; [ ] orbicular. In waste places, introduced. Flo. June.

Daucus carota L. **Wild Carrot.**
Subsp. *carota*. ¶Leaf lobes lanceolate, acute; umbels concave in fr[ ] spines hooked at tip, separate below. Common near the sea and o[ ] calcareous soil. Flo. June–Aug. ✿.
Subsp. *gummifer* Hook. f. *D. gummifer* Lam., non All., *D. gingidiu[ ]* auct. ¶Leaf lobes more ovate, obtuse; umbels flatter; spin[ ] straight at tip, confluent at base. Cliffs by the sea in S. and V[ ] England. Not very distinct.

* *Caucalis latifolia* L. **Great Bur-Parsley.** ¶Leaves simply pinnate[ ] flo. 5 mm.; bracts 3–5; inner flo. long pedicelled, male. Casual i[ ] cultivated fields, not native. Flo. July.

* *Caucalis platycarpos* L. **Small Bur-Parsley.** *C. lappula* Grande[ ] *C. daucoides* L. 1767, non L. 1753. ¶Leaves 2–3, pinnate; flo. 2 mm[ ] bracts 0; outer flo. long pedicelled, male, not native. Flo. June[ ] July. ✿.

Torilis arvensis (Huds.) Link. **Spreading Hedge Parsley.** *T. infes[ ]* (L.) Spreng. ¶Umbels long pedicelled; rays 3–5; bracts 0–1; f[ ] spines curved, not hooked; style glabrous. Probably introduced, i[ ] cultivated fields, scarce. Flo. July–Sept. ✿.

Torilis japonica (Houtt.) DC. **Hedge Parsley.** *Caucalis anthriscus* (L[ ] Huds. ¶Umbels long pedicelled; rays 5–12; bracts 4–10; fr. spin[ ] hooked; style hairy. Common in hedgerows. Flo. July–Aug. ✿.

Torilis nodosa (L.) Gaertn. **Knotted Hedge Parsley.** ¶Stem pro[ ] trate; umbels nearly sessile, short rayed; bracts 0; carpels wit[ ] straight or hooked spines. In dry places, mostly on calcareous an[ ] alluvial soils, chiefly in S. and E. England. Flo. May–July. ✿.

ANGELICA
SYLVESTRIS.

×4

×6

LIGUSTICUM
SCOTICUM.

PEUCEDANUM
PALUSTRE.

PEUCEDANUM
OFFICINALE.

PASTINACA
SATIVA.

HERACLEUM
SPHONDYLIUM.

DAUCUS CAROTA.

TORILIS
JAPONICA.

CAUCALIS PLATYCARPOS.

TORILIS
ARVENSIS.

TORILIS NODOSA.

Plate 41

❀ indicates plant is illustrated

BUXACEAE

Buxus sempervirens L. **Box.** ¶Leaves coriaceous; flo. clusters 1 female and several male with 4 stamens. On calcareous soil, Gloucestershire to Kent, introduced elsewhere. Flo. April–May. ❀.

ARALIACEAE

Hedera helix L. **Ivy.** ¶Flowers tomentose, 5-merous; styles united; fr. black, globose. Climbing everywhere. Flo. Oct.–Nov. ❀.

CORNACEAE

Chamaepericlymenum suecicum (L.) Aschers. & Graebn. **Dwarf Cornel.** *Cornus suecica* L. ¶Stem creeping with erect shoots; flo. surrounded by 4 white bracts. Among heather on mountains in Scotland, local and rare in N. England. Flo. July–Aug. ❀.

Swida sanguinea (L.) Opiz. **Dogwood Cornel.** *Cornus sanguinea* L., *Thelycrania sanguinea* (L.) Fourr. ¶Shrub 6–10 ft; twigs red; petals 4, valvate; calyx teeth very small. Common on calcareous and other soils in S. England, local in Wales and Ireland, probably introduced in N. England and Scotland. Flo. June–July. ❀.

ADOXACEAE

Adoxa moschatellina L. **Moschatel.** ¶Rhizome creeping, white; lateral flo., with 5 petals, facing N.S.E. and W. as clock tower; upper flo., with 4 petals facing sky; fr. green. In shady lanes and banks. Flo. April. ❀.
A symbol of Christian watchfulness.

CAPRIFOLIACEAE

Sambucus nigra L. **Elder.** ¶Shrub or small tree; stipules 0 or small; flo. 5 together, cream-white. Common in hedges and waste places, except in N. Scotland. Flo. June–July. ❀.

Sambucus ebulus L. **Danewort.** ¶Stem about 4 ft, herbaceous; stipules prominent, ovate; flo. 3 together, pinkish white. In waste places, local. Flo. July–Aug. ❀.

Sambucus racemosa L. **Red-berried Elder.** ¶Shrub; leaves oval lanceolate; stipules replaced by large glands; flo. creamy white dense panicle-like cymes; berry globose, scarlet. Bird-sown fro gardens and naturalized in woods and hedges, particularly in N. England and E. Scotland. Flo. April–May.

Viburnum lantana L. **Wayfaring Tree.** ¶Leaves oval, wrinkle pubescent; fr. oval, becoming black; flo. all equal. In hedges, co mon in the S., especially on calcareous soils, introduced elsewher Flo. June–July. ❀.

Viburnum opulus L. **Guelder Rose.** ¶Leaves lobed, glabrous abov outer flo. enlarged and sterile; fr. globose, scarlet. In woods a very damp hedgerows. Flo. June–July. ❀.

Symphoricarpos rivularis Suksd. **Snowberry.** *S. albus* auct., racemosus* auct. ¶Small shrub; twigs slender; leaves orbicul entire; flo. small, pink, campanulate, 3–6 in terminal spikes; ber ½ in., white. Garden escape. Widely naturalized in hedges a thickets. Flo. June–Aug.

Linnaea borealis L. ¶Stems slender, pubescent, creeping, forming mat; flo. pendulous, pink; fr. an achene. In shade, E. Scotlan rare. Flo. June–Aug. ❀.

Lonicera periclymenum L. **Honeysuckle.** ¶Climbing to 30 ft; upp leaves free, often downy beneath; flo. yellow, numerous. Comme in woods and hedgerows. Flo. June–Sept. ❀.

Lonicera xylosteum L. **Fly Honeysuckle.** ¶Stem slender, climbin leaves broadly ovate, pubescent; flo. ½ in. long, in pairs peduncles ½ in.; berry red. Possibly native in a few woods calcareous soils in Sussex, elsewhere bird-sown or escaped fro gardens, rare. Flo. May. ❀.

Lonicera caprifolium L. **Perfoliate Honeysuckle.** ¶Stems glabro climbing; leaves ovate, green above, glaucous below; upp leaves united at their bases; flo. pale yellow, in terminal whor sometimes with additional axillary whorls; bracts large; ber orange-red. Bird-sown or escaped from gardens and naturalized hedges and thickets, rare. Flo. May–June.

Leycesteria formosa Wall. **Flowering Nutmeg.** ¶Shrub, leav opposite, ovate-acuminate; flo. ¾ in., purplish, funnel-shape sessile, in whorls enclosed by large claret-coloured leaf-like brac berry ¾ in., dark purplish brown. Bird-sown from gardens a naturalized in woods and hedges. Flo. June–Sept.

HEDERA HELIX

BUXUS
SEMPERVIRENS.

CHAMAEPERICLYMENUM
SUECICUM

THELYCRANIA
SANGUINEA.
DOGWOOD.

ADOXA
MOSCHATELLINA.
MOSCHATEL.

SAMBUCUS
EBULUS.

VIBURNUM
OPULUS.

VIBURNUM   LANTANA.

×2½

ELDER
SAMBUCUS NIGRA.

LINNAEA BOREALIS.

LONICERA
PERICLYMENUM.

LONICERA XYLOSTEUM.

Plate 42   ❀ indicates plant is illustrated

RUBIACEAE

Rubia peregrina L. **Madder.** ¶Stems climbing by downward prickles; leaves shining; flo. yellowish, 5 cleft; fr. black. In hedgerows near the sea and on sea cliffs, chiefly in S. and S.W. England, Wales and W. Ireland. Flo. June–Aug. ❀.

Cruciata ciliata Opiz. **Crosswort.** *C. laevipes* Opiz., *C. chersonensis* (Willd.) Ehrend., *Galium cruciata* (L.) Scop. ¶Stem 1½ ft; leaves 4 in whorl, 3 veined, hairy; flo. yellow; fr. small, smooth. Common, especially on calcareous soils but rare in W. Wales, and N. Scotland, and introduced in Ireland. Flo. May–June. ❀.

Galium boreale L. **Northern Bedstraw.** ¶Stems 1 ft; leaves 4 in whorl, 3 veined; flo. white; fr. bristles hooked. In moist rocky places in N. England, Scotland and Ireland. Flo. July–Aug. ❀.

Galium verum L. **Lady's Bedstraw.** ¶Stems 1½ ft; leaves many, narrow, 1 veined, downy beneath; flo. yellow; fr. smooth. Common in dry places. Flo. July–Sept. ❀.

Galium album Mill. subsp. *album.* **Hedge Bedstraw.** *Galium mollugo* auct., non. L., *G. erectum* Huds. pro parte. ¶Stems 1–3 ft, trailing on hedges or upright; leaf margins rough with forward prickles; flo. branches spreading; fr. 1–2 mm. Common on banks, in pastures, etc., especially on calcareous soils, in S. England, local in the Midlands, N. England and Wales, rare in Scotland and Ireland. Flo. June–Sept. ❀.

Galium × pomeranicum Retz. (*G. album* subsp. *album × verum*). *G. × ochroleucum* Wolf ex Schweigg. & Koerte. ¶Intermediate between the two parents, with pale yellow flo., sometimes occurs where the parents grow together.

Galium saxatile L. **Heath Bedstraw.** *G. harcynicum* Weig. ¶Stems procumbent, matted, 4 angled, glabrous; flo. branches shorter than internodes; fr. with tubercles. Common on peaty heaths. Flo. July–Aug. ❀.

Galium pumilum Murr. **Slender Bedstraw.** ¶Stems often hairy below; leaves lanceolate, margin revolute, ciliate; flowering branches usually longer than internodes; fr. faintly granular. On limestone and chalk from S. England northwards to Lincoln, local. Flo. June–Aug. ❀.

Galium sterneri Ehrend. *G. pumilum* Murr. subsp. *septentrionale* Sterner ex Hyland. ¶Similar to *G. pumilum* but more prostrate; leaves oblanceolate to linear; flo. cymes more compact, forming a pyramidal panicle (panicle open in *G. pumilum*); fr. covered with tubercles. On calcareous and limestone slopes and rocks from mid Wales to N. Scotland, also in W. and N.E. Ireland, local. Flo. June–Aug.

Galium palustre L. **Marsh Bedstraw.** ¶Stem 3 ft, nearly smoo supported by other plants, black when dry; flo. 3–4 mm. wic fruit rugose. Common in wet meadows. Flo. June–Aug. ❀. Var. *elongatum* C. Presl. ¶ More robust, less branched, flo. 4·5 m

Galium debile Desv. **Pond Bedstraw.** ¶Stem nearly smooth; leav narrow, linear, subglabrous, margin slightly rough; flo. pinki white; fr. granular. In ponds, rare, Devon, Hampshire a Channel Islands. Flo. May–July. ❀.

Galium uliginosum L. **Fen Bedstraw.** ¶Slender stems and le margins rough with backward prickles; leaves 6–8 in who mucronate, green when dry; fr. granular. In fens and bog, meadows, local. Flo. July–Aug. ❀.

Galium parisiense L. **Wall Bedstraw.** *G. anglicum* Huds. ¶Sma slender stems with backward prickles; leaves with forward prickl flo. very small, greenish white; fr. small, granular. On walls a dry places, mostly S.E. England, rare. Flo. June–July. ❀.

Galium aparine L. **Goose Grass, Cleavers.** ¶Climbing, 3–4 ft, ster and leaves with deflexed prickles; fr. large, 4–6 mm., with hook prickles. Common in hedge banks. Flo. June–Aug. ❀.

Galium tricornutum Dandy. **Corn Bedstraw.** *G. tricorne* Stokes p parte. ¶1 ft stems and leaf margins very rough with backwa prickles; fr. large, 3–4 mm., granular, recurved. Calcareous fiel mostly S. England and S. Midlands, local. Flo. June–Sept. ❀.

Galium spurium L. **False Cleavers.** *G. vaillantii* DC. ¶Similar to *G aparine* but branches with more numerous 3–9 flo., greenish, wi only 2 floral bracts instead of a whorl; fr. glabrous or with hooke hairs. In arable fields, in S. and E. England, local. Flo. July.

Galium odoratum (L.) Scop. **Sweet Woodruff.** *Asperula odorata* ¶Rhizomatous; stem 1 ft; flo. funnel shaped, tube equalling lim white, fragrant; fr. with hooked hairs. Woods chiefly on ca careous soil. Flo. May–June. ❀.

Asperula cynanchica L. **Squinancy Wort.** ¶Stock woody; branch prostrate; flo. few, funnel shaped, pale pink; fr. tubercled. On d calcareous soils, chiefly in S. and E. England, S. Wales and Ireland, local. Flo. July–Aug. ❀.

Sherardia arvensis L. **Field Madder.** ¶Stems prostrate; flo. involucre, pink, tube much exceeding limb; sepals 4, 2 bifi crowning the fr. Arable land, common in S. Britain, local Ireland and in N. Scotland where it is mainly confined to the coast sand dunes. Flo. June–July. ❀.

RUBIA
PEREGRINA
MADDER

GALIUM BOREALE.

CRUCIATA
LAEVIPES.

GALIUM
VERUM.

GALIUM
ERECTUM.

GALIUM
ULIGINOSUM.

GALIUM
PALUSTRE.

×3 GALIUM
MOLLUGO

×5

GALIUM
SAXATILE

GALIUM
APARINE.

SHERARDIA
ARVENSIS

SWEET
WOODRUFF.

ALIUM
UMILUM

×2

GALIUM TRICORNUTUM

GALIUM
PARISIENSE
VAR. ANGLICUM.

GALIUM
DEBILE.

ASPERULA
CYNANCHICA.

GALIUM
ODORATUM

Plate 43

VALERIANACEAE

Valeriana dioica L. **Lesser Valerian.** ¶Plant stoloniferous; stem 1 ft; lower leaves entire; flo. dioecious, pale pink. Local in marshes, throughout England and Wales. Flo. May–June. ❀.

Valeriana officinalis L. **Valerian.** *V. sambucifolia* Mikan f. ¶Stolons short or 0; stem 3 ft; leaves all pinnate, very variable. Common in ditches, damp woods and on chalk downs. Flo. June–Sept. ❀.

Valeriana pyrenaica L. **Pyrenean Valerian.** ¶Stolons absent; stem 2 ft, downy, erect; basal leaves large, petiolate, cordate, toothed; upper leaves pinnate; lower pairs of leaflets oblong-acuminate; terminal leaflet broadly ovate-cordate; leaflets deeply and irregularly serrate; flo. pale pink, rarely white, in terminal corymbs; fr. glabrous. Naturalized in woods chiefly in S.W. and N. England and Scotland. Flo. June–July.

Centranthus ruber (L.) DC. **Red Valerian.** ¶Stem 2 ft; leaves ovate; flo. rose-red, sometimes white, with slender tube and long spur. Garden escape. Naturalized on walls, rocks and banks, chiefly in S. England, the Midlands, Wales and E. Ireland. Flo. June–Aug.

Valerianella locusta (L.) Betcke. **Lamb's Lettuce.** *V. olitoria* (L.) Poll. ¶Fr. suborbicular, corky; calyx 0 or 1 minute point. Common in cultivated soil and hedge banks, chiefly in S. England. Flo. April–June. ❀.

Valerianella carinata Lois. ¶Fr. oblong, nearly square in section, not corky; calyx faintly 1 toothed, sterile cells nearly confluent, as figure. Chiefly in S. and S.W. England, local. Flo. April–June. ❀.

Valerianella rimosa Bast. ¶Inflo. lax; calyx teeth minute; sterile cells together larger than fertile one, and confluent. Cultivated ground, chiefly in S. England, local. Flo. July–Aug. ❀.

Valerianella dentata (L.) Poll. ¶Inflo. lax; calyx 4 lobed, 3 lobes ver small; fr. not corky. In fields, chiefly in S. and E. England, loca Flo. June–July. ❀.

Valerianella eriocarpa Desv. ¶Fruit pilose; calyx deeply 5 lobed an strongly net veined. Naturalized in a few places. Flo. May–Jun ❀ (fruit only).

DIPSACEAE

Dipsacus fullonum L. **Common Teasel.** *D. sylvestris* Huds. ¶Ste 4–5 ft; involucre long erect; bracteoles exceeding purple flo. an ending in flexible or stiff spine. In fields and hedge banks, on strea banks, waste ground, etc., chiefly in S. and E. England. Fl July–Aug. ❀.

Dipsacus pilosus L. **Small Teasel.** ¶Stems 3–4 ft; bracteoles short than white flo., heads subglobose. In ditches and by calcareo streams, in England, local. Flo. Aug. ❀.

Knautia arvensis (L.) Coult. **Field Scabious.** *Scabiosa arvensis* ¶Stem 2 ft; bracts ovate; bracteoles 0; calyx teeth 8; petals 5. O dry banks and pastures. Flo. May–June. ❀.

Scabiosa columbaria L. ¶Stem 2 ft; bracts and bracteoles linear; caly teeth 5; petals 5. On calcareous banks and pastures, but very rar in Scotland and absent from Ireland. Flo. July–Aug. ❀.

Succisa pratensis Moench. **Devil's Bit Scabious.** *Scabiosa succisa* ¶Stem 18 in.; bracteoles elliptic; calyx teeth 4; petals 4, blu purple. In fens and damp meadows, common. Flo. June–Sept. ❀

VALERIANELLA
DENTATA.

×7

DIPSACUS
FULLONUM.

VALERIANELLA
RIMOSA.

×5

V. ERIOCARPA.
Fruit.

×8

VALERIANA DIOICA.

×3

×6

VALERIANA
OFFICINALIS.

VALERIANELLA
LOCUSTA.

VALERIANELLA
CARINATA.

×6

×4

KNAUTIA
ARVENSIS.

FIELD
SCABIOUS.

SCABIOSA
COLUMBARIA.

SUCCISA PRATENSIS.

DIPSACUS
PILOSUS.

Plate 44   ✿ indicates plant is illustrated

COMPOSITAE

Eupatorium cannabinum L. **Hemp Agrimony.** ¶Stem 3 ft; inflo. of many small heads; each with oblong bracts and 5–6 reddish florets. Common in ditches and sides of streams, but local in N. England and Scotland. Flo. July–Sept. ✿

Solidago virgaurea L. **Golden Rod.** ¶Stem 1–2 ft; flo. bracts in many rows; flo. golden; achenes ribbed. Common on heaths, dry banks and cliffs chiefly in the S. and W. Flo. July–Sept. ✿

*Solidago altissima L. **Tall Golden Rod.** *S. canadensis* auct., non L. ¶Stem pubescent, 3–5 ft; leaves lanceolate, 3 veined, unequally toothed, roughish above, pubescent below; flo. small, golden yellow in numerous recurved racemes, forming a large pyramidal panicle. Garden escape. Naturalized by rivers, streams and lakes, and established on waste ground, etc., very common. Flo. Aug–Nov.

*Solidago gigantea Ait. *S. serotina* Ait. ¶Similar to *S. altissima*, but stem glabrous below, up to 3 ft; leaves 3 veined, glabrous below except on midrib; flo. larger, ray florets exceeding disk florets, golden yellow, in compact erect corymbose panicles. Garden escape. Naturalized by rivers, streams and lakes, and established on waste ground, etc., common. Flo. Aug.–Nov.

*Solidago graminifolia (L.) Salisb. *S. lanceolata* L. ¶Stems glabrous, up to 3 ft; leaves linear-lanceolate, 3–5 veined entire, glabrous except on veins beneath; flo. small, ray florets not exceeding disk florets, golden yellow, in erect corymbose panicles. Garden escape. Naturalized on hedge banks, etc., rare. Flo. July–Sept.

Bellis perennis L. **Daisy.** ¶Plants forming a close mat; achenes without pappus. Abundant in short grass. Flo. all the year. ✿

Aster tripolium L. **Sea Aster.** ¶Stem 18 in.; leaves fleshy; ray florets mauve or absent. Common in salt marshes. Flo. July–Sept. ✿ Several alien species of *Aster* are spreading from gardens.

Crinitaria linosyris (L.) Less. **Goldilocks.** *Aster linosyris* (L.) Bernh. ¶Stem 1 ft; leaves linear; flo. all tubular, golden and fertile. On limestone cliffs, rare, S. Devon, Somerset, Wales, Lancashire. Flo. Aug.–Sept. ✿

*Conyza canadensis (L.) Cronq. *Erigeron canadensis* L. ¶Stem 18 in.; leaves linear; heads many, small, $\frac{1}{8}$ in. across, white. Alien in cultivated and waste ground, chiefly in S. and E. Britain. Flo. Aug.–Sept. ✿

Erigeron acer L. **Blue Fleabane.** ¶Stem 10–12 in.; heads many, small; ray florets small, mauve; pappus red. On dry sandy and calcareous banks, chiefly in S. and E. Britain. Flo. July–Aug. ✿

Erigeron borealis (Vierh.) Simmons. **Alpine Fleabane.** *E. alpinus* auct., non L. ¶Stem 6 in.; leaves mostly basal; heads solitary, $\frac{3}{4}$ in.; rays mauve. Rock ledges at about 3000 ft, mid Scotland. Flo. July– Aug. ✿

*Erigeron mucronatus DC. ¶Stem slender, up to 6 in.; basal leav obovate-cuneate, 3 lobed or coarsely toothed at apex; upp leaves linear-lanceolate; rays in 2 rows, white above, purp below. Naturalized in S. and S.W. England and the Chann Islands. Flo. July–Aug.

Filago vulgaris Lam. **Cudweed.** *F. germanica* auct. ¶Flo. in spheric clusters of about 30 heads, not overtopped by leaves. Common sandy and acid heaths. Flo. July–Aug. ✿

Filago lutescens Jord. *F. apiculata* G. E. Sm. ¶Flo. in clusters of abou 15 heads, overtopped by leaves; flo. bracts red tipped. Sand fields in S. and Central England, rare. Flo. July–Aug. ✿

Filago pyramidata L. *F. spathulata* C. Presl. ¶Branches horizonta clusters of about 12 5-angled heads, overtopped by leaves; fl bracts yellow tipped. S. England, rare. Flo. July–Aug. ✿

Filago minima (Sm.) Pers. ¶Flo. in small clusters of 3–6 heads, n overtopped by leaves; tips of flo. bracts blunt, yellowish. Commo on sandy and gravelly soils. Flo. June–Sept. ✿

Filago gallica L. ¶Flo. in small clusters of 2–6 heads, overtopped b leaves; tips of flo. bracts yellowish. In S. and E. England o gravel, rare. Flo. July–Aug. ✿

Antennaria dioica (L.) Gaertn. ¶Dioecious and stoloniferous; ste 3–6 in.; leaves woolly, white beneath; flo. bracts often pink. O heaths and mountains, chiefly in N. Britain and W. Ireland Flo. June–July. ✿

*Anaphalis margaritacea (L.) Benth. **Everlasting.** ¶Dioecious; ste 1–2 ft and leaves very woolly; flo. yellowish with woolly bract Garden escape. Naturalized in meadows, by streams and o wall tops, chiefly in Wales and Scotland. Flo. Aug.

Gnaphalium uliginosum L. **Marsh Cudweed.** ¶Stem 4–5 in. wit woolly branches; flo. bracts pale brown, overtopped by leave Common in damp places and waysides. Flo. July–Aug. ✿

Gnaphalium luteoalbum L. **Jersey Cudweed.** ¶Stem 12 in., branched leaves oblong; flo. bracts yellowish, not overtopped by leave Native in Channel Islands, introduced in E. England. Fl June–Aug.

Gnaphalium sylvaticum L. **Wood Cudweed.** ¶Stem 6–9 in.; leave linear-lanceolate; heads in a long leafy spike; bracts brown an green. Woods and heaths on acid soil, local. Flo. July–Sept. ✿

Gnaphalium norvegicum Gunn. ¶Leaves lanceolate; heads in a sho spike, $\frac{1}{4}$ length of stem; bracts dark brown. On mountains i Central Scotland. Flo. Aug. ✿

Gnaphalium supinum L. **Creeping Cudweed.** ¶Stems creeping ascending 2–3 in.; heads very few; bracts dark brown. Mountain in Scotland. Flo. July–Aug. ✿

EUPATORIUM
CANNABINUM.

×3.

ERIGERON
ACER.

CRINITARIA
LINOSYRIS.

ASTER
TRIFOLIUM.

×1½

CONYZA
CANADENSIS.

SOLIDAGO
VIRGAUREA.

ERIGERON
BOREALIS.

FILAGO
SPATHULATA.

ANTENNARIA
DIOICA.

BELLIS
PERENNIS.

FILAGO
GERMANICA.

GNAPHALIUM
NORVEGICUM.

GNAPHALIUM SUPINUM.

GNAPHALIUM
ULIGINOSUM.

FILAGO
APICULATA.

FILAGO GALLICA.

FILAGO
MINIMA.

GNAPHALIUM
SYLVATICUM.

Plate 45 ✸ indicates plant is illustrated

COMPOSITAE (*continued*)

Inula helenium L. **Elecampane.** ¶Stem 3–4 ft; flo. heads 2–3 in. across, golden; bracts broad. Fields and waste places. Flo. July–Aug. ✸.

Inula conyza DC. **Ploughman's Spikenard.** *I. squarrosa* (L.) Bernh. ¶Stem tough, 2 ft; inner flo. bracts purplish; outer florets tubular or very shortly ligulate. On dry calcareous soil, mostly in S. and mid Britain. Flo. July–Sept. ✸.

Inula salicina L. ¶Stem 18 in.; leaves elliptical, cordate at base; flo. few, 1 in.; ligules narrow, golden. Beside Lough Derg, Ireland. Flo. July–Aug.

Inula crithmoides L. **Golden Samphire.** ¶Stems and narrow leaves bright green, thick and fleshy; flo. golden. Salt marshes and wet rocks by the sea, S. and W. coasts. Flo. July–Aug. ✸.

Telekia speciosa (Schreb.) Baumg. *Buphthalmum speciosum* Schreb. ¶Plant robust, hairy, strongly aromatic, superficially resembling *Inula helenium*; stem 3–4 ft; leaves alternate, glabrous above, hairy below; lower leaves triangular-cordate, double toothed, stalked; upper leaves ovate, sessile, with simple teeth; florets subtended by linear filiform scales (absent in *Inula*); flo. heads large with orange-yellow ray florets and very large prominent disk; bracts ovate, mucronate. Garden escape. Naturalized in wet places, chiefly in Scotland, though long known at Woodwalton Fen, Huntingdon. Flo. July–Sept.

Pulicaria dysenterica (L.) Bernh. **Fleabane.** ¶Stem 2 ft, woolly; leaf base cordate; flo. heads 1 in.; outer florets spreading, golden. Common in wet meadows and ditches, but local in mid Wales and Ireland and very rare in Scotland. Flo. Aug.–Sept. ✸.

Pulicaria vulgaris Gaertn. **Lesser Fleabane.** ¶Stem 1 ft; leaf base rounded; flo. heads 1¼ in., pale yellow; outer florets erect. Wet, muddy places in S. England, very rare. Flo. Aug.–Sept. ✸.

Bidens cernua L. **Nodding Bur-Marigold.** ¶Leaves simple, lanceolate, serrate; flo. heads nodding; sometimes (var. *radiata* DC.) with broad, yellow rays. In ponds and ditches, mostly S. and mid Britain and Ireland. Flo. July–Sept. ✸.

Bidens tripartita L. **Bur-Marigold.** ¶Leaves usually tripartite, stalked; terminal leaflet broad; flo. heads erect, yellow. In ponds and ditches. Flo. July–Sept. ✸.

Bidens frondosa L. ¶Leaves usually pinnate with 3–6 separate leaflets; flo. heads erect on long stalks; disk florets yellow; achenes blackish, densely tubercled. By canals and rivers, chiefly in W. Midlands and S. Wales, introduced from N. America. Flo. July–Oct.

Galinsoga parviflora Cav. ¶1–2 ft, much branched; leaves ova[ ] flo. heads small; rays short, white; disk yellow; pappus of silve[ ] scales, not awned. Alien, common in London area. Flo. May–Se[ ]

Galinsoga ciliata (Raf.) Blake. *G. quadriradiata* auct. ¶Close[ ] resembles *G. parviflora* but stem is thickly clothed with spreadi[ ] hairs; pappus scales awned. Alien, common in London area.

Ambrosia artemisiifolia L. **Ragweed.** *A. elatior* L. ¶Annual; ste[ ] erect, shortly hairy, up to 2 ft; leaves short stalked, in pai[ ] pinnatifid, dark green above, grey felted beneath; flo. sma[ ] greenish yellow; male flo. short stalked in clusters on droopi[ ] terminal spikes; female flo. solitary, or in small clusters in axils[ ] upper leaves. Established on waste ground, though often on[ ] casual. Flo. July–Oct.

Ambrosia psilostachya DC. ¶Similar to *A. artemisiifolia*, but stem [ ] to 18 in.; leaves smaller, thicker, less pinnatifid and more heavi[ ] grey felted beneath. Naturalized on dunes in Lancashire a[ ] Ayrshire. Flo. July–Oct.

Achillea millefolium L. **Yarrow, Milfoil.** ¶Stoloniferous; stem 1 [ ] leaves finely divided; flo. heads ¼ in., white or pink. Comm[ ] in grass. Flo. June–Aug. ✸.

Achillea ptarmica L. **Sneezewort.** ¶Stoloniferous; stem 2 ft; leav[ ] linear-lanceolate; flo. heads few, ½ in., white. Common in w[ ] meadows and on moors. Flo. July–Aug. ✸.

Otanthus maritimus (L.) Hoffmanns. & Link. *Diotis maritima* (L.) De[ ] ex Cass. ¶Stem woolly, 6–10 in.; leaves woolly, white; flo. hea[ ] yellow, bracts woolly. Sandy sea-shores in S. England and S.[ ] Ireland, almost extinct. Flo. Aug. ✸.

Anthemis tinctoria L. **Yellow Chamomile.** ¶Perennial; stem 2 [ ] ray florets golden; disk scales lanceolate, subulate. Garden escap[ ] Naturalized in fields, etc. Flo. July–Aug. ✸.

Anthemis cotula L. **Stinking Chamomile.** ¶Annual; stem 18 i[ ] foetid; flo. heads ¾ in.; ray florets white; disk scales linea[ ] achenes tubercled. On basic soils, common in England, but loc[ ] in Wales and very rare in Scotland and Ireland. Flo. July–Sept. [ ]

Anthemis arvensis L. **Corn Chamomile.** ¶Annual; slightly scente[ ] flo. heads 1 in.; ray florets white; disk scales lanceolate, cuspidat[ ] achenes rugose at top. On basic soil, local, and very rare [ ] Ireland. Flo. June–July. ✸.

Chamaemelum nobile (L.) All. **Sweet Chamomile.** *Anthemis nobilis* [ ] ¶Perennial; sweetly aromatic; flo. heads 1 in.; rays white; di[ ] scales oblong; achenes 3 ribbed. Sandy soil and moorland border[ ] mostly S. Britain and S. Ireland, introduced elsewhere. Fl[ ] June–July. ✸.

INULA
CONYZA.

INULA
CRITHMOIDES.

PULICARIA
VULGARIS.

OTANTHUS
MARITIMUS

PULICARIA
DYSENTERICA.

INULA
ELENIUM

ACHILLEA
MILLEFOLIUM

ACHILLEA
PTARMICA.

BIDENS
CERNUA.
VAR.
RADIATA.

×4

BIDENS
TRIPARTITA.

×4

ANTHEMIS
TINCTORIA.

ANTHEMIS
ARVENSIS.

ANTHEMIS COTULA.

CHAMAEMELUM NOBILE.

Plate 46   ✿ indicates plant is illustrated

COMPOSITAE (continued)

Chrysanthemum segetum L. **Corn Marigold.** ¶Annual; stem 1 ft, thickened below the flo.; rays yellow; bracts with broad scarious margins. In cultivated fields. Flo. June–Aug. ✿.

Chrysanthemum leucanthemum L. **Ox-eye Daisy.** ¶Perennial; stem 18 in.; leaves simple; flo. heads solitary; rays white. Common on basic soil and in pasture. Flo. June–Aug. ✿.

Chrysanthemum parthenium (L.) Bernh. **Feverfew, Bachelor's Buttons.** ¶Perennial; stem 18 in.; leaves pinnate; flo. heads many; rays white. In cultivated soil and waste places. Flo. July–Aug. ✿.

Chrysanthemum vulgare (L.) Bernh. **Tansy.** *Tanacetum vulgare* L. ¶Perennial; stem 2 ft, tough; leaves fragrant, lower bipinnate; heads golden; rays o. On hedge banks, common. Flo. July–Sept. ✿.

Tripleurospermum maritimum (L.) Koch. **Scentless Chamomile.**
Subsp. *maritimum*. ¶Leaf segments short, fleshy; disk nearly flat, without scales; achenes with elongate oil glands at top. At the seaside. Flo. July–Sept.
Subsp. *inodorum* (L.) Hyland. ex Vaarama. *Matricaria inodora* L. ¶Leaf segments long and mucronate; oil glands on achenes nearly circular. Common in cultivated land. ✿.

Matricaria recutita L. **Wild Chamomile.** *M. chamomilla* L. ¶ Annual; fragrant; flo. heads ¾ in.; disk conical, without scales; rays white, soon reflexed. On cultivated land, mostly S. and mid England, casual in Scotland and Ireland, local. Flo. June–July. ✿.

Matricaria matricarioides (Less.) Porter. *M. suaveolens* (Pursh.) Buchen. ¶Annual; aromatic; flo. heads greenish; disk conical, hollow; rays none. Alien, common on farm tracks and waste places. Flo. June–July. ✿.

Cotula coronopifolia L. ¶Aromatic, stem ascending; leaves toothed or pinnatifid, with sheathing base; heads ¼ in., yellow; rays o; marginal achenes winged. Established on waste ground, etc., rare. Flo. July–Aug.

Artemisia vulgaris L. **Mugwort.** ¶Aromatic; stem 3 ft, tough, grooved, reddish; leaves dark green above, white beneath. Waysides and waste places. Flo. July–Sept. ✿.

Artemisia verlotorum Lamotte. **Chinese Mugwort.** ¶Similar to *A. vulgaris*, but with long rhizomes and lower part of scape semi-woody and naked; leaflets longer and narrower, darker green, less white beneath and very aromatic; inflo. much more leafy. Naturalized by rivers, streams and roadsides and established on waste ground, common in the London area especially near the Thames. Flo. Oct.–Dec.

Artemisia norvegica Fr. **Norwegian Mugwort.** ¶Plant tufted, greyish, hairy, up to 4 in.; basal leaves stalked with toothed cuneate lobes; upper leaves sessile, pinnate; flo. heads yellow, up to ½ in. across, usually solitary, but sometimes 2–4 together, nodding; bracts with greenish midrib and wide dark brown margins. In mountains in W. Ross, very rare. Flo. July–Sept.

Artemisia stellerana Bess. **Dusty Miller.** ¶Stem creeping, ascending, 1 ft; leaves white felted, with rounded lobes; heads ⅜ in.; bract white; flo. yellow. Garden escape. Naturalized in hedge banks, ditches, etc., mostly S.W. England. Flo. July–Sept.

Artemisia absinthium L. **Wormwood.** ¶Stem silky, 2 ft; leaf segments blunt, silky both sides; bracts silky; heads hemispherical. In waste places, especially by the sea. Flo. July. ✿.

Artemisia maritima L. **Sea Wormwood.** ¶Aromatic; stem 15 in, downy; leaf segments blunt, woolly above and beneath. On sandy seasides, chiefly in S. and E. England and S. Wales. Flo. Aug.–Sept. ✿.

Artemisia campestris L. **Breckland Wormwood.** ¶Scentless; stem 18 in., glabrous; leaf segments narrow, linear, acute; bract reddish. On sandy heaths of E. Anglia only. Flo. Aug.–Sept. ✿.

Tussilago farfara L. **Coltsfoot.** ¶Perennial with deep rhizomes; flo. rays very many, female, bright yellow. Common on basic soils, a troublesome weed. Flo. March. ✿.

Petasites albus (L.) Gaertn. **White Butterbur.** ¶Perennial with thick rhizomes; leaves roundish, cordate, up to 1 ft wide, glabrous above, white pubescent beneath; leaf stems hairy; flo. heads many, white, scented, long stalked, appearing before the leaves; bracts narrow, pale green, glabrous. Garden escape. Naturalized in woods and plantations, by roadsides, etc., mostly in N.E. Scotland. Flo. March–May.

Petasites japonicus (Sieb. & Zucc.) F. Schmidt. ¶Low creeping perennial; leaves roundish, cordate, deeply toothed, glabrous, bright green, up to 3 ft wide; flo. heads many, whitish, in dense corymbs, appearing before the leaves; bracts broad, oblong, pale green. Garden escape. Naturalized by lakes, etc., chiefly in S. England, rare. Flo. March–April.

Petasites fragrans (Vill.) C. Presl. **Winter Heliotrope.** ¶Perennial with deep rhizomes; scapes with 6–8 heads of pale lilac flo.; leaves surviving winter. Established in hedge banks. Flo. Feb. ✿.

Petasites hybridus (L.) Gaertn., Mey. & Scherb. *Butterbur*. ¶Perennial with deep thick rhizomes; leaves 2 ft wide; flo. heads many, pink. Native, streamsides and wet meadows, mostly male except in N.W. Flo. April. ✿.

Homogyne alpina (L.) Cass. ¶Leaves 1 in. across, reniform, dark green above, paler beneath; leaf stalks hairy; flo. heads similar to those of *Tussilago farfara*, solitary, purplish, on stem up to 6 in. Introduced. Naturalized in mountains in Clova and Outer Hebrides. Flo. May–Aug.

Doronicum pardalianches L. **Leopard's Bane.** ¶Leaves ovate amplexicaul; scape 18 in., with several heads, 1½–2 in., yellow. Introduced in a few plantations. Flo. May–July.
A similar plant with leaves narrowed into petiole and solitary heads 2½ in. wide is *D. plantagineum* L., sometimes found outcast from gardens.

CHRYSANTHEMUM
LEUCANTHEMUM

CHRYSANTHEMUM
PARTHENIUM

TUSSILAGO
FARFARA.

PETASITES HYBRIDUS

*PETASITES
FRAGRANS.

C. SEGETUM.

CHRYSANTHEMUM
VULGARE.

MATRICARIA
RECUTITA.

ARTEMISIA
MARITIMA.

ARTEMISIA
VULGARIS.

ARTEMISIA
CAMPESTRIS.

ARTEMISIA
ABSINTHIUM

TRIPLEURO-
-SPERMUM INODORUM.

*MATRICARIA MATRICARIOIDES.

Plate 47

COMPOSITAE (*continued*)

Senecio vulgaris L. **Groundsel.** ¶Flo. heads with involucre cylindrical; bracts linear, outer black tipped; rays none. Abundant in cultivated ground. Flo. all the year. ✿.
Some varieties have a few ray florets. The figure is labelled var. *radiatus*. ✿.

Senecio sylvaticus L. **Wood Groundsel.** ¶Leaves softly pubescent; flo. heads with involucre conical, glandular; rays revolute. Common in woods on sandy soils. Flo. July–Sept. ✿.

Senecio × *viscidulus* Scheele. (*S. sylvaticus* × *viscosus*). ¶Intermediate between the parents, sometimes occurs where the two grow together.

Senecio viscosus L. **Sticky Groundsel.** ¶Stem stout, very glandular; heads with involucre ovoid, conical; rays revolute. In waste ground, locally common. Flo. July–Sept. ✿.

Senecio squalidus L. **Oxford Ragwort.** ¶Stem 1 ft; leaves glabrous, toothed or pinnatifid; heads ¾ in.; rays rather broad. Introduced, spreading on railways, etc., locally abundant, but rare in Scotland and N. Ireland. Flo. June–Sept. ✿.

Senecio × *londinensis* Lousley. (*S. squalidus* × *viscosus*). ¶Intermediate between the parents, sometimes occurs where the two grow together.

Senecio squalidus × *vulgaris*. ¶Intermediate between the parents, sometimes occurs where the two grow together.

Senecio erucifolius L. **Hoary Ragwort.** ¶Stem 2–3 ft; leaves with linear-acute lobes, cottony beneath. On calcareous and heavy soils, mainly in S. and E. England. Flo. July–Aug. ✿.

Senecio jacobaea L. **Ragwort.** ¶Stem 2–3 ft; leaves glabrous with lobes broadly toothed and blunt. Abundant on neglected pastures. Flo. July–Oct. ✿.

Senecio aquaticus Hill. **Marsh Ragwort.** ¶Stem 1–3 ft, purplish; upper leaves pinnatifid with forward pointing lobes, lower undivided or pinnatifid. Wet meadows. Flo. July–Aug. ✿.
Var. *pennatifidus* Gren. & Godr. ¶Leaves with lobes at right angles.

Senecio × *ostenfeldii* Druce. (*S. aquaticus* × *jacobaea*). ¶Intermediate between the parents, often occurs where the two grow together, especially in Scotland and Wales.

Senecio doria L. ¶3 ft; leaves elliptical, fleshy, glaucous, entire toothed; heads ½ in.; rays few, 4–6. Established on a few strea. sides. Flo. July–Sept.

Senecio fluviatilis Wallr. **Broad-leaved Ragwort.** *S. sarracen* auct. ¶Stoloniferous; stem 3 ft; leaves elliptical, glabro 7 × 1½ in.; heads 1 in.; involucre pubescent. Introduced, strea sides. Flo. Aug.

Senecio paludosus L. **Great Fen Ragwort.** ¶Stem 4–5 ft; leaves lo lanceolate, serrate, cottony beneath; rays many. Fen ditches, E. England, very rare, almost extinct. Flo. May–July. ✿.

Senecio palustris (L.) Hook. **Marsh Fleawort.** *S. congestus* (R. B DC. ¶Stem stout, woolly, 2–3 ft; leaves broadly lanceola involucre without shorter scales; heads ¾ in., crowded. Fen ditch in E. England, apparently extinct. Flo. June.

Senecio integrifolius (L.) Clairv. **Field Fleawort.** *S. campestris* (Ret DC. ¶Stem 6–8 in., wiry, cottony; lower leaves lanceolate, na rowed to stalk. On chalk downs and limestone grassland, England to Lincolnshire, local. Flo. June–July. ✿.

Senecio spathulifolius Turcz. **Spathulate Fleawort.** ¶Stem 18 i stout; lower leaves narrowed abruptly to stalk; stem leav amplexicaul. Cliffs in Anglesey and Micklefell, Yorkshire. Fl June–July. ✿.

Senecio cineraria DC. ¶Stem shrubby and woolly; leaves pinnatifi white felted beneath; heads many. Naturalized on sea cliffs, and S.W. Flo. June–Aug. ✿.

Carlina vulgaris L. **Carline Thistle.** ¶Leaves and outer brac spinous; inner bracts whitish, spreading like rays; florets purpl On calcareous grassland, local. Flo. July–Sept. ✿.

Arctium lappa L. **Great Burdock.** *A. majus* Bernh. ¶Leaf petiol solid; heads few, 1½–2 in., long stalked, open in fruit; brac green. Scattered in waste places mostly in S. and mid Britain. Fl July–Sept. ✿.

Arctium pubens Bab. **Common Burdock.** *A. nemorosum* auct. *vulgare* auct. ¶Petioles hollow; heads 1–1½ in., stalked and webbe wide open in fr.; all bracts subulate, equalling the flo. In wood scrub, etc., local. Flo. July–Sept. ✿.

Arctium minus Bernh. **Lesser Burdock.** ¶Smaller plant; heads sho stalked or sessile, ¾–1 in., ovate, closed in fr.; bracts distinct shorter than flo., subulate. In waste places, by roadsides, etc common. Flo. July–Sept. ✿.

SENECIO SYLVATICUS.

S. VULGARIS RADIATUS.

SENECIO SQUALIDUS.

SENECIO JACOBAEA.

x6

SENECIO ERUCIFOLIUS.

SENECIO VULGARIS.

SENECIO AQUATICUS.

MARSH RAGWORT.

SENECIO CINERARIA.

SENECIO VISCOSUS.

ARCTIUM PUBENS.

NECIO TEGRIFOLIUS.

ARCTIUM LAPPA.

x2

SENECIO SPATHULIFOLIUS

SENECIO PALUDOSUS.

CARLINA VULGARIS.

ARCTIUM MINUS

Plate 48 ❀ indicates plant is illustrated

COMPOSITAE (*continued*)

Carduus pycnocephalus L. **Plymouth Thistle.** ¶Wings on stems interrupted below heads; leaves cottony beneath; heads ¾ in., florets exceeding bracts. Long established on Plymouth Hoe. Flo. June– August.

Carduus tenuiflorus Curt. **Slender-flowered Thistle.** ¶Stem winged and spinous throughout; leaves less cottony; heads ½ in.; florets not exceeding bracts. On sea cliffs, rare inland. Flo. June–Aug. ❀.

Carduus nutans L. **Nodding Thistle.** ¶Stem wings interrupted; heads 2 in., nodding; inner bracts contracted above base. On calcareous soils, local in N. England and rare in Scotland and Ireland. Flo. May–Aug. ❀.

Carduus acanthoides L. **Welted Thistle.** *C. crispus* auct. ¶Stem wings almost continuous; heads ¾ in., erect; inner bracts not contracted above base. Waste places, rare in Scotland and W. Ireland. Flo. June–Aug. ❀.

Cirsium vulgare (Savi) Ten. **Spear Thistle.** *Carduus lanceolatus* L. ¶Stem leaves ½–1 ft, decurrent, with few lobes; heads 1–1½ in.; involucre ovate, hairy. Common. Flo. July–Sept. ❀.

Cirsium eriophorum (L.) Scop.
Subsp. *britannicum* Petrak. **Woolly Thistle.** ¶Leaves 1–2 ft, not decurrent, lobes deep and bifid; heads 2–3 in., globose, woolly. On calcareous soil, mainly in S. and E. England and Midlands, local. Flo. Aug. ❀.

Cirsium palustre (L.) Scop. **Marsh Thistle.** *Carduus palustris* ¶Stem 3–5 ft; leaves decurrent, pinnatifid, spinous; heads ¾ in clustered. Common in wet places. Flo. June–Sept. ❀.

Cirsium dissectum (L.) Hill. **Meadow Thistle.** *Carduus pratensis* Hud ¶Stoloniferous; stem 2 ft, simple, cottony; leaves mostly bas toothed or lobed, prickles soft. In wet meadows, mainly S. a mid Britain and Ireland. Flo. June–July. ❀.

Cirsium tuberosum (L.) All. **Tuberous Meadow Thistle.** ¶Simil to *C. dissectum*, but with tuberous roots and no stolons; bas leaves deeply lobed. In calcareous pastures, rare and loc Wiltshire, Gloucestershire, Glamorgan and Cambridgeshi Flo. Aug.

Cirsium heterophyllum (L.) Hill. **Melancholy Thistle.** ¶Stolonifero stem 3 ft; leaves broad, cordate, not prickly, white beneath. wet mountainous places, mid Wales to Scotland, very rare Ireland. Flo. July–Aug. ❀.

Cirsium acaule Scop. **Ground Thistle.** *C. acaulonauct.* ¶Stemless nearly so; flo. heads sessile on basal leaf rosette. On calcareo pastures from Yorkshire southwards. Flo. July–Aug. ❀.

Cirsium arvense (L.) Scop. **Creeping Thistle.** ¶Roots creepi and white; stem 2 ft without wings; heads dioecious, brac appressed. In grass, abundant. Flo. July–Sept. ❀.

*Cirsium oleraceum (L.) Scop. ¶Stem 3 ft, wingless; leaves ova uppermost yellowish exceeding flo. heads. Locally establish in plantations. Flo. July.

CARDUUS
NUTANS.
NODDING
THISTLE.

CIRSIUM
PALUSTRE.

CARDUUS
TENUIFLORUS.

CARDUUS
ACANTHOIDES.

CIRSIUM
VULGARE.
(LANCEOLATUM)

SPEAR THISTLE.

CIRSIUM
HETEROPHYLLUM
MELANCHOLY
THISTLE.

CIRSIUM
ERIOPHORUM

CIRSIUM
ARVENSE.
CREEPING
THISTLE.

RSIUM
SECTUM

CIRSIUM
ACAULON.

Plate 49   ✽ indicates plant is illustrated

COMPOSITAE (*continued*)

Onopordon acanthium L. **Scottish Thistle.** ¶Stem 3–5 ft, broadly winged; leaves elliptic, woolly, spinous; heads nearly globose. Doubtfully native. By roadsides, in waste places, etc., mainly E. England. Flo. July–Aug. ✽.

*Silybum marianum (L.) Gaertn. **Milk Thistle.** ¶Stem 4 ft; leaves large, green, variegated with milk-white beside veins; heads 2 in. Naturalized locally. Flo. June–July.

Saussurea alpina (L.) DC. **Alpine Saw-wort.** ¶3–12 in.; stem and underside of leaves cottony; flo. scented, blue. On alpine rocks, Scotland to N. Wales and Ireland. Flo. Aug.–Sept. ✽.

Serratula tinctoria L. **Saw-wort.** ¶Stem 1–2 ft, slender, grooved; leaves mostly pinnate; margin finely toothed. In moist meadows and moors in England and Wales, very rare in Ireland and absent from Scotland. Flo. June–Aug. ✽.

*Centaurea jacea L. ¶Leaves lanceolate, mostly subentire; bract appendages pale brown, rounded and jagged. In pastures, S. England, introduced, rare. Flo. Aug.–Sept. ✽.

Centaurea nigra L. **Knapweed, Hardheads.** *C. obscura* Jord. ¶Stem swollen below the heads; bract appendages blackish, concealing base. Frequent in grassy places on heavy soils, especially in the N. Flo. July–Sept. ✽.

Centaurea nemoralis Jord. **Brown Knapweed.** ¶Stem slender, n swollen below heads; bract appendages brown; outer flo. oft enlarged. Common in grassy places on calcareous and light soi especially in S. England. Flo. July–Sept. ✽.

Centaurea scabiosa L. **Great Knapweed.** ¶Leaves pinnatifid; brac pale green, not fully covered by dark fringe. Mostly on calcareo soils, but frequent by railways as an introduction. Flo. Jul Sept. ✽.

Centaurea cyanus L. **Cornflower.** ¶Stem, and upper linear-lance late leaves cottony; bract fringe silvery; flo. blue. Cornfiel and waste land. Flo. June–Aug. ✽.

*Centaurea paniculata L. ¶Leaves pinnatifid, lobes linear cotton bract teeth small pale; flo. purple. Established in Jersey. Fl July.

Centaurea aspera L. ¶Leaves narrow; bract fringe reflexed yellowis palmate, spinous. Channel Islands. Flo. July–Aug. ✽.

Centaurea calcitrapa L. **Star Thistle.** ¶Flo. red-purple; bracts endi in long spreading spurs and smaller spines. Gravelly and san places, mainly S. England, rare. Flo. July–Sept. ✽.

*Centaurea solstitialis L. **Yellow Star Thistle.** ¶Stem broad winged; bracts palmately spinous; terminal spine and fl yellow. Introduced in cultivated land. Flo. July–Sept.

SERRATULA
TINCTORIA.

CENTAUREA
ASPERA.

CENTAUREA NIGRA.

ONOPORDON
ACANTHIUM.

SCOTTISH
THISTLE.

SAUSSUREA
ALPINA.

CENTAUREA
CALCITRAPA.

CENTAUREA
NEMORALIS.

CENTAUREA SCABIOSA.

CENTAUREA
JACEA.

CENTAUREA CYANUS.

Plate 50 ✿ indicates plant is illustrated

COMPOSITAE (*continued*)

Cichorium intybus L. **Chicory.** ¶Stem 3 ft, branched and tough; heads clustered in axils; flo. blue. In fields, by roadsides, etc., chiefly on calcareous and alluvial soils, probably introduced in Scotland and Ireland. Flo. July–Sept. ✿.

Arnoseris minima (L.) Schweigg. & Koerte. **Swine's Succory.** *A. pusilla* Gaertn. ¶Leaves radical; stems hollow, widening above; bracts united; flo. yellow. On sandy soils in S. and E. counties. Flo. June–Aug. ✿.

Lapsana communis L. **Nipple-wort.** ¶Stem 2 ft, branched and leafy; bracts linear, erect; florets few in each head, pale yellow. Common, except in N. Scotland. Flo. July–Sept. ✿.

Picris hieracioides L. **Hawkweed Ox-tongue.** ¶Stem 2 ft, with hooked bristles; stiff bristles on leaves; beak of fr. short. Mostly on calcareous soils in S. Britain, very rare in Ireland. Flo. July–Sept. ✿.

Picris echioides L. **Bristly Ox-tongue.** *Helmintia echioides* (L.) Gaertn. ¶Stem 2 ft; leaves and bracts with hairs on white tubercles; fr. long beaked. On calcareous soils and sea cliffs mostly in S. and E. England and Wales, very rare in Ireland, and introduced in Scotland. Flo. June–Sept. ✿.

Crepis foetida L. **Stinking Hawk's-beard.** ¶Stem 2 ft, branched and leafy below; buds drooping; bracts downy; inner fr. long beaked. Mostly on chalk, S. England, rare. Flo. June–Aug. ✿.

**Crepis vesicaria.*
Subsp. *taraxacifolia* (Thuill.) Thell. **Beaked Hawk's-beard.** *C. taraxacifolia* Thuill. ¶Stem 1½ ft, branched above; heads many, erect in bud; fr. beaked. In waste ground, fields, by roadsides, etc., common in S. and E. England and the Midlands, local in Wales and Ireland, and rare, but increasing in N. England and Scotland. Flo. June–July. ✿.

*Crepis setosa Haller f. **Bristly Hawk's-beard.** ¶Stem 2 ft; leaves pinnate, hispid; bracts bristly; flo. pale yellow; fr. beaked. Introduced, mostly in clover fields, rare. Flo. July–Aug.

Crepis capillaris (L.) Wallr. **Smooth Hawk's-beard.** *C. virens* ¶Stem 2 ft; leaves pinnate, upper sagittate, glabrous; heads ½ in fr. 10 ribbed. Common. Flo. June–Sept. ✿.

Crepis nicaeensis* Balb. **French Hawk's-beard. ¶Leaves pinnate sagittate, roughly hairy; heads 1 in.; bracts glandular; d ciliate. Introduced in cultivated land, rare. Flo. June–July.

Crepis biennis L. **Greater** or **Rough Hawk's-beard.** ¶Stem 3 leaves hispid, pinnate, broad; heads 1½ in.; inner bracts dow within. On calcareous soils, native in S. and E. England, probab introduced elsewhere, local. Flo. June–July. ✿.

Crepis mollis (Jacq.) Aschers. **Soft Hawk's-beard.** ¶Stem 1½ leaves entire; outer bracts short, appressed, glandular; fr. wi 20 ribs. In woods in the N., local. Flo. July–Aug. ✿.

Crepis paludosa (L.) Moench. **Marsh Hawk's-beard.** ¶Stem 2 leaves tapering to point; bracts woolly, glandular; pappus brow In wet meadows from S. Wales to N. Scotland and Ireland. Fl July–Sept. ✿.

Hypochoeris glabra L. **Smooth Cat's-ear.** ¶Stem 3–10 in.; leav radical; heads ½ in., bracts glabrous; inner fr. beaked. San heaths and dunes, mostly in the southern half of Britain, loca rare in Scotland and Ireland, opening in morning sun only. Fl June–Oct. ✿.

Hypochoeris radicata L. **Common Cat's-ear.** ¶Stem 1½ ft; fork and bracteate; leaves radical, hispid; heads 1½ in. across. Ve common. Flo. May–July. ✿.

Hypochoeris maculata L. **Spotted Cat's-ear.** ¶Stem 1½ ft; leav hispid, purple spotted; heads broad; involucre blackish, hispi On calcareous banks and cliffs, mostly E. England, very loca very rare in the Channel Islands, Cornwall, N. Wales an Lancashire. Flo. July–Aug. ✿.

ORIUM
YBUS

LAPSANA
COMMUNIS.

PICRIS
ECHIODES.

PICRIS
HIERACIOIDES.

ARNOSERIS
MINIMA.

CAT'S EAR
HYPOCHOERIS
RADICATA.

HYPOCHOERIS
MACULATA.

HYPOCHOERIS GLABRA.

×2

ACIFOLIA. CREPIS
PALUDOSA.

CREPIS
FOETIDA.

CREPIS
MOLLIS.

CREPIS CAPILLARIS

CREPIS BIENNIS.

COMPOSITAE (*continued*)

Genus HIERACIUM

Botanists who wish to identify *Hieracia* should study H. W. Pugsley's 'Prodromus of the British Hieracia' in the *Journal of the Linnean Society of London* (Botany), vol. 54. This is sold at the Society's rooms at Burlington House, Piccadilly, London W.1. Mr Pugsley has given us a clear picture of the genus with descriptions of 260 species and their distribution. The following notes are only abbreviated extracts from Mr Pugsley's summary of sections, together with short descriptions of 23 sample species, 15 of them figured, in order to show the kind of gradation which may be recognized among them.

Section 1. *Amplexicaulia.* ¶Leaves mostly in a radical rosette, densely clothed with many stalked glands; stem with a few amplexicaul leaves; heads large; ligules with pilose tips. Unlike the rest of the genus the 3 species in this section seem to be fairly recently introduced, e.g. *Hieracium amplexicaule* L.

Section 2. *Alpina.* ¶Leaves in a radical rosette, with long pilose hairs and sparingly clothed with stalked glands; stem leaves 0 or bract-like; heads solitary, rather large; involucre (floral bracts) incumbent in bud, densely clothed with long pilose hairs; ligules (strap-shaped corolla) pilose at tip. 15 species including:

Hieracium holosericeum Backh. ¶Leaves light green, narrow, obtuse, subentire, all clothed with long silky pilose hairs. Chiefly in N. Scotland. ✿
The scarcer *H. alpinum* L. has leaves darker green, more obovate, with less silky heads.

Section 3. *Subalpina.* ¶Leaves in a radical rosette, pilose, and with a few fine yellow glands; stem leaves 1–few, small, lanceolate; inflo. of 2–5 large heads, often very glandular or pilose. 22 species including:

Hieracium lingulatum Backh. ¶Radical leaves long, lanceolate, subentire, rough with stiff pilose hairs; head large, blackish, pilose; flo. bracts broad, erect in bud. Central to N. Scotland. ✿

Section 4. *Cerinthoidea.* ¶Stem and leaves without glands, in rosette, clothed with long denticulate hairs, rather glaucous; stem leaves semi-amplexicaul; heads large, with densely pilose incumbent bracts; ligules with pilose tips. 14 species including:

Hieracium anglicum Fr. ¶Radical leaves ovate, denticulate, narrowed below to petiole; stem leaves 2, upper bract-like; heads 1–4 with long glandular peduncles; flo. bracts densely clothed with long black-based hairs and few glands; styles livid. Widely distributed in Scotland, N. England and Ireland. ✿

Section 5. *Oreadea.* ¶Leaves in rosette, narrowed below (except nos. 1–3), often glaucous, without glands but with long rigid hairs (setae); stem leaves not amplexicaul; heads less pilose than in sections 2–4; flo. bracts erect; ligules mostly glabrous tipped; styles yellow. 19 species including:

Hieracium lasiophyllum Koch. ¶Leaves oblong, obtuse, little toothed, rounded below, upper surface rough with setae; flo. bracts greyish green. England (W. Midlands), Wales, Scotland and Ireland.

Hieracium eustomon (E. F. Linton) Roffey. ¶Leaves broadly oval,

rounded below, toothed, with setae on margin only; flo. br. dark green. In Devon, W. Somerset and Wales.

Hieracium schmidtii Tausch. ¶Leaves oval, toothed, usually taper below, with stiff hairs on margin only; 1 stem leaf; flo. br. dark green. England, Wales, Scotland, Ireland. ✿

Hieracium argenteum Fr. ¶Plant more slender; leaves narrow lanceolate, glaucous, toothed, with fewer stiff hairs; 2 st leaves; flo. bracts dark green. In N. England, Wales, Scotl. and Ireland.

Section 6. *Suboreadea.* ¶Leaves in rosette, glaucous, someti. purple spotted, rather broad, rounded or angled below; s. leaves 0–3, narrowed below, with hairs less rigid than in section bracts usually erect in bud; styles yellow. 17 species including

Hieracium britannicum F. J. Hanb. ¶Leaves ovate-lanceolate, scar. glaucous, unspotted, sharply toothed; stem leaf 0 or 1; bracts long, narrow, greyish green; ligules glabrous. Wales, a from Cheddar, Derby dales, Teesdale to Scotland and Ireland.

Section 7. *Vulgata.*

Subsection *Bifida.* ¶Leaves in rosette, mostly glabrous abo. peduncles and flo. bracts not very glandular, but more or . pilose and with stellate hairs. 13 species of limited distribut. in N. England and Scotland.

Subsection *Stellatifolia.* ¶Leaves in a rosette, these and the bracts clothed with stellate hairs. 2 species of limited distribut. in England and Wales.

Subsection *Glandulosa.* ¶Leaves in rosette, usually more or . clothed with long pilose hairs; flo. bracts clothed with da. strong glandular hairs; stem leaves 0–1. 21 species including:

Hieracium pellucidum Laest. ¶Leaves dark green, subglabrous abo. purplish beneath, broadly oval, with broad toothed base; he. small; flo. bracts blackish green; styles livid. In England, Wa. and Ireland.

Hieracium exotericum Jord. ex Bor. ¶Leaves light green, softly pil. on both surfaces, oval with broad toothed base; styles yelle. England, Wales, Ireland, rare in Scotland.
Forma *grandidens* (Dahlst.) Pugsl. ¶Leaves more deeply tooth. styles livid. ✿

Subsection *Sagittata.* ¶Leaves mostly in rosette, pilose, with spre. ing teeth at base; flo. bracts densely glandular and someti. with long or stellate hairs. 12 species in Scotland, N. Engla. Wales.

Subsection *Caesia.* ¶Plants with more stem leaves, glaucous, n. rowed below flo. bracts with dense stellate hairs and a few gl. dular. 23 species mostly in Scotland and N. England.

Subsection *Eu-vulgata.* ¶Plants with several stem leaves, taper. to petiole; flo. bracts densely glandular and with stellate ha. 22 species, mostly in England and Wales, including:

Hieracium vulgatum Fr. ¶Radical leaves narrow with sharp ascend. teeth, purplish beneath; stem leaves 2–5; flo. bracts greyish gre. incumbent in bud, with pilose hairs and a few short glands. Scotland, N. and mid England. Wales, Ireland. ✿

HIERACIUM
EXOTERICUM
VAR.
GRANDIDENS.

ERACIUM
HOLOSERICEUM.

HIERACIUM
PILOSELLA.

HIERACIUM
BRITANNICUM.

HIERACIUM
LINGULATUM.

HIERACIUM
ANGLICUM.

HIERACIUM
SCHMIDTTII.

HIERACIUM
VULGATUM.

Plate 52

COMPOSITAE (*continued*)

Hieracium maculatum Sm. ¶Radical leaves narrow, dark green, spotted, dentate, with stiff hairs on both surfaces; stem leaves 3–5; flo. bracts greyish green, with short glandular and few longer pilose hairs. In England. ❀.

Hieracium diaphanum Fr. *H. anglorum* (Ley) Pugsl. ¶Plant robust; radical leaves often few, ovate, dentate; stem leaves 3–5; heads small; flo. bracts with dense, dark glandular hairs and a few stellate. In many counties of England, rare in Ireland.

Hieracium lachenalii C. C. Gmel. ¶Plant robust; radical leaves few, with rough hairs, ovate, sharply dentate; stem leaves 4–12; flo. bracts deep olive-green, with stellate hairs; ligules with pilose tips. In 47 counties of England and Wales. ❀.

Section 8. *Alpestria*. ¶Stem leaves numerous, rounded below, amplexicaul; heads few, often on branches from upper leaf axils; flo. bracts dark, obtuse, finely glandular, without stellate hairs; ligules glabrous. 18 species in N. Scotland.

Section 9. *Prenanthoidea*. ¶Radical leaves 0; stem leaves numerous, green reticulate below, semi-amplexicaul; heads many, small; peduncles and flo. bracts densely clothed with dark glandular hairs; styles livid. 2 species.

Section 10. *Tridentata*. ¶Plants often tall; stem leaves many, green, serrate, with thickened edges and narrowed base; flo. bracts incumbent in bud, less clothed than in sections 1–9, often microglandular; ligules glabrous. 32 species mostly of very limited distribution, but including:

Hieracium trichocaulon (Dahlst.) Johans. *H. tridentatum* Fr. ¶Leaves elliptic-lanceolate with sharp erect teeth, subglabrous; heads many, small, pale; flo. bracts olive-green with pale edges, with some pilose hairs and some glandular. In 27 counties of England and Wales. ❀.

Section 11. *Foliosa*. ¶Leaves all on the stem, numerous, paler and reticulate beneath; upper semi-amplexicaul, margins thickened; heads rather large, numerous; flo. bracts with glandular hairs and some pilose. 16 species, mostly in Scotland and N. England, including:

Hieracium latobrigorum (Zahn) Roffey. ¶Leaves dull or yellowish green, shortly or sparingly dentate, lower tapering below, upper rounded; peduncles with stellate hairs; flo. bracts dark olive-green, with dark glandular hairs and micro-glands; styles yellow. In 19 counties of Scotland, 4 of England. ❀.

Section 12. *Umbellata*. ¶Leaves numerous, not reticulate beneath, margins recurved, base narrow, attenuate; inflo. subumbellate; outer flo. bracts with reflexed tips, nearly glabrous. 3 species including:

Hieracium umbellatum L. subsp. *umbellatum*. ¶Leaves numerous, dark green, paler beneath, linear-lanceolate with few small spreading teeth; flo. bracts blackish green; styles yellow. In 63 counties England, Wales and Scotland, 11 in Ireland. ❀.

Hieracium umbellatum L. subsp. *bichlorophyllum* (Druce & Za P. D. Sell & C. West. *H. bichlorophyllum* (Druce & Zahn) Pu ¶Leaves numerous, clear green, paler beneath, oblong-lanceol subentire or with 1–2 broad shallow teeth; inflo. with lon branches; flo. bracts olive-green; styles yellow. In S.W. Engla Wales and Ireland.

Section 13. *Sabauda*. ¶Stems hirsute; leaves numerous, lower lanc late, upper ovate, often densely pilose beneath, not reticula flo. bracts appressed or the outer lax, dark green with fine gla and pilose or subglabrous; styles livid. 11 species mostly in Engla and Wales.

Hieracium perpropinquum (Zahn) Druce. *H. bladonii* Pugsl. ¶Lo stem clothed with long whitish hairs; leaves dark green, broa lanceolate, with sharp ascending teeth; peduncles with stell and pilose hairs; flo. bracts with some glandular hairs and lo whitish hairs at base; outer bracts loose. In 36 counties of Engla and Wales, 7 of Scotland. ❀.

Section 14. *Pilosellina*. ¶Plants with stolons, basal rosettes and headed flo. stems; ligules pale yellow, red beneath.

Pilosella officinarum C. H. & F. W. Schultz. **Mouse-ear Hawkwe** *Hieracium pilosella* L. ¶Stolons long and creeping; leaves set above and on the margins, white beneath with soft hairs; bracts clothed with dense stellate, glandular and pilose ha Generally distributed and common. ❀ on plate 51.

Pilosella peleteriana (Mérat) C. H. & F. W. Schultz. *Hieracs peleterianum* Mérat. ¶Stolons short and thick; leaves deep gre with dense pilose hairs above, grey beneath with stellate ha flo. bracts tapering, clothed with long, pale black-based ha Channel Islands and Cornwall to Merioneth and Derbyshi very local. ❀.

Section 15. *Pratensina*. ¶Plants with stolons and few stem leav leaves entire with long stiff hairs; heads many.

Pilosella aurantiaca* (L.) C. H. & F. W. Schultz. **Orange Hawkwe *Hieracium aurantiacum* L.
Subsp. *aurantiaca*. ¶Plant with few stolons; leaves obovate; brick-red or reddish orange. Garden escape. Naturalized grassy places, rare.
Subsp. *brunneocroceum* (Pugsl.) P. D. Sell & C. West. *Hieraci brunneocroceum* Pugsl. ¶Plant with many long quick-growi stolons; leaving oblong or oblanceolate; flo. smaller than those subsp. *aurantiaca*, brownish orange. Garden escape. Naturaliz in grassy places, rather common.

**Pilosella caespitosa* (Dumort.) P. D. Sell & C. West. subsp. *colli formis* (Naeg. & Peter) P. D. Sell & C. West. *Hieracium collinifo* (Naeg. & Peter) Roffey. ¶Stem hairy; heads 12–30 in a comp corymb; flo. yellow with dark styles. Naturalized in a few scatter localities from the W. Midlands to N. Scotland, rare.

HIERACIUM
LACHENALII.

HIERACIUM
UMBELLATUM

HIERACIUM
LATOBRIGORUM

HIERACIUM
PERPROPINQUUM

HIERACIUM
TRICHOCAULON.

ERACIUM
ACULATUM.

HIERACIUM PELETERIANUM.

Plate 53   ❀ indicates plant is illustrated

COMPOSITAE (*continued*)

Leontodon taraxacoides (Vill.) Mérat. **Hawkbit.** *L. leysseri* (Wallr.) Beck. ¶Stem slender, subglabrous; head solitary, drooping in bud; outer fr. with crown of scales, inner with pappus. Locally common in dry grassy places, but rare in N. England and very rare in Scotland. Flo. June–Sept. ❀.

Leontodon hispidus L. **Rough Hawkbit.** ¶Stem hairy; head solitary, densely hairy, drooping in bud; fr. with 2 rows of pappus. Locally common in grassy places, especially on calcareous soils, but very rare in Scotland and N. Ireland. Flo. June–Sept. ❀.

Leontodon autumnalis L. **Smooth Hawkbit.** ¶Stem glabrous, branched, scaly; leaves usually glabrous, often pinnatifid; fr. with 1 row of pappus. Common in grassy places. Flo. July–Oct. ❀. Var. *pratensis* Koch. ¶Involucre clothed with black hairs. Mostly on mountains.

Taraxacum officinale Weber. **Dandelion.** ¶Leaves with tooth-like lobes; outer flo. bracts long, recurved; heads large; fr. light brown. Very common in fields, lawns, waste places, by roadsides, etc. Flo. March–July. ❀.

Taraxacum palustre (Lyons) DC. **Little Marsh Dandelion.** *T. paludosum* (Scop.) Schlecht. ex Crep. ¶Leaves narrow, subentire or teeth few; heads small; flo. bracts broadly ovate, closely appressed. In marshes, fens, wet meadows, etc., local. Flo. May–July. ❀.

Taraxacum spectabile Dahlst. **Bog Dandelion.** ¶Leaves large, dark green, midrib red; flo. bracts loosely appressed; ligules red at back. In marshes, wet meadows, by streamsides, on mountains, etc., local. Flo. May–July.

Taraxacum laevigatum (Willd.) DC. **Lesser Dandelion.** *T. erythrospermum* Andrz. ex Bess. ¶Leaves deeply divided, segments narrow, with intermediate smaller ones; outer flo. bracts spreading, inner with a dorsal appendage at apex; fr. red. In dry places, common. Flo. May–July. ❀.

Taraxacum obliquum (Fr.) Dahlst. ¶Has fr. pale brown and brighter yellow flo.

Lactuca virosa L. **Acrid Lettuce.** ¶Stem 3 ft; lower leaves with broad segments; beak equalling smooth black fr. On waste ground,

banks, etc., especially near the sea, mainly E. England, local common. Flo. July–Aug. ❀.

Lactuca serriola L. **Prickly Lettuce.** *L. scariola* L. ¶Stem 4 ft; low leaves with narrow distant curved segments; beak equalling fr. O sand dunes and waste places, mostly S. and E. England. Fl July–Aug. ❀.

Lactuca saligna L. **Least Lettuce.** ¶Stem 2 ft; upper leaves line lower pinnate, segments narrow, acute; inflo. narrow; beak lon On banks near S. and E. coasts, local. Flo. July–Aug.

Mycelis muralis (L.) Reichb. **Wall Lettuce.** *Lactuca muralis* (I Gaertn. ¶Stem 2 ft; leaves thin, lobes irregular; inflo. wi spreading; beak of fr. very short. On calcareous rocks, walls a in woods, local in N. England and rare in Scotland and Irelan Flo. July–Aug. ❀.

Cicerbita alpina (L.) Wallr. **Alpine Lettuce.** *Lactuca alpina* (L.) Gray. ¶Stem 3–4 ft, glandular above; leaves with large termin lobe; involucre glandular; flo. blue. Clova Mountains, very ra Flo. July–Aug. ❀.

Cicerbita macrophylla (Willd.) Wallr. **Blue Sowthistle.** *Lactu macrophylla* (Willd.) A. Gray. ¶Stem up to 3 ft, with creepi rhizome; glabrous below, glandular above; lower leaves larg lyrate, with triangular terminal lobe; upper leaves smaller, oft sessile; involucre glandular, hairy; flo. lilac-blue in a simple compound terminal raceme. Garden escape. Naturalized grassy places and established on waste ground, widespre throughout Britain and Ireland. Flo. July–Aug.

Sonchus oleraceus L. **Common Sowthistle.** ¶Leaves not spinou basal auricles acute, spreading; involucre glabrous; fr. 6 ribbe rugose. On cultivated land, common. Flo. June–Aug. ❀.

Sonchus asper (L.) Hill. **Prickly Sowthistle.** ¶Leaves spinous, bas auricles round and clasping; involucre glabrous; fr. 6 ribbe smooth. On cultivated land, common. Flo. June–Aug. ❀.

Sonchus arvensis L. **Corn Sowthistle.** ¶Stoloniferous; leaf spines so basal auricles round; inflo. with yellow glands; fr. 10 ribbed; f golden. Cultivated land, common. Flo. Aug.–Sept. ❀.

Sonchus palustris L. **Fen Sowthistle.** ¶Stem 6 ft; lower leaves deep pinnatifid, basal lobes acute; inflo. with blackish glands; flo. lemo colour. Fens and ditches, E. England, rare. Flo. July–Aug. ❀.

LEONTODON
HISPIDUS.

LEONTODON
TARAXACOIDES.
COMMON HAWKBIT.

LEONTODON
AUTUMNALIS.

TARAXACUM
LAEVIGATUM.

×2

TARAXACUM
OFFICINALE.
DANDELION.

MYCELIS
MURALIS.

TARAXACUM
PALUSTRE.

WALL
LETTUCE.

ALPINE
LETTUCE.

CICERBITA
ALPINA.

LACTUCA
VIROSA.

LACTUCA
SERRIOLA.

SONCHUS
ASPER

SONCHUS OLERACEUS

SONCHUS PALUSTRIS.

CORN
SOW-THISTLE.

SONCHUS
ARVENSIS.

Plate 54   ❀ indicates plant is illustrated

COMPOSITAE (*continued*)

Tragopogon pratensis L. **Goat's-beard.**
Subsp. *pratensis.* ¶Flo. rather pale yellow, equalling pale-edged involucre; anthers yellow; outer fr. smooth, 15–20 mm. Rare in waste places in Britain, common on Continent.
Subsp. *minor* (Mill.) Wahlenb. **Lesser Goat's-beard.** *Tragopogon minor* Mill. ¶Flo. bright yellow, shorter than red-edged involucre; anthers brownish; outer fr. rugose, 10–12 mm. Locally common in grassy places, waste places, etc., but rare in Scotland and Ireland. Flo. June–July. ❀.

*Tragopogon porrifolius L. **Salsify.** ¶Stem much thickened at top; flo. purple. Escape from cultivation. Naturalized in rough grassy places, etc., chiefly S. England. Flo. June–Aug.

Scorzonera humilis L. ¶Leaves lanceolate acuminate; flo. pale yellow, exceeding involucre, woolly below. Marshy fields in Dorset and meadow in Warwickshire. Flo. May–July.

LOBELIACEAE

Lobelia dortmanna L. **Water Lobelia.** ¶Aquatic; leaves radical submerged, linear, of 2 tubes; flo. pale lilac. In gravelly lakes, Wales, Lake District, Scotland and Ireland. Flo. July. ❀.

Lobelia urens L. **Blue Lobelia.** ¶Terrestrial; stem 1–2 ft, angular, leafy, with acrid juice; flo. blue. In heathy fields and woods, local. Cornwall, S. Devon, Hampshire, Sussex and formerly in S. Wales. Flo. Aug. ❀.

CAMPANULACEAE

Jasione montana L. **Sheep's-bit.** ¶Stem 1 ft, base leafy, pilose; heads solitary; flo. blue, petals narrow. On dry sandy and acid soils, especially in the W. Flo. May–Aug. ❀.

Wahlenbergia hederacea (L.) Reichb. **Ivy-leaved Bell-flower.** *Campanula hederacea* L. ¶Stems slender, trailing; leaves thin, glabrous; flo. pale blue; capsule opening at top. Acid moors and peat bogs, chiefly in the W. Flo. July–Aug. ❀.

Phyteuma tenerum R. Schulz. **Round-headed Rampion.** *P. orbiculare* auct., non L. ¶Lower leaves ovate; bracts triangular; flo. deep blue-purple, in globose heads. On chalk pastures mainly in S.E. England. Flo. July. ❀.

Phyteuma spicatum L. **Spiked Rampion.** ¶Lower leaves cordate; bracts linear; flo. cream colour, in oblong spike. Very local in woods, E. Sussex. Flo. July. ❀.

Campanula glomerata L. **Clustered Bell-flower.** ¶Stem 6–8 in., downy; leaves rounded below; flo. sessile, terminal, deep blue-purple. On calcareous downs, alluvial grassland and railway banks, chiefly S. and E. England, rare in S.W. England, Wales and Scotland. Flo. May–Sept. ❀.

Campanula trachelium L. **Nettle-leaved Bell-flower.** ¶Stem 2–3 hispid; upper leaves shortly petioled, teeth coarse and blu peduncles 2–3 flowered. In shady places and woods on calcare and stiff soils chiefly in the S. half of Britain. Flo. July–Sept.

Campanula latifolia L. **Greater Bell-flower.** ¶Stem 3–4 ft; upp leaves sessile, serrate; peduncles with 1 large blue-purple flo. open woods and hedge banks, chiefly in the N. Flo. July. ❀.

*Campanula rapunculoides L. **Creeping Bell-flower.** ¶Stolonifero stem 1½ ft; calyx tube with stiff appressed hairs; flo. blue-purp Garden escape. Naturalized in grassy places, on hedge and ra way banks and established in waste ground. Flo. July–Aug. ❀.

*Campanula lactiflora Bieb. ¶Stem hispid, 3–5 ft, branched abov leaves sessile, ovate-lanceolate, deeply serrate, pale beneath; f large, open-campanulate, variable in colour from milky wh tinged with blue to pale and dark blue, in loose leafy panicl calyx lobes broad-ovate, acute, about half as long as the corol Garden escape. Naturalized by rivers, chiefly in Scotland. F June–Sept.

Campanula rotundifolia L. **Harebell, Bluebell** (in Scotland). ¶Stolo ferous; stem 1 ft, decumbent below; radical leaves orbicula upper linear. In dry grassy places, common except in S.W. Englan and Ireland where it is local. Flo. July–Sept. ❀.

*Campanula persicifolia L. ¶Leaves long, linear-lanceolate, glabrou flo. few, a broad open cup 1½ in. wide. Naturalized in a few shad places. Flo. June–Aug.

*Campanula rapunculus L. ¶Tall, 3 ft; lower leaves truncate at bas flo. small, ½ in.; upper peduncles 1 flowered, lower 2–3 flowere Locally naturalized on sandy soil, rare. Flo. July–Aug. ❀.

Campanula patula L. **Spreading Bell-flower.** ¶2 ft; lower leav narrowed into petiole; flo. large, 1–1½ in., calyx lobes toothed base. Shady places in England and Wales, local. Flo. July–Aug. ❀

*Campanula alliariifolia Willd. ¶Stem downy, 3–4 ft; radical leav large, ovate-cordate to reniform, pubescent above, densely gr tomentose beneath, coarsely and irregularly toothed; upp leaves much smaller; flo. creamy white, 1–2 in. long, borne sing on short pedicels in the axils of the leaf-like bracts, the who forming a loose terminal 1-sided raceme; calyx teeth separated oblong to lanceolate appendages; stigmas 3. Garden escap Naturalized on railway banks, chiefly in Devon and Cornwal Flo. July–Sept.

*Campanula medium L. **Canterbury Bell.** ¶Stem hispid, 1–3 f leaves sessile, ovate-lanceolate, crenate; flo. large, inflate campanulate, dark blue to white; calyx teeth separated by broa reflexed appendages. Garden escape. Naturalized in chalk railway cuttings, chiefly S. England and Midlands. Flo. May July.

Legousia hybrida (L.) Delarb. **Venus' Looking-glass.** *Specular hybrida* (L.) A.DC. ¶8–10 in. hispid; leaves oblong, wavy; fl small, erect, purple; capsule long. On cultivated land, chiefly and E. England, local. Flo. June–Sept. ❀.

TRAGOPOGON
MINOR
GOAT'S
BEARD

CAMPANULA PATULA.

×3
JASIONE
MONTANA

PHYTEUMA
SPICATUM

WAHLENBERGIA
HEDERACEA.

CAMPANULA
LATIFOLIA.

CAMPANULA
RAPUNCULUS.

CAMPANULA
GLOMERATA.

×2

×2

PHYTEUMA
TENERUM

LEGOUSIA
HYBRIDA.

CAMPANULA
ROTUNDIFOLIA.

LOBELIA
URENS

LOBELIA
DORTMANNA.

CAMPANULA TRACHELIUM.

CAMPANULA
RAPUNCULOIDES.

Plate 55   ✿ indicates plant is illustrated

ERICACEAE

Vaccinium vitis-idaea L. **Cowberry.** ¶Leaves evergreen, leathery, dotted beneath, margins revolute; flo. pale pink; berries scarlet. On peat moors, common in N., local in Wales and Ireland. Flo. May–July. ✿.

Vaccinium myrtillus L. **Bilberry, Whortleberry.** ¶Leaves deciduous, ovate, acute, serrate, green; flo. subglobose; berry black. Common on moors though rare in S.E. England, E. Anglia and Midlands. Flo. April–June. ✿.

Vaccinium × intermedium Ruthe. (*V. myrtillus × vitis-idaea*). ¶Semi-evergreen; leaves elliptic, slightly serrate, with faint glandular dots beneath; fr. purplish, rarely produced. Occurs with the parents on Cannock Chase, Staffordshire and in Derbyshire, and probably elsewhere.

Vaccinium uliginosum L. **Bog Whortleberry.** ¶Leaves deciduous, oval, obtuse, entire, bluish green, net veined; berry black. On moors in Scotland and N. England, local. Flo. May–June. ✿.

Vaccinium oxycoccus L. **Cranberry.** *Oxycoccus palustris* Pers. ¶Stems slender; leaves small, ovate, with sides parallel; pedicels downy; fr. subglobose, red. Wet boggy heaths, chiefly in the N. half of Britain, local. Flo. June–Aug. ✿.

Vaccinium microcarpum (Rupr.) Hook. f. **Small Cranberry.** *Oxycoccus microcarpus* Turcz. ex Rupr. ¶Leaves triangular ovate, widest near base; pedicels glabrous; fruit more elongate. Bogs in central Scotland. Flo. July.

*Vaccinium macrocarpon Ait. *Oxycoccus macrocarpos* (Ait.) Pursh. ¶Similar to *V. oxycoccus* but leaves oblong, up to twice as long and less glaucous beneath; flo. up to twice as large and up to 10 in a raceme (up to 4 in *V. oxycoccus*); fr. twice as large, red, edible. Bird-sown from gardens, etc., and naturalized on moors and heaths, chiefly N. England and Scotland. Flo. June–Aug.

Arbutus unedo L. **Strawberry Tree.** ¶Shrub 10–25 ft; leaves leathery, glabrous; flo. cream; fr. a warty berry. Native in S.W. Ireland. Flo. Sept.–Oct. ✿.

Arctostaphylos uva-ursi (L.) Spreng. **Bear Berry.** ¶Stem trailing; leaves thick, shining, evergreen; flo. pink-tipped; berry red. Common on stony moors in Scotland, N. England and W. Ireland. Flo. June. ✿.

Arctous alpinus (L.) Nied. **Alpine Bear Berry.** *Arctostaphylos alpinus* (L.) Spreng. ¶Stem trailing; leaves thin, wrinkled, not evergreen; flo. white; fr. black. On moors in N. Scotland. Flo. May. ✿.

Andromeda polifolia L. **Marsh Andromeda.** ¶Stem woody, prostrate below; leaves evergreen, glaucous beneath; fr. a subglobose capsule. Peat bogs, mid Scotland to mid England, mid Wales and Ireland. Flo. May–Sept. ✿.

*Gaultheria shallon Pursh. ¶Evergreen shrub, up to 3 ft, spreading by underground stems; leaves alternate, ovate, acute, toothed; flo. urceolate, ¼ in., pinkish, in panicles; berry ¼ in., black, hairy. Planted for pheasant cover and naturalized on sandy heaths and peaty bogs. Flo. May–June.

*Pernettya mucronata (L. f.) Gaudich. ex Spreng. ¶Erect evergreen shrub, up to 5 ft, stems freely suckering; leaves alternate, ovate, acute, mucronate, leathery, toothed; flo. campanulate, ¼ in., white, axillary, nodding; berry ½ in., white, pink, crimson, deep purple or black. Garden escape. Naturalized on heaths and banks, especially in Ireland. Flo. May–June.

Calluna vulgaris (L.) Hull. **Ling.** ¶Leaves minute, evergreen; calyx large, pink like corolla, with 4 ovate bracteoles. Common on moors and woodland banks. Flo. Aug.–Sept. ✿.

Erica ciliaris L. **Ciliate Heath.** ¶Leaves 3 in whorl, glandular, whi beneath; stamens included; anthers not awned. Local in Cornwa Devon and Dorset. Flo. Aug.–Sept. ✿.

Erica × watsonii Benth. (*R. ciliaris × tetralix*). ¶Intermediate betwee the parents, occurs commonly where they grow together.

Erica tetralix L. **Cross-leaved Heath.** ¶Leaves 4 in whorl, glandula margins revolute to midrib; anthers awned. Common on bogg heaths. Flo. July–Aug. ✿.

Erica mackaiana Bab. **Mackay's Heath.** ¶Leaves wider, marg revolute, glabrous above, white beneath; calyx glabrous exce apex; anthers awned. Wet moors in Galway and Donegal. Fl Aug.–Sept. ✿.

Erica × praegeri Ostenf. (*E. mackaiana × tetralix*). ¶Intermediate b tween the parents, sometimes occurs where they grow together.

Erica cinerea L. **Purple Heather, Fine-leaved Heath.** ¶Stem wit short leafy shoots; leaves 3 in whorl; stamens included; anthe awned. Common on dry heaths. Flo. July–Aug. ✿.

Erica vagans L. **Cornish Heath.** ¶Leaves 4–5 in whorl; flo. pal pedicels long; stamens exserted; anthers not awned. Abundant o Lizard Head, Cornwall, perhaps also native in Fermanagh. Fl Aug.–Sept. ✿.

Erica hibernica (Hook. & Arn.) Syme. **Irish Heath.** *E. mediterrane* auct. ¶Stem 3–5 ft; leaves 4–5 in whorl; flo. pale pinl; anthers exserted, not awned. On heaths in W. Ireland. Flo. April–May. ✿

Ledum palustre L. ¶Stem 2 ft; leaves brown felted beneath, marg revolute; pedicels glandular; flo. white, petals free. In bog Stirlingshire and W. Perthshire, introduced elsewhere. Fl June–July. ✿.

*Ledum groenlandicum Oeder. *L. latifolium* Jacq. ¶Similar to *l palustre* but leaves elliptic, more densely felted beneath; pedice slightly pubescent; capsule a little larger. Garden escape. Natura ized in bogs, etc., chiefly N. Britain, rare. Flo. June–July.

*Rhododendron ponticum L. ¶Large evergreen shrub; leaves elliptic t oblong; dark green; flo. large, widely campanulate, purpl flecked with brown. Naturalized in woods and on heaths on peat and sandy soils. Flo. May–June.

Phyllodoce caerulea (L.) Bab. **Scottish Menziesia.** *Bryanthus caerulea* (L.) Dippel. ¶Stem 5–6 in., hairy above; leaves evergreen, linea flo. purple. On a moorland in Perthshire. Flo. June–July. ✿.

Daboecia cantabrica (Huds.) C. Koch. **St Dabeoc's Heath.** *Boret cantabrica* (Huds.) Kuntz. ¶Stem 1–2 ft, glandular above; leave alternate, evergreen, white beneath; flo. rose-purple. On heath in Mayo and W. Galway. Flo. Aug. ✿.

Loiseleuria procumbens (L.) Desv. **Trailing Azalea.** *Azalea procumbe* L. ¶Procumbent cushion-like shrubs; leaves evergreen, leathery calyx reddish; corolla pink. On mountains in Scotland. Flo. May July. ✿ on plate 56.

EMPETRACEAE

Empetrum nigrum L. **Crowberry.** ¶Stem prostrate; leaves 3–4 time as long as broad; flo. mostly dioecious. On moors in Scotland, N and W. England to Devon. Flo. May–June. ✿.

Empetrum hermaphroditum Hagerup. ¶Stem not prostrate; leaves 2– times as long as broad; flo. hermaphrodite. On mountains, mostl in Scotland.

VACCINIUM
MYRTILLUS.

VACCINIUM
VITIS-IDAEA

VACCINIUM
ULIGINOSUM.

ARBUTUS
UNEDO.

E. MACKAIANA.

VACCINIUM
OXYCOCCUS   CRANBERRY.

×7

ANDROMEDA
OLIFOLIA.

ARCTOSTAPHYLOS
UVA-URSI.

ERICA
TETRALIX.

ERICA
VAGANS.

ERICA CILIARIS.

LEDUM
PALUSTRE.

×5

ERICA CINEREA.

DABOECIA
CANTABRICA.

HYLLODOCE
AERULEA.

MPETRUM NIGRUM.   ARCTOUS ALPINUS.

ERICA
MEDITERRANEA.   CALLUNA VULGARIS.

Plate 56   ✿ indicates plant is illustrated

PYROLACEAE

Pyrola rotundifolia L. **Large Wintergreen.**
Subsp. *rotundifolia* ¶Flo. White, ½ in. across; pedicels 4–6 mm.; calyx lobes triangular, lanceolate, acute; style 7–8 mm., curved; stigma with 5 small erect lobes. In fens and damp woods, on rock ledges, etc., local in mid Scotland; very rare in England, S. Wales and Ireland. Flo. July–Sept. ✿.
Subsp. *maritima* (Kenyon) E. F. Warb. ¶Similar to subsp. *rotundifolia*, but pedicels shorter; calyx lobes ovate; style smaller and more curved. On dune slacks in N. Wales and Lancashire, rare.

Pyrola media Sw. **Medium Wintergreen.** ¶Flo. pinkish white, ⅜ in. (10 mm.); style straight, with 5 lobes above a thick ring. In woods and moors, mostly N. England, Scotland and N. Ireland, very local. Flo. June–Aug. ✿.

Pyrola minor L. **Lesser Wintergreen.** ¶Flo. pink, globose, ¼ in.; style very short; stigma with 5 spreading lobes. In woods, moors and dunes, mostly in the N. half of Britain, local. Flo. June–Aug. ✿.

Orthilia secunda (L.) House. *Pyrola secunda* L. *Ramischia secunda* (L.) Garcke. ¶Flo. greenish white, secund; style exserted; stigma with 5 spreading lobes. Woods and damp rocks, Scotland, N. England, Wales and Ireland, very local except in N. Scotland. Flo. July–Aug. ✿.

Moneses uniflora (L.) A. Gray. **One-flowered Wintergreen.** *Pyrola uniflora* L. ¶Flo. solitary, white, drooping; disk large; stigma with 5 spreading lobes. Pine woods in Scotland, local and rare. Flo. June–Aug. ✿.

MONOTROPACEAE

Monotropa hypophegea Wallr. **Yellow Bird's-nest.** ¶Saprophyte, without green colour; flo. glabrous inside; fr. subglobose. The name means 'under beech wood', also on dunes mostly S. England, local. Flo. June–Aug.

Monotropa hypopitys L. ¶Similar saprophyte; flo. many, clothed inside with stiff hairs; fr. ovoid. The name means 'under pine wood', mostly S. England, local. Flo. June–Aug. ✿.
For other saprophytes—cf. plates 66 and 81.

PLUMBAGINACEAE

Limonium vulgare Mill. **Sea Lavender.** *Statice limonium* L. ¶Leaves large, pinnately veined; spikelets crowded; calyx lobes with teeth between them. In muddy salt marshes, locally common in S. and E. England, rather rare in Wales and the N. Flo. July–Sept. ✿.

Limonium humile Mill. **Lax-flowered Sea Lavender.** *Statice rariflora* Drej. ¶Leaves pinnately veined; flo. separated on branches; calyx lobes with teeth between them. In muddy salt marshes, rather local. Flo. July–Aug. ✿.

Limonium bellidifolium (Gouan) Dumort. ¶Leaves small, obovate, stems spreading with many barren branches; calyx without teeth between. Drier saltings, Norfolk and Suffolk, and formerly in Lincolnshire. Flo. July. ✿.

Limonium auriculae-ursifolium (Pourr.) Druce. *Statice lychnidifolia* Girard. ¶Plant robust; leaves large, obovate, glaucous, 5 veined; calyx without teeth between. On seaside rocks, Jersey and Alderney. Flo. June–Sept.

Limonium binervosum (G. E. Sm.) C. E. Salmon. **Rock Sea Lavender.** ¶Leaves obovate or oblanceolate, 3 veined below; calyx without teeth between; spikes in 2 rows. On sea cliffs, England and Wales. Flo. July–Sept. ✿.

Limonium recurvum C. E. Salmon. ¶Leaves obovate; petiole 3 veined; barren branches 0; spikes dense; calyx teeth shallow, blunt. On cliffs at Portland, very rare. Flo. July–Sept.

Limonium transwallianum (Pugsl.) Pugsl. ¶Leaves narrow, oblanceolate, 1 veined; flo. small, 4 mm.; calyx teeth deep; petals narrow blue. Sea cliffs, Pembrokeshire. Flo. July–Sept. ✿.

Limonium paradoxum Pugsl. ¶Branches short, erect, from near base; leaves 1 veined; flo. in small round heads. St David's Head, Wales and Donegal. Flo. July–Sept.

Armeria maritima (Mill.) Willd. **Thrift, Sea Pink.** *Statice armeria* L.
Subsp. *maritima*. ¶Leaves narrow, linear, 1 veined; calyx teeth acute or very shortly awned. Common on sea cliffs. Flo. March–Sept. ✿.
Var. *planifolia* Syme. ¶Leaves a little broader, often 3 veined. Scottish mountains.
Subsp. *elongata* (Hoffm.) Bonnier. ¶Leaves 4 in.: scape tall, 18 in. On heaths, around Grantham, Lincolnshire and Leicestershire.

Armeria arenaria (Pers.) Schult. **Jersey Thrift.** *A. plantaginea* Willd. ¶Leaves 3–5 veined, margin membranous; calyx teeth with long awns equal to ½ their length. On sand dunes in Jersey. Flo. June–July.

LOISELEURIA
PROCUMBENS.

PYROLA
MEDIA.

PYROLA
MINOR.

LIMONIUM
HUMILE.

×3

LIMONIUM
VULGARE.

×3

×3

×3

ORTHILIA
SECUNDA.

LIMONIUM BINERVOSUM.

LIMONIUM
TRANSWALLIANUM

MONOTROPA
HYPOPITYS.

ARMERIA
MARITIMA.

×1½

PYROLA
ROTUNDIFOLIA.

MONESES UNIFLORA.

LIMONIUM
BELLIDIFOLIUM.

×3

Plate 57   ✤ indicates plant is illustrated

DIAPENSIACEAE

Diapensia lapponica L. ¶Stems forming a mat; leaves mostly in rosette, nearly linear; flo. pale yellow. Hill-tops at 2600 ft in Inverness-shire, discovered in 1951. Flo. July. ✤.

PRIMULACEAE

Hottonia palustris L. **Water Violet.** ¶Stems and leaves submerged; pedicels glandular; flo. lilac with yellow eye; fr. globose. In ponds and ditches, mostly in E. England. Flo. May–June. ✤.

Primula vulgaris Huds. **Primrose.** ¶Scape short or 0; pedicels long; leaves narrowed gradually below; throat of corolla narrow. Common in woods and shady banks. Flo. Feb.–May. ✤.

Primula veris L. **Cowslip.** ¶Scape 8–10 in.; pedicels short; leaves abruptly narrowed below; flo. small. Locally common in meadows on basic and calcareous soils, but rare in Scotland and N. Ireland. Flo. April–May. ✤.

Primula veris × vulgaris. ¶This hybrid occurs with parent species. Variable and compared with *P. elatior* more hairy; flo. larger, yellower, with narrower throat.

Primula elatior (L.) Hill. **Oxlip.** ¶Leaves abruptly narrowed below; flo. facing one way; throat without folds, more open than in the hybrid. In woods on boulder clay, Essex, Hertfordshire, Bedfordshire, Huntingdonshire and E. Anglia. Flo. April–May. ✤.

Primula × media Petermann. (*P. elatior × veris*). ¶Intermediate between the parents, sometimes occurs where they grow together.

Primula × digenea Kerner (*P. elatior × vulgaris*). ¶A very variable hybrid; leaves usually intermediate between the parents; flo. similar to *P. vulgaris*, but usually paler yellow, and often with an orange eye; pedicels long, erect, pubescent; peduncle and calyx with long woolly hairs. Frequent where the parents grow together.

Primula farinosa L. **Bird's-eye Primrose.** ¶Leaves crenulate, mealy beneath; flo. petals not contiguous, lobes oblong, pale lilac, heterostylous. In damp meadows, N. England and S. Scotland. Flo. May–July. ✤.

Primula scotica Hook. ¶Leaves not crenulate, mealy beneath; pet contiguous, obcordate; red-purple styles all alike. In da meadows, N. Scotland. Flo. May–June. ✤.

*Cyclamen hederifolium Ait. *C. neapolitanum* Ten. ¶Root a cor leaves angled; peduncles erect and nodding in flo., coiled in corolla lobes reflexed. Locally naturalized, mostly in woods in England. Flo. Aug.–Sept. ✤.

Lysimachia thyrsiflora L. *Naumbergia thyrsiflora* (L.) Reichb. ¶St erect 2 ft; leaves glandular; flo. small, yellow; peduncles axilla at middle of stem. At edge of ponds and canals, mostly N. Engla S. Scotland. Flo. June. ✤.

Lysimachia vulgaris L. **Yellow Loosestrife.** ¶Rhizomes stout; st erect 3 ft; leaves glandular; flo. not glandular. In ditches, fens a riversides. Flo. July–Aug. ✤.

*Lysimachia punctata L. ¶Stem 2 ft; leaves ovate, margins cilia calyx and 1 in. corolla glandular, ciliate. Garden escape. Natur ized in wet places. Flo. July–Sept.

*Lysimachia ciliata L. ¶Stem 2 ft; leaves ovate-acuminate; peti ciliate; petals very glandular at base; spreading by rhizom Garden escape. Naturalized by streams, ditches, etc., and esta lished on waste ground. Flo. June–July. ✤.

*Lysimachia terrestris (L.) Britton, Sterns & Poggenb. ¶Stem ere bearing bulbils in axils of narrow leaves; flo. yellow and purple. shores of Lake Windermere.

Lysimachia nemorum L. **Yellow Pimpernel.** ¶Stems weak and pr trate; leaves ovate, glabrous; flo. pedicels slender. Common woods, especially on stiff soils. Flo. May–Sept. ✤.

Lysimachia nummularia L. **Creeping Jenny.** ¶Stems matted; lea suborbicular; gland dotted; flo. large; calyx ovate. On da grassy places, in wet woods, etc., local, but rare in Ireland an garden escape in S.W. England and N. Scotland.

Trientalis europaea L. **Chickweed Wintergreen.** ¶Rhizomes slend stem 8 in.; leaves mostly in whorl at top; flo. white. High moors a pine woods, mostly Scotland and N. England, very rare in Suffo Flo. June–July. ✤.

PRIMROSE.
PRIMULA VULGARIS

TTONIA
USTRIS.

OXLIP
PRIMULA
ELATIOR

PRIMULA
VERIS.
COWSLIP.

PRIMULA
SCOTICA

PRIMULA
FARINOSA

P VERIS x 4

DIAPENSIA
LAPPONICA.

LYSIMACHIA
THYRSIFLORA.

. x2

LYSIMACHIA
VULGARIS

TRIENTALIS
EUROPAEA.

CYCLAMEN
HEDERIFOLIUM.

LYSIMACHIA
NEMORUM

*LYSIMACHIA
CILIATA.

LYSIMACHIA
NUMMULARIA.

Plate 58 �֎ indicates plant is illustrated

PRIMULACEAE (*continued*)

Glaux maritima L. **Saltwort, Sea Milkwort.** ¶Stems trailing; flo. small, axillary, sessile; corolla o; calyx petaloid pink. On estuary mud and seaside rocks. Flo. June–Aug. ֎.

Anagallis arvensis L. **Scarlet Pimpernel.**
Subsp. *arvensis.* ¶Flo. petals overlapping, fringed with gland hairs, usually scarlet, rarely pink or blue; fr. pedicels longer than leaves. Common on cultivated and waste land, dunes, etc., but rare in mid and N. Scotland.
Subsp. *foemina* (Mill.) Schinz & Thell. ¶Petals obovate, not overlapping, glands few; fr. pedicels not longer than leaves. On cultivated land, S. England, rare. ֎.

Anagallis tenella (L.) L. **Bog Pimpernel.** ¶Stem prostrate; leaves nearly orbicular; flo. erect, funnel shaped, pink, On wet peaty heaths mostly in S. half of England, W. Scotland and W. Ireland. Flo. June–Aug. ֎.

Anagallis minima (L.) E. H. L. Krause. **Chaff Weed.** *Centunculus minimus* L. ¶Stem 1–3 in.; flo. sessile, axillary, minute, pinkish, chaff-like. On bare sandy ground, mostly S. England, W. Wales and W. Scotland. Flo. June–July. ֎.

Samolus valerandi L. **Brook Weed.** ¶Stem erect, 1 ft; leaves obtuse, glabrous; flo. white, pedicels bent. On wet ground, mostly near the sea, locally common, but very rare in E. Scotland. Flo. June–Aug. ֎.

OLEACEAE

Fraxinus excelsior L. **Ash.** ¶Tall tree; flo. in small racemes, without sepals or petals; stamens crimson; fr. winged. Native in woods, mostly on calcareous soils, but frequently planted elsewhere, and readily regenerating.

Ligustrum vulgare L. **Privet.** ¶Shrub, up to 10 ft; young shoots puberulous; leaves lanceolate; corolla limb equalling tube. Common on calcareous soils in S. England. Flo. June–July. ֎.
The commonly planted shrub with glabrous shoots, ovate leaves and longer corolla limb is *L. ovalifolium* Hassk.

BUDDLEJACEAE

*Buddleja davidii Franch. **Butterfly Bush.** ¶Shrub, up to 15 ft; branchlets downy; leaves lanceolate, acuminate, serrate, up to 1 ft long, green above, white felted below; flo. small, campanulate, lilac to deep purple with an orange eye, in dense long narrow drooping spikes, up to 1 ft long. The flowers are very attractive to butterflies. Garden escape. Naturalized in chalk pits, and established on waste ground, old walls, etc., mostly S. half of Britain and S. Ireland. Flo. June–Oct.

APOCYNACEAE

Vinca minor L. **Lesser Periwinkle.** ¶Stems rooting freely; leaves lanceolate, 1½ in.; calyx lobes glabrous; flo. 1 in., blue-mauve, solitary. In woods, local, fr. rarely found. Flo. March–May and autumn. ֎.

*Vinca major L. **Greater Periwinkle.**
Subsp. *major.* ¶Plant larger than *V. minor*; flo. stems not rootin leaves ovate, 2 in.; calyx lobes ciliate; flo. 2–3, 1½–2 in. wic blue-mauve. Garden escape. Naturalized in hedge banks, woo etc., mostly in S. half of Britain. Flo. April–June.
Subsp. *hirsuta* (Boiss.) Stearn. *Vinca herbacea* auct., non Waldst. Kit. ¶Similar to subsp. *major*, but leaves narrower, lanceolate; fl deep violet, with much narrower lobes. Garden escape. Natur ized in woods and plantations, etc., in Devon, Essex, Kent a Glamorgan.

GENTIANACEAE

Cicendia filiformis (L.) Delarb. **Yellow Gentianella.** *Microcala fi formis* (L.) Hoffmans. & Link. ¶Slender, erect, 1–4 in.; leav small; flo. small, ⅛ in., yellow. In sandy places, especially near t sea, S. England, W. and N. Wales and S.W. Ireland, rare. Fl Aug.–Sept. ֎.

Exaculum pusillum (Lam.) Caruel. *Cicendia pusilla* (Lam.) Grise ¶Stems several, short, slender; leaves linear; flo. small, ⅛ in., pin Sandy places in Guernsey, very rare. Flo. July–Sept. ֎.

Centaurium pulchellum (Sw.) Druce. **Lesser Centaury.** *Erytha pulchella* (Sw.) Fr. ¶Plant erect, without basal rosette; flo. ped celled, not clustered; lobes 3–4 mm., deep pink. Damp grass places on stiff soils, often near the sea in S. England. Flo. June Sept. ֎.

Centaurium tenuiflorum (Hoffmans. & Link) Fritsch.
¶Similar to *C. pulchellum* but branches more strict and erec Corolla tube constricted above petals narrower. I. of Wight an Dorset.

Centaurium erythraea Rafn. **Common Centaury.** *C. umbellatum* auc ¶Erect from basal rosette; flo. subsessile; clusters subumbellat stamens inserted at top of tube. Common in dry grassy plac wood borders, etc., especially on calcareous soil, also on dunes. Fl June–Oct. ֎.
Sometimes found, var. *subcapitatum* (Corb.) Gilmour, with dwa capitate growth rather resembling the following species, but wit stamens inserted at top of corolla tube. ֎.

Centaurium capitatum (Willd.) Borbás. **Tufted Centaury.** ¶Dwa plant branched from basal rosette; flo. capitate; stamens inserte at base of corolla tube. Dry calcareous downs near sea, mostly England and S. Wales, rare. Flo. July–Aug. ֎.

Centaurium littorale (D. Turner) Gilmour. **Sea Centaury.** ¶Erect fro rosette; leaves linear, basal spathulate; flo. few, sessile, lobes 6– mm. Sand dunes near the sea, mostly N. and N.W. coasts. Fl July–Aug. ֎.

Centaurium scilloides (L. f.) Samp. *C. portense* (Brot.) Butcher. ¶Stem decumbent, often barren; leaves obovate; flo. pedicelled; corol lobes 8–9 mm. Cliffs in Pembrokeshire and W. Cornwall. Fl July–Aug. ֎.

Blackstonia perfoliata (L.) Huds. **Yellow-wort.** *Chlora perfoliata* L ¶Erect, 1 ft; very glaucous; cauline leaves connate in pairs; fl bright yellow. On calcareous pastures and dunes, mostly Englan and Ireland. Flo. June–Oct. ֎.

ANAGALLIS ARVENSIS.

ANAGALLIS TENELLA.

ANAGALLIS FOEMINA.

ANAGALLIS MINIMA.

GLAUX MARITIMA.

LIGUSTRUM VULGARE.

SAMOLUS VALERANDI.

CENTAURIUM PULCHELLUM.

EXACULUM PUSILLUM.

ASH.

FRAXINUS EXCELSIOR.

VAR. SUBCAPITATUM.

CENTAURIUM ERYTHRAEA.

INDIA FORMIS.

BLACKSTONIA PERFOLIATA.

CENTAURIUM CAPITATUM.

CENTAURIUM LITTORALE.

PERIWINKLE. VINCA MINOR.

CENTAURIUM PORTENSE.

Plate 59 ✿ indicates plant is illustrated

GENTIANACEAE (*continued*)

Gentiana pneumonanthe L. **Marsh Gentian.** ¶Stems suberect, 1 ft; leaves linear; flo. large, 1¼–1½ in., blue, narrowed below. On wet heaths, mostly S. and E. England, very local. Flo. July–Sept. ✿.

Gentiana verna L. **Spring Gentian.** ¶Leaves ovate, in rosettes; flo. solitary, ¾ in., deep blue, lobes spreading; tube cylindric. In grassy places on limestone, N. England and W. Ireland. Flo. April–June. ✿.

Gentiana nivalis L. **Small Alpine Gentian.** ¶Annual; erect, 1–6 in.; leaves ¼ in.; flo. small, deep blue; tube cylindric. On rocks in Perthshire and Angus at about 3000 ft. Flo. July–Sept. ✿.

Gentianella campestris (L.) Börner. **Field Felwort.** *Gentiana campestris* auct. ¶Stem 2–8 in.; sepals 4, 2 outer larger overlapping inner; flo. purple. In meadows, on dunes, etc., chiefly on acid soils in Ireland, Scotland, N. England to Berkshire and Devon. Flo. July–Oct. ✿. Var. *baltica* (Murb.) H. Sm. *Gentiana baltica* auct. ¶Annual; stem subsimple; cotyledons persisting; is, now, no longer regarded as distinct. ✿.

Gentianella germanica (Willd.) Börner. **Scarce Autumn Felwort.** *Gentiana germanica* Willd. ¶Stem 6–10 in., branched; calyx lobes 5, lanceolate unequal; corolla 1 in., lilac, tapering below. Grassy places on calcareous soil, S. England, local. Flo. Aug.–Sept. ✿.

Gentianella amarella (L.) Börner. **Autumn Felwort.** *Gentiana amarella* L.
Subsp. *amarella*. ¶Stem 3–9 in., subsimple; stem leaves ovate-lanceolate; calyx lobes 5 subequal; corolla ½–¾ in., cylindric, purple. On pastures and downs on calcareous soil, dunes, chiefly in England, Wales N. and E. Scotland. Flo. Aug.–Oct. ✿.
Subsp. *hibernica* Pritchard. ¶Similar to subsp. *amarella*, but basal leaves usually linear-lanceolate; corolla slightly larger, dull purple, rarely pale blue or white. In pastures on calcareous soil, Ireland. Flo. Aug.–Oct.
Subsp. *septentrionalis* (Druce) Pritchard. **Northern Felwort.** *Gentianella septentrionalis* (Druce) E. F. Warb., *Gentiana septentrionalis* (Druce) Druce. ¶Annual; 2–3 in.; calyx lobes unequal; corolla creamy white suffused with purplish red outside, whitish within. Dunes by the sea and limestone meadows near the sea, Scotland. Flo. July–Aug.
Subsp. *druceana* Pritchard. ¶Similar to subsp. *amarella* and subsp. *septentrionalis*, but middle and upper stem leaves ovate-lanceolate to lanceolate; flo. colour and shape similar to subsp. *septentrionalis*. Shell-sand dune slacks and limestone pastures, mid and N. Scotland, local. Flo. Aug.–Oct.

Gentianella × pamplinii (Druce) E. F. Warb. (*Gentianella amarella × germanica*) *Gentiana × pamplinii* Druce. ¶Intermediate between the parents and occurs rarely where they grow together.

Gentianella amarella × uliginosa. ¶Intermediate between the parents often occurs where they grow together.

Gentianella anglica (Pugsl.) E. F. Warb. **Dwarf English Felwo** *Gentiana anglica* Pugsl.
Subsp. *anglica*. ¶2–4 in., branched from base; basal leaves narrow spathulate, obtuse; stem leaves lanceolate, acute; corolla ½ long, about 1½ times as long as calyx teeth; calyx teeth unequ Chalk grassland from Devon to Lincolnshire, local. Flo. Apr June. ✿.
Subsp. *cornubiensis* Pritchard. ¶Similar to subsp. *anglica*, but sligh smaller; basal leaves broadly spathulate; stem leaves linear linear-lanceolate, obtuse; corolla slightly larger; calyx teeth su equal. Sea cliffs, W. Cornwall, local. Flo. March–June.

Gentianella uliginosa (Willd.) Börner. **Dune Felwort.** *Genti uliginosa* Willd. ¶Annual; 3–4 in.; often branched from ba cotyledons persisting; calyx lobes unequal; leaves lanceolate; l 4–5-merous. Sand dunes, S. Wales. July–Oct.

Menyanthes trifoliata L. **Bogbean.** ¶Aquatic; leaves large, tri-foli and flo. pale pink, fimbriate, both held above water. Common watery bogs. Flo. May–July. ✿.

Nymphoides peltata (S. G. Gmel) Kuntze. *Limnanthemum peltatum* S. Gmel. ¶Leaves orbicular, floating; petioles long; flo. yelle fringed, fimbriate at base. In slow streams and ponds, mainly England, local. Flo. July–Aug. ✿.

POLEMONIACEAE

Polemonium caeruleum L. **Jacob's Ladder.** ¶2–3 ft; leaves pinna lower petioles winged; flo. deep blue; filaments hairy below. woods and by streams, N. half of England, occurs elsewhere a naturalized garden escape. Flo. June–July. ✿.

BORAGINACEAE

Cynoglossum officinale L. **Hound's Tongue.** ¶Stem woody; lea softly hairy; fr. with hooked bristles and thickened bord Downs, wood borders, etc., on dry soils, especially near the s mainly in the S. half of Britain. Flo. June–Aug. ✿.

Cynoglossum germanicum Jacq. **Green Hound's Tongue.** *C. montan* auct. ¶Stem slender, green; leaves subglabrous above; fr. bris without a thickened border. Shady places in mid S. and England, rare. Flo. May–July. ✿.

Omphalodes verna Moench. ¶Stoloniferous perennial; stem pubesce up to 6 in.; basal leaves cordate; stem leaves broadly lanceolate ovate; flo. sky-blue, ½ in. across, similar to a large forget-me-n but throat closed by obtuse scales, in few-flowered cymes on stems; calyx 5-toothed, hairy; nutlets smooth with ciliate margi Garden escape. Naturalized in hedge banks and woods. F March–May.

Asperugo procumbens L. **Madwort.** ¶Stems procumbent and brist leaves oblong, hispid; flo. small, axillary, becoming blue. Int duced, in fields and waste places, rare. Flo. May–July.

GENTIANA NIVALIS.

GENTIANELLA AMARELLA.

GENTIANELLA GERMANICA

×4

GENTIANELLA CAMPESTRIS

GENTIANA VERNA.

GENTIANA PNEUMONANTHE.

GENTIANELLA CAMPESTRIS VAR. BALTICA.

GENTIANELLA ANGLICA.

×2

NYANTHES TRIFOLIATA

OG BEAN

CYNOGLOSSUM OFFICINALE.

CYNOGLOSSUM GERMANICUM.

JACOB'S LADDER

POLEMONIUM COERULEUM.

NYMPHOIDES PELTATA.

BORAGINACEAE (continued)

Symphytum officinale L. **Comfrey.** ¶Stem winged with decurrent leaves; calyx teeth twice as long as tube; flo. cream or purple. Common by rivers and canals. Flo. May–June. ❊.

*\ *Symphytum asperum* Lepech. **Rough Comfrey.** ¶Stems covered with short hooked bristles; upper leaves shortly stalked; flo. becoming blue. Garden escape. Established in waste places, rare. Flo. June–July. ❊.

*\ *Symphytum × uplandicum* Nyman (*S. asperum × officinale*). **Blue Comfrey.** *S. peregrinum* auct. ¶Stem tall, branched, bristly, not winged; calyx teeth acuminate, twice length of tube; flo. blue. Naturalized in rough grassy places in waste places, by roadsides, etc. Flo. June–Aug.

*\ *Symphytum orientale* L. ¶Leaves ovate, softly pubescent, petioled; calyx teeth obtuse, ½ length of tube; flo. white. Garden escape. Naturalized in grassy places, by roadsides, etc., mainly S. England. Flo. April–May.

*\ *Symphytum caucasicum* Bieb. ¶Stems rough, hairy, angular, 1½–2 ft; leaves ovate-lanceolate, acuminate, slightly decurrent, softly hairy above, grey felted beneath; flo. blue, campanulate, in terminal twin racemes; calyx teeth obtuse, hispid. Garden escape. Naturalized in woods and plantations. Flo. May–June.

Symphytum tuberosum L. **Tuberous Comfrey.** ¶Root tuberous; stems 1–1½ ft; calyx teeth acute, 3 times length of tube; flo. cream. In woods, mainly N. England and Scotland, introduced elsewhere. Flo. June–July. ❊.

*\ *Symphytum grandiflorum* DC. ¶Similar to *S. tuberosum* but with slender rhizomes and smaller leaves; calyx deeply divided; teeth linear-lanceolate, obtuse; flo. cream or yellowish white. Garden escape. Naturalized in woods and hedge banks, chiefly S. England and Midlands. Flo. April–May.

*\ *Borago officinalis* L. **Borage.** ¶Leaves large, ovate, hispid; flo. ¾ in., deep blue; anthers exserted, black. Garden escape. Established on waste ground, etc. Flo. June–July.

*\ *Pentaglottis sempervirens* (L.) Tausch. **Alkanet.** *Anchusa sempervirens* L. ¶Leaves broad, ovate, hispid; peduncles axillary, forked; flo. bright blue. Garden escape. Naturalized in woods, grassy places, by roadsides, etc., widespread. Flo. May–Aug. ❊.

*\ *Trachystemon orientalis* (L.) G. Don. ¶Stem hispid, thick, up to 1 ft; radical leaves ovate, long stalked; flo. bluish violet, similar to those of *Borago officinalis*, but smaller with a longer corolla tube. Garden escape. Naturalized in hedge banks and woods, mainly S. England, rare. Flo. March–May.

Lycopsis arvensis L. **Lesser Bugloss.** ¶Leaves oblong, hispid with tuberous hairs; inflo. forked; flo. bright blue; corolla tube with double bend. Arable land, cornfields, etc., chiefly on light soils, especially near the sea, widespread but very rare in W. Ireland. Flo. June–July. ❊.

Pulmonaria longifolia (Bast.) Bor. **Narrow-leaved Lungwort.** *P. angustifolia* auct., non L. ¶Leaves narrow, lanceolate, not always blotched; flo. pink then bright blue. In woods on cl soil in Hampshire, Dorset and I. of Wight, rare. Flo. April–June.

*\ *Pulmonaria officinalis* L. **Lungwort.** ¶Leaves broadly ovate, alwa with pale blotches; flo. pale purple. Garden escape. Naturaliz in woods, chiefly in S. half of Britain, rare. Flo. April–May. ❊

Mertensia maritima (L.) Gray. **Northern Shore-wort.** ¶Ste procumbent; leaves fleshy, glaucous, rough with hard poin flo. pink becoming bluish. On northern sea-shores. Flo. Jun July. ❊.

Myosotis scorpioides L. **Water Forget-me-not.** *M. palustris* (I Hill. ¶Cyme not bracteate; calyx hairs appressed; teeth sho triangular; flo. ¼ in., style equalling calyx tube. Common ponds and streams. Flo. May–Oct. ❊.

Myosotis secunda A. Murr. **Marsh Forget-me-not.** *M. repens* au ¶Stoloniferous; cyme bracteate; calyx hairs appressed; teeth calyx length; fr. pedicels long, 3–5 times calyx. Wet places heaths, etc., particularly on peaty soils, widespread, but ve rare in E. Anglia. Flo. May–Aug. ❊.

Myosotis stolonifera Gay. **Short-leaved Forget-me-not.** *M. bre folia* C. E. Salmon. ¶Leaf length not exceeding twice its breadt bluish green; calyx teeth obtuse; flo. paler. Wet hilly places, England, S. Scotland. Flo. June–Aug. ❊.

Myosotis caespitosa K. F. Schultz. **Lesser Water Forget-me-no** ¶Stems, leaves and calyx with appressed hairs; cyme bractea flo. small, ⅛ in.; style short, ½ calyx tube. Common in wate places. Flo. May–Aug. ❊.

Myosotis sicula Guss. **Jersey Forget-me-not.** ¶Stem 2–6 i subglabrous below; calyx subglabrous; teeth oblong, obtuse, length of calyx. On dunes in Jersey, rare. Flo. April–June.

Myosotis alpestris Schmidt. **Alpine Forget-me-not.** ¶Stem a leaves with spreading hairs; flo. large, ¼ in.; calyx with spreadi and few hooked hairs. Mountain rocks, Teesdale and Perthshi rare. Flo. July–Aug. ❊.

Myosotis sylvatica Hoffm. **Wood Forget-me-not.** ¶Stems and leav with spreading hairs; calyx ¾ cleft, with straight and hooked hair flo. ¼–⅜ in. In woods except S.W. England, S. Wales, N. Scotla and Ireland, occurs also in grassy places, etc., as a naturaliz garden escape. Flo. May–July. ❊.

Myosotis arvensis (L.) Hill. **Common Forget-me-not.** ¶Stem a leaves with spreading hairs; calyx with many hooked hairs; fl ⅛–³⁄₁₆ in.; style short. Woods, cultivated lands, dunes, etc., commo and widespread. Flo. April–Sept. ❊.

Myosotis discolor Pers. **Yellow Forget-me-not.** *M. versicolor* Sr ¶Inflo. in fr. not much longer than leafy stem; calyx closed in fr flo. yellow becoming blue. Grassy places on light soils, widesprea Flo. May–June. ❊.

Myosotis ramosissima Rochel. **Early Forget-me-not.** *M. hispi* Schlecht., *M. collina* auct. ¶Inflo. in fr. much longer than lea stem; calyx open in fr.; flo. bright blue. Common on dry ban and wall tops, mainly S. half of Britain. Flo. April–June. ❊.

SYMPHYTUM
TUBEROSUM.

S ASPERUM.

PULMONARIA
OFFICINALIS.

SYMPHYTUM
OFFICINALE.

PENTAGLOTTIS
SEMPERVIRENS.

PULMONARIA
LONGIFOLIA.

MERTENSIA
MARITIMA

LYCOPSIS
ARVENSIS.

MYOSOTIS
ALPESTRIS.

MYOSOTIS
CAESPITOSA.

MYOSOTIS HISPIDA.

MYOSOTIS
SCORPIOIDES

MYOSOTIS
BREVIFOLIA.

MYOSOTIS SECUNDA.

MYOSOTIS
ARVENSIS.

MYOSOTIS
DISCOLOR.

MYOSOTIS
SYLVATICA.

Plate 61   ✿ indicates plant is illustrated

BORAGINACEAE (continued)

Lithospermum purpurocaeruleum L. **Blue Gromwell.** ¶Stems long, creeping and trailing, flo. portion erect, forked, supported by shrubs; flo. deep blue. Thickets on chalk and limestone, mostly S.W. England and S. Wales, rare, occurs elsewhere as a garden escape. Flo. May–July. ✿.

Lithospermum officinale L. **Gromwell.** ¶Perennial; 1½ ft; leaves acute, lateral nerves obvious; nutlets smooth and white. Bushy places, mostly on calcareous soil. Flo. June–July. ✿.

Lithospermum arvense L. **Corn Gromwell.** ¶Annual; 1 ft; leaves obtuse, lateral nerves obscure; nutlets rugose, grey or brownish. Locally common on cultivated land in S. and E. England, rare elsewhere. Flo. May–July. ✿.

Echium vulgare L. **Viper's Bugloss.** ¶Upper leaves rounded at base; lower with no obvious lateral veins; flo. blue, 4 stamens exserted. Calcareous downs, dry pastures, dunes, sea cliffs, etc., widespread in England and Wales, local in Scotland and Ireland. Flo. June–Aug. ✿.

Echium lycopsis L. **Purple Bugloss.** *E. plantagineum* L. ¶Upper leaves cordate at base; lower with obvious lateral veins; flo. purple, 2 stamens exserted. Sea cliffs and dunes. Cornwall and Jersey, occurs elsewhere as a garden escape. Flo. June–Aug.

CONVOLVULACEAE

Calystegia sepium (L.) R. Br. **Bindweed.**
Subsp. *sepium*. ¶Stems long, glabrous, climbing; flo. white, rarely pink (f. *colorata* Lange); flo. bracts ½ in. long, cordate, not inflated. On hedges, in marshes, ditches and gardens, etc., widespread, but less common in Scotland. Flo. June–Aug. ✿.
Subsp. *roseata* Brummitt. ¶Stems usually hairy; leaf apex often more attenuate; flo. pink. On hedges, in marshes and ditches in coastal and subcoastal areas in the west from Cornwall to mid Scotland. Flo. June–Aug.

Calystegia × *lucana* (Ten.) G. Don. (*C. sepium* × *silvatica*). ¶Intermediate between the two parents and often frequent where they grow together, especially in S. England and Midlands.

Calystegia pulchra Brummitt & Heywood. *C. dahurica* auct., non (Herbert) G. Don. ¶Stems long, climbing; peduncles hairy; bracteoles slightly inflated; flo. bright pink, usually with white bands on the throat, intermediate in size between *C. sepium* and *C. silvatica*. Garden escape. Naturalized in hedge banks and thickets, etc., usually near habitation, rather common. Flo. June–Aug.

Calystegia silvatica (Kit.) Griseb. **Great Bindweed.** *C. sylvestris* (Willd.) Roem. & Schult. ¶Stems very long, climbing; flo. bracts 1 in. long, triangular, inflated. Garden escape. Naturalized in hedges and thickets and established on waste ground, widespread. Flo. June–Aug.

Calystegia soldanella (L.) R. Br. **Sea Bindweed.** ¶Stem short, 6–12 in., procumbent; leaves reniform; flo. bracts ½ in.; flo. pink. On sandy sea-shores, widespread, but rare in Scotland. Flo. June–Aug. ✿.

Convolvulus arvensis L. **Lesser Bindweed.** ¶Stem climbing; flo bracts very small, low in peduncle; flo. 1 in., pink and white. Common in cultivated soil, but rare in N. Scotland. Flo. June–Aug. ✿.

Cuscuta europaea L. **Greater Dodder.** ¶Parasitic, string-like, climbing; heads ½–¾ in.; corolla scales small; styles shorter than ovary. On nettles and hops, S. England, rare. Flo. July–Sept. ✿.

Cuscuta epithymum (L.) L. **Lesser Dodder.** ¶Parasitic, thread-like, red; heads smaller, pink; corolla scales nearly closing tube; styles longer than ovary. On heather and gorse (sometimes white flo. on clover, *Lotus*, etc.), chiefly S. and E. England. Flo. July–Sept. ✿.

SOLANACEAE

Solanum dulcamara L. **Woody Nightshade.** ¶Perennial; shrubby; leaves cordate, upper hastate; flo. ½ in., blue-purple; berry scarlet. Common in hedgerows, copses and marshes, but local in Scotland. Flo. June–Aug. ✿.

Solanum nigrum L. **Black Nightshade.** ¶Annual; stem herbaceous, angled; leaves ovate; flo. ¼ in., white; berry black. On sea cliffs and cultivated land in England and Wales, introduced in Scotland and Ireland. Flo. July–Sept. ✿.

Lycium barbarum L. *L. halimifolium* Mill. ¶Stem with a few straight spines; leaves lanceolate, grey-green; petals short. Garden escape. Naturalized in hedges and thickets and established on waste ground. Flo. June–Aug.

Lycium chinense Mill. **Duke of Argyle's Tea-tree.** *L. barbarum* auct. ¶Usually without spines; leaves a little wider, bright green; corolla lobes equalling tube. Garden escape. Naturalized in hedges, etc., especially near the sea. Flo. Aug.–Oct. ✿.

Atropa bella-donna L. **Deadly Nightshade.** ¶Stem 3 ft; leaves in unequal pairs; flo. dull purple; berries black; very poisonous. Native in woods and thickets on calcareous soil in England and Wales; elsewhere on waste ground, etc., as an introduction. Flo. June–Aug. ✿.

Datura stramonium L. **Thorn-apple.** ¶Leaves very broad, coarsely toothed; flo. erect, 2 in., funnel shaped, white; fr. covered with spines, very poisonous. Introduced. Flo. June–July.

Hyoscyamus niger L. **Henbane.** ¶Stem 2 ft; leaves downy; flo. with many dark purple veins; fr. enclosed in calyx. In sandy waste places especially near the sea, chiefly in the S. half of Britain. Flo. May–Aug. ✿.

Physalis alkekengi L. **Winter Cherry.** ¶Perennial with a creeping root; stem pubescent, 1–1½ ft; leaves in pairs, entire, variable in shape from ovate-acute to ovate-deltoid, acuminate, on long stems; flo. rotate, dirty white, solitary, axillary; calyx ovate, inflated reddish yellow, enclosing the orange-red berry which resembles a small cherry. Garden escape. Established on waste ground. Flo. June–Aug.

LITHOSPERMUM
PURPURO-
CAERULEUM.

LITHOSPERMUM
OFFICINALE.

LITHOSPERMUM
ARVENSE.

ECHIUM
VULGARE.

CALYSTEGIA
SEPIUM.

CUSCUTA
EPITHYMUM.

CUSCUTA
EUROPAEA.

CONVOLVULUS
ARVENSIS.

CALYSTEGIA SOLDANELLA

SOLANUM
DULCAMARA.

SOLANUM
NIGRUM.

LYCIUM CHINENSE.

ATROPA BELLA-DONNA.

HYOSCYAMUS NIGER

Plate 62   ✿ indicates plant is illustrated

SCROPHULARIACEAE

Verbascum thapsus L. **Common Mullein.** ¶Leaves decurrent, clothed with soft wool; sepals ovate, upper filaments with white hairs, lower subglabrous. Common on dry soil, chiefly in England and Wales, mostly casual in Scotland and Ireland. Flo. June–Aug. ✿.

**Verbascum thapsiforme* Schrad. ¶Similar to *V. thapsus*, but corolla larger, and flat; filaments shorter with decurrent anthers. Naturalized on banks, etc., rare. Flo. June–Aug.

**Verbascum phlomoides* L. ¶Similar to *V. thapsiforme*, but leaves non-decurrent. Garden escape. Established on waste ground, chiefly in S. England. Flo. June–Aug.

Verbascum pulverulentum Vill. **Hoary Mullein.** ¶Leaves not decurrent, clothed with mealy white wool; sepals lanceolate; all filaments with white hairs. Norfolk and Suffolk, introduced elsewhere. Flo. July–Aug. ✿.

**Verbascum speciosum* Schrad. ¶Plant clothed with thick white wool; corolla yellow, larger than in *V. pulverulentum*; sepals lanceolate; all filaments with white hairs. Introduced. Naturalized on banks, waste ground, etc. Flo. July–Aug.

Verbascum lychnitis L. **White Mullein.** ¶Leaves green above, white woolly beneath; sepals linear; all filaments with white hairs; flo. white or yellow. Calcareous banks and quarries, chiefly in S. England. Flo. July–Aug. ✿.

Verbascum nigrum L. **Dark Mullein.** ¶Leaves dark green above, pubescent beneath; filaments with purple hairs. Calcareous banks, chiefly in S. England, rare in Wales, and introduced in Scotland and Ireland. Flo. June–Sept. ✿.

**Verbascum chaixii* Vill. Similar to *V. nigrum*, but leaves rounded at base; flo. 2–4 in axils of branches. Established on waste ground, etc. Rare.

Verbascum virgatum Stokes. **Slender Mullein.** ¶Stem and leaves green but glandular; flo. large, clustered in axils; subsessile filaments with purple hairs. Native in Cornwall and Devon, introduced elsewhere. Flo. June–Sept. ✿.

Verbascum blattaria L. **Moth Mullein.** ¶Plant green, glandular above; flo. solitary, axillary, pedicelled; filaments with purple hairs. In waste places, chiefly S. and E. England. Flo. June–Sept.

The following hybrids have been noted in Britain:
Verbascum lychnitis × thapsus = V. × thapsi L.; *V. lychnitis × pulverulentum = V. × regelianum* Wirtg.; *V. lychnitis × nigrum = V. × schiedeanum* Koch; *V. pulverulentum × thapsus = V. × godronii* Bor.; *V. nigrum × thapsus = V. × semialbum* Chaub.; *V. nigrum × pulverulentum = V. × wirtgenii* Franch.

Cymbalaria muralis* Gaertn., Mey. & Scherb. **Ivy-leaved Toadflax. *Linaria cymbalaria* (L.) Mill. ¶Stems weak, trailing; leaves 5 lobed, glabrous; flo. mauve, lip white and yellow. Introduced, comm on old walls. Flo. May–Sept. ✿.

Kickxia elatine (L.) Dumort. **Fluellen.** *Linaria elatine* (L.) Mill. ¶St prostrate; leaves with basal lobes; pedicels glabrous; flo. sp straight. Cornfields and arable land in England and Wales, ra in Ireland. Flo. July–Oct. ✿.

Kickxia spuria (L.) Dumort. **Round-leaved Fluellen.** *Linaria spu* (L.) Mill. ¶Stem prostrate; leaves ovate or orbicular; pedic hairy; flo. spur curved. Cornfields and arable land in mid, S. a E. England, very rare in Wales, and casual elsewhere. Flo. Ju Oct. ✿.

Chaenorhinum minus (L.) Lange. **Small Toadflax.** *Linaria minor* (Desf. ¶Stem erect, 6 in., glandular; flo. solitary, axillary, mauv spur short. On cultivated land, railways, in chalk pits, rath common, but rare in Scotland. Flo. May–Sept. ✿.

Linaria pelisseriana (L.) Mill. **Jersey Toadflax.** ¶Stem ere $\frac{1}{2}$–1 ft; flo. few, violet with white lip; spur long and straig On heaths in Jersey. Flo. May–July.

*Linaria purpurea (L.) Mill. **Purple Toadflax.** ¶Perennial; ere 2–3 ft; flo. dense, violet; spur long and curved. Introduce rather common on old walls, waste ground, etc. Flo. June–Sept. ✿

Linaria repens (L.) Mill. **Pale Toadflax.** ¶Stem from rhizome ere 1–2 ft; flo. pale mauve with purple veins; spur short. On stony calcareous land, railway tracks, local. Flo. June–Sept. ✿.

Linaria repens × vulgaris = L. × sepium Allman. ¶Flo. yellowish, strip with purple; foliage intermediate between the parents; variabl Sometimes occurs where the parents grow together.

Linaria vulgaris Mill. **Common Toadflax.** ¶Stem from rhizom erect, 2 ft; leaves linear, rarely lanceolate; flo. large, yellow, l orange. Common in England, Wales and S. Scotland, local N. Scotland and Ireland. Flo. July–Oct. ✿.

*Linaria supina (L.) Chazelles. ¶Stem glaucous; branches prostra and ascending; flo. $\frac{1}{2}$ in., few, close, yellow with orange li Sandy places near Par, Cornwall and Plymouth. Flo. June–Sep

*Linaria arenaria DC. **Sand Toadflax.** ¶Stems 4–6 in., mu branched, sticky with glands; flo. small, bright yellow; spt slender. Naturalized on sand dunes, N. Devon. Flo. May Sept. ✿.

Antirrhinum majus* L. **Snapdragon. ¶Bracts short, ovate; caly lobes ovate, much shorter than corolla. Plentifully naturalize on old walls and rock cuttings. Flo. July–Sept.

Misopates orontium (L.) Raf. **Weasel's Snout.** *Antirrhinum orontium* ¶Bracts linear; calyx lobes long, linear, equalling pink coroll On cultivated land, mostly in S. and E. England and Wales. Fl July–Sept. ✿.

VERBASCUM NIGRUM

V. PULVERULENTUM

*LINARIA
PURPUREA

KICKXIA
SPURIA × 4

LINARIA
VULGARIS.

ERBASCUM
THAPSUS

K. SPURIA

KICKXIA
ELATINE.

*CYMBALARIA
MURALIS.

VERBASCUM VIRGATUM

VERBASCUM
LYCHNITIS.

LINARIA
REPENS

CHAENORHINUM
MINUS.

*LINARIA
ARENARIA.

MISOPATES
ORONTIUM.

Plate 63   ❀ indicates plant is illustrated

SCROPHULARIACEAE (continued)

Scrophularia auriculata L. **Water Figwort.** *S. aquatica* auct. ¶Stems narrowly 4 winged; leaves crenate; bracts small; staminode orbicular. Common by ponds and wet ditches in England, local in Wales and Ireland, rare in Scotland. Flo. June–Sept. ❀.

Scrophularia umbrosa Dumort. **Scarce Water Figwort.** *S. ehrhartii* Stevens., *S. alata* Gilib. ¶Stem broadly 4 winged; leaves serrate; bracts leafy; flo. fewer; staminode 2 lobed. In wet shady places, rare. Flo. July–Sept. ❀.

Scrophularia nodosa L. **Figwort.** ¶Root knobbed; stem 4 angled, not winged; leaves coarsely serrate at base. Common in woods and hedge banks. Flo. June–Sept. ❀.

Scrophularia scorodonia L. **Balm-leaved Figwort.** ¶Stem and leaves pubescent; leaves very rugose, doubly serrate; teeth mucronate. In Cornwall, S. Devon and Channel Islands. Flo. June–Aug. ❀.

*Scrophularia vernalis L. **Yellow Figwort.** ¶Glandular, hairy; sepals subacute, without a border; flo. greenish yellow; staminode 0. Naturalized in a few shady places. Flo. April–June.

*Mimulus guttatus DC. **Monkey Flower.** ¶Glabrous excepting pubescent calyx; flo. yellow with red spots; lower lip much the longest. Garden escape. Naturalized by streams in many places. Flo. June–Aug. ❀.

*Mimulus luteus L. **Blotched Monkey Flower.** ¶Glabrous throughout; flo. with large red blotches; lower lip but little longer than upper. Garden escape. In similar places, mainly northern. Flo. June–Sept.

*Mimulus moschatus Dougl. ex Lindl. **Musk.** ¶Plant glandular, hairy; formerly fragrant; calyx teeth subequal; flo. $\frac{1}{4}-\frac{1}{2}$ in., yellow. Garden escape. Naturalized by sides of streams, etc. Flo. July–Aug.

Limosella aquatica L. **Mudwort.** ¶Leaves spathulate; calyx longer than corolla tube; corolla white or mauve; lobes triangular. On mud at margin of pools, rare and decreasing. Flo. June–Oct. ❀.

Limosella subulata Ives. ¶Leaves all subulate; calyx short; corolla white with longer orange tube; lobes ovate. In Wales at margin of pools, very rare. Flo. June–Oct.

Sibthorpia europaea L. **Cornish Moneywort.** ¶Very slender; stems and leaves hairy; upper lobes of corolla yellowish, lower pink. On shady stream banks, very rare in S. England, and local in S.W. England and Wales. Flo. July–Oct. ❀.

Digitalis purpurea L. **Foxglove.** ¶Stems 3–6 ft; leaves 6–12 in.; flo.
pink-purple, pollinated by humble bees. Common in wood land clearings and heaths. Flo. July–Sept. ❀.

*Erinus alpinus L. ¶Perennial; plant small, tufted; stems man leaves obovate, the basal ones forming a rosette; corolla slende tubular, purple; capsule ovoid. Garden escape. Naturalized rocky woods and established on old walls, particularly in England and Scotland. Flo. April–Oct.

*Veronica filiformis Sm. **Round-leaved Speedwell.** ¶Stems slende creeping; leaves suborbicular, pubescent; pedicels long; flo. blu Garden escape, spreading without setting fr. Locally abundant meadows, by streams, also as a pest of lawns in many places. Fl Mar.–May. ❀.

Veronica hederifolia L. **Ivy-leaved Speedwell.** ¶Stems decumber hairy; leaves with basal lobes; sepals cordate; flo. small, lila Common on hedge banks, cultivated ground, by streamsides an as a garden weed. Flo. March–May. ❀.

Veronica polita Fr. **Grey Speedwell.** ¶Leaves grey-green, pubescen equalling pedicels; sepals ovate; capsule lobes erect. Common cultivated ground. Flo. March–Nov. ❀.

Veronica agrestis L. **Field Speedwell.** ¶Leaves yellow-green; sepa oblong, spreading beside capsule lobes; flo. blue and white pink. In cultivated land, less common. Flo. March–Nov. ❀.

*Veronica persica Poir. **Persian Speedwell.** *V. buxbaumii* Te ¶Leaves bright green; flo. large; pedicels long; capsule lob divergent, keeled. An old introduction, now the commone species. Flo. all months. ❀.

*Veronica praecox All. ¶Stem erect; leaves conspicuously dentat pedicels not twice as long as calyx; fr. longer than broad. Chief in sandy fields in E. Anglia. Flo.

Veronica triphyllos L. **Fingered Speedwell.** ¶Leaves with 3–7 finge like lobes; sepals spathulate; flo. deep blue. On sandy field chiefly in E. Anglia. Flo. April–June. ❀.

Veronica verna L. **Spring Speedwell.** ¶Stems erect, 2–4 in.; leav pinnate, 3–7 lobed; sepals linear-lanceolate, unequal; fl lilac, small. Dry pastures, Norfolk and Suffolk, rare. Flo. Ma June. ❀.

*Veronica peregrina L. **American Speedwell.** ¶Erect, 2–8 in. leaves ovate, subentire; bracts longer than blue flo.; style almo wanting. Cultivated land in Scotland, N.W. Ireland, and else where. Flo. April–July.

*Veronica repens Clarion ex DC. **Corsican Speedwell.** ¶Stem creeping; leaves broadly ovate, subentire; flo. few, 3–6, pink pedicels longer than bracts. Garden escape. N. England. Fl April–May.

SCROPHULARIA
UMBROSA.

SCROPHULARIA
NODOSA.

SCROPHULARIA
SCORODONIA.

SCROPHULARIA
AQUATICA.

MIMULUS GUTTATUS.

X 10

SIBTHORPIA EUROPAEA.

LIMOSELLA
AQUATICA.

VERONICA
HEDERIFOLIA.

VERONICA
TRIPHYLLOS.

V. PERSICA.

DIGITALIS
PURPUREA.

VERONICA
POLITA.

VERONICA
AGRESTIS.

V FILIFORMIS.

VERONICA VERNA.

Plate 64   ❀ indicates plant is illustrated

SCROPHULARIACEAE (continued)

Veronica arvensis L. **Wall Speedwell.** ¶Leaves ovate, pubescent; bracts mostly leaf-like; spike elongating; flo. bright blue. Common on dry soils, banks and walls. Flo. March–Sept. ❀.

Veronica serpyllifolia L. **Thyme-leaved Speedwell.**
Subsp. *serpyllifolia*. ¶Stem creeping; leaves ovate, glabrous; spike erect; flo. whitish; fr. shorter than calyx. Common on cultivated land and heaths. Flo. March–Oct. ❀.
Subsp. *humifusa* (Dickson) Syme. ¶Leaves suborbicular; inflo. glandular; flo. blue. On mountains.

Veronica alpina L. **Alpine Speedwell.** ¶Leaves subglabrous; flo. few, small, dull blue; fr. longer than broad. On mountain rocks in Scotland, local. Flo. July–Aug. ❀.

Veronica fruticans Jacq. **Shrubby Speedwell.** *V. saxatilis* Scop. ¶Stem wiry; leaves glabrous; corolla large, bright blue with red eye; fr. longer than calyx. On high mountain rocks, mid Scotland. Flo. July–Aug. ❀.

Veronica spicata L. **Spiked Speedwell.**
Subsp. *spicata*. ¶Stem 1 ft, slender; leaves gradually narrowed to petiole; flo. deep blue-purple. On dry grassland in E. Anglia, rare. Flo. July–Sept. ❀.
Subsp. *hybrida* (L.) E. F. Warb. ¶Plant stouter, 1–2 ft; leaves abruptly narrowed to broader petiole, and more crenate. On limestone rocks, Avon Gorge, Wales, Yorkshire, and Westmorland, rare. Flo. July–Sept.

Veronica officinalis L. **Common Speedwell.** ¶Stem creeping; leaves ovate, hairy; flo. lilac; spike rather dense; pedicels short. Common on dry heaths and banks. Flo. May–Aug. ❀.

Veronica chamaedrys L. **Germander Speedwell.** ¶Stem hairy on 2 sides; leaves hairy; flo. large and blue; ft. shorter than calyx. Common on cultivated ground, in grassy places, etc. Flo. March–Aug. ❀.

Veronica montana L. **Wood Speedwell.** ¶Stem hairy all round; leaves yellow-green; flo. lilac; capsule exceeding calyx. In woods on damp or stiff soils. Flo. April–July. ❀.

Veronica scutellata L. **Marsh Speedwell.** ¶Leaves linear-lanceolate; flo. spikes lax, alternate; flo. pale lilac. On wet meadows and moors. Flo. June–Aug. ❀.

Veronica anagallis-aquatica L. **Water Speedwell.** ¶Stem green; leaves long; spikes long; flo. blue; fruiting pedicels ascending. In edges of ponds and watery places, mostly S. and E. England, rare elsewhere. Flo. June–Aug. ❀.

Veronica catenata Pennell. **Pink Water Speedwell.** *V. aquatica* Bernh., non Gray. ¶Stem purple; leaves and spikes shorter; flo. pink; fruiting pedicels spreading. In similar watery places, mostly S. and E. England, local in Wales and Ireland, very rare in Scotland. Flo. June–Aug. ❀.

Veronica beccabunga L. **Brooklime.** ¶Stems creeping, fleshy; leaves obtuse; spikes opposite; flo. bright blue; capsule suborbicular. In small streams and watery places. Flo. May–Sept. ❀.

Euphrasia micrantha Reichb. **Common Slender Eyebright.** ¶Slender, erect, subsimple; leaves many small; flo. coloured, lower lip longer; capsule narrow. From Cornwall and Devon to Shetland. Flo. July–Sept. ❀.

Euphrasia scottica Wettst. **Slender Scottish Eyebright.** ¶Stem slender, erect, subsimple; leaves fewer, wider; flo. white; lower lip equalling upper. On moors and mountains, S. Wales to Shetland. Flo. July–Aug. ❀.

Euphrasia rhumica Pugsl. ¶Stem slender, erect, purplish; leaves narrow, with fine white bristles on both surfaces; flo. small, white, tinged with blue; capsule ovate-oblong. Isle of Rhum (Inner Hebrides). Flo. Aug.

Euphrasia frigida Pugsl. ¶Plant suberect, lax; lower leaves distant, obtuse; flo. white, lower lip longer; capsule large, broad, deeply cut. Teesdale to Shetland. Flo. July–Aug.

Euphrasia foulaensis Townsend ex Wettst. ¶Shorter, less slender; leaves broad, obtuse; flo. violet (or white), lip not much longer; capsule broad. N. Scotland to Shetland. Flo. July–Aug.

Euphrasia eurycarpa Pugsl. ¶Plant suberect, slender, purplish; leaves small, broad, oval; flo. white with bluish upper lip; capsule small, as broad as long. Isle of Rhum (Inner Hebrides). Flo. Aug.

Euphrasia campbelliae Pugsl. ¶Plant erect, slender, purplish; leaves with thick white bristles on margins and nerves; flo. white with purplish upper lip; capsule medium, oblong. Isle of Lewis (Outer Hebrides). Flo. July.

Euphrasia rotundifolia Pugsl. ¶Erect with short branches; leav rounded, crenate, hirsute; flo. small, white; capsule large ar broad. On sea cliffs in Sutherland, etc. Flo. July.

Euphrasia marshallii Pugsl. ¶Erect and branched; leaves broa obtuse, hirsute; flo. medium, white; capsule large and broa Sea cliffs in W. Sutherland and Caithness. Flo. July–Aug.

Euphrasia curta (Fr.) Wettst. **Hairy-leaved Eyebright.** ¶Ere with basal branches; leaves small, acute, hirsute; flo. smal white; capsule small and narrow. Local on grassy mountai •slopes and seasides. Flo. June–Sept.

Euphrasia cambrica Pugsl. **Dwarf Welsh Eyebright.** ¶Very dwar ½–1 in.; leaves obtuse, sparingly hirsute; flo. small, whitish, li subequal; capsule large and broad. High Welsh mountains an Kirkstone Pass. Flo. July.

Euphrasia tetraquetra (Bréb.) Arrondeau. **Broad-leaved Eyebrigh** *E. occidentalis* Wettst. ¶Dwarf, 2–4 in.; branches basal, stou leaves large, hiding internodes; flo. small, white; capsule 6–8 mr Sea cliffs, especially in S.W. Flo. May–Aug.

Euphrasia nemorosa (Pers.) Wallr. **Common Eyebright.** ¶Ste erect, 5–10 in.; branches several, suberect; leaves glabrou teeth acute or aristate; flo. white or purplish above, lower l longer. Common. Flo. July–Sept. ❀.
Var. *calcarea* Pugsl. ¶Dwarf but coarse, with small flo. On cha downs.
Var. *collina* Pugsl. ¶Small but coarse, with flo. larger. On hi in W.
Var. *sabulicola* Pugsl. ¶Small, with flo. very small, white. San in Scotland.

Euphrasia heslop-harrisonii Pugsl. ¶Plant suberect, slender, flexuou leaves small, with blunt shallow teeth; flo. small, white with pa blue upper lip; capsule narrow, oblong. Isle of Rhum (Out Hebrides) and West Ross.

Euphrasia confusa Pugsl. **Little Kneeling Eyebright.** ¶Dwar 1–4 in.; many slender kneeling branches; leaves many, smal flo. small; capsule small but broad. Grassy cliffs and moor W. England to N. Scotland. Flo. July–Sept. ❀.

Euphrasia pseudokerneri Pugsl. **Chalk Hill Eyebright.** ¶Erec branches many, spreading; leaves small, paler below; flo. larg white; capsule small, 5 mm., not exceeding calyx. Chalk down Flo. June–Sept.

Euphrasia arctica Lange ex Rostrup. **Greater Eyebright.** *E. boreal* auct. ¶Plant large, with coarse growth; leaves large, thick, dar green; flo. large, white; capsule large, Scotland and N. Englanc rare in S. Flo. July–Aug.

Euphrasia brevipila Burnat & Gremli. **Short-haired Eyebrigh** ¶Plant large, growth coarse; leaves more yellowish, with shor glands and bristles; flo. large, lilac or white. Common in Scotlanc local in England. Flo. June–Aug. ❀.

Euphrasia rostkoviana Hayne. **Large-flowered Sticky Eyebrigh** ¶Basal branches many, slender; leaves rather small, clothe with glandular hairs; flo. large, lower lip much the large Meadows in W., local. Flo. July–Aug.

Euphrasia montana Jord. **Mountain Sticky Eyebright.** ¶Ster simple or little branched; leaves clothed with glandular hairs flo. white, large, elongating from 10 to 13 mm. Mountain pastures N. England. Flo. June–July.

Euphrasia rivularis Pugsl. **Snowdon Eyebright.** ¶Stem slender subsimple; leaves small, glandular, hairy; flo. large, 8–9 mm. lilac; capsule broad and short. On Snowdon range only. Flo early summer.

Euphrasia anglica Pugsl. **English Sticky Eyebright.** ¶Whol plant densely clothed with glandular hairs; leaves broad; flo large, whitish. On moist heaths and meadows, common in S.W England. Flo. May–Sept. ❀.

Euphrasia vigursii Davey. ¶Plant erect, robust; leaves covered wit glandular hairs of varying sizes; flo. large, purplish to lilac capsule elliptic. Heaths, Cornwall and S. Devon, local. Flo June–Sept.

Euphrasia hirtella Jord. ex Reut. **Small-flowered Sticky Eye bright.** ¶Stem subsimple; upper internodes crowded, densel glandular; leaves large, with deep teeth; flo. small. In Wales Flo. early summer.

Euphrasia salisburgensis Funck. **Narrow-leaved Eyebright.** ¶Leave very small, less than half as broad as long, upper linear; fl small. On limestone, mid Yorkshire and in Ireland. Flo. July– Aug. ❀.

VERONICA
FRUTICANS.

VERONICA
SPICATA.

VERONICA
ARVENSIS.

VERONICA
SERPYLLIFOLIA.

VERONICA
OFFICINALIS.

VERONICA
MONTANA.

ERONICA
PINA.

VERONICA
CATENATA.

VERONICA
BECCABUNGA.

RONICA
UTELLATA.

VERONICA
CHAMAEDRYS.

VERONICA
ANAGALLIS-AQUATICA.

HRASIA
RANTHA.

EUPHRASIA
SCOTICA.

EUPHRASIA
NEMOROSA.

×2.

EUPHRASIA CONFUSA.

EUPHRASIA
BREVIPILA.

×2

EUPHRASIA ANGLICA.

EUPHRASIA
SALISBURGENSIS.

Plate 65

�֎ indicates plant is illustrated

SCROPHULARIACEAE (*continued*)

Odontites verna (Bellardi) Dumort. **Red Bartsia.** *Bartsia odontites* (L.) Huds.
Subsp. *verna.* ¶Branches ascending; leaves lanceolate, toothed; bracts exceeding pink flo. Common in Scotland, less so in England. Flo. June–July. .
Subsp. *serotina* Corb. ¶Branches horizontal; leaves narrow, subentire; bracts not longer than flo. Common in arable fields in S. England. Flo. July–Aug.

Parentucellia viscosa (L.) Caruel. **Yellow Bartsia.** *Bartsia viscosa* L. ¶Plant 6–18 in.; viscid with glandular hairs; flo. yellow, lower lip longer. In damp grass, mostly near S. and W. coasts. Flo. June–Sept. ✶.

Bartsia alpina L. **Alpine Bartsia.** ¶Rhizome short; plant pubescent; bracts purplish; flo. dull purple, lips subequal. In mountain pastures, Yorkshire to Perthshire. Flo. June–Aug. ✶.

Pedicularis palustris L. **Red Rattle.** ¶Annual 8–18 in., much branched below; leaf pinnae many; calyx pubescent; flo. pink and crimson. Watery places on heaths and moors. Flo. May–Sept. ✶.

Pedicularis sylvatica L. **Lousewort.** ¶Perennial, 3–6 in.; branches few basal; leaf pinnae few; calyx glabrous outside; flo. few. Common on heaths and hill pastures. Flo. April–July. ✶.

Rhinanthus serotinus (Schönh.) Oborny. **Greater Hayrattle.** *R. major* Ehrh., non L.
Subsp. *aperus* (Fr.) Hyland. ¶Plant robust; leaves long, teeth many, acute; bracts acuminate; inflo. crowded; corolla 20–22 mm., tube slightly curved; purple teeth longer than broad. In cornfields, arable ground, grassy places, etc., rare. Flo. June–Sept. ✶.

Rhinanthus minor L. **Hayrattle.**
Subsp. *minor.* ¶Less robust; branches short; leaves crenate, intercalary none; corolla 15 mm., straight; purple teeth broader than long; lowest bract teeth less deep. Common in pastures on ba soils. Flo. May–June. ✶.
Subsp. *stenophyllus* (Schur.) Swartz. *Rhinanthus stenophyllus* (Schu Druce. ¶Flo. branches many; intercalary leaves 2–4, line lanceolate, teeth often prominent. Common in Scotland and England, often on limestone. Flo. June–Aug. ✶.
Subsp. *calcareus* (Wilmott) E. F. Warb. *Rhinanthus calcareus* Wilmo ¶Flo. branches many, slender; intercalary leaves 2–4, sm linear, teeth appressed. On chalk and limestone, S. England a Scotland. Flo. July–Aug.
Subsp. *monticola* (Sterneck) Swartz. *Rhinanthus monticola* Sterne *R. spadicens* Wilmott. ¶Lower internodes crowded, bearing sh flowerless branches; calyx often violet tinted. On lower mount pastures, N. England and Scotland. July–Aug. ✶.
Subsp. *borealis* (Sterneck) P. D. Sell. *Rhinanthus borealis* (Sterne Marshall. ¶Stem simple, 4–8 in., leaves broad, blunt, pubesce calyx hairy. On mountains in Scotland and Kerry. Flo. Ju Aug. ✶.
Subsp. *lintoni* (Wilmott) P. D. Sell. *Rhinanthus lintoni* Wilmott. *drummond-hayi* auct. ¶Stem 4–8 in., subsimple, slender; lea narrow, tapering; calyx pubescent, elongate. On mountains Scotland. Flo. July–Aug. ✶.

Melampyrum cristatum L. **Crested Cow-wheat.** ¶Flo. in dense spi yellow and purple tinted; bracts with wider, pink, finely pectin base, lower with long points. Woods, S. and E. England, loc Flo. June–Sept. ✶.

Melampyrum arvense L. **Field Cow-wheat.** ¶Flo. pink and yel in lax spike; bracts finely pinnate, points less long. In cornfie S. and E. England, local and rare. Flo. June–Sept. ✶.

Melampyrum pratense L. **Common Cow-wheat.** ¶Flo. in separ leaf axils; calyx small; corolla ¾ in., yellow in woods, or wh splashed with pink on moors. Common. Flo. June–Aug. ✶.

Melampyrum sylvaticum L. **Wood Cow-wheat.** ¶Flo. in separ leaf axils; calyx lobes long, equalling smaller yellow coro Mountain woods, chiefly in Scotland, local. Flo. June–Aug. ✶

PARENTUCELLIA
VISCOSA.

BARTSIA
ALPINA.

PEDICULARIS
SYLVATICA.

ONTITES VERNA.

PEDICULARIS
PALUSTRIS.

MELAMPYRUM
PRATENSE.

RHINANTHUS
SEROTINUS.

COW-WHEAT.

RHINANTHUS
STENOPHYLLUS.

RHINANTHUS
SPADICEUS.

HAY
RATTLE.

RHINANTHUS
BOREALIS.

RINANTHUS
MINOR

R. LINTONI.

MELAMPYRUM
CRISTATUM

MELAMPYRUM
SYLVATICUM

MELAMPYRUM
ARVENSE.

Plate 66

OROBANCHACEAE

Orobanche purpurea Jacq. **Purple Broomrape.** *O. caerulea* Vill. ¶Stem simple, bluish; flo. dull bluish purple, with 1 bract and 2 bracteoles; stigma lobes white, united. On *Achillea*, Channel Islands, common; S. and E. England, rare. Flo. June–July. ✗.

Orobanche ramosa L. **Branched Broomrape.** ¶Stem with a few basal branches; flo. ½ in., cream with purple edges; 1 bract and 2 bracteoles. Channel Islands, introduced in S.E. England. Flo. July–Sept. ✗.

Orobanche rapum-genistae Thuill. **Greater Broomrape.** ¶Stem 2 ft; flo. large, yellowish; bract 1 only; stamens basal; stigma lobes yellow, distant. On gorse and broom, chiefly in England and Wales, rare and decreasing. Flo. May–July. ✗.

Orobanche alba Steph. ex Willd. **Red Broomrape.** ¶Stem 3–6 in., red; flo. deep red (in Britain); stigma lobes red, contiguous. On thyme, chiefly near the S. coast of Cornwall, W. coast of Scotland and N.E. and W. coasts of Ireland. Flo. June–Aug. ✗.

Orobanche caryophyllacea Sm. **Clove Scented Broomrape.** ¶Flo. large, yellowish, purple tinted, densely glandular; stamens subbasal; stigma lobes distant, purple. On *Galium*, coast of E. Kent, rare. Flo. July. ✗.

Orobanche elatior Sutton. **Tall Broomrape.** *O. major* auct. ¶Stem 1–2 ft; flo. pale yellow, tinted purple, glandular; stigma lobes yellow; stamens inserted 5 mm. above base. On *Centaurea scabiosa*, S. and E. England, local. Flo. July. ✗.

Orobanche reticulata Wallr.
Subsp. *pallidiflora* (Wimm. & Grab.) Hegi. **Thistle Broomrape.** ¶Stem 1 ft, glandular; flo. yellowish with purple edges; stamens 3–4 mm. above base; stigmas purple. On thistles, mostly in Yorkshire, rare. Flo. June–Aug.

Orobanche minor Sm. **Lesser Broomrape.** *O. apiculata* Wallr. ¶Spike lax, yellow tinted purple; corolla curved and equal throughout; stigma lobes purple, contiguous; filaments subglabrous. On Leguminosae, mostly S. and E. England, S. Wales and S. Ireland. ✗.
Var. *flava* Regel. ¶Stems, flo. and stigma lobes yellow. In Channel Islands.
Var. *compositorum* Pugsl. ¶Corolla long and narrow; filaments hairy. On *Crepis*.

Orobanche picridis F. W. Schultz ex Koch. **Picris Broomrape.** ¶Flo. pale, whitish yellow, tinted purple, glandular; filaments very hairy below, inserted 4 mm. above base. On *Picris* and *Crepis*, S. England, rare. Flo. June–July. ✗.

Orobanche hederae Duby. **Ivy Broomrape.** ¶Corolla straight, cream veined purples; stamens inserted 3 mm. above bas[e] stigma lobes yellow, united. On ivy, S. England, Wales, ar Ireland, mainly coastal. ✗.

Orobanche maritima Pugsl. **Carrot Broomrape.** *O. amethystea* auc[t] ¶Flo. many, dull yellow veined purple; central lobe large stigma lobes purple, partly united. Chiefly on *Daucus*, S. coasts England and Wales, rare. Flo. June–July.

Lathraea squamaria L. **Toothwort.** ¶Root parasite without gre[en] colour; stem 6 in.; calyx glandular; flo. cream. On roots of haz[el] and elm in woods, copses and shady places. Flo. March–May. ✗

LENTIBULARIACEAE

Utricularia vulgaris L. **Common Bladderwort.** ¶Aquatic wi[th] bladders on green capillary leaves; upper lip of flo. equalli[ng] palate, lower lip deflexed. In ponds, local and decreasing. Fl[o.] July–Aug. ✗.

Utricularia neglecta Lehm. **Western Bladderwort.** *U. major* auc[t.] ¶Aquatic with bladders on green leaves; upper lip of flo. long[er] than palate, lower lip margins flat. In ponds, chiefly in [W.] England. Flo. July–Aug. ✗.

Utricularia intermedia Hayne. ¶Aquatic with bladders mostly [on] colourless leaves under mud; flo. bright yellow streaked red. [In] peaty water, chiefly in N. England, Scotland and W. Irelan[d] very local. Flo. rare, July–Sept. ✗.

Utricularia minor L. **Lesser Bladderwort.** ¶Aquatic with bladde[rs] on small colourless and green leaves; flo. pale and small, 6–8 m[m.] In boggy pools and ditches, chiefly N.W. England, Scotland a[nd] Ireland. local. Flo. July–Sept. ✗.

Pinguicula vulgaris L. **Common Butterwort.** ¶Flo. ½–¾ in., viol[et] with white throat; lobes of lip spreading; spur 5–6 mm., acu[te] On wet rocks and bogs, chiefly N. England, Scotland and [N.] Ireland. Flo. May–June. ✗.

Pinguicula grandiflora Lam. **Greater Butterwort.** ¶Flo. larg[e] 1 in., violet with white throat; lobes of lip broad, overlappi[ng] spur 10 mm. Bogs in S.W. Ireland, naturalized in S.W. Englan[d.] Flo. May–June. ✗.

Pinguicula alpina L. ¶Flo. ¾ in., white with yellow mouth; sp[ur] conical, 2–3 mm.; capsule oval. Ross, probably extinct. Fl[o.] June.

Pinguicula lusitanica L. **Pink Butterwort.** ¶Flo. ¼ in., pinkish lila[c] and yellow; spur cylindrical; capsule globose. In wet heaths a[nd] peaty bogs, mostly S.W. England, W. Scotland, and W. Irelan[d.] Flo. June–Sept. ✗.

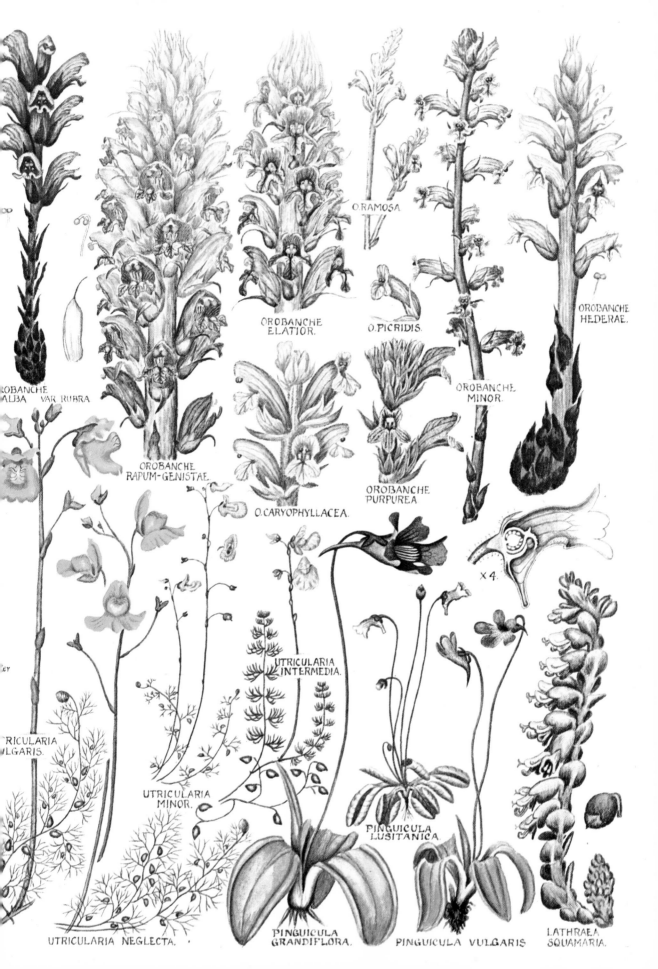

OROBANCHE
ALBA VAR RUBRA.

OROBANCHE
RAPUM-GENISTAE.

OROBANCHE
ELATIOR.

O.RAMOSA.

O.PICRIDIS.

OROBANCHE
HEDERAE.

OROBANCHE
MINOR.

O.CARYOPHYLLACEA.

OROBANCHE
PURPUREA

× 4.

UTRICULARIA
VULGARIS.

UTRICULARIA
INTERMEDIA.

UTRICULARIA
MINOR.

PINGUICULA
LUSITANICA.

UTRICULARIA NEGLECTA.

PINGUICULA
GRANDIFLORA.

PINGUICULA VULGARIS

LATHRAEA
SQUAMARIA.

Plate 67   ✤ indicates plant is illustrated

VERBENACEAE

Verbena officinalis L. **Vervain.** ¶Stem 18 in., tough, hispid; branches few, spreading; flo. few, pale lilac. In England and Wales, rather local. Flo. July–Sept. ✤.

LABIATAE

Mentha suaveolens Ehrh. **Round-leaved Mint.** *M. rotundifolia* auct., non (L.) Huds. ¶Leaves nearly round, much wrinkled; bracts lanceolate; flo. in compact spike. Near S.W. coasts and local elsewhere, England and Wales. Flo. late summer. ✤.

Mentha spicata × suaveolens. **French Mint.** *M. alopecuroides* Hull. ¶Very robust; leaves large, broadly ovate, softly wrinkled; bracts subulate; flo. in a spike. Commonly naturalized from gardens. Flo. late summer.

Mentha longifolia (L.) Huds. **Horse Mint.** ¶Leaves lanceolate, woolly white beneath; bracts subulate; flo. spike dense. Commonly naturalized from gardens. Now regarded as merely a hairy form of *M. spicata*. Flo. late summer. ✤.

Mentha spicata L. **Spear Mint.** ¶Leaves sessile, lanceolate, glabrous; flo. in spike; bracts linear; lower stamens exserted. Commonly naturalized from gardens. Flo. Aug. ✤.

Mentha × piperita L. = *M. aquatica × spicata.* **Pepper Mint.** ¶Stem red; leaves ovate, stalked, subglabrous, purple tinted; spike interrupted below; stamens included. In ditches, local. Flo. late summer. ✤.

Mentha aquatica L. **Water Mint.** ¶Stem and ovate leaves robust, hairy; inflo. of 2–3 whorls, lower separate; stamens exserted. I ditches and wet places. Flo. late summer. ✤.

Mentha × smithiana R. A. Graham = *M. aquatica × arvensis × spicata.* *N rubra* Sm., non Mill. ¶Stems often red; leaves broadly ovate obtuse, subglabrous; bracts leaf-like; calyx teeth twice as long a broad; stamens exserted. Flo. late summer. ✤.

Mentha × gentilis L. = *M. arvensis × spicata.* ¶Leaves ovate-lanceolate hairy; bracts leaf-like; pedicels and calyx subglabrous; teeth twice as long as broad; flo. small, 3 mm.; stamens not exserted. ✤

Mentha × verticillata L. = *M. aquatica × arvensis.* *M. sativa* L. ¶Robust leaves ovate, hairy; bracts leaf-like; pedicels and calyx hairy teeth twice as long as broad; stamens not exserted. Common. Flo late summer.

Mentha arvensis L. **Corn Mint.** ¶Leaves ovate, hairy; whorls axillary distant; bracts leaf-like; calyx teeth triangular, hairy, as long a broad; stamens exserted. Common in cornfields. Flo. late summe ✤.

Mentha pulegium L. **Penny Royal.** ¶Stem prostrate below; leave small, oval, ¼–½ in.; whorls distant; bracts leaf-like; flo. swolle below mouth. Damp sandy places, local. Flo. late summer. ✤.

Lycopus europaeus L. **Gipsy-wort.** ¶Stem 2–3 ft; leaves lobed c dentate; calyx spine pointed; flo. white, spotted purple. Commo in ditches and river banks. Flo. June–Sept. ✤.

Origanum vulgare L. **Marjoram.** ¶Stem wiry, branched as shown bracts leaf-like, small; bracteoles purple; flo. pale rose. Commo on calcareous soils. Flo. July–Sept. ✤.

VERBENA
OFFICINALIS.

MENTHA
ROTUNDIFOLIA.

MENTHA
LONGIFOLIA.

MENTHA
PIPERITA.

MENTHA AQUATICA.

MENTHA
SPICATA.

MENTHA PULEGIUM.

MENTHA
GENTILIS.

MENTHA
SMITHIANA.

MENTHA
ARVENSIS

LYCOPUS
EUROPAEUS.

ORIGANUM
VULGARE.

MARJORAM.

Plate 68   ✳ indicates plant is illustrated

LABIATAE (*continued*)

Thymus serpyllum L. **Wild Thyme.** ¶Creeping stems many, long; flo. stems hairy all round; leaves 4–6 mm.; flo. in 1 head. In E. England. Flo. June–Aug. ✳.

Thymus drucei Ronn. **Common Wild Thyme.** ¶Creeping stems many, dense; flo. stems hairy on 2 sides only; leaves 5–8 mm.; flo. in 1 head. Common on dry banks and heaths. Flo. June–Aug.

Thymus pulegioides L. **Larger Wild Thyme.** *T. chamaedrys* Fr. ¶Creeping stems few; stem angles sharp and hairy; leaves up to 10 mm.; inflo. with separate whorl below. Calcareous and dry soils, S. and E. England. Flo. July–Aug. ✳.

Clinopodium vulgare L. **Cushion Calamint.** *Calamintha clinopodium* Benth. ¶Stems 1½ ft; flo. rose-red in terminal and axillary heads; bracteoles subulate, ciliate. Common in England. Flo. July–Sept. ✳.

Acinos arvensis (Lam.) Dandy. **Basil Thyme.** *Calamintha acinos* (L.) Clairv. ¶Stem 6–8 in., ascending; flo. blue in small whorls; calyx curved, swollen below. Fairly common, especially on calcareous soils. Flo. Aug.–Sept. ✳.

Calamintha nepeta (L.) Savi. **Lesser Calamint.** ¶Stem 1 ft; leaves small, greyish, hairy; calyx teeth nearly alike, internal hairs protruding; flo. mauve. Mainly S. England, rare. Flo. July–Aug. ✳.

Calamintha ascendens Jord. **Common Calamint.** *C. officinalis* auct. ¶Stem 1 ft; leaves larger, green; calyx with lower teeth much longer; flo. pale lilac, spotted. On basic or calcareous banks, England. Flo. July–Sept. ✳.

Calamintha sylvatica Bromf. **Wood Calamint.** *C. intermedia* auct. ¶Stem 2 ft; leaves large; flo. large, 15–20 mm., deeply purple blotched. Very local on chalk, I. of Wight. Flo. Aug.–Sept. ✳.

✳Melissa officinalis L. **Balm.** ¶Stems many, 2 ft; leaves ovate, wrinkled; calyx with 2 unequal lips; flo. white. Naturalized mainly in S. England. Flo. May–July. ✳.

Salvia horminoides Pourr. **Wild Sage, Clary.** ¶Leaves coarsely toothed or lobed; upper teeth of calyx united; flo. often shorter than calyx, violet with 2 white spots. Mostly S. England. Flo. May–July. ✳.

Salvia verbenaca L. ¶Leaves coarsely toothed or lobed; upper teeth of calyx united; flo. usually longer than calyx, purple unspotted. Vazon Bay, Guernsey. Flo. June–Aug.

Salvia pratensis L. **Meadow Clary.** ¶Upper leaves and bracts ovate; corolla large, up to 1 in., 3 times length of calyx, deep violet. On calcareous pastures, very local. Flo. June–July. ✳.

✳Salvia verticillata L. ¶Bracts small, brown, reflexed; calyx with upper teeth distinct; flo. ½ in., violet, with a ring of hairs within. In waste places. Flo. June–July.

Nepeta cataria L. **Cat Mint.** ¶Stem 2–3 ft; leaves pubescent, white beneath; inflo. dense; flo. white. Mostly on calcareous soil, local. Flo. July–Sept. ✳.

Glechoma hederacea L. **Ground Ivy.** *Nepeta glechoma* Benth. ¶Stem creeping; leaves reniform, soft; flo. blue-purple, sometimes small and female. Common. Flo. April–June. ✳.

Scutellaria galericulata L. **Skull-cap.** ¶Stem 1 ft, from rhizome; leaves rounded or cordate below; flo. ½–¾ in., blue-violet. Edges of ponds and streams. Flo. July–Sept. ✳.

✳Scutellaria hastifolia L. ¶Stem 1 ft, from rhizome; leaves hastate below; flo. in terminal spike, ¾–1 in., blue-violet. In a wood, W. Norfolk, introduced. Flo. July–Sept.

Scutellaria minor L. **Lesser Skull-cap.** ¶Stem 6 in., from rhizome; leaves round below; flo. in leaf axils ⅜ in., pale pink. Common on wet heaths. Flo. July–Sept. ✳.

THYMUS
SERPYLLUM.

THYMUS
PULEGIOIDES.

CLINOPODIUM
VULGARE.

CALAMINTHA
NEPETA.

CALAMINTHA ASCENDENS

CALAMINTHA
SYLVATICA.

ACINOS ARVENSIS.

MELISSA
OFFICINALIS

SALVIA
PRATENSIS.

SALVIA
HORMINOIDES.

GLECHOMA
HEDERACEA

NEPETA CATARIA.

SCUTELLARIA
MINOR.

SCUTELLARIA
GALERICULATA.

Plate 69

LABIATAE (*continued*)

Prunella vulgaris L. **Self-heal.** ¶Leaves ovate, subentire, rounded below; upper teeth of calyx united; flo. blue-violet, rarely pink. Flo. June–Sept. ❀.

Prunella laciniata (L.) L. ¶Upper leaves lobed or pinnate, cuneate below; upper teeth of calyx more distinct; flo. creamy white. On chalk downs in S. England, local. Flo. June–Aug. ❀.

Melittis melissophyllum L. **Bastard Balm.** ¶Stem 1–2 ft; leaves strong smelling; flo. large, white blotched red-purple. In woods and banks, S.W. England and S. Wales. Flo. May–June. ❀.

Marrubium vulgare L. **White Horehound.** ¶Stem and leaves hoary or woolly; calyx with 10 subulate hooked teeth; flo. whitish. On downs and chalk cliffs. Flo. July–Oct. ❀.

Betonica officinalis L. **Betony.** *Stachys betonica* Benth. ¶Stem 1 ft; leaves distant; flo. mostly in dense head, red-purple, without internal hairs. In hedge banks, common. Flo. June–Sept. ❀.

Stachys palustris L. **Marsh Woundwort.** ¶Stem 3 ft, from rhizome; leaves lanceolate; bracteoles equalling pedicels; flo. pale lilac. By ditches and streams, common. Flo. July–Sept. ❀.

Stachys sylvatica L. **Wood Woundwort.** ¶Leaves ovate; petioles long; bracteoles equalling pedicels; flo. claret colour. Common. Flo. July–Sept. ❀.

Stachys alpina L. **Alpine Woundwort.** ¶Stem 2 ft; leaves often purplish; bracteoles exceeding pedicels; flo. red with yellow eye, downy. In woods, Gloucestershire and Denbighshire, very rare. Flo. July–Aug. ❀.

Stachys germanica L. **Downy Woundwort.** ¶Plant stoloniferous, clothed with long white hairs; flo. in dense spike, pale rose. Calcareous soil in Oxfordshire, etc., very rare. Flo. July–Aug. ❀.

Stachys arvensis (L.) L. **Field Woundwort.** ¶Annual, 6–10 in. branched at base; flo. ¼ in., pale lilac. Cultivated fields, common in W. England. Flo. June–Aug. ❀.

*Stachys annua (L.) L. ¶Annual, 6–10 in.; leaves oblong, 1–2 in.; fl ½ in., pale yellow. On cultivated land, casual. Flo. June–Sept. ❀

*Galeopsis ladanum L. ¶Stem softly hairy, not thickened at nodes; lea width ½–1 in.; side 3–8 toothed; flo. small, lilac. Cultivated an waste land, casual. Flo. July–Sept.

Galeopsis angustifolia Ehrh. ex Hoffm. ¶Stem soft, not thickened a nodes; leaves linear-lanceolate, ¼–½ in. wide; teeth few; flo. larg ¾–1 in., pale rose. Cultivated land. Flo. July–Sept. ❀.

Galeopsis segetum Neck. *G. dubia* Leers. ¶Stem not thickened at node leaves very soft, downy; flo. large, pale yellow. On sandy cornfield rare. Flo. July–Aug. ❀.

Galeopsis tetrahit L. **Common Hemp-nettle.** ¶Stem thickened a nodes, hispid; flo. ¾ in., rose-purple and yellow; mid lobe of lip fla entire, margin pale. Woods and hedge banks. Flo. July–Sept. ❀

Galeopsis bifida Boenn. ¶Thickened at nodes, more evenly hispid; flo ½ in.; mid lobe of lip convex notched, deeply coloured to margir Probably hybrid. Arable land. Flo. July–Sept.

Galeopsis speciosa Mill. **Large-flowered Hemp-nettle.** ¶Thickene at nodes, evenly hispid; flo. ¾ in., pale yellow, and lip mostl violet. Arable land, especially on peaty soil of Fen District. Fl July–Sept. ❀.

*Leonurus cardiaca L. **Motherwort.** ¶Stem 3 ft; lower leaves 5 lobec upper 3 lobed; flo. in dense whorls, white or pink, purple spotted Introduced, rare. Flo. July–Sept.

PRUNELLA
VULGARIS.

PRUNELLA
LACINIATA.

MELITTIS
MELISSOPHYLLUM.

MARRUBIUM
VULGARE

STACHYS
ALPINA

BETONICA
OFFICINALIS

BETONY

GALEOPSIS
ANGUSTIFOLIA.

GALEOPSIS
SPECIOSA.

STACHYS
ANNUA

STACHYS
PALUSTRIS.

GALEOPSIS
TETRAHIT
HEMP
NETTLE.

GALEOPSIS SEGETUM

STACHYS
GERMANICA

STACHYS
SYLVATICA.

STACHYS
ARVENSIS.

LABIATAE (*continued*)

Lamium amplexicaule L. **Henbit.** ¶Bract leaves sessile, like an involucre; calyx short and closing; corolla pink with crimson hood. In cultivated ground, chiefly S. and E. Britain. Flo. April–Aug. ❀.

Lamium moluccellifolium Fr. **Intermediate Dead-nettle.** *L. intermedium* F. ¶Upper bracts sessile; calyx deeply cut, spreading; corolla ½ in., pale pink. Cultivated ground in N. England and Scotland, rare elsewhere. Flo. June–Sept. ❀.

Lamium hybridum Vill. **Cut-leaved Dead-nettle.** *L. incisum* Willd. ¶Leaves all stalked, truncate at base, teeth deeply cut; corolla short, ring of hairs within faint or 0. In cultivated ground, local. Flo. April–June. ❀.

Lamium purpureum L. **Purple Dead-nettle.** ¶Leaves cordate at base, teeth rounded; corolla pink, with ring of hairs inside. Very common. Flo. April–Aug. ❀.

*Lamium maculatum L. **Spotted Dead-nettle.** ¶Leaves usually blotched with white; corolla pink with ring of hairs. Introduced. Flo. May–Aug.

Lamium album L. **White Dead-nettle.** ¶Flo. large and white, lateral lobes of lower lip with small teeth. Waste ground and roadsides. Flo. April–June and autumn. ❀.

Lamiastrum galeobdolon (L.) Ehrend. & Polatschek. **Yellow Archangel.** *Galeobdolon luteum* Huds., *Lamium galeobdolon* (L.) L. ¶Stolons widely spreading; flo. yellow, lower lip with 3 subequal lobes. In woods, especially on stiff soils, chiefly in S. England and Midlands. Flo. May–July. ❀.

Ballota nigra L. **Horehound.**
**Subsp. *nigra.* ¶Stem 1–2 ft., hairy, strong smelling; calyx tube short; calyx teeth lanceolate, 2–4 mm. long; flo. pale purple. Introduced, waste ground, etc., very rare. Flo. June–Sept.

Subsp. *foetida* Hayek. ¶Differs from subsp. *nigra* in its longer cal tube and broadly ovate calyx teeth, becoming abruptly acumina 1–2 mm. long; flo. pale purple. Common in hedge banks, was ground, etc., in England and Wales, local in Scotland a Ireland. Flo. June–Sept. ❀.

Teucrium botrys L. **Cut-leaved Germander.** ¶Stem 8 in.; leaves a pinnatifid; calyx gibbous; flo. pale purple. On chalk in S. Englan rare. Flo. July–Sept. ❀.

Teucrium scordium L. **Water Germander.** ¶Plant 1 ft, stoloniferou stems and leaves softly hairy; flo. pale purple. Wet places, an hollows on sand dunes. S. and E. England and Ireland, very loca Flo. July–Sept. ❀.

* Teucrium chamaedrys L. **Wall Germander.** ¶Stem 1 ft; leaves da green, cuneate below, uppermost smaller; flo. purple. Introduce on walls and ruins, rare. Flo. July–Sept. ❀.

Teucrium scorodonia L. **Wood Sage.** ¶Stem 1 ft; leaves wrinkled; fl yellowish green, in pairs. Common. Flo. July–Sept. ❀.

Ajuga reptans L. **Bugle.** ¶Stolons leafy; stem hairy on 2 sides; uppe most leaves shorter than blue flo. Common on damp ground. Fl May–July. ❀.

Ajuga pyramidalis L. **Pyramidal Bugle.** ¶Stem 6 in., hairy all roun upper leaves longer than pale mauve flo. Rock crevices in Scotlan N. England, Ireland, scarce. Flo. May–July. ❀.

Ajuga genevensis L. ¶Rhizomatous; stem hairy all round; upper leav shorter than deep blue flo. Chalk pastures in Berkshire, perha introduced. Flo. May–July. ❀.

Ajuga chamaepitys (L.) Schreb. **Ground-pine.** ¶Stem 6 in.; leaves 3 narrow lobes; flo. short, in pairs, yellow. In chalky fields, S. England, local. Flo. May–Sept. ❀.

LAMIUM HYBRIDUM.

LAMIUM MOLUCCELLIFOLIUM.

LAMIUM PURPUREUM.

BALLOTA NIGRA.

...MIUM ...PLEXICAULE.

GALEOBDOLON LUTEUM.

TEUCRIUM SCORODONIA.

TEUCRIUM BOTRYS.

LAMIUM ALBUM.

...ENEVENSIS.

AJUGA PYRAMIDALIS.

TEUCRIUM CHAMAEDRYS.

AJUGA CHAMAEPITYS.

AJUGA REPTANS.

TEUCRIUM SCORDIUM.

Plate 71

❀ indicates plant is illustrated

PLANTAGINACEAE

Plantago major L. **Great Plantain.** ¶Leaves abruptly contracted below to a petiole; spike of flo. brownish; capsule many seeded. Common. Flo. May–Sept. ❀.

Plantago media L. **Hoary Plantain, Lamb's-tongue.** ¶Leaves gradually narrowed below, subsessile, pubescent; flo. whitish; stamens purple. On basic and chalky soils, chiefly in England. Flo. June–Sept. ❀.

Plantago lanceolata L. **Ribwort Plantain.** ¶Leaves lanceolate, ribbed; scape furrowed; spike ovate; flo. brown. Common in pastures. Flo. April–Aug. ❀.

Plantago maritima L. **Sea Plantain.** ¶Leaves long, linear, fleshy; flo. brown; stamens pale yellow. In salt marshes and on mountains. Flo. June–Aug. ❀.

Plantago coronopus L. **Buck's-horn Plantain.** ¶Leaves pinnatifid and pubescent, but very variable. In gravelly places, commonest near the sea. Flo. May–Aug. ❀.

*Plantago indica L. *P. psyllium* L. ¶Stem long, leafy and branched; leaves linear, opposite. Introduced in cultivated ground and sand dunes. Flo. July–Aug.

Littorella uniflora (L.) Aschers. **Shore-weed.** *L. lacustris* L. ¶Submerged, with slender stolons; male flo. stalked, female sessile with long slender stigmas. On gravel in lakes and reservoirs, local. Flo. June–Aug. ❀.

ILLECEBRACEAE

Illecebrum verticillatum L. **Knot-grass.** ¶Branches prostrate; sepals thick, white, hooded and awned; petals minute, white. On moist sand in S. England, introduced elsewhere, very local. Flo. July–Sept. ❀.

Herniaria glabra L. **Rupture-wort.** ¶Leaves narrowed below; fr. acute, longer than sepals, which are glabrous. Dry sandy places, mostly in E. Anglia, rare. Flo. July–Sept. ❀.

Herniaria ciliolata Melderis. **Ciliate Rupture-wort.** *H. ciliata* Bab., non Clairv. ¶Leaves ovate, usually ciliate; sepals tipped with a bristle; fr. obtuse, equalling sepals. Lizard Head and Channel Islands. Flo. July–Aug.

*Herniaria hirsuta L. ¶Branches and leaves clothed with spreading hairs; leaves lanceolate, narrowed at both ends. Casual, Hampshire and S. Devon. Flo. July–Sept.

Corrigiola litoralis L. **Strap-wort.** ¶Plant glaucous or reddish; leaves tapering below, stipulate; flo. clustered, white tipped with red. Gravelly bank of Slapton Ley and in Channel Islands, elsewhere adventive on railway tracks. Flo. July–Aug. ❀.

Scleranthus annuus L. **Knawel.** ¶Stems erect; calyx lobes acute, ◻ narrow white margin, spreading in fr. In sandy fields. Flo. Ju◻ Aug. ❀.

Scleranthus perennis L. **Perennial Knawel.** ¶Stem procumb◻ calyx lobes rounded with broad white margins, closed in fr. Sa◻ fields in Norfolk and Suffolk, and in Radnorshire. Flo. Ju◻ Aug.
Subsp. *perennis.* ¶Stems ascending to erect, woody below; se◻ oblong, blunt, with broad white margins; closed in fr. On rock◻ Radnorshire only. Flo. June–Aug.
Subsp. *prostratus* P. D. Sell. ¶Similar to subsp. *perennis* but with l◻ procumbent or slightly ascending stems and smaller leaves and◻ Sandy heaths in Norfolk and Suffolk. Flo. June–Aug. ❀.

AMARANTHACEAE

*Amaranthus retroflexus L. ¶Stout, erect, pubescent, leafless abc◻ leaves ovate; flo. in dense spikes; sepals 5. Casual; alien, in cu◻ vated land. Flo. July–Sept.

CHENOPODIACEAE

Chenopodium polyspermum L. **Many-seeded Goose-foot.** ¶Lea◻ ovate, green; flo. spikes small, leafless; sepals 5, not keeled; test◻ seed has pits with sinuous margin. Cultivated ground, chiefly◻ England. Flo. July–Sept. ❀.

Chenopodium vulvaria L. **Stinking Goose-foot.** *C. olidum* Cu◻ ¶Leaves rhomboid-oval, mealy; flo. spikes dense; sepals ◻ keeled; seed testa with faint furrows. Waste places, chiefly◻ England. Flo. Aug.–Sept. ❀.

Chenopodium album L. **Fat Hen.** ¶Stem often reddish; leaves thi◻ variable, dentate, mealy; inflo. branched; sepals keeled; test◻ seed faintly striate or reticulate. Arable land, common. F◻ July–Aug. ❀.

Chenopodium suecicum. J. Murr. *C. viride* auct. ¶Similar to *C. Album*, ◻ stem green; leaves thin, bright glaucous green; seed testa regula◻ pitted, obtusely keeled.

*Chenopodium pratericola Rydb. ¶Leaves linear oblong, glauc◻ beneath; sepals strongly keeled; seed testa with small netwo◻ Casual on rubbish tips.

*Chenopodium opulifolium Schrad. ex Koch & Ziz. ¶Stem 2 ft; lea◻ broad, obtuse, dentate, mealy below; sepals keeled; testa f◻ rowed and finely papillose. Waste places. Flo. Aug.–Sept.

PLANTAGO CRONOPUS

PLANTAGO MEDIA

×7

CHENOPODIUM POLYSPERMUM

CHENOPODIUM VULVARIA

×6

PLANTAGO MAJOR.

PLANTAGO LANCEOLATA

PLANTAGO MARITIMA.

CHENOPODIUM ALBUM

HERNIARIA GLABRA

SCLERANTHUS PERENNIS.

ILLECEBRUM VERTICILLATUM

×10

SCLERANTHUS ANNUUS.

×4

×10.

CORRIGIOLA LITORALIS.

LITTORELLA UNIFLORA.

Plate 72

CHENOPODIACEAE (*continued*)

Chenopodium ficifolium Sm. **Fig-leaved Goose-foot.** ¶Lower leaves with pair of ascending lobes; sepals white with green keel; seed testa furrowed. Cultivated and waste land, locally common in S. and E. England, rare elsewhere. Flo. July–Sept. ✿.

*Chenopodium berlandieri Moq. ¶Leaves 3 lobed, mealy; flo. clusters in lax spikes; seed testa with honeycomb pattern. In docks and rubbish tips.

*Chenopodium hircinum Schrad. ¶Leaves 3 lobed, mealy, white and smelling; flo. clusters in short dense spikes; testa with furrows and pits. In docks and rubbish tips. Flo. late summer.

Chenopodium murale L. **Sowbane, Nettle-leaved Goose-foot.** ¶Stem leafy almost to top; leaves sharply toothed; flo. branches short; testa with dense minute pits. In cultivated and waste ground. Flo. Aug. ✿.

Chenopodium hybridum L. **Sowbane.** ¶Lower leaves subcordate, teeth few and large; flo. spikes spreading; sepals hardly keeled; testa with large pits. Cultivated land, chiefly S. and E. England, rare. Flo. late summer.

Chenopodium urbicum L. ¶Leaves glabrous, triangular, dentate; flo. spikes short, erect; clusters small; seeds black; testa reticulate. Cultivated land. Flo. late summer.

Chenopodium rubrum L. **Red Goose-foot.** ¶Stem often red; leaves rhomboidal, coarsely toothed; sepals of lateral flo. 3–4, free to middle; seed red-brown; testa pitted. Cultivated and waste ground, pond verges, etc., common in S. and E. England. Flo. Aug. ✿.

Chenopodium botryodes Sm. ¶Leaves subentire, triangular; sepals of lateral flo. 2–4, united almost to apex, keeled at top. Salt marshes, S. and E. England. Flo. Sept. ✿.

Chenopodium glaucum L. **Oak-leaved Goose-foot.** ¶Leaves small, oak shaped, green above, white beneath; flo. spikes many, small; seeds reddish. In rich ground, chiefly S. England. Flo. Sept. ✿.

*Chenopodium bonus-henricus L. **Good King Henry.** ¶Perennial, 1½ ft; leaves broad, green; inflo. pyramidal; stigmas long. In rich soils and farmyards, not native. Flo. May–Aug. ✿.

Beta vulgaris
Subsp. *maritima* (L.) Arcangeli. **Sea Beet.** *B. maritima* L. ¶Stems mostly decumbent; leaves thick, green and glossy; fruiting sepals corky. On sea-shores. Flo. July–Sept. ✿.
Cultivated forms of *B. vulgaris*, with erect stem and thick root, sometimes occur as outcasts.

Atriplex littoralis L. **Grass-leaved Orache.** ¶Leaves linear, entire toothed; flo. spike long, leafless above; fruiting sepals rhombo tuberculate. On sea-shores. Flo. July–Aug. ✿.

Atriplex patula L. **Common Orache.** ¶Leaves tapering to pedi lobes ascending; sepals smooth or little tuberculate. In cultiva and waste ground, common. Flo. Aug.–Sept. ✿.

Atriplex hastata L. **Hastate Orache.** ¶Leaves triangular, abrup contracted below; sepals mostly truncate below, less than h united. Waste ground, common, especially near the sea. F Aug.–Sept. ✿.

Atriplex glabriuscula Edmondst. **Babington's Orache.** ¶Ste spreading; leaves triangular, subentire; inflo. leafy; sepals 5– mm., tubercled, united along the base.
Var. *babingtonii* (Woods) Moss. ¶Leaves much toothed; sep 5 × 5 mm. On sea-shores, common. Flo. July–Sept. ✿.

Atriplex laciniata L. **Frosted Orache.** *A. sabulosa* Rouy. ¶Pla silvery white, decumbent; leaves rhomboid-ovate, very mea flo. spikes short. Sandy sea-shores, local. Flo. July–Sept. ✿.

Halimione portulacoides (L.) Aellen. **Sea Purslane.** *Atriplex por lacoides* L. ¶Perennial, dense, shrubby plants; leaves mos opposite, entire; sepals 3 lobed. Locally abundant in salt marsh Flo. July–Sept. ✿.

Halimione pedunculata (L.) Aellen. *Atriplex pedunculata* L. ¶Annu erect; leaves alternate, entire; sepals 3 lobed; fr. pedicelled. In s marshes, E. England, very rare. Flo. July–Sept. ✿.

Salicornia perennis Mill. **Perennial Glasswort.** ¶Perennial, mu branched, in large tussocks; fertile segments 4–8; central separ ing 2 lateral. Salt marshes, S. England. Flo. Aug.–Sept.

Salicornia dolichostachya Moss. ¶Annual; spikes long, 3–5 in.; segmer 15–30; central flo. larger, almost separating the lateral. Tidal s marshes. Flo. Aug.–Sept.

Salicornia europaea L. *S. stricta* Dumort. ¶Bright green; spikes lor blunt, segments 6–16; flo. nearly equal, central, not separating lateral. In muddy, tidal marshes. Flo. Aug.–Sept. ✿.

Salicornia ramosissima Woods. **Prostrate Glasswort.** *S. prostr* auct. ¶Stems usually becoming prostrate and reddish; branches short and tapering, segments 2–6, oval; central flo. lar but not separating lateral ones; young plants sometimes erect a variable in angle of branching. Flo. Aug.–Sept. ✿.

Salicornia pusilla Woods. **Fragile Glasswort.** *S. disarticulata* Mc ¶Stems erect; flo. branches very short, segments 1–2, all separ ing when ripe; flo. solitary not in threes. Drier parts of salt marsh S. and E. coasts. Flo. Aug.–Sept.

×10

CHENOPODIUM
BOTRYODES.

CHENOPODIUM
RUBRUM.

CHENOPODIUM
GLAUCUM.

CHENOPODIUM
MURALE.

ENOPODIUM
CIFOLIUM.

CHENOPODIUM
BONUS-HENRICUS.

×5

ATRIPLEX
GLABRIUSCULA

ATRIPLEX
PATULA.

RIPLEX
TTORALIS.

BETA
MARITIMA.

HALIMIONE
PORTULACOIDES.

×2

ATRIPLEX
LACINIATA.

HALIMIONE PEDUNCULATA.

SALICORNIA
EUROPAEA.

SALICORNIA RAMOSISSIMA.

ATRIPLEX
HASTATA.

Plate 73   �indicates plant is illustrated

CHENOPODIACEAE (*continued*)

Suaeda fruticosa Forsk. **Shrubby Sea-blite.** ¶Perennial shrub, 2–3 ft; leaves rounded at ends; stigmas 3; seeds smooth. On shingle, S. and E. coasts. Flo. July–Sept. ✀.

Suaeda maritima (L.) Dumort. **Annual Sea-blite.** ¶Annual, mostly spreading or prostrate, glaucous and reddish; leaves acute; stigmas 2; seeds reticulate. Common on sea-shores. Flo. July–Sept. ✀.

Salsola kali L. **Saltwort.** ¶Prostrate and prickly; stems striped; leaves succulent, spinous; flo. axillary; sepals thick and green. On sandy sea-shores. Flo. July–Sept. ✀.

POLYGONACEAE

Polygonum convolvulus L. **Black Bindweed.** ¶Stem 3 ft, twining; flo. subsessile or pedicels 1–2 mm.; outer sepals keeled. On cultivated ground. Flo. July–Sept. ✀.

Polygonum dumetorum L. **Copse Buckwheat, Bindweed.** ¶Stem 5 ft, twining; flo. pedicels 8 mm. long; outer sepals broadly winged. In hedges and thickets, chiefly S. England, rare. Flo. July–Sept. ✀.

Polygonum aviculare L. **Common Knotgrass.** *P. heterophyllum* Lindm. ¶Stems mostly prostrate; leaves lanceolate, very unequal; ochreae silvery, torn; sepals pinkish, united at base only. In cultivated and waste ground, etc., common. Flo. July–Aug. ✀.

*Polygonum aubertii L. Henry. **Russian Vine.** *P. baldschuanictum* auct., non Regel. ¶Rampant woody climber; leaves cordate to hastate; flo. white in axillary and terminal panicles. Garden escape, or outcast, naturalized in hedges and thickets and on waste ground. Flo. Aug.–Nov.

Polygonum rurivagum Jord. ex Bor. ¶Leaves unequal, linear-lanceolate, acute; ochreae long, 8–10 mm.; fr. 2 mm. On arable calcareous land, local.

Polygonum arenastrum Bor. *P. aequale* Lindm. ¶Stems matted; leaves small, blunt, nearly equal; sepals green and white, united half-way; fr. 2·5 mm. Paths and farm gateways. ✀.

Polygonum boreale (Lange) Small. ¶Leaves oblong-ovate to spathulate; petioles projecting from ochreae; fr. 3·5–4·5 mm. Arable land, Sutherland, Orkney and Shetland.

Polygonum oxyspermum Mey. & Bunge ex Ledeb. subsp. *raii* (Bab.) D. A. Webb & A. O. Chater. **Ray's Knotgrass.** *P. raii* Bab. ¶Stems prostrate, woody; leaf margins flat; ochreae silvery, torn, with simple veins; fr. 5–6 mm., exceeding sepals. On sea-shores. Flo. June–Sept. ✀.

Polygonum maritimum L. **Sea Knotgrass.** ¶Stems prostrate, woody; leaf margins revolute; ochreae with many-branched veins; fr. 4 mm. On sea-shores in S.W. England and Channel Islands, very rare. Flo. July–Sept.

Polygonum hydropiper L. **Water Pepper, Biting Persicaria.** ¶Stems suberect, 1–2 ft, nodding; flo. greenish; sepals with yellow glands. Common in damp places. Flo. July–Sept. ✀.

Polygonum mite Schrank. **Lax-flowered Persicaria.** *P. laxiflorum* Weihe. ¶Similar to *P. hydropiper* but not acrid, suberect; ochreae much fringed; flo. interrupted pink, without glands. In ditches a wet places, local. Flo. June–Sept. ✀.

Polygonum minus Huds. **Lesser Persicaria.** ¶Stem ½–1 ft; lea narrow, 2–5 mm. wide; ochreae much fringed; flo. smaller, pi fr. only 2–2·5 mm. Edges of pools and streams, local. Flo. Au Sept. ✀.

Polygonum persicaria L. **Common Persicaria.** ¶Leaves often d blotched; ochreae fringed; inflo. dense, obtuse; flo. pink, with glands. In cultivated and damp ground, common. Flo. June–Se ✀.

Polygonum lapathifolium L. **Pale Persicaria.** ¶Leaves often bl blotched or downy; ochreae unfringed except uppermost; in dense, obtuse; flo. greenish white, sometimes glandular. F June–Sept. ✀.

Polygonum nodosum Pers. **Spotted Persicaria.** *P. maculatum* (Gr Dyer ex Bab. ¶Undersides of leaves dotted with glands; ochr shortly fringed; inflo. lax and acute; flo. pink; peduncle glandul In damp ground, local. The specimen figured was exceptiona large, but determined by an expert. Flo. July–Sept. ✀.

Polygonum amphibium L. **Amphibious Persicaria.** ¶Aquatic; lea usually ovate-oblong, floating; flo. in a stout spike, pink, In po and slow streams. Flo. July–Sept. ✀.

Polygonum bistorta L. **Snakeweed, Bistort.** ¶Rhizome twisted; st simple, erect; young leaves folded lengthwise; flo. pink. In mo meadows. Flo. June–Aug. ✀.

*Polygonum campanulatum Hook. f. ¶Plant superficially resembling *bistorta*, but leaves very tomentose, whitish to buff benea Garden escape, naturalized in ditches, wet places, etc., especia in Ireland, rare. Flo. June–Sept.

Polygonum viviparum L. **Alpine Bistort.** ¶Rhizome creeping; st erect ½–1 ft; spike slender; flo. pink mixed with red bulbils. (mountain pastures in N. England and Scotland. Flo. June–A ✀.

*Polygonum cuspidatum Sieb. & Zucc. **Japanese Polygonu** ¶Rhizome deep; plant very large; leaves broadly ovate, trunc at base; inflo. of many-flowered axillary panicles; flo. whi Persistent garden escape, common on waste ground, etc. F Aug.–Oct.

*Polygonum sachalinense F. Schmidt. ¶Resembling *P. cuspidatum* l taller and stouter; leaves ovate-acute, cordate at base; in shorter and more compact; flo. white. Garden escape, establish in waste ground, etc. Flo. Aug.–Oct.

*Polygonum polystachyum Wall. ex Meisn. ¶Rhizome creeping; ste stout, erect; leaves oblong-lanceolate, acuminate, truncate cuneate at the base; sometimes hairy beneath, with red veins; white in lax leafy panicles. Garden escape, established on wa ground, etc. Flo. Aug.–Oct.

*Polygonum amplexicaule D. Don. ¶Stems erect; leaves large, ova cordate; lower leaves stalked, upper leaves sessile, clasping ste flo. dark red in dense cylindrical spikes. Garden escape, natur ized in thickets, hedge banks, etc. Flo. July–Sept.

*Polygonum sagittatum L. ¶Stems weak with many short hook prickles; leaves oblong-sagittate, glabrous; flo. white in sm spikes. Garden escape, naturalized in ditches in Ireland, etc. F July–Sept.

SUAEDA MARITIMA

SALSOLA KALI

POLYGONUM CONVOLVULUS.

POLYGONUM RAII

ÆDA TICOSA.

POLYGONUM MINUS.

POLYGONUM DUMETORUM

POLYGONUM MITE.

POLYGONUM LAPATHIFOLIUM

POLYGONUM PERSICARIA

×2

POLYGONUM AVICULARE.

POLYGONUM BISTORTA.

POLYGONUM ARENASTRUM.

POLYGONUM HYDROPIPER

×4

YGONUM ODOSUM.

POLYGONUM AMPHIBIUM.

POLYGONUM VIVIPARUM.

Plate 74   ✽ indicates plant is illustrated

POLYGONACEAE (continued)

Fagopyrum esculentum Moench. **Buckwheat.** *F. sagittatum* Gilib. ¶Stem 1–2 ft, branched; leaves cordate at base; flo. pink or white; fr. 6 mm., much exceeding sepals. Cultivated alien, casual. Flo. July–Aug.

Koenigia islandica L. ¶Annual; stem mostly 1–2 in.; leaves small, $\frac{1}{4} \times \frac{1}{8}$ in., obovate; ochreae short; flo. small, clustered; fr. trigonous. Mountains of Skye. Flo. Aug.–Sept.

Oxyria digyna (L.) Hill. **Mountain Sorrel.** ¶Stem 6–10 in.; leaves radical, reniform; inflo. leafless; inner sepals enlarging in fr. On damp mountain rocks, chiefly in Scotland. Flo. July–Aug. ✽.

Rumex conglomeratus Murr. **Sharp Dock.** ¶Leaves oblong, sometimes narrowed centrally; fr. sepals oblong, entire, all with tubercles. Common on waste ground, etc. Flo. July–Aug. ✽.

Rumex rupestris Le Gall. **Shore Dock.** ¶Leaves oblong, blunt, glaucous; fr. sepals oblong, entire, 4 mm., all with long tubercles, 2·5–3 mm. On sea cliffs in S.W. England, Wales and Channel Islands. Flo. June–Aug. ✽.

Rumex sanguineus L. var. *viridis* Sibth. **Red-veined Dock.** ¶Leaves ovate-lanceolate, with green or with red veins; fr. sepals oblong, entire, only 1 with a globular tubercle. In woods and shady places. Common except in Scotland, where it is local or rare. Flo. June–Aug. ✽.

Rumex maritimus L. **Golden Dock.** ¶Upper leaves linear-lanceolate; fr. sepals acute, with long, slender teeth and slender pedicels; plant golden in fruit. Wet ground near pools, chiefly in England rare. Flo. June–Sept. ✽.

Rumex palustris Sm. **Yellow Marsh Dock.** ¶Like above but fr. sepals and tubercles obtuse with shorter teeth; pedicles shorter, thicker. In wet ground near pools, chiefly S. and E. England, local. Flo. June–Sept. ✽ (fr. only).

Rumex pulcher L. **Fiddle Dock.** ¶Branches nearly horizontal; leaves oblong or fiddle shaped; fr. sepals ovate, toothed, all tubercled. In grassy places, mainly S. and E. England. Flo. June–July. ✽.

Rumex obtusifolius L. **Broad-leaved Dock.** ¶Lower leaves very broad, ovate-oblong; fr. sepals triangular, toothed, 1 with tubercle. Very common in cultivated and waste ground and field margins. Flo. July–Oct. ✽.

Rumex crispus L. **Curled Dock.** ¶Branches erect; leaves oblong-lanceolate, margins crisped; fr. sepals ovate, subentire, 1 or all tubercled. Common in cultivated and waste ground, etc. Fl June–Oct. ✽.

Rumex crispus × obtusifolius = R. × acutus L., *R. pratensis* Mert. & Koc ¶Intermediate between the parents. Common.

Rumex longifolius DC. **Long-leaved Dock.** *R. domesticus* Hartm *R. aquaticus* auct., non L. ¶Stem 1–4 ft; leaves very long, marg undulate; fr. sepals broadly cordate, entire; tubercles o. W places, N. England and Scotland. Flo. June–Aug. ✽.

Rumex patientia L. ¶Very tall; leaves ovate-acute; fr. sepals broad ovate, subentire, 1 with tubercle. Introduced in waste plac mainly in S. England. Flo. June–July.

Rumex hydrolapathum Huds. **Great Water Dock.** ¶Stem stou 5–6 ft; leaves ovate-lanceolate; ft. sepals 6–8 mm., triangula shortly dentate and tubercled. Margins of canals and poo common in S. England and Midlands, local in W. England, Wal and Ireland, and rare in Scotland. Flo. July–Sept. ✽.

Rumex aquaticus L. **Scottish Water Dock.** ¶Stem 5–6 ft; leav broad, cordate; fr. sepals ovate-triangular, entire, 5–8 mm tubercles o; pedicels slender. Watery places, W. Scotland, ve rare. Flo. July–Aug.

Rumex alpinus L. **Monk's Rhubarb.** ¶Rhizome creeping; leav rounded, as broad as long; fr. sepals ovate, entire; tubercles Introduced, near buildings, mainly in N. Flo. July–Aug.

Rumex scutatus L. **French Sorrel.** ¶Leaves 1–1½ in., rounded, broad as long, basal lobes diverging; flo. bisexual. Introduce Flo. June–July.

Rumex acetosa L. **Common Sorrel.** ¶Leaves oblong, hastate wi downward lobes; flo. unisexual, outer sepals reflexed. Comm in pastures. Flo. May–June. ✽.

Rumex acetosella L. **Sheep's Sorrel.** ¶Smaller, 6–10 in.; leav lanceolate, hastate, lobes spreading; flo. unisexual, outer sep erect. Common on heaths and acid soils. Flo. May–Aug. ✽.

Rumex tenuifolius (Wallr.) Löve. ¶Like above, but leaves very narro margins inrolled; fr. 1 mm. On poorest soils. Flo. May–Aug.

RUMEX
SANGUINEUS.

RUMEX
CONGLOMERATUS.

RUMEX
LONGIFOLIUS.

R. PALUSTRIS
FRUIT.
×2

RUMEX
RUPESTRIS.

RUMEX
MARITIMUS.
×2

RUMEX
PULCHER.

OXYRIA
DIGYNA.

RUMEX
OBTUSIFOLIUS.

RUMEX
CRISPUS.

RUMEX
HYDROLAPATHUM.

RUMEX
ACETOSA.
×2
×4

RUMEX
ACETOSELLA.

3→

Plate 75

ELAEAGNACEAE

Hippophae rhamnoides L. **Sea Buckthorn.** ¶Thorny shrub, 6–8 ft; leaves clothed with silvery scales; flo. small, green; fr. globose, orange. Sand dunes mainly on E. and S.E. coasts. Flo. March–April. ❀.

LORANTHACEAE

Viscum album L. **Mistletoe.** ¶Shrubby parasite, 2 ft; leaves thick; flo. mostly unisexual; petals yellowish; fr. white. On branches of apple, poplar and other trees, mainly in S. and E. England, local. Flo. Feb.–April. ❀.

SANTALACEAE

Thesium humifusum DC. **Bastard Toadflax.** ¶Slender, prostrate, root parasite; flo. small, with 3 bracteoles, cream. On various roots in chalky soil in S. and E. England. Flo. June–Aug. ❀.

EUPHORBIACEAE

Euphorbia peplis L. **Purple Spurge.** ¶Procumbent, purple; leaves lopsided with narrow stipules; bracts leaf-like; glands entire, rounded. Sandy shores, mainly in S.W. England and Channel Islands, very rare. Flo. July–Sept. ❀.

Euphorbia helioscopia L. **Sun Spurge.** ¶Erect 1½ ft; leaves obovate, narrowed below; bracts leaf-like; glands entire, green; capsule smooth. Common in cultivated land. Flo. May–Oct. ❀.

Euphorbia platyphyllos L. **Broad-leaved Spurge.** ¶Leaves oblong, base cordate; upper bracts different, deltoid; glands oval; capsule with warts. Arable land, chiefly S. England, local. Flo. June–Aug. ❀.

Euphorbia stricta L. **Upright Spurge.** ¶Similar to *E. platyphyllos*; leaves smaller, clasping; bracts changing gradually to leaves; capsule smaller, 1·5–2 mm., warts more prominent, cylindrical. In limestone woods, W. Gloucestershire and Monmouthshire, very rare. Flo. June–Sept.

Euphorbia hyberna L. **Irish Spurge.** ¶Perennial; leaves large, 3 in.; bracts ovate, rounded below; glands entire; capsule 5–6 mm., with prominent warts. Locally common in woods in S.W. Ireland, and very rare in woods in S.W. England. Flo. April–July. ❀.

*Euphorbia dulcis L. **Sweet Spurge.** ¶Perennial; leaves oblanceolate; upper bracts deltoid, truncate below; glands entire, green becoming purple; capsule 2–3 mm., warts prominent. Alien. Flo. June–Aug.

*Euphorbia corallioides L. ¶Tall, 2–3 ft; leaves lanceolate, woolly; bracts pilose; glands entire; capsule woolly. Introduced in Sussex, and elsewhere. Flo. May–June.

*Euphorbia pilosa L. **Hairy Spurge.** ¶Rhizome stout; stems 2–3 ft; leaves large, oblong, pilose; upper bracts oval; glands entire; capsule nearly smooth. Woods near Bath, probably extinct. Flo. May–June.

Euphorbia amygdaloides L. **Wood Spurge.** ¶Stem 2 ft, pubescent; upper bracts yellowish, united in pairs; glands with horns. Common in S. England. Flo. March–June. ❀.

*Euphorbia uralensis Fisch. ex Link. **Russian Spurge.** *E. virgata* Waldst. & Kit., non Desf. ¶Rhizome creeping; branches long; leaves 2½ in., narrowly oblong; glands with long horns. Locally naturalized, mostly S. and E. England. Flo. May–July.

Euphorbia esula L. ¶Rhizome creeping; branches short; leaves 1½ in. oblanceolate, widest near apex; glands with short horns. In woods, rare, and much confused with *E. uralensis*. Flo. May–July.

Euphorbia cyparissias L. **Cypress Spurge.** ¶Rhizome creeping; leaves narrowly linear, numerous; bracts yellowish; glands with short horns. Perhaps native on calcareous soils in S.E. England, but mainly garden escape. Flo. June–Sept. ❀.

Euphorbia paralias L. **Sea Spurge.** ¶Leaves oblong, blunt, thick and fleshy; glands with short horns; seeds smooth. On sandy sea shores, mainly S. and W. England, Wales and Ireland. Flo. Aug.–Sept. ❀.

Euphorbia portlandica L. **Portland Spurge.** ¶Leaves obovate-lanceolate, apiculate, glaucous; glands with long horns; seeds pitted. On sandy shores, S. and W. coasts of England and Wales and N. and E. coasts of Ireland. Flo. June–Sept. ❀.

Euphorbia peplus L. **Petty Spurge.** ¶Stem 6–10 in.; leaves ovate, stalked; bracts ovate; umbel rays 3; glands with long horns. Common weed in cultivated ground. Flo. May–Oct. ❀.

Euphorbia exigua L. **Dwarf Spurge.** ¶Stem 4–8 in.; slender; leaves linear, tapering, acute; bracts lanceolate; glands with long horns. Common in cultivated ground, chiefly S. and E. England. Flo. June–Aug. ❀.

Euphorbia lathyrus L. **Caper Spurge.** ¶Stem 2–3 ft; leaves large, narrowly oblong; bracts ovate-acute; glands with horns; capsule large. In woods, local, mostly a garden weed, chiefly in S. half of Britain. Flo. June–July. ❀.

Mercurialis perennis L. **Dog's Mercury.** ¶Rhizome perennial; stem unbranched, hairy; female flo. long stalked. Very common in woods, in England, Wales, and S. Scotland, local in Ireland, and very rare in N. Scotland. Flo. March–April. ❀.

Mercurialis annua L. **Annual Mercury.** ¶Annual; stem branched, subglabrous; female flo. subsessile in leaf axils. In cultivated soil, common in S. and E. England, local or rare elsewhere. Flo. July–Sept.

EUPHORBIA PEPLIS.

×5

×2½

EUPHORBIA
HYBERNA.

EUPHORBIA
PLATYPHYLLOS

×3½

EUPHORBIA
AMYGDALOIDES.

MERCURIALIS
PERENNIS.

EUPHORBIA
HELIOSCOPIA.

EUPHORBIA LATHYRUS.

EUPHORBIA
PEPLUS.

×3

×4

×3

EUPHORBIA
CYPARISSIAS.

VISCUM ALBUM.

HIPPOPHAE
RHAMNOIDES.

×4
PHORBIA PORTLANDICA

EUPHORBIA
EXIGUA

EUPHORBIA
PARALIAS.

THESIUM
HUMIFUSUM.

Plate 76   ❋ indicates plant is illustrated

ARISTOLOCHIACEAE

Asarum europaeum L. **Asarabacca.** ¶Rhizome thick; stem very short, pubescent, bearing 2 leaves, 2 scales and 1 purplish flo. In woods, rare, perhaps native. Flo. May–Aug. ❋.

Aristolochia clematitis* L. **Birchwort. ¶Rhizome long; stem 2 ft, flo. tube dull yellow; fr. ¾ in., pear shaped. Naturalized in a few places. Flo. June–Sept. ❋.

THYMELAEACEAE

Daphne mezereum L. **Mezereon.** ¶Erect shrub, 2 ft; leaves thin, not evergreen; flo. red-purple; fr. scarlet. Calcareous woods, mainly in England, introduced elsewhere, rare. Flo. Feb.–March. ❋.

Daphne laureola L. **Spurge Laurel.** ¶Erect shrub, 2 ft; leaves evergreen, thick and glossy; flo. green; fr. black. Calcareous woods, mainly S. and E. England. Flo. Feb.–May. ❋.

ULMACEAE

Ulmus glabra Huds. **Wych Elm.** *U. montana* Stokes. ¶Leaves obovate, 2–6 in., with long tapering point, base of longer side rounded, hiding petiole. Common in hedges, etc. Flo. Feb.–March. ❋.

Ulmus procera Salisb. **English Elm.** *U. campestris* auct. ¶Tall spreading tree; leaves 2–3 in., suborbicular or ovate-acute, unequal at base, teeth curved. Widespread in England, Wales and Ireland, rare in Scotland. Flo. Feb.–March. ❋.

Ulmus angustifolia (Weston) Weston. **Cornish Elm.** *U. stricta* (Ait.) Lindl. ¶Smaller tree; branches erect; leaves narrowly ovate, with blunt teeth. In S.W. England. Flo. Feb.–March.

Ulmus coritana Melville. ¶Spreading tree, 60 ft; leaves narrowly or broadly ovate, biserrate, glabrous above, glandular beneath; base asymmetrical. Mid and E. England. Flo. Feb.–March.
The hybrid. *U. coritana × glabra* is fairly common.

Ulmus carpinifolia Gled. **Smooth Elm.** *U. nitens* Moench. ¶Leaves long, obovate-lanceolate, acuminate, shining, biserrate, base unequal, lower part of long side often straight. Fairly common in E. England. Flo. Feb.–March.
Var. *plotii* (Druce) Tutin. ¶Branches spreading; leaves elliptic, subglabrous, base nearly equal sided. In Midlands and E. England.

CANNABINACEAE

Humulus lupulus L. **Hop.** ¶Stems long, climbing; male inflo. much branched; female with broad bracts. Common in hedges, etc., in S. and E. England, the Midlands, local in N. England, Wales and Ireland, and rare in Scotland. Flo. July–Aug. ❋.

URTICACEAE

Urtica dioica L. **Stinging Nettle.** ¶Stoloniferous; stem 2–3 ft; leaves 2½ in., cordate; flo. spikes 2–3 in. Too common. Flo. June–Sept. ❋.

Urtica urens L. **Small Nettle.** ¶Annual; stem 1 ft; leaves 1½ in. ovate, all hairs stinging; flo. spike ½ in. Cultivated ground, mostly on light soils, common in the E. half of Britain, local in the W. half of Britain, and in Ireland. Flo. June–Sept. ❋.

Parietaria judaica L. **Pellitory of the Wall.** *P. diffusa* Mert. & Koch *P. officinalis* auct. ¶Red stems and leaves softly hairy; female flo. terminal, male lateral; filaments elastic. In crevices of old walls etc., common in S. and E. England, the Midlands and Ireland, mainly coastal in Wales, local in N. England, and rare in Scotland. Flo. June–Sept. ❋.

Soleirolia soleirolii* (Req.). Dandy. **Mother of Thousands *Helxine soleirolii* Req. ¶Stems slender, creeping, matted; leaves small, round; flo. small. Spreading from rock gardens, common in hedge banks, walls, etc., in S.W. England. Flo. May–Sept.

MYRICACEAE

Myrica gale L. **Bog Myrtle, Sweet Gale.** ¶Stem 3 ft; leaves grey-green, with fragrant yellow glands; inflo. catkins; bracts and anthers red. In wet heaths and fens, chiefly in N.W. England Scotland and W. Ireland. Flo. April–May. ❋.

BETULACEAE

Betula pendula Roth. **Silver Birch.** *B. verrucosa* Ehrh. ¶Bark white twigs long, pendulous; leaves doubly serrate, glabrous; catkin scales reflexed. Common in woods, on heaths, etc. Flo. April– May. ❋.

Betula pubescens Ehrh. **Brown Birch.** ¶Stems more bushy, dark brown; leaves singly serrate, downy; catkin scales straight. Common on damp heaths, etc. Flo. April–May. ❋.
Subsp. *odorata* (Bechst.) E. F. Warb. ¶Young twigs and leaves have brown resinous warts, viscid buds and smaller leaves. Scottish Highlands. Flo. April–May.

Betula nana L. **Dwarf Birch.** ¶Dwarf shrub, 1–3 ft; leaves small suborbicular, crenate; catkins short, oval. Locally common on mountains in Mid and N. Scotland, and very rare in a solitary locality in Upper Teesdale, N. England. Flo. May. ❋.

ASARUM EUROPAEUM.

D.LAURE-
-OLA. ×4

DAPHNE
LAUREOLA.

DAPHNE
MEZEREUM.

ARISTOLOCHIA
CLEMATITIS.

URTICA DIOICA.

×3

PARIETARIA
DIFFUSA.

ENGLISH
ELM.

ULMUS
PROCERA.

ULMUS GLABRA.
WYCH ELM.

BETULA
NANA.

URTICA
URENS.

HOP.

MYRICA GALE
SWEET GALE.

HUMULUS
LUPULUS.

BETULA
PENDULA.

BETULA
PUBESCENS.

Plate 77   ❀ indicates plant is illustrated

BETULACEAE (continued)

Alnus glutinosa (L.) Gaertn. **Alder.** *A. rotundifolia* Stokes. Leaves blunt, green, veins few. In wet woods, by streamsides, etc., common. Flo. Feb.–March. ❀.

Alnus incana (L.) Moench. ¶Leaves acute, pale below, veins many. Planted, particularly in Scotland. Flo..March.

CORYLACEAE

Carpinus betulus L. **Hornbeam.** ¶Leaves plaited, ovate, serrate; fr. subtended by a very large 3-lobed bract. Common in woods and hedges in England, particularly the S.E., local in Wales and rare in Scotland and Ireland. Flo. May. ❀.

Coryllus avellana L. **Hazel.** ¶Leaves rounded, cordate, stipulate; female flo. small, enclosed in green bracts. In woods and hedges, common. Flo. March–April. ❀.

FAGACEAE

Quercus robur L. **Pedunculate Oak.** ¶Leaves subglabrous, mostly with a projecting auricle at base; flo. and fr. pedunculate. In woods, hedges, etc., common, especially on basic soils. Flo. April–May. ❀.

Quercus petraea (Mattuschka) Liebl. **Sessile Oak.** *Q. sessiliflora* Salisb. ¶Leaves with stellate hairs below, without auricle at base; flo. and fr. subsessile. In woods, hedges, etc., common, especially on acid soils. Flo. April–May. ❀.

Quercus petraea × robur = Q. × rosacea Bechst. ¶Intermediate between the two parents, it is sometimes found where they grow together.

Quercus ilex L. **Evergreen Oak, Holm Oak.** ¶Leaves evergreen, dark green, glossy above; whitish-grey tomentose beneath; entire, or lightly toothed; fr. cup with small ovate scales. Planted in woods and hedges where it sometimes regenerates, chiefly S. and E. England. Flo. April–May.

Quercus borealis Michx. f. var. *maxima* (Marsh.) Ashe. **Red Oak.** *Q. rubra* L. sec. Duroi, *Q. maxima* Marsh. Leaves oblong, with 3–5 pairs of triangular-acute pointed lobes reaching half-way to midrib; glabrous except for reddish-brown tufts of hair on the primary veins beneath; fr. cup shallow, saucer shaped, enclosing only base of fr. which is light brown and smooth. Planted in woods where it sometimes regenerates. Flo. May.

Quercus cerris L. **Turkey Oak.** ¶Leaves with many acute lobe fr. cup with spreading scales. Often planted in woods and hedge and regenerating freely. Flo. May.

Castanea sativa Mill. **Spanish Chestnut.** ¶Tree 70 ft; leaves oblon lanceolate, serrate; fr. 1–3 in a spinous involucre. Introduced, woods, hedges, etc. Flo. May.

Fagus sylvatica L. **Beech.** ¶Leaves ovate, silky; male catkins tasse like; fr. triquetrous in woody spinous involucre. Woods, especial on chalky soil. Flo. March–April. ❀.

SALICACEAE

Salix pentandra L. **Bay Willow.** ¶Stem 20 ft; leaves lanceolate, gloss catkin scales yellowish; stamens 5; capsule glabrous. Wet plac mainly in N. England, Scotland and N. Ireland, introduce elsewhere. Flo. May–June. ❀.

Salix triandra L. **Almond Willow.** ¶Stem 20 ft; leaves glabrou paler below; catkin scales yellowish; stamens 3; capsule glabrou Sides of streams and osier beds, chiefly in S. and E. England. Fl April. ❀.

Salix fragilis L. **Crack Willow.** ¶Stem 50 ft; twigs fragile at joint leaves long; catkins long, pendulous; scales yellowish; stamens By streams, ponds, etc. Common. Flo. April. ❀.

Salix alba L. **White Willow.** ¶Stem 50 ft; leaves white and silk catkin scales yellowish; stamens 2; stigma bifid. By stream ponds, etc. Common. Flo. April–May. ❀.

Salix purpurea L. **Purple Willow.** ¶Stem 4–10 ft; leaves blu green above, paler below; catkin scales dark at tip; stame connate, purple. In fens and osier beds, local. Flo. March–April. ❀

Salix viminalis L. **Common Osier.** ¶Stem 10–15 ft; twigs long an straight; leaves long, silky below; catkin scales dark at tip; anthe yellow. By streams and in osier beds, common. Flo. April–May. ❀

Salix lapponum L. **Downy Willow.** ¶Stem 30 ft; leaves oblon silky especially below; scales dark at tip; anthers yellow an brown. Wet mountain rocks, Scotland and N. England. July. ❀

Salix aurita L. **Eared Willow.** ¶Stem 4–6 ft with raised striatio under bark; leaves wrinkled, downy below, stipules large; scal dark at tip. In damp woods, on heaths, by moorland streams, etc throughout the British Isles, but especially frequent in Scotlan and N. Ireland. Flo. April–May. ❀.

ALNUS
GLUTINOSA.   ALDER.

CARPINUS
BETULUS.
HORNBEAM

HAZEL

QUERCUS
PETRAEA.
SESSILE
OAK

CORYLUS
AVELLANA

COMMON
OAK
QUERCUS
ROBUR.

FAGUS
SYLVATICA.

SALIX
TRIANDRA.

SALIX
ALBA.

SALIX
PENTANDRA.

SALIX
FRAGILIS.

SALIX
PURPUREA.

SALIX
VIMINALIS.

SALIX LAPPONUM.

SALIX AURITA.

Plate 78   ❀ indicates plant is illustrated

SALICACEAE (*continued*)

Salix caprea L. **Great Sallow.** ¶Stem 25 ft; twigs without striations; leaves ovate, grey tomentose beneath; catkin scales dark at tip. In woods and hedgerows. Flo. March–April. ❀.

Salix cinerea L. **Fen Sallow.**
Subsp. *cinerea*. ¶Stem 25 ft; twigs downy, with raised striations under bark; leaves obovate, grey beneath; anthers yellow. In fens, etc., in E. England, local. Flo. March–April.
Subsp. *oleifolia* Macreight **Common Sallow.** *S. atrocinerea* Brot., *S. cinerea* subsp. *atrocinerea* (Brot.) Silva & Sobrinho. ¶Stem 12–15 ft; twigs subglabrous, with raised striations under bark; leaves obovate, with rust-coloured hairs beneath; catkin scales dark at tip; anthers reddish. Common by streams. Flo. March–April. ❀.

Salix repens L. **Creeping Willow.** ¶Stems mostly prostrate; leaves oblong-lanceolate with silky hairs; catkin scales brown at tip. On wet heaths and sand dunes, common. Flo. April–May. ❀.

Salix nigricans Sm. **Dark-leaved Willow.** ¶Stems 6–12 ft, spreading, striate under bark; leaves deep green, paler pubescent below, black when dry; scales dark at tip. Mountains in the N. Flo. May. ❀.

Salix phylicifolia L. **Tea-leaved Willow.** ¶Stems 6–12 ft, striate under bark; leaves glabrous, glaucous below, not black when dry; scales dark tipped. Wet rocks in the N. Flo. April–May. ❀.

Salix hibernica Rech. f. ¶Similar to *S. phylicifolia* but not striate under bark; leaves broadly lanceolate to elliptical, almost entire, broadly cuneate at base, apex shortly acuminate (not tapering as in *S. phylicifolia*). Rocks, etc., in N.W. Ireland. Flo. April–May.

Salix arbuscula L. **Little Tree Willow.** ¶Low shrub; twigs striate; leaves glabrous above, glaucous beneath; scales brown tipped, with white hairs; anthers reddish. Mountains, Perthshire and Argyll. ❀.

Salix lanata L. **Woolly Willow.** ¶Large shrub; buds large, woolly; leaves silky above, woolly beneath; scales with long yellow hairs. Mountain rocks in Scotland, rare. Flo. June. ❀.

Salix myrsinites L. **Myrtle-leaved Willow.** ¶Low shrub; twigs not striate; leaves green and shining; scales purple, dark tipped, hairy; anthers purple. Wet mountain rocks, Scotland. Fl May–June. ❀.

Salix herbacea L. **Least Willow.** ¶Plant small, from rhizom leaves ½ in., suborbicular, bright green; catkins terminal. C mountain tops, plentiful in Scotland, local in N. England, Wal and Ireland. Flo. June–July. ❀.

Salix reticulata L. **Reticulate Willow.** ¶Stem creeping, rootin leaves 1 in., becoming subglabrous, oval, glaucous and retic late beneath. Rocks in Highlands of Scotland. Flo. June–July. ❀

*Populus alba L. **Lobed** or **White Poplar.** ¶Buds downy; leav suborbicular, snowy white beneath; catkin scales crenat stigmas linear, cruciform. Planted, not native. Flo. Marc April. ❀.

Populus canescens (Ait.) Sm. **Grey Poplar.** ¶Buds downy; leav grey beneath, broadly ovate, with 4–5 blunt teeth each sid scales laciniate. Damp woods mainly in S. England. Flo. Marc ❀ (leaf only).

Populus tremula L. **Aspen.** ¶Buds rather sticky; leaves glabrou broader than long, petiole compressed; catkin scales deep laciniate. In woods, on heaths, etc., common. Flo. March. ❀.

Populus nigra L. **Black Poplar.**
*Subsp. *nigra*. ¶Branches spreading; buds sticky; leaves glabrou acuminate, with many small crenate teeth; catkin scales laciniat Introduced, planted in woods, hedges, etc., not common. Fl April.
Subsp. *betulifolia* (Pursh) W. Wettst. *P. betulifolia* Pursh. ¶Similar subsp. *nigra* but with smaller leaves, and a delicate pubescence petioles, inflo. and young shoots. Perhaps native by streamsid in wet woods, etc., in S. and E. England and the Midlands, loca Flo. April.
Both subspecies are frequently confused with *P. × canadensis* va *serotina* which is common.
Var. *italica* Duroi, *P. italica* (Duroi) Moench. **Lombardy Popla** ¶Branches and twigs all closely erect, fastigiate; leaf blad smaller. Often planted.

*Populus × canadensis Moench var. *serotina* (Hartig) Rehd. **Hybri Black Poplar.** *P. serotina* Hartig. ¶Very similar to *P. nigr* branches ascending; buds longer; leaves with teeth a little deepe often with 2 glands at base of blade. Planted. Flo. April.

SALIX ARBUSCULA.

SALIX APREA

SALIX ATROCINEREA

SALIX PHYLICIFOLIA

SALIX MYRSINITES.

SALIX HERBACEA.

SALIX NIGRICANS.

SALIX RETICULATA

SALIX REPENS.

SALIX LANATA

POPULUS NIGRA.

POPULUS TREMULA.

P ×CANESCENS

POPULUS ALBA.

Plate 79 ❄ indicates plant is illustrated

Monocotyledones

ALISMATACEAE

Baldellia ranunculoides (L.) Parl. **Lesser Water Plantain.** *Alisma ranunculoides* L. ¶Stems 1 ft; leaves narrow, lanceolate; flo. whorled, lilac; fr. head spherical. Beside streams and ponds, local. Flo. May–Aug. ❄.
Var. *repens* Davies. ¶Has flo. larger, ¾ in., on creeping stems. Lakesides, Wales and Ireland.

Luronium natans (L.) Raf. **Floating Water Plantain.** *Alisma natans* L. ¶Stems long, floating; leaves long petioled, small obtuse; flo. solitary, white. In lakes and canals, chiefly in Wales, rare. Flo. Aug. ❄.

Alisma plantago-aquatica L. **Water Plantain.** ¶Leaves ovate, rounded at base; flo. pinkish white; anthers twice as long as broad; style lateral, long. Beside ponds and ditches, common, except in Scotland, where it is local. Flo. July–Aug. ❄

Alisma lanceolatum With. **Lanceolate Water Plantain.** ¶Leaves lanceolate, narrowed below; anthers as long as broad; style short near top of ovary. Mainly in S. and E. England, less common. Flo. July–Aug. ❄.

Alisma lanceolatum × *plantago-aquatica.* ¶Intermediate between the parents, it often occurs where the two grow together.

Alisma gramineum Lejeune. ¶Leaves very long, strap-like, ¼–½ in. wide, submerged, or oblong, petiolate; flo. below or above water; stigma curled; fruit widest at top; stalk arcuate. River Glen and other streams in Lincolnshire and near Droitwich, Worcestershire. Flo. July–Sept.

Damasonium alisma Mill. **Thrumwort, Star-fruit.** *D. stellatum* Thuill. ¶Leaves floating, oblong, 5 veined; flo. white; carpels with long beak, star-like. In ponds and ditches, with gravelly or sandy bottoms in S. England, rare. Flo. June–July. ❄.

Sagittaria sagittifolia L. **Arrowhead.** ¶Stoloniferous; aerial leaves arrow-shaped; flo. white with purple centre. In mud by streams and ponds, common in S. and E. England and the Midlands, local in Ireland, rare in Wales, and introduced and very rare in S.W. England and Scotland. Flo. July–Aug. ❄.

BUTOMACEAE

Butomus umbellatus L. **Flowering Rush.** ¶Stem 3 ft; leaves linear, triquetrous; flo. pink. By ponds and dikes, local, but widespread in most of England except the N. where it is rare, rather rare in Wales and Ireland, and introduced and very rare in Scotland. Flo. July–Sept. ❄.

HYDROCHARITACEAE

Hydrocharis morsus-ranae L. **Frog-bit.** ¶Stems floating; leaves in tufts; flo. dioecious, white, springing from pellucid sheaths. canals and ponds, locally common in S. and E. England and Midlands, rare in Wales, N. England and Ireland and absent from Scotland. Flo. July–Aug. ❄.

Stratiotes aloides L. **Water Soldier.** ¶Stem submerged, rising surface for flo.; leaves spinous-serrate, aloe-like; flo. dioecious white. Ponds and ditches in E. England, introduced elsewhere rare. Flo. June–Aug. ❄.

Elodea nuttalii (Planch.) St. John. *Hydrilla verticillata* auct. ¶Stem submerged, very long; leaves linear, acute, with small sharp teeth and small scales near the base. In Esthwaite Water, N. Lancs. and W. Galway, Ireland. Flo. not recorded from the British Isles.

*Elodea canadensis Michx. **Canadian Pondweed.** ¶Stem submerged leaves oblong, dark green, 3 in whorl; flo. with long, slender tube, purplish. In still waters, introduced, common, except in Scotland. Flo. May–Sept. ❄.

*Elodea ernstae St. John, *E. callitrichoides* auct., non (Rich.) Casp. ¶Stems submerged; leaves lanceolate, acute or acuminate, translucent, dark green, lightly toothed, usually in whorls of 3; flo. dioecious, small, solitary, whitish; male flo. on pedicels 20–30 mm long; female flo. submerged with very long stigmas which reach the surface of the water. Introduced. Naturalized in ponds and streams, chiefly S. England. Female plants only have so far been found in Britain. Flo. Oct.–Nov.

*Lagarosiphon major (Ridl.) Moss. ¶Stems stout, rigid, submerged long, leafy throughout, superficially resembling a robust, luxuriant form of *Elodea canadensis*; leaves thick, dark green, translucent linear-acute, with short blunt triangular-shaped teeth; flo. dioecious, small, whitish, enclosed in long spathes; male spathe ovate, many flowered, flo. floating free on water on reaching the surface; female spathe ovate or oblong; 1 flowered. Introduced. Naturalized in ponds, lakes, slow streams, etc., chiefly S. England. Flo. June–Sept.

JUNCAGINACEAE

Triglochin palustris L. **Marsh Arrow-grass.** ¶Leaves filiform semicylindrical to tip; fr. linear; carpels adhering at tip. marshy places, local, but widespread. Flo. June–Aug. ❄.

Triglochin maritima L. **Sea Arrow-grass.** ¶Leaves linear, flattened at tip; fr. ovoid, carpels separating. Sea-shores and salt marsh Flo. July–Sept. ❄.

SCHEUCHZERIACEAE

Scheuchzeria palustris L. ¶Stem 6 in.; leaves linear, semicylindrical with a pore at top; flo. yellowish green. In wet moss, Perthshire and Argyll, Scotland and Offaly, Ireland, formerly known from Shropshire and elsewhere, very rare. Flo. June–Aug. ❄.

LURONIUM NATANS.

BUTOMUS
UMBELLATUS.

FLOWERING
RUSH.

BALDELLIA
RANUNCULOIDES.

ALISMA
LANCEOLATUM.

SAGITTARIA
SAGITTIFOLIA
ARROW
HEAD.

ALISMA
PLANTAGO-
-AQUATICA.

GLOCHIN
RITIMA.

DAMASONIUM
ALISMA.

TRIGLOCHIN
PALUSTRIS.

SCHEUCHZERIA
PALUSTRIS.

HYDROCHARIS
MORSUS-RANAE.

FROG-BIT.

WATER
SOLDIER.

STRATIOTES ALOIDES.

ELODEA
CANADENSIS.

Plate 80

❀ indicates plant is illustrated

ORCHIDACEAE

Hammarbya paludosa (L.) Kuntze. **Little Bog Orchid.** *Malaxis paludosa* (L.) Sw. ¶Stem 1–4 in.; leaves concave, bearing tiny bulbils; flo. green, with lip at back. In sphagnum bogs, mostly northern, very rare in S. Flo. Aug.–Sept. ❀

Liparis loeselii (L.) Rich. **Fen Orchid.** ¶Stem 4–6 in.; flo. yellowish green, lip oblong, mostly upwards; leaves lanceolate or ovate (var. *ovata* Riddelsd. ex Godfery, Glamorgan and Carmarthen dunes). Mostly in fens in E. England. Flo. July. ❀

Corallorhiza trifida Chatel. **Coral Root.** ¶Root fleshy with rounded lobes or branches; saprophyte with brown scales; flo. yellowish, lip white, purple spotted. Boggy woods in Scotland and N. England. Flo. June–Aug. ❀

Neottia nidus-avis (L.) Rich. **Bird's-nest Orchid.** ¶Roots many, thick, interlaced; saprophyte with brown scales; flo. brown. In shady woods, especially of beech, chiefly in S. half of Britain. Flo. June–July. ❀

Listera ovata (L.) R. Br. **Twayblade.** ¶Stem 18 in.; leaves 2, large, 4–6 in., ribbed; flo. spike long and green. In damp woods and shady pastures, locally common except in N. Scotland. Flo. June–July. ❀

Listera cordata (L.) R. Br. **Lesser Twayblade.** ¶Stem 6–8 in.; leaves small, 1 in., opposite; flo. spike small, reddish. In sphagnum under heather and in woods, Scotland, N.W. England, rare in S.W. England, Wales and Ireland. Flo. July–Sept. ❀

Spiranthes spiralis (L.) Chevall. **Lady's Tresses.** *S. autumnalis* Rich. Tubers ovate; leaves radical, ovate; flo. white in 1 spiral. In pasture, often calcareous, chiefly in S. half of Britain and S. Ireland, absent from Scotland. Flo. Aug.–Sept. ❀

Spiranthes aestivalis (Poir.) Rich. **Summer Lady's Tresses.** ¶Roots cylindrical; stem bearing lanceolate leaves; flo. white in 1 spiral. Formerly in marshy ground in the New Forest, Hampshire, and in the Channel Islands, but probably now extinct. Flo. July–Aug. ❀

Spiranthes romanzoffiana Cham. **Threefold Lady's Tresses.** ¶Roots cylindrical; leaves cauline; flo. in 3 spiral rows. Flo. Aug.–Sept. Subsp. *gemmipara* (Sm.) Clapham. ¶Cauline leaves fairly broad, not acuminate; flo. close together, white. In S.W. Ireland and W. Devon, very rare. Subsp. *stricta* (Rydb.) Clapham. ¶Leaves long, narrow, acuminate; flo. greenish white; spike long and lax. N.E. Ireland, Hebrides and Argyll, in boggy pastures.

Goodyera repens (L.) R. Br. **Creeping Lady's Tresses.** ¶Rhizome creeping; stem glandular; leaves net veined; flo. white; lip pouched. Pine woods in Scotland and N. England, also in E. Anglia where it may have been introduced. Flo. Aug. ❀

Epipogium aphyllum Sw. **Leafless Epipogium.** ¶Stem 3–7 saprophyte with brown scales; flo. few; petals long, lanceol yellowish; lip upwards, cordate, white with purple spots. Wood deep shade in S. England, formerly in Herefordshire and Shr shire, very rare.

Cephalanthera rubra (L.) Rich. **Red Helleborine.** ¶Leaves lanceola acute; flo. rose-red; lip white tipped with purple; ovary dow shorter than bract. In calcareous woods, in Gloucestershire a Buckinghamshire, very rare. Flo. June–July. ❀

Cephalanthera longifolia (L.) Fritsch. **Long-leaved Hellebori** *C. ensifolia* (Schmidt) Rich. ¶Leaves long and narrow; flo. wh petals acute; ovary glabrous, longer than bracts. Woods calcareous soil, local and rare. Flo. May–July. ❀

Cephalanthera damasonium (Mill.) Druce. **White Helleborine.** *grandiflora* Gray. ¶Leaves ovate-oblong; petals white, oblo blunt; lip with yellow spot. Woods, especially beech, on calcare soil, chiefly in S. England. Flo. May–June. ❀

Epipactis phyllanthes G. E. Sm. ¶Flo. cernuous or hanging dov open or closed until fertilized, pale green; lip-like lateral pet not fully differentiated. Woods and sand dunes on calcare soil. Flo. July–Aug. Var. *pendula* (C. Thomas) D. P. Young. ¶Lip more differ tiated, depression at base (hypochile) as long as reflexed (epichile). Northern. Var. *vectensis* (T. & T. A. Stephenson) D. P. Young. ¶Lip w small green hypochile and longer straight tip (epichile). Southe Var. *degenera* D. P. Young. ¶Lip with shallow, rudiment depression at base.

Epipactis leptochila (Godfery) Godfery. **Narrow-lipped Hel borine.** ¶Flo. spreading and open, green; lip green with hy chile red spotted within, tip long, spreading. Shady woods mai in S. England. Flo. June–Aug. ❀

Epipactis dunensis (T. & T. A. Stephenson) Godfery. ¶Flo. completely open; epichile as broad as long. Lancashire a Anglesey dunes.

Epipactis helleborine (L.) Crantz. **Broad Helleborine.** *E. latifolia* (All. ¶Leaves broadly ovate; sepals green; lip purple, fu differentiated, tip recurved; ovary subglabrous. In woods, loca common, except in Scotland where it is rare. Flo. July–Sept.

Epipactis purpurata Sm. **Violet Helleborine.** *E. sessilifolia* Peter ¶Leaves narrower, ovate-lanceolate, purple beneath; bra long; sepals greenish; lip whitish with recurved tip; ovary hai Calcareous woods, mainly in S. England and Midlands, loc Flo. Aug.–Sept.

Epipactis atrorubens (Hoffm.) Schult. **Dark-red Helleborine.** *atropurpurea* Raf. ¶Leaves small, elliptic; petals dark red-purp lip broad with rugose swellings and reflexed tip. Limestone roc N. Wales, N. England, N. Scotland and W. Ireland, local a rare. Flo. June–July. ❀

MMARBYA
LUDOSA.

LIPARIS
LOESELII.

CORALLORHIZA
TRIFIDA

NEOTTIA
NIDUS-AVIS.

EPIPACTIS
ATRORUBENS

EPIPACTIS
HELLEBORINE.

EPIPACTIS
LEPTOCHILA

CEPHALANTHERA
RUBRA.

PIRANTHES
PIRALIS.

LISTERA
OVATA.

SPIRANTHES
AESTIVALIS.

LISTERA
CORDATA

GOODYERA REPENS

CEPHALANTHERA
LONGIFOLIA.

CEPHALANTHERA
DAMASONIUM.

Plate 81

❀ indicates plant is illustrated

❀ ORCHIDACEAE (*continued*)

Epipactis palustris (L.) Crantz. **Marsh Helleborine.** ¶Rhizome creeping; outer sepals greenish, inner white flushed with pink; lip crenate, with red veins and yellow spots. In fens, marshes and dunes, widespread, but local. Flo. June–Aug. ❀.

Anacamptis pyramidalis (L.) Rich. **Pyramidal Orchid.** *Orchis pyramidalis* L. ¶Spike pyramidal; flo. rose; lip with 3 oblong lobes and 2 tubercles; spur long and slender. On calcareous soils, widespread, but local in England and Ireland, rare in Wales and Scotland. Flo. July. ❀.

Himantoglossum hircinum (L.) Spreng. **Lizard Orchid.** *Orchis hircina* (L.) Crantz. ¶Plant tall, 2–3 ft; flo. green and brown; lip with 3 linear lobes, central lobe very long and twisted. Wood margins and rough grassy places usually on calcareous soil, mainly S. and E. England, very rare. Flo. May. ❀.

Aceras anthropophorum (L.) Ait. f. **Man Orchid.** ¶Tubers ovoid; sepals green, forming a hood; lip yellowish with 4 linear lobes; spur o. On chalk mainly in S. and E. England, local. Flo. June–July. ❀ on plate 82.

Orchis simia Lam. **Monkey Orchid.** ¶Tubers ovoid; flo. pale or crimson, hooded; lip with 4 narrow crimson lobes; spur cylindrical. On chalk, in S. England, very rare. Flo. May. ❀.

Orchis militaris L. **Soldier Orchid.** ¶Tubers ovoid; flo. pale purple with darker veins; lip 4 lobed with upturned ends. In woods on chalk in S. and E. England, very rare. Flo. May. ❀.

Orchis purpurea Huds. **Lady Orchid.** ¶Tubers ovoid; sepals forming hood, veined dark purple; lip broad, whitish, spotted red. Woods and shady places on chalk, mainly in Kent. Flo. May. ❀.

Orchis ustulata L. **Dwarf Orchid.** ¶Tubers ovoid; stem 6 in.; flo. small; hood dark purple, becoming white; lip white, spotted red. On calcareous hills, mainly S. England, local. Flo. June. ❀.

Orchis morio L. **Green-winged Orchid.** ¶Tubers ovoid; flo. hood with dark green veins; lip crimson-purple with pale centre. In moist meadows, mainly in S. half of Britain, and mid Ireland, locally plentiful. ❀.

Orchis mascula (L.) **Early Purple Orchid.** ¶Tubers ovoid; leaves blotched; flo. rich red-purple; lip nearly flat, spotted on pale centre. In shady places, common. Flo. April–May. ❀.

Orchis laxiflora Lam. **Jersey Orchid.** ¶Tubers ovoid; leaves ribbed, not blotched; sides of lip recurved, centre not spotted. W meadows in Channel Islands. Flo. May–June. ❀.

Dactylorhiza incarnata (L.) Soó. *Dactylorchis incarnata* (L.) Vermeu *Orchis strictifolia* Opiz. ¶Stem hollow; leaves yellow-gree unspotted; flo. flesh colour; sides of lip reflexed. Wet meadow and marshes, widespread, but local. Flo. May–July. ❀.
Subsp. *coccinea* (Pugsl.) Soó. ¶Flo. smaller, bright red. Dunes in N.W
Subsp. *pulchella* (Druce) Soó. ¶Flo. reddish purple, lip nearly flat.

Dactylorhiza kerryensis (Wilmott) P. F. Hunt & Summerhaye *Dactylorchis majalis* auct. ¶Stem 1 ft, hollow; 6 leaves, 2 × ⅞ ir with or without ring-shaped spots; flo. red-purple; lip 8 × mm., mid lobe triangular; spur narrow, 2·5 mm. Marsh meadows, Ireland, etc. Flo. May–June.
Subsp. *occidentalis* (Pugsl.) P. F. Hunt & Summerhayes. ¶Ste 6–10 in.; leaves much spotted, often arcuate; flo. spike shor deep red-purple. W. Ireland and N.W. Scotland.

Dactylorhiza praetermissa (Druce) Soó. *Dactylorchis praetermissa* (Druc Vermeul. *Orchis praetermissa* Druce. ¶Stem 18 in., hollow; 6 leave 6 × 1 in., mostly unspotted; flo. deep red-purple; lip 9 × 11 mm mid lobe short; spur broad. Basic marshes, S. and E. Englan Midlands and S. Wales. Flo. May–June. ❀.

Dactylorhiza purpurella (T. & T. A. Stephenson) Soó. *Dactylorch purpurella* (T. & T. A. Stephenson) Vermeul. ¶Stem 8 in., slight hollow; 6 leaves, 4½ × ¾ in., slightly spotted; flo. very deep re purple; lip 6 × 8 mm., entire; spur broad. Mainly Wales, N England, Scotland and N. Ireland. Flo. June–July. ❀.

Dactylorhiza traunsteineri (Sauter) Soó. *Dactylorchis traunsteineri* (Saute Vermeul. ¶Stem 1 ft, slightly hollow; 4 leaves, lanceolate, 4½ × in., transversely marked; flo. deep red-purple; lip deltoid, m lobe triangular. In calcareous fens from S. and E. England Wales and S. Scotland, local and rare. Flo. May–July.

Dactylorhiza maculata (L.) Soó. *Dactylorchis maculata* (L.) Vermeu
Subsp. *ericetorum* (E. F. Linton) P. F. Hunt & Summerhaye ¶Stem solid; lower leaves acute, spotted; flo. pale lilac or whitis spotted; outer lobes of lip broad, rounded; spur slender. Pe moors, heaths, etc. Flo. May–July. ❀.

Dactylorhiza fuchsii (Druce) Soó. *Dactylorchis fuchsii* (Druce) Vermeu *Orchis fuchsii* Druce. ¶Stem solid; lower leaves blunt, spotted; fl lilac or whitish; lip with 3 rather deep triangular lobes. In wood meadows, marshes, etc., on basic soils, widespread, but local. Fl June–Aug. ❀.
Subsp. *hebridensis* (Wilmott) Soó. ¶Lobes of lip rounded, deep re In Hebrides only.

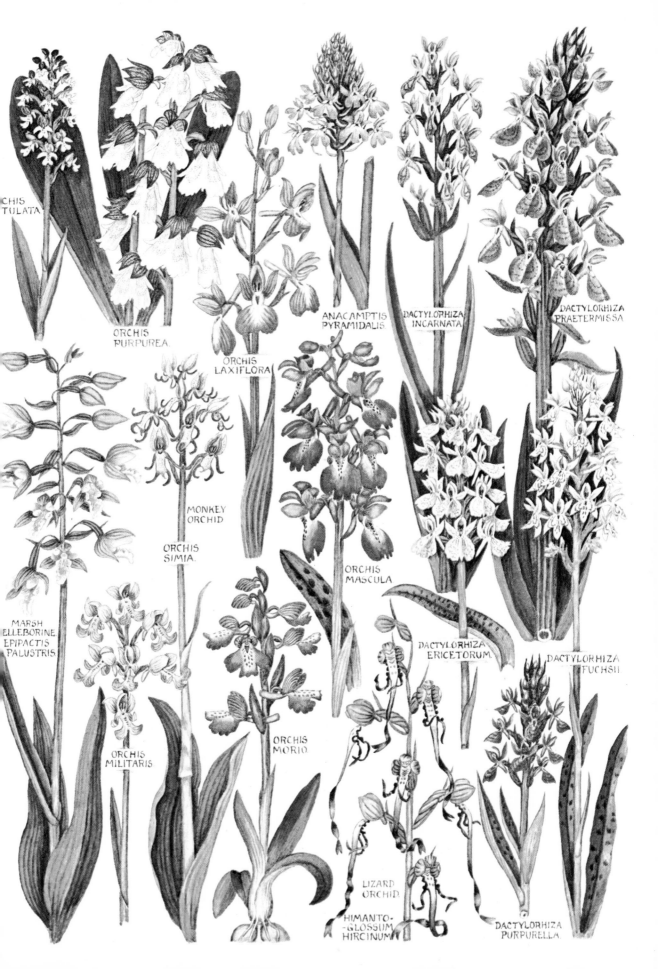

CHIS
TULATA

ORCHIS
PURPUREA.

ANACAMPTIS
PYRAMIDALIS.

DACTYLORHIZA
INCARNATA.

DACTYLORHIZA
PRAETERMISSA

ORCHIS
LAXIFLORA

MONKEY
ORCHID

ORCHIS
SIMIA.

ORCHIS
MASCULA

MARSH
ELLEBORINE
EPIPACTIS
PALUSTRIS

DACTYLORHIZA
ERICETORUM.

DACTYLORHIZA
FUCHSII

ORCHIS
MILITARIS.

ORCHIS
MORIO.

LIZARD
ORCHID

HIMANTO-
GLOSSUM
HIRCINUM

DACTYLORHIZA
PURPURELLA.

Plate 82   ❈ indicates plant is illustrated

ORCHIDACEAE (*continued*)

Ophrys apifera Huds. **Bee Orchid.** ¶Sepals pink or whitish, inner small; lip very convex with tip recurved and hidden; side lobes hairy. On calcareous and basic soils, chiefly S. and E. England and the Midlands, rare in N. England and Ireland, mainly coastal in Wales, and absent from S.W. England and Scotland. Flo. June–July. ❈.
Var. *trollii* (Heg.) Druce. ¶Lip more yellow, nearly flat, tip spreading. ❈.

Ophrys fuciflora (Crantz) Moench. **Late Spider Orchid.** *O. arachnites* (L.) Reichard. ¶Outer sepals pink; inner narrow, downy; lip broad, brown, velvety, becoming convex; tip upturned. On chalk downs, S.E. England, very rare. Flo. June–July. ❈.

Ophrys sphegodes Mill. **Early Spider Orchid.** *O. aranifera* Huds. ¶Outer sepals green, inner green or brown; lip broad, brown, velvet with green edges, without a point. On chalk downs, S. England. Flo. April–June. ❈.

Ophrys insectifera L. **Fly Orchid.** *O. muscifera* Huds. ¶Plant slender; outer sepals green, inner filiform; lip narrow, oblong, rich brown with pale blue centre. On chalky soil. Mainly in S. half of Britain. Flo. May–June. ❈.

Herminium monorchis (L.) R. Br. **Musk Orchid.** ¶Stem 4–6 in.; flo. very small; sepals greenish; lip narrow, green, 3 lobed, pouched below. On calcareous soil in S. England, rare. Flo. June–July. ❈.

Gymnadenia conopsea (L.) R. Br. **Sweet-scented Orchid.** *Habenaria conopsea* (L.) Benth. ¶Flo. many, rose-pink or variable, fragrant; lip with 3 equal lobes and long slender spur. On basic or calcareous soil, locally plentiful. Flo. June–July. ❈.

Neotinea intacta (Link) Reichb. f. ¶Leaves oblong, often slightly spotted; flo. pinkish white; lip with lateral lobes narrow; spur short. Limestone pastures in W. Ireland, and in a solitary locality in the I. of Man. Flo. April–June.

Leucorchis albida (L.) E. Mey. ex Schur. **Small White Orchid.** *Habenaria albida* (L.) R. Br. ¶Root of fleshy fibres; flo. small, pendulous, greenish white; lip 3 lobed; spur short. On hill pastures, mainly in the N. Flo. June–July. ❈.

Coeloglossum viride (L.) Hartm. **Frog Orchid.** ¶Stem 3–8 in.; flo. green; lip linear, brownish green, tubercled; spur short. In upland pastures, widespread, but local. Flo. June–Aug. ❈.

Platanthera chlorantha (Custer) Reichb. **Butterfly Orchid.** *Habenaria chlorantha* Bab. ¶Stem 18 in.; flo. white, scented; pollinia diverging below; spur curved downwards. In moist woods on basic and chalky soils, widespread, but local. Flo. May–July. ❈.

Platanthera bifolia (L.) Rich. **Lesser Butterfly Orchid.** *Habenaria bifolia* (L.) R. Br. ¶Stem 10 in.; flo. white, scented; pollinia parallel; spur slender, horizontal. Open woods, pastures, heaths etc., on basic and chalky soils. Flo. May–July. ❈.

Cypripedium calceolus L. **Lady's Slipper.** ¶Flower sepals maroon, lateral twisted, 2 lower often connate; lip large, inflated, yellow. Woods on limestone, Yorkshire and Durham, very rare. Flo. May–June. ❈.

×3½

O. FUCIFLORA.

OPHRYS
APIFERA.

OPHRYS
INSECTIFERA

OPHRYS
SPHEGODES.

HERMINIUM
MONORCHIS.

×4½

VAR. TROLLII.

ACERAS
ANTHROPOPHORUM

GYMNADENIA
CONOPSEA.

PLATANTHERA
CHLORANTHA

LEUCORCHIS
ALBIDA.

LADY'S SLIPPER
CYPRIPEDIUM CALCEOLUS

COELOGLOSSUM
VIRIDE.

PLATANTHERA BIFOLIA.

×4

Plate 83   ❀ indicates plant is illustrated

IRIDACEAE

Iris pseudacorus L. **Yellow Flag.** ¶Stem 3 ft; leaves stiff, sword-like; flo. large, bright yellow; seeds brown. In wet fields and marshes, common. Flo. May–July. ❀.

Iris foetidissima L. **Stinking Iris.** ¶Stem 2 ft; leaves weak; flo. mauve with dark veins, rarely yellow; seeds scarlet. Woods and thickets on dry calcareous soils, chiefly in S. half of Britain, elsewhere as an introduction. Flo. May–July. ❀.

*Iris spuria L. ¶Stem 3 ft; leaves linear; flo. violet and whitish; capsule with long point. Naturalized in fen dikes in Lincolnshire. Flo. June–July. ❀.

*Hermodactylus tuberosus (L.) Mill. *Iris tuberosa* L. ¶Tubers finger-like; stem 1 ft; leaves linear, 4 angled; flo. sepals dark purple, inner thread-like. Naturalized in Cornwall and Channel Islands. Flo. April.

*Crocus nudiflorus Sm. **Naked Autumn Crocus.** ¶Corm stoloni-ferous; leaves in spring; flo. in autumn, purple; stigma finely divided. Meadows mainly in the Midlands, not native. Flo. Sept.–Oct.

*Crocus purpureus Weston. **Purple Crocus.** *C. vernus* auct. ¶Corm not stoloniferous; leaves with the purple or white flo.; stigmas blunt, orange. In meadows, mainly in S. and E. England, local, not native. Flo. March–April. ❀.

Romulea columnae Seb. & Mauri. **Warren Crocus.** *R. parviflora* Bub. ¶Corm ¼ in.; leaves very narrow, recurved; flo. pale lilac, midribs darker; fr. recurved. Sand near the sea, S. Devon and Channel Islands. Flo. April. ❀.

Sisyrinchium bermudiana L. **Blue-eyed Grass.** *S. angustifolium* Mill. ¶Leaves grass-like; spathe 2–3 flowered; flo. blue, paler outside; filaments united. Wet meadows and hills, W. Ireland. Flo. July. ❀.

Gladiolus illyricus Koch. ¶Stem 2 ft; leaves glaucous; flo. sepals crimson-purple or paler with dark centres; anthers shórter than filaments. Bushy heaths, Hampshire, Dorset, and formerly in the I. of Wight. Flo. July. ❀.

*Gladiolus segetum Ker-Gawl. ¶Flo. larger, crimson-purple; anther longer than filaments. A garden escape.

AMARYLLIDACEAE

Narcissus pseudonarcissus L. **Wild Daffodil.** ¶Stem 6–9 in.; flo petals pale; corona deep yellow, irregularly lobed. In damp woods and riversides, locally plentiful. Flo. March–April. ❀.

Narcissus obvallaris Salisb. **Tenby Daffodil.** ¶Stem 10–12 in. flo. petals deep yellow; corona distinctly 6 lobed, spreading In grass near Tenby, Pembrokeshire. Flo. April. ❀.

*Narcissus hispanicus Gouan. **Spanish Daffodil.** *N. major* Curt ¶Stem 18 in.; flo. petals deep yellow; corona spreading, obscurely lobed. A garden escape. Flo. April.

*Narcissus majalis Curt. **Pheasant's Eye.** *N. poeticus* auct. ¶Flo petals white; corona very short, yellow with red rim. Flo. May.

*Narcissus × biflorus Curt. **Primrose Peerless.** ¶Stem with flo.; petals white; corona short, yellow. A hybrid, garden escape not fruiting. Flo. April–May. ❀.

Galanthus nivalis L. **Snowdrop.** ¶Leaves glaucous; flo. white pendulous, with green spot on short inner petals. Perhaps native in damp woods in S.W. England, Wales and adjacent counties elsewhere as an introduction. Flo. Jan.–March. ❀.

Leucojum aestivum L. **Summer Snowflake.** ¶Stem 18 in.; spath green at apex, with 3–6 flo. white with green tips. In wet meadow and withy beds, chiefly S. England, elsewhere as an introduction local. Flo. May. ❀.

Leucojum vernum L. **Spring Snowflake.** ¶Stem 8 in.; spathe gree in middle, with 1 flo. white with green tips. In Dorset and Somer set, elsewhere as an introduction, very rare. Flo. Feb.–March. ❀

IRIS
PSEUDACORUS

ROMULEA
COLUMNÆ

IRIS
FOETIDISSIMA.

CROCUS
PURPUREUS.

SISYRINCHIUM
BERMUDIANA.

IRIS
SPURIA.

LEUCOJUM
AESTIVUM

LEUCOJUM
VERNUM.

NARCISSUS
PSEUDO-
NARCISSUS.

NARCISSUS
OBVALLARIS.

TENBY
DAFFODIL.

DIOLUS
RICUS.

×NARCISSUS
BIFLORUS.

LENT
LILY.

GALANTHUS
NIVALIS.
SNOWDROP.

Plate 84 ✿ indicates plant is illustrated

DIOSCOREACEAE

Tamus communis L. **Black Bryony.** ¶Root a tuber; stem very long, twining; flo. dioecious, yellow-green; berry red. In woods and hedgerows, common in England and Wales, except in the N., introduced and very rare in Scotland, and absent from Ireland. Flo. May–July. ✿.

LILIACEAE

Ruscus aculeatus L. **Butcher's Broom.** ¶Stem 2 ft; flo. small, greenish, in centre of leaf-like branch or cladode; berry red. In woods and on cliffs, mostly in S. and E. England and S. Wales, elsewhere as an introduction. Flo. Feb.–April. ✿.

Asparagus officinalis L.
Subsp. *prostratus* (Dumort.) E. F. Warb. **Wild Asparagus.** ¶Stems prostrate; leaves minute, scarious; cladodes clustered, rigid; flo. yellow-green; berry red. On sea cliffs and sand, S. and S.W. England, Channel Islands, Wales and E. Ireland. Flo. June–Aug. ✿.
Subsp. *officinalis.* ¶Stems erect, tall; cladodes slender and flexuous; flo. yellow-green; berry red. Introduced. Garden escape. Naturalized in grassy places, etc., common in S. and E. England. Flo. July–Oct.

Polygonatum verticillatum (L.) All. **Whorled Solomon's Seal.** ¶Leaves whorled; flo. constricted in the middle; filaments papillose; berry red. Mountain woods in Northumberland, Dumfries-shire, Perthshire, rare. Flo. June–July. ✿.

Polygonatum odoratum (Mill.) Druce. **Lesser Solomon's Seal.** ¶Stem 6–8 in.; flo. cylindrical, often solitary; filaments glabrous; berry bluish black. In calcareous woods, W. and N. England and Wales, elsewhere as an introduction, very local. Flo. June–July. ✿.

Polygonatum multiflorum (L.) All. **Solomon's Seal.** ¶Stem 2 ft; flo. constricted in the middle; filaments downy; berry black. In woods, mostly S. England and Wales, local. Flo. May–June. ✿.

A hybrid of the last two species is sometimes found, outcast from gardens.

Maianthemum bifolium (L.) Schmidt. **May Lily.** ¶Stem 4–8 in.; leaves 2 only; flo. petals 4, whitish, fragrant; fr. red. In woods, N. Yorkshire and N. Lincolnshire, and formerly in Middlesex, very rare. Flo. May–June. ✿.

Convallaria majalis L. **Lily of the Valley.** ¶Stem 6–8 in., angular leaves large; bracts scarious; flo. white, scented; berry red. In hilly calcareous woods, widespread, but local throughout Britain introduced in Ireland. Flo. May. ✿.

Simethis planifolia (L.) Gren. & Godr. *S. bicolor* (Desf.) Kunth ¶Stem 6–18 in.; leaves grass-like; flo. purple outside, whitish within; very rare. On a heath, Co. Kerry and introduced near Bournemouth. Flo. June–July. ✿.

Allium ampeloprasum L. **Wild Leek.** ¶Stem 3–4 ft; leaves 1½ in wide; umbel compact; flo. many; usually without bulbils Rocky coasts, Cornwall, Steep Holm, Pembrokeshire, Guernsey Flo. July–Aug.

Allium babingtonii Borrer. ¶Stem 3–4 ft; leaves broad; umbel irregular, with secondary heads and many large bulbils. Coasts of Cornwall and W. Ireland. Flo. August.

Allium scorodoprasum L. **Sand Leek.** ¶Stem 2–3 ft; leaves ¼–½ in wide; spathes 2; flo. rose with purple bulbils. Dry soils mainly in N. England and Scotland. Flo. July–Aug. ✿.

Allium sphaerocephalon L. **Round-headed Leek.** ¶Leaves tubular spathes 2; umbels without bulbils; flo. rose; stamens with lateral points shorter than anthers. St Vincent rocks, Bristol and Jersey Flo. June–July.

Allium vineale L. **Crow Garlic.** ¶Stem 2 ft; leaves tubular; spathe 1 flo. rose with many bulbils; stamens with lateral points longer than anthers. Common in S. half of Britain, less frequent in N., becoming rare in Scotland, very local in Ireland. Flo. June–Aug. ✿.

CONVALLARIA
MAJALIS.

POLYGONATUM
MULTIFLORUM.

TAMUS
COMMUNIS.

POLYGONATUM
ODORATUM.

ALLIUM
SCORODOPRASUM.

MAIANTHEMUM
BIFOLIUM.

POLYGONATUM
VERTICILLATUM.

SIMETHIS
PLANIFOLIA.

ALLIUM VINEALE.
CROW GARLIC.

ASPARAGUS
PROSTRATUS.

RUSCUS
ACULEATUS.

Plate 85   ❀ indicates plant is illustrated

LILIACEAE (continued)

Allium oleraceum L. **Field Garlic.** ¶Leaves fleshy, solid; spathes 2, long; flo. few, pink or brownish, with bulbils, stamens not trifid, equalling petals. Field borders, etc., widely distributed but rare. Flo. July–Aug. ❀.

*Allium carinatum L. ¶Similar to *A. oleraceum*, but leaves flat, grooved; petals bright pink; stamens longer than petals. Introduced, mainly N. England and Scotland. Flo. Aug.

Allium schoenoprasum L. **Chives.** ¶Leaves cylindrical; spathes 2; flo. umbel dense, globose; stamens half as long as spreading pink petals. On limestone, W. and N. England, Wales, elsewhere as an introduction, rare. Flo. June–July. ❀.
A. sibiricum auct. of W. Cornwall and Pembrokeshire is now said to be only a form of *A. schoenoprasum*. ❀.

*Allium roseum L. ¶Leaves linear, flat; spathes 2–4, short; flo. pink, with bulbils. Locally naturalized. Flo. June.

*Allium triquetrum L. **Triangular-stalked Garlic.** ¶Stem triquetrous; leaves radical, linear, keeled; spathes 2, short; flo. large, white. Naturalized in woods, etc., in W. Cornwall, S. Wales, S.W. Ireland and Guernsey. Flo. April–June. ❀.

*Allium paradoxum (Bieb.) G. Don. ¶Similar to *A. triquetrum*, but smaller, with brighter green stem and leaves; inflo. 1–4 flowered with numerous bulbils; flo. small, white. Naturalized in woods, thickets, plantations, by roadsides, etc., widely distributed, and increasing, though as yet rather rare. Flo. April–May.

Allium ursinum L. **Ransoms, Wood Garlic.** ¶Stem triquetrous; leaves broad, elliptic; flo. white, petals acute. Common in moist woods. Flo. April–June. ❀.

Muscari atlanticum Boiss. & Reut. **Grape Hyacinth.** *M. racemosum* auct. ¶Stem 6 in.; leaves narrow, flaccid; bracts minute; flo. dark blue, uppermost smaller, sterile. Sandy fields in E. England. Flo. April–May. ❀.

Scilla autumnalis L. **Autumn Squill.** ¶Leaves autumnal; flo. pale purple, without bracts; anthers purple. Dry pastures, usually near the sea, in S. England, elsewhere as an introduction. Flo. July–Sept. ❀.

Scilla verna Huds. **Spring Squill.** ¶Leaves in spring; flo. pale blue, with bracts; anthers blue. Mainly in W. coastal pastures, locally plentiful. Flo. April–May. ❀.

Endymion non-scriptus (L.) Garcke. **Bluebell.** *Scilla nutans* Sm. ¶Flo. nodding, cylindrical, petal tips recurved; anthers yellow. Woods, abundant over most of Britain, less frequent in Ireland. Flo. May (April–June). ❀.

*Endymion hispanicus (Mill.) Chouard. ¶Flo. erect, paler; petals more open, tips not recurved; anthers purple. A garden escape. Flo. May.

*Endymion hispanicus × non-scriptus. ¶Intermediate between the parents, it is commonly grown in gardens, and occurs in scrub, fields, etc., as an outcast or escape. Flo. May.

Ornithogalum umbellatum L. **Star of Bethlehem.** ¶Leaves green with white midrib; flo. subumbellate, erect, large, white. Perhaps native in grassy places in S. and E. England, elsewhere as an introduction. Flo. April–June. ❀.

*Ornithogalum nutans L. ¶Leaves glaucous; flo. in a nodding raceme, greenish white, petals 1 in. long. Introduced. Naturalized in grassy places, mostly S. and E. England, rare. Flo. April–May. ❀.

Ornithogalum pyrenaicum L. **Spiked Star of Bethlehem, Bath Asparagus.** ¶Leaves in spring, fading early; flo. many in erect spike, petals spreading. In woods, local, common near Bath. Flo. June–July. ❀.

*Lilium pyrenaicum Gouan. **Pyrenean Lily.** ¶Leaves alternate, lanceolate; flo. nodding, yellow with black spots. Naturalized in woods and hedge banks, N. Devon, etc. Flo. June–July. ❀.

*Lilium martagon L. **Turk's-cap Lily.** ¶Stem 2–3 ft; leaves mostly whorled; flo. nodding, pale purple with dark warts. Naturalized in woods, mostly S. England, local. Flo. Aug.–Sept.

Fritillaria meleagris L. **Fritillary, Snake's-head.** ¶Leaves few, linear; flo. nodding, red-purple, chequered dark and light; fr. erect. Damp meadows in S. and E. England, and the Midlands, local. Flo. May. ❀.

Tulipa sylvestris L. **Wild Tulip.** ¶Leaves linear; flo. bright yellow; fr. oblong, trigonous. Naturalized in meadows, etc., mainly in S. and E. England. Flo. April–May. ❀.

LILIUM
PYRENAICUM.

ALLIUM
SCHOENOPRASUM.

"ALLIUM
SIBIRICUM."

ALLIUM
OLERACEUM.

ALLIUM
URSINUM.

ALLIUM
TRI-
QUETRUM.

FRITILLARIA
MELEAGRIS.

TULIPA
SYLVESTRIS.

SCILLA
AUTUMNALIS.

IUSCARI
ANTICUM

SCILLA
VERNA.

ENDYMION
NON-SCRIPTUS.

ORNITHOGALUM
NUTANS.

ORNITHOGALUM
PYRENAICUM.

ORNITHOGALUM
UMBELLATUM.

Plate 86

LILIACEAE (*continued*)

Gagea lutea (L.) Ker-Gawl. **Yellow Star of Bethlehem.** ¶Bulb small; stem 6–8 in. with 1 hooded radical leaf and 2 bracts; flo. greenish yellow. Woods and grassy places in Britain, widespread, but very local. Flo. March–May. ❀.

Lloydia serotina (L.) Reichb. **Mountain Spiderwort.** ¶Stem 3–6 in.; leaves slender, triquetrous; flo. white with red-purple veins. Snowdon, very rare. Flo. June–July. ❀.

Colchicum autumnale L. **Meadow Saffron.** ¶Leaves large, oblong, 8–12 in. in spring; flo. in autumn, pale purple, like crocus but with 6 stamens. Meadows, mainly in S. half of Britain, very local, and very rare in Ireland. Flo. Sept.–Oct. ❀.

Narthecium ossifragum (L.) Huds. **Bog Asphodel.** ¶Leaves radical, rigid, linear; flo. bright yellow; anthers orange. Common in bogs on acid moors, chiefly W. and N. Britain, widespread in Ireland. Flo. July–Sept. ❀.

Tofieldia pusilla (Michx.) Pers. **Scottish Asphodel.** ¶Leaves sword-shaped; spike dense; bracts small, 3 lobed; flo. greenish white. By mountain streams, Scotland and N. England. Flo. June–Aug. ❀.

Paris quadrifolia L. **Herb Paris.** ¶Leaves 4, whorled; flo. solitary; sepals 8, acute, green; fr. a black berry. Woods on chalky soil, widespread, but very local over most of England except the S.W., where it is rare; rare in Wales, very rare in Scotland, and absent from Ireland. Flo. May–July. ❀.

JUNCACEAE

Juncus bufonius L. **Toad Rush.** ¶Dwarf 1 in. or 6–8 in.; flo. solitary or 2–3 together; sepals long or short, acuminate, green with hyaline border. Ditches and muddy places, common. ❀.

Juncus trifidus L. **Three-leaved Rush.** ¶Rhizome creeping; stems crowded, with 1 leaf; flo. 1–3 between 2 long leafy bracts. Mountain tops in Scotland. Flo. June–Aug. ❀.

Juncus squarrosus L. **Heath Rush.** ¶Leaves rigid, pressed to ground; bracts broad; inflo. terminal; flo. brown. Acid heaths and moors, abundant. Flo. June–July. ❀.

Juncus compressus Jacq. **Round-fruited Rush.** ¶Stems tufted; infl terminal, shorter than bract; flo. about 30; anthers equalli filaments; capsule subglobose. On basic soils, widespread, b local, in England; rare in Wales and absent from Scotland a Ireland. Flo. June–July. ❀.

*Juncus subulatus Forsk. ¶Rhizomatous; stems leafy, 2–3 ft; leav glaucous, hollow; bract short; flo. many, green; stamens 6, shor styles twisted; capsule trigonous. Spreading in new salt mars Berrow, Somerset.

Juncus gerardii Lois. **Salt Mud Rush.** ¶Rhizome creeping; inf terminal, few flowered, longer than bract; anthers 3 times leng of filaments; capsule acute. Salt marshes, common. Flo. June–Jul ❀.

*Juncus tenuis Willd. **Slender Rush.** *J. macer* S. F. Gray. ¶Leav with long auricles; inflo. terminal, overtopped by long bracts; f straw coloured. Waysides, heaths and woodland tracts, spreadin Flo. Aug. ❀.

Juncus balticus Willd. **Baltic Rush.** ¶Rhizome widely creeping; le sheaths broad; inflo. lateral at $\frac{2}{3}$ height; flo. about 12, brow stamens 3. Dune slacks in Scotland and Lancashire. Flo. Jun Aug. ❀.

Juncus filiformis L. **Thread Rush.** ¶Rhizome creeping; stems slende inflo. lateral at $\frac{1}{2}$ height; flo. 6–8, pale; stamens 6. Lakesides, etc mostly N. England and S. Scotland, local. Flo. June–Sept. ❀.

Juncus inflexus L. **Hard Rush.** *J. glaucus* Sibth. ¶Stem 2 ft, glaucou with 12–18 striae; pith interrupted; inflo. lateral, lax, wi straight branches. Wet basic soils, common. Flo. June–Aug. ❀.

Juncus effusus L. **Soft Rush.** *J. communis* auct. ¶Stem 2½ ft, gloss green; inflo. lateral; bract not expanded; flo. greenish; capsu yellowish, retuse, not apiculate. Wet meadows, common. Fl June–Aug. ❀.

Juncus subuliflorus Drej. **Common Rush.** *J. conglomeratus* auc ¶Stem 2½ ft, greyish green; inflo. dense, subglobose; base of bra expanded; flo. brown; capsule retuse, apiculate. Wet heaths, field etc., locally common. Flo. May–July. ❀.

GEA
TEA.

PARIS
QUADRIFOLIA.

TOFIELDIA
PUSILLA.

LLOYDIA
SEROTINA.

JUNCUS
CONGLOMER-
-ATUS.

NARTHECIUM
OSSIFRAGUM.

COLCHICUM
AUTUMNALE.

JUNCUS
GERARDII.

JUNCUS
BALTICUS.

JUNCUS
TRIFIDUS.

JUNCUS
INFLEXUS

JUNCUS
COMPRESSUS

JUNCUS
FILIFORMIS.

x2

JUNCUS
TENUIS

x2

JUNCUS
SQUARROSUS.

JUNCUS
EFFUSUS

x2

JUNCUS
BUFONIUS

Plate 87 ❅ indicates plant is illustrated

JUNCACEAE (*continued*)

Juncus maritimus Lam. **Sea Rush.** ¶Stem and leaves wiry, pointed; inflo. shorter than bract, erect; sepals lanceolate, outer acute, pale straw coloured. Salt marshes, common. Flo. July–Aug. ❅.

Juncus acutus L. **Sharp Sea Rush.** ¶Stem tall, stout, sharply pointed; sepals ovate, blunt, reddish brown with scarious margins. On sea sands, England, Wales and S. Ireland, rare. Flo. June. ❅.

Juncus subnodulosus Schrank. **Blunt-flowered Rush.** *J. obtusiflorus* Ehrh. ex Hoffm. ¶Stem 2–3 ft; leaves septate; secondary branches on inflo. at a wide angle; sepals obtuse; capsule ovoid. Marshes on basic soil, locally abundant in E. England, widely distributed elsewhere though rather rare. Flo. July–Sept. ❅.

Juncus acutiflorus Ehrh. ex Hoffm. **Sharp-flowered Rush.** *J. sylvaticus* auct. ¶Stem 2½ ft; leaves septate; secondary branches of inflo. at acute angle; sepals very acute, shorter than acute tapering capsule. Marshes, especially on acid soils, common. Flo. July–Sept. ❅.

Juncus articulatus L. **Jointed Rush.** *J. lampocarpus* Ehrh. ex Hoffm. ¶1–2 ft; leaves curved, septate; inflo. branches few; sepals acute; capsule shining, blackish, ovoid-acuminate. Common, especially on acid soil. Flo. June–Aug. ❅.

Juncus alpinoarticulatus Chaix. **Alpine Rush.** *J. alpinus* Vill. ¶Leaves septate; inflo. small; sepals obtuse, outer mucronate; capsule obtuse, mucronate. Wet places on mountains, N. England and Scotland, rare. Flo. July–Aug.

Juncus nodulosus Wahlenb. ¶Similar to *J. alpinus* but with inflo. irregular, some flo. subsessile, others on long peduncles in small umbels. Shore of Loch Ussie, E. Ross and near Braemar, Aberdeenshire.

Juncus bulbosus L. **Bulbous Rush.** *J. supinus* Moench. ¶Stems and leaves slender, often prostrate or floating; inflo. irregular; stamens 3; anthers equalling filaments; flo. viviparous. Wet heaths, bogs, pond verges, etc., on acid soils, common. Flo. June–Sept. ❅.

Juncus kochii F. W. Schultz. ¶Similar to *J. bulbosus*, more upright; stamens 6; anthers shorter than filaments. Probably common, but confused with *J. bulbosus*. Flo. June–Sept. ❅.

Juncus castaneus Sm. **Chestnut Rush.** ¶Stem 6–12 in.; leaves and long bract tapering to blunt point; heads 1–3; flo. very large, rich brown; capsule ¼ in. On high mountains, Scotland. Flo. June–July. ❅.

Juncus triglumis L. **Three-flowered Rush.** ¶Stems 3–6 in.; terete; leaves of 2 tubes; auricles large; flo. usually 3, level, capsule ovate. Wet places on high mountains, N. England, Scotland. Flo. June–July. ❅.

Juncus biglumis L. **Two-flowered Rush.** ¶Stems 2–6 in., channelled; leaves of 1 tube; auricles small; flo. 2, 1 above; capsu retuse. High mountains in Scotland, very rare. Flo. June–July. ◀

Juncus capitatus Weigel. **Capitate Rush.** ¶Annual, 1–4 in.; leav setaceous, without auricles; flo. clusters terminal, sessile, ov topped by a bract. W. Cornwall, Anglesey, Hebrides. F May–June. ❅.

Juncus mutabilis Lam. **Pigmy Rush.** *J. pygmaeus* Rich. ¶Annu 1–2 in., purplish; leaf sheath long, auricled; flo. cylindrical purplish, sessile clusters. W. Cornwall and Hebrides. Flo. Ma June. ❅.

Luzula forsteri (Sm.) DC. **Forster's Wood-rush.** ¶Branches su erect in flo. and fr.; leaves narrow; flo. reddish; capsule sho acuminate; seed appendage short. Basic soils, S. England a Wales. Flo. April–June. ❅.

Luzula pilosa (L.) Willd. **Hairy Wood-rush.** ¶Branches spreadin deflexed in fr.; flo. brown; leaves 4 mm. wide; capsule obpyrifor to cover long seed appendages. Woods, common througho Britain, except E. Anglia, where it is rare; local in Ireland. F April–June. ❅.

Luzula sylvatica (Huds.) Gaudin. **Great Wood-rush.** *L. maxi* (Reichard) DC. ¶Large tussocks; leaves ¼–½ in. wide; infl broadly spreading; flo. brown. In woods, especially on acid so common over most of Britain, especially in the N., but rare in Anglia; local in Ireland. Flo. May–June. ❅.

Luzula luzuloides (Lam.) Dandy & Wilmott. *L. albida* (Hoffm.) D ¶Similar to *L. sylvatica* but smaller; leaves ¼ in. wide; flo. din white or pinkish. Introduced in woods, chiefly in N. England, rar Flo. June–July.

Luzula spicata (L.) DC. **Spiked Wood-rush.** ¶Stem 6 in.; leav small; inflo. drooping, dense, spike-like; sepals finely pointed. C mountains, mainly Scotland. Flo. June–July. ❅.

Luzula arcuata Sw. **Curved Wood-rush.** ¶Dwarf, 2–3 in.; leav narrow; flo. clusters on few arcuate branches; sepals exceedir capsule. On high mountains, N. Scotland. Flo. June–July. ❅.

Luzula campestris (L.) DC. **Field Wood-rush.** ¶6 in.; inflo. of sessile and a few stalked clusters; anthers prominent, much long than filaments; seeds subglobose. Common in grassy places, et Flo. April–May. ❅.

Luzula multiflora (Retz.) Lejeune. **Many-flowered Wood-rus** *L. erecta* Desv. ¶1–1½ ft; inflo. dense, subspherical or of sever short-stalked clusters; anthers equalling filaments; seeds oblon Peaty moors, open woods on acid soils, etc., common. Flo. Apri June. ❅.

Luzula pallescens Sw. **Fen Wood-rush.** ¶Stem 6–12 in.; inflo. su umbellate of several clusters; flo. small, pale; capsule obovoi seeds oblong. In fens, Huntingdonshire, introduced elsewher very rare. Flo. April–May.

JUNCUS
CAPITATUS.

JUNCUS
MUTABILIS.

JUNCUS
ACUTIFLORUS.

JUNCUS
ARTICULATUS.

JUNCUS
MARITIMUS

JUNCUS
ACUTUS.

JUNCUS
BIGLUMIS.

JUNCUS
TRIGLUMIS.

JUNCUS
SUBNODULOSUS.
BLUNT FLOWERED
RUSH

LUZULA
MULTIFLORA

LUZULA
PILOSA.

LUZULA
FORSTERI.

JUNCUS
CASTANEUS.

LUZULA
SPICATA.

LUZULA
ARCUATA.

LUZULA
SYLVATICA.

LUZULA
CAMPESTRIS.

JUNCUS
STOCHII.

JUNCUS BULBOSUS.

x2

Plate 88　❄❄ indicates plant is illustrated

TYPHACEAE

Typha latifolia L. **Bulrush, Reedmace.** ¶6–7 ft; leaves $\frac{1}{2}$–$\frac{3}{8}$ in. wide; male and female inflo. contiguous, female without bracteoles. Beside streams and ponds, common throughout most of England, but local in Wales and Ireland, and rare in Scotland. Flo. June–July. ❄❄.

Typha angustifolia L. **Narrow-leaved Reedmace.** ¶6–7 ft; leaves $\frac{1}{8}$–$\frac{1}{4}$ in. wide; male and female inflo. separated, female with slender bracteoles. Beside streams and ponds, chiefly in S. and E. England, local. Flo. June–July. ❄❄.

SPARGANIACEAE

Sparganium erectum L. **Branched Bur-reed.** *S. ramosum* Huds. ¶Stem branched, whitish below; leaves keeled; fr. $\frac{1}{4}$ in., angled, abruptly contracted to beak. Beside ponds and ditches, common. Flo. June–Aug. ❄❄.
Var. *neglectum* (Beeby) Fiori & Paol. *S. neglectum* Beeby. ¶Stem red below; fr. $\frac{3}{8}$ in., terete, tapering to beak. More local.

Sparganium emersum Rehm. **Unbranched Bur-reed.** *S. simplex* Huds. ¶Stem unbranched; leaves keeled; male heads with elongate anthers; lowest fr. head stalked. By ponds and ditches on basic soils, common, but less frequent than *S. erectum*. Flo. June–July. ❄❄.

Sparganium augustifolium Michx. **Floating Bur-reed.** *S. natans* auct. ¶Leaves floating, base expanded; anthers small; fr. tapering above and below; lowest head stalked. Mostly in mountain lakes and streams in Wales, N. England, Scotland and Ireland. Flo. July–Sept. ❄❄.

Sparganium minimum Wallr. **Small Bur-reed.** ¶Leaves thin, floating, base not expanded; male flo. head usually solitary; fr. oval. Lakes and pools, especially on acid soils, mostly in Wales, N. England, Scotland and Ireland, local. Flo. June–July. ❄❄.

ARACEAE

Arum maculatum L. **Lords-and-Ladies, Cuckoo-pint.** ¶Leaves early spring, spotted or not; midrib dark green; spadix usua purple, $\frac{1}{2}$ length of erect spathe. Hedge banks, common throug out most of England, Wales and Ireland, local in Scotland. F April–May. ❄❄.

Arum italicum Mill. ¶Leaves before winter, unspotted; midrib lig green; spadix orange, $\frac{1}{3}$ length of pale green, drooping spat Mostly near S. coast of England, local. Flo. April–May. ❄❄.

*Acorus calamus L. **Sweet Flag.** ¶Stem 4 ft; spathe stem-like; lea with wavy edges, scented when crushed; flo. crowded. Introduce margins of pools, mostly in England. Flo. June–July. ❄❄.

*Calla palustris L. ¶Stem creeping; leaves broadly cordate or rounde spathe oval, whitish; spadix crowded with flo. Introduced, swam and pond sides, Surrey and elsewhere. Flo. June.

LEMNACEAE

Lemna trisulca L. **Ivy Duckweed.** ¶Frond thin, stalked, mostly su merged, branching at right angles; 1 root to each frond. In pon etc., locally common in England and Ireland, rare in Wales a Scotland. Flo. June–July. ❄❄.

Lemna minor L. **Lesser Duckweed.** ¶Frond ovate, budding free with single root. In ponds, etc., common, except in N. Scotlar Flo. June–July. ❄❄.

Lemna gibba L. **Gibbous Duckweed.** ¶Frond hemispherical, fla tish above, rounded below, with single root. In ponds, etc., mai S. and E. England and the Midlands, local. Flo. rare, summer. ❄

Spirodela polyrhiza (L.) Schleid. **Great Duckweed.** *Lemna polyrhiza* ¶Frond $\frac{1}{4}$–$\frac{3}{8}$ in. wide; roots many. In ponds, mostly S. and England and the Midlands, local. Flo. very rare, July. ❄❄.

Wolffia arrhiza (L.) Hork. ex Wimm. ¶Frond only 1 mm., ovoi rootless. In still waters, mainly S. England.

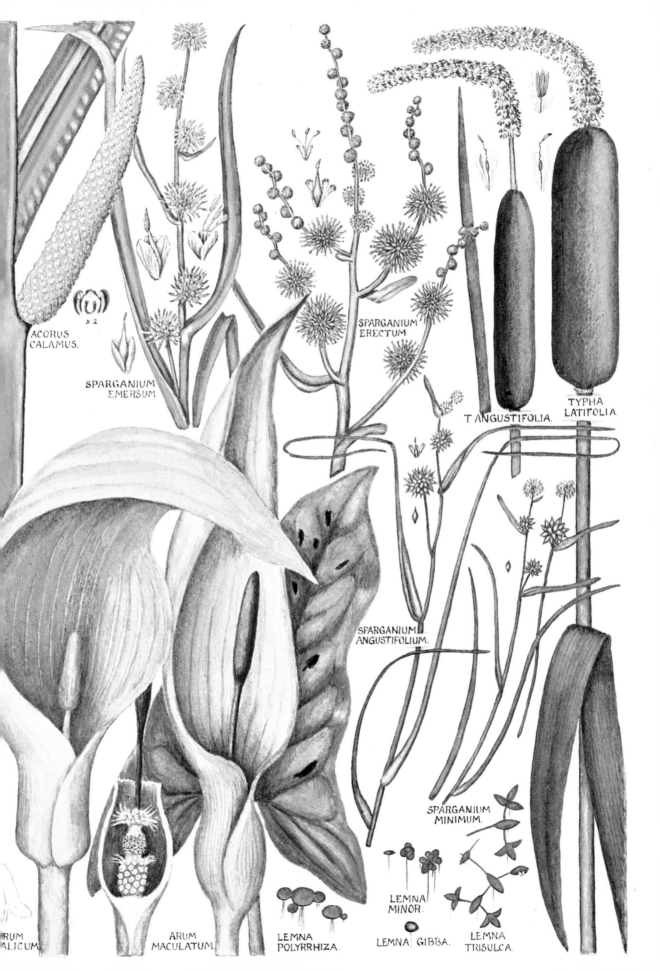

ACORUS
CALAMUS.

× 2

SPARGANIUM
EMERSUM.

SPARGANIUM
ERECTUM.

T. ANGUSTIFOLIA.

TYPHA
LATIFOLIA.

SPARGANIUM
ANGUSTIFOLIUM.

SPARGANIUM
MINIMUM.

RUM
ALICUM.

ARUM
MACULATUM.

LEMNA
POLYRRHIZA.

LEMNA
MINOR.

LEMNA GIBBA.

LEMNA
TRISULCA.

Plate 89

POTAMOGETONACEAE

Groenlandia densa (L.) Fourr. **Opposite-leaved Pondweed.** *Potamogeton densus* L. ¶Leaves opposite; stipules o except in involucre, where they adhere to the leaves; spike very short, recurved. Clear streams and ponds, mostly in England. Flo. May–Aug. ❊.

Potamogeton natans L. **Floating Pondweed.** ¶Submerged leaves without blades; blade of floating leaves elliptical, jointed at base. Lakes and ponds, common. Flo. May–Aug. ❊.

Potamogeton polygonifolius Pourr. **Bog Pondweed.** *P. oblongus* Viv. ¶Blade of submerged leaves lanceolate, of floating leaves elliptical, not jointed at base. Bogs and acid pools, common, except in mid and E. England, where it is local or rare. Flo. June–Sept. ❊.

Potamogeton coloratus Hornem. **Fen Pondweed.** ¶Leaves mostly elliptical, stalked, thin, beautifully net veined; fr. very small, green; stalk slender. Calcareous fen pools, mainly E. England and Ireland, local. Flo. June–July. ❊.

Potamogeton lucens L. **Shining Pondweed.** ¶Leaves all submerged, large, oblong, short stalked; stipules large; fr. spike 2 in.; stalk thickened above. Ponds, streams, etc., mostly S. and E. England and the Midlands, locally common. Flo. June–Sept. ❊.

Potamogeton alpinus Balb. **Reddish Pondweed.** *P. rufescens* Schrad. ¶Leaves narrowly oblong, reddish, short stalked; fr. spike 1½ in., stalk not thickened. Lakes and ditches, widespread, but local. Flo. June–Sept. ❊.

Potamogeton nodosus Poir. **Loddon Pondweed.** ¶Leaves long stalked, elliptical, beautifully net veined; fr. stalk long, stout, not thicken above. In R. Thames, Avon, Stour and Loddon, local. Flo. Aug Sept. ❊.

Potamogeton gramineus L. **Various-leaved Pondweed.** *P. hete phyllus* Schreb. ¶Densely branched at base; submerged lea lanceolate, sessile; floating leaves oblong, long stalked; fr. st thickened above. Chiefly in acid waters in E. Anglia, N. Engla Scotland and Ireland. Flo. Aug.–Sept. ❊.

Potamogeton × zizii Koch ex Roth.= *P. gramineus × lucens*. Like *lucens* but with some oblong, stalked floating leaves; submerg leaves sessile. Local.

Potamogeton × nitens Weber= *P. gramineus × perfoliatus*. Little branch at base; submerged leaves cordate below; floating leaves lo stalked or o.

Potamogeton epihydrus Raf. **American Pondweed.** ¶Submerg leaves very long, linear, ¼ in. wide; with broad air tissue; floati leaves broad, elliptical, stalked; peduncle slender. Hebrid introduced in W. Yorkshire.

Potamogeton praelongus Wulf. **Long-stalked Pondweed.** ¶Leav submerged, strap shaped, narrowed to apex, rounded at sess base; fr. stalk long. Lakes, etc., mainly Midland counties nor wards. Flo. May–Aug. ❊.

Potamogeton perfoliatus L. **Perfoliate Pondweed.** ¶Leaves claspi the stem, cordate-ovate, but sometimes narrower; stipule sma soon falling; fr. stalk stout. Ponds, streams, etc., common. F June–Aug. ❊.

POTAMOGETON
POLYGONIFOLIUS.

POTAMOGETON
GRAMINEUS.

AMOGETON
IATANS.

POTAMOGETON
COLORATUS

POTAMOGETON
LUCENS

POTAMOGETON
PERFOLIATUS.

POTAMOGETON
PRAELONGUS.

POTAMOGETON
ALPINUS.

POTAMOGETON NODOSUS.

GROENLANDIA
DENSA.

Plate 90   ❄ indicates plant is illustrated

POTAMOGETONACEAE (continued)

Potamogeton crispus L. **Curled Pondweed.** ¶Leaves oblong, blunt, sessile, wavy, denticulate; fr. with a long beak. Ponds, streams, etc., common. Flo. May–Sept. ❄.

Potamogeton rutilus Wolfg. **Shetland Pondweed.** ¶Leaves very narrow, 1 mm. wide or less, tapering to a fine point; stipules strongly veined, acuminate. Lakes, Outer Hebrides, and Shetland. Flo. Aug.

Potamogeton pusillus L. **Small Pondweed.** *P. panormitanus* Biv. ¶Leaves very narrow, 1 mm. wide, blunt; lateral veins faint; stipules ⅔ tubular; beak of fr. nearly central. Ponds, streams, etc., mainly England. Flo. June–Sept. ❄.

Potamogeton berchtoldii Fieb. **Small Pondweed.** ¶Leaves long, narrow, 1–2 mm., acute; lateral veins meeting central at right angles near tip; stipules open. Ponds, streams, etc., common. Flo. June–Sept. ❄.

Potamogeton trichoides Cham. & Schlecht. **Hair-like Pondweed.** ¶Leaf width 1 mm. or less, tapering to long point; stipules open; usually ripening only 1 fr. per flo. Ponds, streams, etc., mostly S. and E. England and the Midlands, local. Flo. June–Aug. ❄.

Potamogeton obtusifolius Mert. & Koch. **Grassy Pondweed.** ¶Leaf width 3–4 mm., rarely 2 mm.; tip rounded apiculate; midrib with air cell, lateral veins rejoining at wide angle; stipules broad; peduncle short. Ponds, streams, etc., widespread, but local.

Potamogeton compressus L. **Grass-wrack Pondweed.** *P. zosteraefolius* Schumach., ¶Stem flattened; leaves very long, 2–4 mm. wide; tip rounded; main veins 3–5, with others smaller. Ponds, streams, etc., mostly Central and E. England. Flo. June–Sept. ❄.

Potamogeton acutifolius Link. **Sharp-leaved Pondweed.** ¶Stem flattened; leaves with air tissue, long, linear, pointed; veins many; fr. stalk short. In still waters, S. and E. England. Flo. June–July. ❄.

Potamogeton friesii Rupr. **Flat-stalked Pondweed.** ¶Stem flattened, with many short, leafy branches; leaves 2–3 mm. wide, 5-veined fr. whorls separated; stalk 1–2 in. Ponds, streams, etc., mostly England, local. Flo. June–Aug. ❄.

Potamogeton filiformis Pers. **Slender-leaved Pondweed.** ¶Leaves slender, of 2 tubes; base sheathing; spike widely interrupted; stalk very long; fr. beak central. Lakes, etc., Scotland, Anglesey and Ireland, mostly near coast. ❄.

Potamogeton pectinatus L. **Fennel-like Pondweed.** *P. flabellatus* Bab. ¶Upper leaves slender, of 2 tubes; sheath long, open; ligule longer; fr. large; beak near inner margin. Lowland waters, common in England, except S.W., rare in Wales and Scotland, and local in Ireland. Flo. June–Sept. ❄.

RUPPIACEAE

Ruppia spiralis L. ex Dumort. **Spiral Tassel Pondweed.** ¶Le. width 1 mm., sheath inflated; peduncle very long, often spiral twisted; fr. ovoid. Ditches near the sea, mostly S. and E. Englan and N.E. Ireland, rare. Flo. July–Aug. ❄.

Ruppia maritima L. **Beaked Tassel Pondweed.** *R. rostellata* Koc ¶Leaves narrower, filiform, sheaths small; peduncle shor equalling pedicels; fr. gibbous. Ditches near the sea, local. Fl June–Aug.

ZANNICHELLIACEAE

Zannichellia palustris L. **Horned Pondweed.** ¶Variable; leav slender; stipules semi-tubular; flo. subsessile in minute spath carpels muricate. In fresh or brackish waters, mostly England. Fl May–Aug. ❄.

NAIADACEAE

Najas flexilis (pronounced Nar-yas) (Willd.) Rostk. & Schmid **Flexible Naiad.** ¶Leaf width less than 1 mm., subentire; sheat ciliate; fr. 3 mm. In lakes, N. England, Scotland, W. Ireland. Fl Aug.

*Najas graminea Del. †Similar, leaves tufted on branches. Alie Formerly in Reddish canal, near Manchester, but now extinct.

Najas marina L. **Greater Naiad.** ¶Leaves with many, large spinous pointed teeth; sheaths entire, not ciliate; fr. 4 mm., ovoi In Hickling Broad, Norfolk. Flo. July–Aug. ❄.

ZOSTERACEAE

Zostera marina L. **Common Grass-wrack.** ¶Leaves very long, 4– mm. wide, rounded at apex; stigma twice as long as style; see ribbed. In the sea below tide-level, widspread, but local. Fl June–Sept. ❄.

Zostera angustifolia (Hornem.) Reichb. **Narrow-leaved Gras wrack.** ¶Leaf width about 2 mm. only; margin of flo. sheath mm.; stigma equalling style; seeds ribbed. Estuary mud, half tid to low tide. Widespread, but local. Flo. June–Sept.

Zostera noltii Hornem. **Dwarf Grass-wrack.** *Z. nana* auct. ¶Leav 3–6 in. × 1 mm.; flo. few, male enclosed in bracts; sheath inflate seeds smooth. Estuary mud, half tide to low tide. Widespread b local. Flo. June–Sept.

ERIOCAULACEAE

Eriocaulon aquaticum (Hill) Druce. **Pipe-wort.** *E. septangulare* Wit ¶Roots and rhizomes white, septate; leaves septate; flo. stalk fu rowed, twisted flo. in scaly head, lead coloured. Watery place Skye and W. Ireland. Flo. July–Sept. ❄.

POTAMOGETON
ACUTIFOLIUS.

POTAMOGETON
FRIESII.

POTAMOGETON
CRISPUS.

×2

OTAMOGETON
ERCHTOLDII.

POTAMOGETON
OBTUSIFOLIUS.

POTAMOGETON
PUSILLUS.

POTAMOGETON
TRICHOIDES.

ERIOCAULON
SEPTANGULARE.

POTAMOGETON
COMPRESSUS.

×2½

RUPPIA
SPIRALIS.

×
2½

ZOSTERA
MARINA.

OTAMOGETON
FILIFORMIS.

POTAMOGETON
PECTINATUS.

NAJAS
MARINA.

ZANNICHELLIA
PALUSTRIS.

CYPERACEAE

Eriophorum angustifolium Honck. **Common Cotton-grass.** ¶Leaves triquetrous, 3–6 mm. wide; upper sheath loose; peduncle smooth; glumes 1 nerved, brown, margin broad, hyaline. Common in acid bogs. Flo. May–June. ✿.

Eriophorum gracile Roth. **Slender Cotton-grass.** ¶Leaves triquetrous, 1–2 mm. wide, short, obtuse; peduncles hairy; glumes ovate, many nerved, not hyaline. In acid bogs, mostly S. and E. England, rare and local. Flo. June–July.

Eriophorum latifolium Hoppe. **Broad-leaved Cotton-grass.** ¶Leaves flat with short triquetrous point; sheath close fitting; peduncles rough; glumes blackish green. Bogs on basic or calcareous soil, mostly in N. Britain. Flo. May–June.

Eriophorum vaginatum L. **Hare's Tail Grass.** ¶Leaf width 1 mm., triquetrous; upper sheath much inflated, usually leafless; spike solitary. In moorland bogs, mostly in N., common. Flo. May. ✿.

Eleocharis parvula (Roem. & Schult.) Link ex Bluff, Nees & Schau. **Dwarf Spike-rush.** *Scirpus parvulus* Roem. & Schult., *Scirpus nanus* Spreng., non Poir. ¶Small; runners whitish, capillary, tipped with tubers; stem 1½ in. with 1 leafless sheath; spikelet 2–3 mm. On estuary mud, S. England, N. Wales and Ireland, very local. Flo. July–Aug.

Eleocharis acicularis (L.) Roem. & Schult. **Slender Spike-rush.** ¶Runners slender, brown; stem 4 angled, subulate; lowest glume ½ length of spikelet; nut ribbed. Wet heathy places, mostly England, local. Flo. July–Aug. ✿.

Eleocharis quinqueflora (F. X. Hartmann) Schwarz. *E. pauciflora* (Lightf.) Link. ¶Rhizome creeping; stem with scales and 1 leafless sheath; obliquely truncate glume more than ½ length of spikelet. Moors and fens, mostly in N. Flo. June–July. ✿.

Eleocharis palustris (L.) Roem. & Schult. **Common Spike-rush.** ¶Rhizome creeping; stem 1 ft; sheath almost transversely truncate; stigmas 2; spikelet ½ encircled by glume; variable. Common in marshes, etc. Flo. May–July. ✿.

Eleocharis austriaca Hayek. ¶Stems less purple, vascular bundles widely open; spikes many, short and conical; fr. with wide style vase, and often with 5 bristles instead of 4. On moorland streamsides and marshes. N. England, local. Flo. May–July.

Eleocharis uniglumis (Link) Schult. **One-glumed Spike-rush.** ¶Similar to above with stigmas 2; but lowest glume encircling spikelet; nut biconvex. In open marshes, mostly near the coast. Flo. June–July. ✿.

Eleocharis multicaulis (Sm.) Sm. **Many-stemmed Spike-rush.** ¶Stems 6 in., tufted; sheath obliquely truncate, acute; stigmas 3; nut trigonous; spikelet often viviparous. Wet acid heaths, mostly in S.W. Flo. July–Aug. ✿.

Scirpus cespitosus L. **Deer Grass.** *Trichophorum cespitosum* (L.) Hartm. ¶Upper sheath fitting tightly, opening 1 mm., with short blade; glumes brown with yellowish midrib. The type on Ingleborough and Ben Lawers. ✿.
Subsp. *germanicus* (Palla) Broddesson. ¶Upper sheath fitting loosely, opening larger; glumes brown with green midrib. Common on acid moors. Flo. May–June.

Scirpus setaceus L. **Bristle Scirpus.** *Isolepis setacea* (L.) R. Br. ¶Bract longer than inflo.; spikelets 1–3; glumes dark brown, margins white, keel green; nut trigonous, ribbed. Sandy soil, fairly common. Flo. June–July. ✿.

Scirpus cernuus Vahl. *S. filiformis* Savi, non Burm. *S. pygmaeus* (Vahl) A. Gray. ¶Bract not exceeding inflo.; longer, usually solitary spikelet; glumes green and brown; nut subglobose, nearly smooth. Sandy places by estuaries, mainly western. Flo. July.

Scirpus fluitans L. **Floating Mud-rush.** *Eleogiton fluitans* (L.) Link.

¶Stem floating, leafy; spike small, solitary, greenish. In ponds an dikes. Flo. June–Aug. ✿.

Scirpus lacustris L. **Common Bulrush** or **Club-rush.** Schoenoplectu *lacustris* (L.) Palla. ¶Stems 4–6 ft, sometimes with long basal leaves bract stem-like; glumes smooth, shortly awned. In rivers an ponds. Flo. Aug.–Sept. ✿.

Scirpus tabernaemontani C. C. Gmel. **Glaucous Club-rush.** Schoeno plectus tabernaemontani (C. C. Gmel.) Palla. ¶Stems 3–4 ft, glaucous bract stem-like; glumes clothed with dark brown papillae. We peaty places, often near the sea. Flo. June–July. ✿.

Scirpus triquetrus L. **Triangular Club-rush.** ¶Stem 3–4 ft, triquetrous bract exceeding inflo.; glumes brown with shallow rounded lobes In muddy estuaries, very local. Flo. Aug–Sept.

Scirpus americanus Pers. **Jersey Club-rush.** ¶Stems triquetrous leaves 2–3; bract long; spikelets dense, sessile; glumes with acut lobes. Ponds near the sea, Jersey. Flo. June–July.

Scirpus maritimus L. **Sea Club-rush.** ¶Stem 1–3 ft; leaves long an keeled; bracts several; spikelets large; glumes chocolate-brown sharply 2 lobed, awned. Estuary mud. Flo. July. ✿.

Scirpus sylvaticus L. **Wood Club-rush.** ¶Stems 2–3 ft; leaves broad bracts many; inflo. compound; spikelets many, green; glume entire. Wet shady places, local. Flo. July. ✿.

Scirpus holoschoenus L. **Round-headed Club-rush.** *Holoschoenu vulgaris* Link. ¶Stem terete, 3–4 ft; upper sheaths with short blade spikes many in stalked globular clusters. On sea sand, N. Devon Somerset, Glamorganshire. Flo. Aug.

Blysmus compressus (L.) Panz. ex Link. **Sedge-like Club-rush** *Scirpus caricis* Retz. ¶Leaves flat, keeled, rough; spikelets 10–12 lowest bract long, green; upper shorter than spikelets, man ribbed. In open marshes, local. Flo. June–July. ✿.

Blysmus rufus (Huds.) Link. **Red Blysmus.** *Scirpus rufus* (Huds. Schrad. ¶Leaves involute, smooth; spikelets 4–8; bracts mostl equalling spikelets, 1–3 ribbed. In salt marshes on N. and W coasts. Flo. June–July. ✿.

Cyperus fuscus L. **Brown Cyperus.** ¶Annual; stem 6 in.; inflo subcapitate or small umbels; glumes reddish. On mud from ditche or dried pools. S. England, rare. Flo. Aug.–Sept. ✿.

Cyperus longus L. **Sweet Galingale.** ¶Rhizome aromatic; stem 3 ft inflo. an irregular umbel; bracts very long. By ponds and ditches mostly in S. England, very local. Flo. Aug.–Sept. ✿.

Schoenus nigricans L. **Black Bog-rush.** ¶Stem wiry, 1–2 ft; sheath black; leaves ¾ length of stem; spikelets 5–10, blackish, sessile. Bog on calcareous or basic soil. Flo. July. ✿.

Schoenus ferrugineus L. **Brown Bog-rush.** ¶Stem 6–12 in.; sheath reddish brown; leaves ¼ length of stem; spikelets 1–3, reddish. B Loch Tummel, Perthshire, only. Flo. July.

Cladium mariscus (L.) Pohl. **Fen Sedge.** ¶Stem 3–6 ft; leaves long sharply serrate; inflo. of many branches, each with small reddis spikelets. In fens and marshes, locally abundant. Flo. Aug. ✿.

Rhynchospora alba (L.) Vahl. **White Beak-sedge.** ¶Stems tufted lower sheaths leafless; bracts about equalling inflo.; spikelets white Bogs on acid moors. Flo. July–Aug. ✿.

Rhynchospora fusca (L.) Ait. f. **Brown Beak-sedge.** ¶Rhizom creeping; lower sheaths mostly with blades; bracts exceeding inflo. spikelets brown. Damp peaty soil, local and rare. Flo. July–Aug ✿.

Kobresia simpliciuscula (Wahlenb.) Mackenzie. *K. caricina* Willd ¶Stem 4–8 in.; leaves slender; upper flo. (or spikelets) male, lowe female, with 2 glumes. Moors, N. England, Perthshire, Argyl local. Flo. June–July. The figure is labelled *K. calicina*. ✿.

SCHOENUS
NIGRICANS.

SCIRPUS
LACUSTRIS.

ERIOPHORUM
ANGUSTIFOLIUM.

ERIOPHORUM
VAGINATUM.

ERIOPHORUM
LATIFOLIUM.

B. RUFUS.

SCIRPUS
SETACEUS.

SCIRPUS
MARITIMUS.

BLYSMUS
COMPRESSUS.

CLADIUM
MARISCUS.

YPERUS
ONGUS.

S. TABERNAE-
-MONTANI.

E.PALUSTRIS.

E.MULTI-
-CAULIS.

KOBRESIA
CALICINA.

SCIRPUS FLUITANS.

CYPERUS
FUSCUS.

SCIRPUS
CESPITOSUS.

RHYNCHOSPORA
ALBA.

RHYNCHOSPORA
FUSCA.

ELEOCHARIS
ACICULARIS.

ELEOCHARIS
QUINQUEFLORA

ELEOCHARIS
UNIGLUMIS.

SCIRPUS
SYLVATICUS.

Plate 92   ✿ indicates plant is illustrated

CYPERACEAE (*continued*)

Carex
See *British Sedges*, by A. C. Jermy and T. G. Tutin (1968).

1. *Primocarex.* ¶Spike solitary, of one or both sexes.

Carex microglochin Wahlenb. ¶Stem 4 in.; leaves short; 4–8 yellow fr. with a bristle exserted at apex beside the stigma. Mountain bogs in Perthshire, very rare. Flo. July. ✿.

Carex pauciflora Lightf. **Few-flowered Sedge.** ¶Stem 4 in.; leaves short; spike male at top; fr. 3–4 only, yellow or reddish, without central bristle. Wet moors in the N. Flo. June. ✿.

Carex pulicaris L. **Flea Sedge.** ¶Stem and leaves 6–10 in.; spike male at top; fr. 5–6 mm., shortly stalked, brown and shiny. Frequent on wet moors. Flo. June. ✿.

Carex dioica L. **Dioecious Sedge.** ¶Stem 4–6 in.; leaves short; male and female spikes usually on separate plants; fr. 3·5 mm., sessile. On wet moors, local. Flo. May. ✿.

Carex rupestris All. **Rock Sedge.** ¶Leaves 2 mm. wide, equalling stem, point wavy; spike male at top; glumes ovate; fr. obovoid. Mountain rocks in Scotland, local. Flo. June–July. ✿.

2. *Arenariae.* ¶Creeping plants; spikes clustered, mostly male at top.

Carex maritima Gunn. **Curved Sedge.** *C. incurva* Lightf. ¶Creeping; terete stems and leaves curved; spikes clustered in dense head, male at top; fr. smooth. Coastal sand dunes, Scotland, N. England. Flo. June. ✿.

Carex arenaria L. **Sand Sedge.** ¶Creeping stems triquetrous, ½–1 ft; spikes separated a little, upper male; fr. ribbed and winged. Coastal sand dunes, common. Flo. June. ✿.

Carex disticha Huds. **Creeping Brown Sedge.** ¶Stems triquetrous, 1–2 ft; lowest and uppermost spikes female, central narrower male; fr. ribbed and serrate. Wet meadows and fens, local. Flo. June. ✿.

Carex divisa Huds. **Salt Meadow Sedge.** ¶Creeping; stems slender; bract often long and green; spikes oval, mostly contiguous, terminal male at top. Meadows near sea or estuaries. Flo. May–June. ✿.

Carex chordorrhiza L. f. ¶Stem stout, trigonous; leaves few, short; bract small; inflo. subcapitate, small. In bogs, W. Sutherland, very rare. Flo. June–July.

3. *Paniculatae.* ¶Spikes many, male at top, inflo. panicled or spike-like; stigmas 2.

Carex diandra Schrank. **Two-stamened Sedge.** *C. teretiuscula* Good. ¶Stem slender; leaves grey-green; ligule very short; glumes 3 mm.; fr. suborbicular, beaked, reddish. Damp meadows, local. Flo. May–June. ✿.

Carex appropinquata Schumach. **Lesser Tussock Sedge.** *C. paradoxa* Willd., non J. F. Gmel. ¶Tufted; stems 2 ft; leaves 1–2 mm. wide; inflo. branched; fr. ribbed below, abruptly narrowed above. Calcareous meadows and fens, local. Flo. June. ✿.

Carex paniculata L. **Greater Tussock Sedge.** ¶Tufted; stems 3–6 ft; leaves 3–7 mm. wide; inflo. branched; fr. gradually narrowed above. Wet shady places, common. Flo. June. ✿.

Carex otrubae Podp. **False Fox Sedge.** *C. vulpina* auct. ¶Stem triquetrous, not winged; ligule long, 10–15 mm.; 1 or 2 bracts very long; fr. greenish, ribbed. Damp, shady places, common. Flo. May–June. ✿.

Carex vulpina L. **Fox Sedge.** ¶Stem angles winged; ligule 2–5 mm.; bracts all short; fr. reddish brown. In damp, grassy places, mostly S. England, local. Flo. May–June. ✿.

4. *Spicatae.* ¶Spikes subsessile, male at top; stigmas 2.

Carex spicata Huds. **Spiked Sedge.** *C. contigua* Hoppe. ¶Leaf width 3–4 mm.; ligule 5 mm.; spikes male at top; glumes long, purplish; fr. tapering at base. On basic and gravelly soil. Flo. June. ✿.

Carex muricata L. **Prickly Sedge.** *C. pairaei* F. W. Schultz. ¶Leaf width 2 mm.; ligule short, 1–2 mm.; spikes male at top; glumes ... mm.; brown fr. rounded at base. On dry basic soil, scarce. Flo. June. ✿.

Carex polyphylla Kar. & Kir. **Chalk Sedge.** *C. leersii* F. W. Schultz non Willd. ¶Stems and leaves rough; ligule short; spikes male at top, upper close, lower separated; glumes brown; fr. tapering at base. Chalky pastures. Flo. May–June. Now regarded as a variety of *C. divulsa*.

Carex divulsa Stokes. **Grey Sedge.** ¶Slender; ligule short; spikes male at top, greyish, more distant, lowest often branched; fr. rounded at base. In woods and hedges, common. Flo. June–July. ✿.

5. *Elongatae.* ¶Spikes male at base; stigmas 2.

Carex echinata Murr. **Star Sedge.** *C. stellulata* Good. ¶Spikes about 4, slightly separate, male at base; glumes reddish brown; fr. spreading, star-like. Common in wet acid meadows. Flo. May–June. ✿.

Carex elongata L. **Elongated Sedge.** ¶Stem 2 ft; spikes several, oblong, overlapping, male at base; glumes 2 mm., brown, edges pale; fruit 4 mm. In marshes, local. Flo. June. ✿.

Carex ovalis Good. **Oval Sedge.** ¶1–1½ ft; spikes oval, clustered, male at base; glumes brown, edges pale; fr. 4–5 mm. Common on acid soils. Flo. June. ✿.

6. *Canescentes.* ¶Spikes male at base; stigmas 2; glumes short and pale.

Carex lachenalii Schkuhr. **Hare's-foot Sedge.** *C. lagopina* Wahlenb. ¶6 in.; spikes 3–4, contiguous, male at base; glumes short, reddish, edges pale; fr. yellow, beak short. Mountain bogs and wet rocks, Scotland. Flo. July.

Carex curta Good. **Pale Sedge.** *C. canescens* auct. ¶1 ft; spikes 4–6, oblong, male at base; glumes 2 mm., white, midrib green; fr. yellowish, beak short. In bogs on acid soils. Flo. July. ✿.

Carex remota L. **Distant-flowered Sedge.** ¶Bracts very long, leaf-like; spikes very distant, male at base; glumes white, midrib green; fr. green. Common in damp shady places. Flo. June. ✿.

CAREX
MICROGLOCHIN.

×2

CAREX
MARITIMA.

CAREX
DIVISA.

CAREX
DIANDRA.

CAREX DISTICHA

AREX DIOICA

CAREX
PULICARIS.

CAREX
PAUCIFLORA.

CAREX
PANICULATA

×2

CAREX
RUPESTRIS.

CAREX ARENARIA.

CAREX
ECHINATA

CAREX
DIVULSA.

CAREX
APPROPINQUATA

CAREX
OTRUBAE.

CAREX
REMOTA.

CAREX
SPICATA.

CAREX
LONGATA

CAREX
MURICATA

CAREX
CURTA.

CAREX VULPINA.

CAREX
OVALIS

Plate 93   ❀ indicates plant is illustrated

CYPERACEAE (*continued*)

7. *Altratae.* ¶Terminal spike partly male; stigmas 3.

Carex norvegica Retz. **Alpine Sedge.** *C. alpina* Liljeb. ¶Bract leaf-like; spikes small, erect, black, terminal male at base; fr. small, obovoid. Wet alpine rocks, Central Scotland. Flo. June–July. ❀.

Carex atrata L. **Black Sedge.** ¶Leaves broad, 5 mm.; bract leaf-like; spikes oval, black, stalked, terminal male at base. Wet rocks on mountains, Scotland, N. England, Caernarvon. Flo. July. ❀.

Carex buxbaumii Wahlenb. **Dark Sedge.** *C. fusca* auct. ¶Leaves narrow, glaucous; bract leaf-like; spikes subsessile, terminal male at base; glumes narrow, blackish; fr. broad, glaucous green. W. Inverness-shire. Flo. July. ❀.

Carex atrofusca Schkuhr. *C. ustulata* Wahlenb. ¶Leaves short and broad; bracts brown, sheathing; spikes black, lower nodding, terminal male above or throughout. Mountain bogs, Perthshire, Hebrides. ❀.

8. *Acutae.* ¶Spikes dense flowered, terminal male; bracts leafy; stigmas 2; beak very short.

Carex recta Boott. **Caithness Sedge.** *C. Kattegatensis* Fr. ex Krecz. ¶Stem 1½ ft; leaf ligule 2–3 mm.; lower spikes long stalked; female glumes long, 4–5 mm., midrib pale excurrent. Estuary sands, N. Scotland. Flo. July–Aug.

Carex elata All. **Tufted Sedge.** *C. hudsonii* A. Benn. ¶Stem 2–3 ft; leaf ligule 5–10 mm.; upper bracts small; spikes long, subsessile; fr. in straight rows. Riversides and fen ditches. Flo. June. ❀.

Carex acuta L. **Slender-spiked Sedge.** *C. gracilis* Curt. ¶Stem 2–3 ft; leaf ligule 2–3 mm.; lowest bract equalling inflo.; spikes long; glumes narrow, black, nerve often excurrent. By ponds, common. Flo. May–June. ❀.

Carex aquatilis Wahlenb. **Mountain Water Sedge.** ¶Stem 2–3 ft; leaf ligule 10 mm.; 2 or 3 bracts equalling inflo.; female spikes narrowed below; glumes dark. By mountain lakes and streams. Flo. July. ❀.

Carex bigelowii Torr. ex Schwein. **Stiff Sedge.** *C. rigida* Good. ¶Stem 6 in., stoutly triquetrous; leaves keeled and recurved; spikes shorter, ½ in.; glumes short and black. Stony places on mountains. Flo. June–July. ❀.

Carex nigra (L.) Reichard. **Common Sedge.** *C. goodenowii* Gay. ¶Stem 1 ft; lower bract leaf-like; spikes dense, cylindrical, obtuse; glumes black, narrower than green fr. Wet grassy places on acid soils. Flo. May–June. ❀.

9. *Limosae.* ¶Peduncles slender; fr. elliptic; beak very short; stigmas 3.

Carex flacca Schreb. **Glaucous Sedge.** *C. glauca* Scop., *C. diversicolor* auct. ¶1 ft stem and leaves glaucous; spikes cylindrical; stalks slender; glumes dark; fr. minutely papillose. Common on calcareous soil. Flo. May–June. ❀.

Carex limosa L. **Mud Sedge.** ¶1 ft stem and narrow leaves rough; spikes nodding, 10–20 flo.; male glumes lanceolate, female glumes ovate; fr. elliptic, ribbed. In peaty pools, local. Flo. June. ❀.

Carex rariflora (Wahlenb.) Sm. **Few-flowered Sedge.** ¶6–8 in. stem and leaves smooth; spikes nodding, 8–10 flo.; male glumes

ovate, female glumes obovate. High mountain bogs in Scotland local. Flo. June.

Carex paupercula Michx. **Broad-leaved Mud Sedge.** *C. magellanic* auct. ¶1 ft stem smooth; leaves broader, 3 mm.; spikes nodding 8–10 flo.; female glumes lanceolate, narrower than pale, ovate fr. Bogs, Scotland, N. England, rare. Flo. June. ❀.

10. *Digitatae.* ¶Inflo. finger-like; flo. few; fr. pale, pubescent beak short.

Carex digitata L. **Fingered Sedge.** ¶6–8 in.; leaf width 3–4 mm. spikes lax, 6–8 flo.; glumes pale; fr. pubescent. On limeston and chalk, N. Somerset to N. England. Flo. April–May. ❀.

Carex ornithopoda Willd. **Bird's-foot Sedge.** ¶3–5 in.; leaves nar rower; spikes small, lax, 4–5 flo.; glume shorter than pyriform fr Limestone banks, Derbyshire to Cumberland, local. Flo. May. ❀.

Carex humilis Leyss. **Dwarf Sedge.** ¶Dwarf, 2 in.; leaves ver narrow; bracts broad, enclosing 3–5 flo., female spike. Dr limestone turf and crevices, Herefordshire to Hampshire. Flo April. ❀.

11. *Montanae.* ¶Spikes sessile subglobose or oblong; fr. pubescent beak short.

Carex montana L. **Mountain Sedge.** ¶Shortly creeping; stem 8–1 in.; leaf width 2 mm.; glume dark, shorter than pubescent fr Calcareous pastures, S. England and Wales. Flo. May. ❀.

Carex ericetorum Poll. **Heath Sedge.** ¶Stems tufted, 3–6 in.; leave wider, 3–4 mm., short; glumes dark, edges pale; fr. obovate pubescent. Calcareous soil, Suffolk to Westmorland. Flo. April May. ❀.

Carex pilulifera L. **Pill Sedge.** ¶Stem 1 ft; leaves narrow, 2 mm. glumes light brown; fr. globose, green; bract sometimes long Damp heaths, common. Flo. May–June. ❀.

Carex caryophyllea Latourr. **Spring Sedge.** *C. praecox* auct. ¶Ste 6–8 in.; bracts sheathing; spikes oblong; glumes ovate, brown midrib green; fr. elliptic, green. In short grass, common. Flo April–May. ❀.

Carex filiformis L. **Downy-fruited Sedge.** *C. tomentosa* auct. ¶1 ft leaves narrow; bracts shortly leaf-like; spikes oblong: fr. small obovoid, very downy. In wet meadows, Gloucestershire t Sussex, local. Flo. May–June. ❀.

12. *Paniceae.* ¶Spikes stalked; fr. large, oval, glabrous, pale.

Carex pallescens L. **Pale Sedge.** ¶1 ft; bract leaf-like; female spike dense, slender stalked; glumes white with green midrib; fr. brigh green. Damp meadows and woods. Flo. June. ❀.

Carex panicea L. **Carnation Grass.** ¶1 ft; leaves very glaucous; brac sheath tight; spikes lax, few flo.; fr. curved. In damp pastures common. Flo. May–June. ❀.

Carex vaginata Tausch. **Wide-sheathing Sedge.** ¶6–12 in.; leave bright green; bract sheath very loose; spikes lax, few flo.; fr curved. On high mountains in Scotland. Flo. July. ❀.

13. *Nutantes.* ¶Lower bract sheath long; spikes nodding; fr. narrow beaked.

Carex capillaris L. **Hair Sedge.** ¶Small, 2–4 in., very slender; spike lax, few flo. nodding; glumes and fr. small, brown, shiny. Moun tain slopes, Teesdale to N. Scotland, local. Flo. June–July. ❀.

CAREX
HUMILIS.

CAREX
LIMOSA

CAREX
PILULIFERA.

× 2

× 2

× 2

CAREX
BUXBAUMII.

CAREX
DIGITATA

C. ORNITHO-
PODA.

CAREX
MONTANA

CAREX
ERICETORUM.

CAREX
ELATA.

CAREX
NIGRA

CAREX
ATRATA.

CAREX
ACUTA

CAREX
PAUPERCULA

× 2

CAREX
ATROFUSCA.

CAREX
FILIFORMIS.

CAREX
PALLESCENS.

CAREX
NORVEGICA.

× 2

CAREX
AQUATILIS.

CAREX
CARYOPHYLLEA

× 2

CAREX
CAPILLARIS.

× 3

CAREX
FLACCA.

CAREX
BIGELOWII.

CAREX
VAGINATA.

CAREX
PANICEA.

Plate 94 ❧ indicates plant is illustrated

CYPERACEAE (continued)

Carex strigosa Huds. **Loose-spiked Wood Sedge.** ¶Stem 2 ft; leaf width ¼ in.; female spikes lax, flo. slender, 2 in. long; fr. lanceolate, green. Damp shady places, local. Flo. May–June. ❧.

Carex pendula Huds. **Pendulous Sedge.** ¶Stem 3–6 ft; leaf width ½ in.; flo. spikes dense, very long, 4–6 in., drooping; fr. lanceolate, green. Damp woods and shady places. Flo. May–June. ❧.

Carex sylvatica Huds. **Wood Sedge.** ¶Stem 1½ ft; female spikes 1–1½ in., lax, nodding; stalks slender; glumes pale; fr. green with long beak. Wood on stiff soils, common. Flo. May–June. ❧.

14. *Distantes.* ¶Bracts long sheathing; spikes distant, oblong; beak long, bifid.

Carex depauperata Curt. ex With. **Starved Wood Sedge.** ¶Spikes with few flo., 3–4 only, lower distant, stalked; fr. very large, 8 mm., ribbed; beak long. N. Somerset and Surrey, very rare. Flo. May.

Carex binervis Sm. **Green-ribbed Sedge.** ¶Spikes distant, lowest 1 in., dense, long stalked; glumes dark; fr. with strong green submarginal ribs. Acid moors and meadows, common. Flo. June. ❧.

Carex distans L. **Distant Sedge.** ¶Spikes distant, ½ in.; stalks included in sheath; glumes greenish brown; fr. many, ribbed. Wet places, mostly near sea. Flo. May–June. ❧.

Carex hostiana DC. **Tawny Sedge.** *C. hornschuchiana* Hoppe, *C. fulva* auct. ¶Spikes distant, ¾ in., lower long stalked; glumes brown with white margin; fr. many, ribbed. On acid moors and meadows. Flo. June.

Carex punctata Gaudin. **Dotted Sedge.** ¶Spikes distant; stalks included in bract sheath; glumes pale reddish; fr. pale green with pellucid dots. Wet places by the sea, local. Flo. June–July.

Carex lasiocarpa Ehrh. **Downy-fruited Sedge.** *C. filiformis* auct. ¶Leaves narrow, glabrous; female spikes distant, subsessile, 1 in.; glumes brown; fr. very downy. Peat bogs and reed swamps, local. Flo. June. ❧.

Carex hirta L. **Hairy Sedge.** ¶Wider leaves and sheaths hairy; spikes distant; glumes long, greenish, awned; fr. green, very pubescent. Damp meadows and shady places, common. Flo. May–June. ❧.

15. *Extensae.* ¶Bracts deflexed; female spikes short, dense; fr. spreading.

Carex extensa Good. **Long-bracted Sedge.** ¶Leaves narrow, involute; bracts very long; spikes subsessile; glumes light brown; fr. ribbed. In salt marshes, locally common. Flo. June. ❧.

Carex serotina Mérat. **Late-flowering Sedge.** ¶Leaves 2–3 mm. wide, channelled; male spike sessile; glumes yellowish; fr. not

curved, abruptly contracted to short beak. Mostly near sea. Fl. July–Aug.

Carex lepidocarpa Tausch. ¶Stems slender; male spike stalked; female spikes rarely contiguous; fr. deflexed, tapering to slender beak. Wet places on basic soils. Flo. May–June. ❧.

Carex demissa Hornem. **Low Sedge.** *C. tumidicarpa* Anderss. ¶Stem spreading; male spike short stalked; lowest female spike often distant and stalked; fr. swollen, green, lower deflexed. Common on acid soils. Flo. July. ❧.

Carex flava L. **Yellow Sedge.** ¶Stems stout; leaves 4–7 mm. wide; terminal spike sessile, often partly female; fr. large, 6–7 mm., deflexed, golden. In peat on limestone, N. Lancashire, W. Yorkshire. Flo. June. ❧.

16. *Vesicariae.* ¶Stems leafy; lower spikes on slender stalks; fr. ovoid; beak long.

Carex pseudocyperus L. **Cyperus Sedge.** ¶Stem 2–3 ft; leaves wide; ligule 12 mm.; female spikes nodding; fr. 5–6 mm., ribbed; beak long. By ponds and slow rivers, local. Flo. May–June. ❧.

Carex laevigata Sm. **Smooth Sedge.** *C. helodes* Link. ¶Stem 2 ft; leaf ligule 10 mm.; male spike 1; lower female spike nodding; glumes 3 mm.; fr. 5–6 mm., ovoid, inflated. Shady places on acid soil. Flo. June. ❧.

Carex rostrata Stokes. **Beaked Sedge, Bottle Sedge.** *C. ampullacea* Good. ¶Stem 1–2 ft; leaf ligule 2–3 mm.; male spikes 2–3; lower female spikes 2 in., suberect; glumes 5 mm.; fr. 5–6 mm., yellowish. Wet peaty soil. Flo. June. ❧.

Carex vesicaria L. **Bladder Sedge.** ¶Stem 1–2 ft; leaf ligule 5–8 mm.; female spikes 1 in. long; glumes 3 mm.; fr. 4–5 mm., ovoid, yellow. Wet places, local. Flo. June.

Carex stenolepis Less. **Thin-glumed Sedge.** *C. grahami* Boott. ¶1–2 ft; leaf ligule 3–4 mm., acute; female spikes broadly oval; fr. 4–5 mm., inflated, ribbed. Mountain bogs in Argyll, Perthshire, Angus, rare. Flo. July. ❧.

Carex saxatilis L. **Russet Sedge.** *C. pulla* Good. ¶½–1 ft; leaves concave; ligule 1 mm., rounded; male spike usually 1; female spikes oval; fr. 3 mm., smooth. Bogs on high mountains, Scotland, local. Flo. July. ❧.

17. *Paludosae.* ¶Plants tall; leaves wide; spikes many, large, erect, dense.

Carex acutiformis Ehrh. **Lesser Pond Sedge.** *C. paludosa* Good. ¶Stem 2–3 ft; leaf width 7–10 mm.; ligule ½–1 in.; male glumes 5–6 mm., obtuse; female spikes 1–1½ in.; glumes 4–5 mm.; fr. 4 mm. Ponds and canals. Flo. May–June. ❧.

Carex riparia Curt. **Great Pond Sedge.** ¶Stem 3–4 ft; leaf width ½ in.; ligule ½ in.; male glumes long, 8 mm., pointed; female spikes 2–3 in.; female glumes 7 mm.; fr. 8 mm. Ponds and dikes. Flo. May–June. ❧.

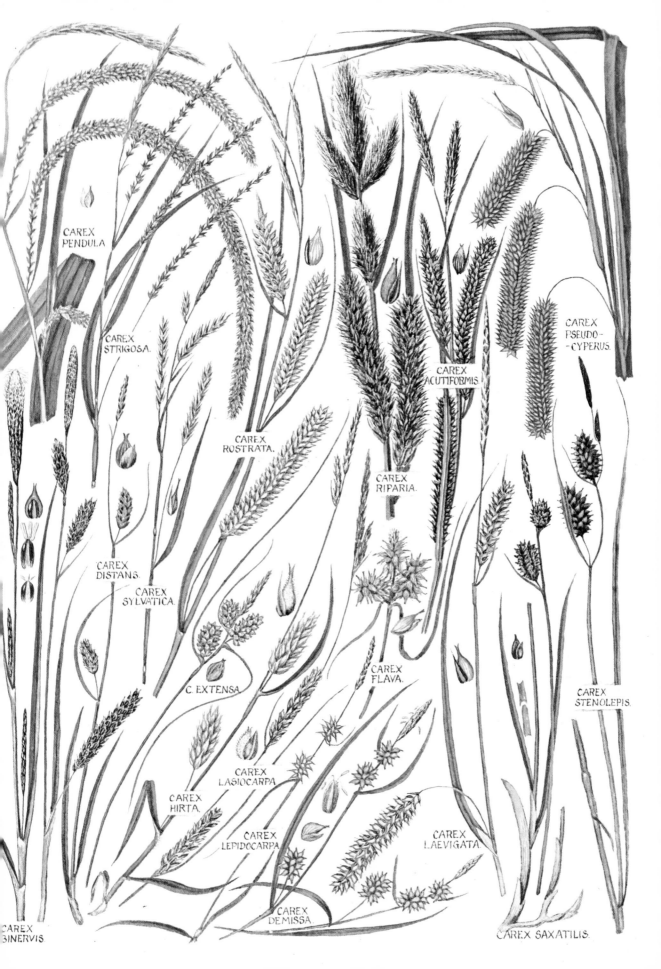

CAREX
PENDULA.

CAREX
STRIGOSA.

CAREX
RUSTRATA.

CAREX
ACUTIFORMIS.

CAREX
PSEUDO-
-CYPERUS.

CAREX
RIPARIA.

CAREX
DISTANS.

CAREX
SYLVATICA.

C. EXTENSA.

CAREX
FLAVA.

CAREX
STENOLEPIS.

CAREX
LASIOCARPA.

CAREX
HIRTA.

CAREX
LEPIDOCARPA.

CAREX
LAEVIGATA.

CAREX
BINERVIS.

CAREX
DEMISSA.

CAREX SAXATILIS.

Plate 95   ✿ indicates plant is illustrated

GRAMINEAE

Much fuller accounts of the Grasses will be found in Dr C. E. Hubbard's *Grasses* (Penguin Series). The lines of that work have been followed here as far as possible. We are also indebted to Dr Hubbard for permission to use some of his 'points of difference' and for looking through the text below and making useful suggestions.

Digitaria ischaemum (Schreb.) Muhl. **Smooth Finger Grass.** *Panicum glabrum* Gaudin. ¶Annual; leaf ligule membranous; spikelets; stalked, on 1 side of axis; lower glume suppressed; lower lemma barren. Arable land, S. and S.E. England. Flo. Aug.

Cynodon dactylon (L.) Pers. **Creeping Finger Grass.** ¶Perennial; leaf ligule a ring of hairs; spikelets sessile on 1 side of axis; glumes narrow, subequal. Coastal sand, S.W. England. ✿ on plate 96.

Setaria viridis (L.) Beauv. **Bristle Grass.** *Panicum viride* L. ¶Annual inflo. spike-like; spikelet stalks bearing long rough bristles; upper glume equalling spikelet, lower very short. Rare weed. Flo. Aug.–Oct.

Spartina maritima (Curt.) Fernald. **Cord Grass.** *S. stricta* (Ait) Roth. ¶Stems 1 ft; leaf width ¼ in.; spikelets ½ in., hairy; upper glume 3 nerved; anthers 4–6 mm. Salt marshes mostly in S. England. Flo. July–Sept.

Spartina × townsendii H. & J. Groves=*S. alterniflora × maritima.* **Rice Grass.** ¶Stems 2–3 ft; leaf width ½ in.; spikelets ¾ in. long, hairy; anthers 8–11 mm. Spreading on coastal mud flats, S. England to Scotland, planted. Flo. July–Nov. ✿.

Spartina alterniflora Lois. **American Cord Grass.** ¶Stems 2–3 ft; leaf width ¼ in.; spikelets ½ in. long, subglabrous; upper glumes 5–9 nerved; anthers 4–6 mm. Mud flats, Hampshire, now very rare. Flo. July–Nov.

Sieglingia decumbens (L.) Bernh. **Heath Grass,** *Triodia decumbens* (L.) Beauv. ¶Stems spreading; leaf ligule of short hairs; spikelets plump and shiny; flo. usually self-fertilizing. Damp peaty soils, common. Flo. July. ✿ on plate 96.

Molinia caerulea (L.) Moench. **Purple Moor Grass.** ¶Stems tufted, 1–3 ft; leaves long, dying in winter; ligule of short hairs; inflo. up to 1 ft long, purple. Moors and fens, common. Flo. July–Sept. ✿ on plate 97.

Phragmites australis (Cav.) Steud. **Common Reed.** *P. communis* Trin., *Arundo phragmites* L. Stems stout, 6–9 ft; leaf width ½ in.; ligule of hairs; inflo. densely branched; spikelet ½ in. Marshes, pools and fens. Common. Flo. Aug.–Oct.

Leersia oryzoides (L.) Sw. ¶Stems 1–3 ft; leaf sheaths hairy, often enclosing inflo.; glumes 0; lemma and palea hairy. Brook sides, Surrey to Somerset and Dorset. Flo. Aug.–Oct.

Nardus stricta L. **Mat Grass.** ¶Stems and inrolled leaves wiry; spikes 1 sided, very slender; spikelets narrow, pointed. Heaths and moors, common. Flo. June–Aug. ✿ on plate 98.

Parapholis strigosa (Dumort.) C. E. Hubbard. **Sea Hard-grass.** *Lepturus filiformis* Trin. ¶Stem ½–1 ft; leaves 1–2 in.; spikes long, narrow; spikelets alternate embedded in the stem; anthers 2–4 mm. Salt marshes. Flo. June–Aug. ✿ on plate 99.

Parapholis incurva (L.) C. E. Hubbard. **Curved Hard-grass.** *Lepturus incurvatus* Trin. ¶Smaller, up to 6 in.; stems and spikes curved; leaves ½–1 in.; anthers very small, 0·5–1 mm. Salt marshes, Somerset and Dorset to Lincolnshire. Flo. June–July.

Phalaris arundinacea L. **Reed Canary Grass.** ¶Stem 3–5 ft; leaf width ½ in.; ligules ¼ in.; panicle with many rough branches; small sterile lemmas and fertile one hairy. Wet places. Flo. June–Aug. ✿.

Phalaris canariensis L. **Canary Grass.** ¶Stem 1–3 ft; inflo. spike-like, 1–2 in. long; glumes large, pale yellowish with green, winged keels. Introduced as bird seed. Flo. July–Sept.

Milium effusum L. **Wood Millet.** ¶Stem 3–4 ft; leaf width ½ in.; ligule long; inflo. long and wide spreading; spikelets isolated, oval, green. In woods. Flo. May–July. ✿.

Alopecurus alpinus Sm. **Alpine Foxtail.** ¶Stem 1 ft; spikes short and broad; glumes very hairy; lemma ovate, awn short or 0. Wet places on mountains, Scotland and N. England. Flo. June–Aug. ✿.

Alopecurus pratensis L. **Meadow Foxtail.** ¶Stem 3 ft; spikes soft, 2 in. long; spikelets 4–6 mm.; glumes acute, united below; lemma awn long. Common in meadows. Flo. April–July. ✿.

Alopecurus geniculatus L. **Marsh Foxtail.** ¶Stem prostrate below; le sheaths pale, inflated; spikelets 3 mm.; glumes blunt, nearly fre Wet margins of pools and ditches. Flo. June–Aug. ✿.

A. geniculatus × pratensis is fairly common. Spikelets 3·5–4·5 mm glumes subacute.

Alopecurus bulbosus Gouan. **Bulbous Foxtail.** ¶Stem ½–1 ft, bulbo at base; upper sheaths inflated; glumes sharply pointed; lemma awn long. Salt marshes in England. Flo. May–Aug. ✿.

Alopecurus aequalis Sobol. **Orange Foxtail.** *A. fulvus* Sm. ¶Prostra at base; sheaths inflated; glumes blunt; lemma awn short; anthe orange. Margins of pools and ditches, local. Flo. June–Sept. ✿

Alopecurus myosuroides Huds. **Slender Foxtail.** *A. agrestis* L. ¶Ste 2 ft; spikes 2–4 in., narrow; glumes pointed, half united; lemma awn long. Arable land, common. Flo. May–Aug. ✿.

Phleum alpinum L. **Alpine Cat's-tail.** *P. commutatum* Gaudin. ¶Ste 1 ft; leaf ligule short; spikes short and broad; glumes truncat keel ciliate; awns 2–3 mm. High mountains, Scotland, N.W England. Flo. July–Aug. ✿.

Phleum pratense L. **Cat's-tail, Timothy Grass.** ¶Stem 2–3 ft; leav rough; ligule 4–6 mm.; spike 3–4 in.; glumes truncate; keel ciliat awn 1 mm. Meadows, common. Flo. June–Aug. ✿.

Phleum bertolonii DC. **Lesser Cat's-tail.** *P. nodosum* auct. ¶Ste swollen at base; leaf ligules 2–4 mm.; spikes 1–2 in., dense; glum truncate, ciliate; awn short. Grassy hills, common. Flo. June–Au ✿.

Phleum phleoides (L.) Karst. **Purple-stalked Cat's-tail.** ¶Leav narrower, ligules 1–2 mm.; spikes 1–3 in.; glumes bluntly na rowed; keel hairs very short. Dry sand and chalk, E. England. Fl June–Aug. ✿.

Phleum arenarium L. **Sand Cat's-tail.** ¶Stem 2–8 in.; leaves sho ligules long; spikes dense, narrowed below; glumes gradual narrowed above. Coast sands, locally common. Flo. May–July. ✿

Lagurus ovatus L. **Hare's-tail.** ¶Stems 1 ft, hairy; leaves short, soft hairy; spikes ovoid, hairy, bristly; glumes narrow, subulate, hair Channel Islands, naturalized in S. England. Flo. July.

Mibora minima (L.) Desv. **Early Sand Grass.** ¶Slender, tufted, 1– in.; leaves small; spike slender, 1 sided; spikelets 1 flo.; glum blunt. Anglesey, Glamorgan and Channel Islands (Dorset). Fl Feb.–May. ✿ on plate 96.

Agrostis stolonifera L. **Creeping Bent.** *A. alba* auct. ¶Stolons leaf stems 1 ft; panicle contracted, branches short, palea ⅔ length lemma. Common everywhere. Flo. July–Aug. ✿.
Var. *palustris* (Huds.) Farw. ¶Stolons leafless; stem 2 ft; panic more open. Wet places.
A. stolonifera × tenuis. ¶Intermediate in form, is widespread.

Agrostis tenuis Sibth. **Common Bent.** *A. vulgaris* With. ¶Rhizom short; stem ½–2 ft; ligule short; panicle spreading, brown; lemm awnless; palea ½ length of lemma. Abundant everywhere. Fl June–Aug. ✿.

Agrostis gigantea Roth. **Black Bent.** *A. nigra* With. ¶Rhizomatou stem 2–3 ft; leaves large; ligule long; panicle open; lemma aw less; palea 1–1·3 mm. On waste and arable land. Flo. June–Au

Agrostis canina L.
Subsp. *canina* **Velvet Bent.** ¶Stolons creeping, bearing tufts slender leaves; panicle branches bare below; lemma awne palea minute. Moors and meadows, abundant. Flo. June–Aug. ✿
Subsp. *montana* (Hartm.) Hartm. ¶With scaly rhizomes and den tufts of leaves. ✿.

Agrostis setacea Curt. **Bristle-leaved Bent.** ¶Many shoots of ve fine leaves; panicle narrow; lemma awned; palea very sma Heaths and moors, mostly in S.W., abundant. Flo. June–July. ✿

Polypogon monspeliensis (L.) Desf. **Annual Beard-Grass.** ¶2 f leaves and ligules long; panicle spike-like; ripe spikelets falling glumes rough, long awned. Coasts and saltings, S. and S.E. Englan Flo. July. ✿.

A. ALPINUS.

ALOPECURUS
AEQUALIS.

ALOPECURUS
PRATENSIS.

ANTHOXANTHUM
ODORATUM

ALOPECURUS
BULBOSUS.

GASTRIDIUM
VENTRICOSUM

SPARTINA
TOWNSENDII

PHALARIS
ARUNDINACEA.

ALOPECURUS
GENICULATUS.

ALOPECURUS
MYOSUROIDES

MILIUM
EFFUSUM.

AGROSTIS
STOLONIFERA.

P. ALPINUM

×2

×4

×4

PHLEUM
PHLEOIDES.

PHLEUM
PRATENSE.

AGROSTIS
CANINA.

POLYPOGON
MONSPELIENSIS

PHLEUM BERTOLONII.

PHLEUM
ARENARIUM

AGROSTIS
SETACEA.

AGROSTIS
TENUIS.

AGROSTIS
CANINA
VAR. MONTANA

Plate 96   ❉ indicates plant is illustrated

GRAMINEAE (*continued*)

Apera spica-venti (L.) Beauv. **Loose Silky Bent, Wind Grass.** ¶1–3 ft; leaves and ligules long; panicle branches long, spreading; lemma awn long; anthers 2 mm. On light soils in S.E. England. Flo. June–Aug.

Apera interrupta (L.) Beauv. **Dense Silky Bent.** ¶Stems and leaves short; panicle branches short, erect, dense; anthers minute. Sandy soil, W. Norfolk and Suffolk, rare elsewhere. Flo. June–July.

Gastridium ventricosum (Gouan) Schinz & Thell. *G. lendigerum* (L.) Desv. ¶Stems 1 ft; leaves short; panicle spike-like, pale green; spikelets swollen at base, shiny. Calcareous land, S. England, scarce. Flo. June–Aug. ❉ on plate 95.

Calamagrostis epigejos (L.) Roth. **Wood Small-reed.** ¶3–6 ft; leaves wide, glabrous; ligule long; panicle dense; glumes narrow; hairs much exceeding lemma. Damp woods and fens. Flo. June–July. ❉.

Calamagrostis canescens (Weber) Roth. **Purple Small-reed.** *C. lanceolata* Roth. ¶Stem 3–4 ft; leaves hairy above; panicle loose; glumes rather narrow; hairs slightly exceeding lemma. Marshes and fens, rather rare. Flo. June–July. ❉.

Calamagrostis stricta (Timm) Koel. **Narrow Small-reed.** *C. neglecta* auct. ¶1–3 ft; leaves hairy above; ligule short; panicle narrow, dense; glumes 3–4 mm., broadly lanceolate; hairs shorter than lemma. Northern bogs, rare. Flo. July.

Calamagrostis scotica (Druce) Druce. **Scottish Small-reed.** ¶Stem 1–3 ft; leaves hairy above; panicle rather narrow, dense; glumes 4–6 mm., lanceolate; hairs shorter than lemma. Bogs, N. Caithness, very rare. Flo. July–Aug.

Ammophila arenaria (L.) Link. **Marram Grass.** *A. arundinacea* Host. ¶Rhizomes long; stem 3 ft; leaves inrolled, sharp pointed; ligule 1 in.; panicle large, spike-like; glumes ½ in. Coastal sands, abundant. Flo. July. ❉.

The hybrid *Ammophila arenaria* × *Calamagrostis epigejos* is found on the E. coast; leaves flatter; inflo. purplish; lemma hairs longer; anthers small.

Anthoxanthum odoratum L. **Scented Vernal Grass.** ¶Perennial; stem unbranched; spike 2–3 in.; glumes hairy, unequal; awns of sterile lemmas not conspicuous. Abundant everywhere. Flo. April–June. ❉ on plate 95.

*Anthoxanthum puelii Lecoq & Lamotte. **Annual Vernal Grass.** *A. aristatum* auct. ¶Annual; stem branched; spike ½–1 in.; glumes glabrous; awns of sterile lemmas conspicuous. Sandy fields, rare. Flo. June–Aug.

Hierochloe odorata (L.) Beauv. **Holy Grass.** ¶Creeping; stem 1 ft; upper leaves short, pointed; panicle spreading; spikelets rounded; glumes broad. Wet places, N. Scotland, N. Ireland. Flo. March–May.

Holcus mollis L. **Creeping Soft Grass.** ¶Rhizomes creeping; stems hairy at nodes; glumes ovate, acute, hairy; upper lemma long awned. Grassland, cultivated ground, troublesome weed. Flo. June–Aug. ❉.

Holcus lanatus L. **Yorkshire Fog.** ¶Tufted; stems downy; glumes ovate, blunt, hairy, upper aristate; upper lemma short awned. Common. Flo. May–Aug. ❉.

Aira caryophyllea L. **Silvery Hair Grass.** ¶Stems 2–12 in., slender; leaf sheaths rough; panicle spreading; glumes silvery; lemmas awned. Dry soils, banks and wall tops, common. Flo. May–July. ❉.

Aira praecox L. **Early Hair Grass.** ¶Tufted, 2–6 in., slender; leaves very small; sheaths smooth; panicle spike-like; glumes shiny; lemmas awned. Sandy and acid soils, common. Flo. April–June. ❉.

Corynephorus canescens (L.) Beauv. **Grey Hair Grass.** *Aira canescen* L. ¶Tufted; leaves many, very slender, rough; panicle narrow; lemma awn with apex club-like. Sand dunes, Norfolk, Suffolk, Channel Islands. Flo. June–July. ❉.

Deschampsia setacea (Huds.) Hack. **Bog Hair Grass.** ¶Leaves very narrow, bristle-like; sheaths smooth; ligules long, pointed; lemma broad, unequally 4 pointed. Boggy heaths, local. Flo. July–Aug. ❉.

Deschampsia flexuosa (L.) Trin. **Wavy Hair Grass.** ¶Leaves narrow, bristle-like; sheaths slightly rough; ligules blunt; lemma ovate, apical teeth microscopic. On moors, abundant. Flo. June–July. ❉. Var. *montana* Huds. ¶Has smaller panicles, with larger spikelet. Alpine.

Deschampsia cespitosa (L.) Beauv. **Tufted Hair Grass.** ¶Large tussocks; stem 2–4 ft; leaves flat, coarse, ribs rough; ligule long; lemma tip toothed. Wet fields and moors, common. Flo. June– Aug. ❉.

Deschampsia alpina (L.) Roem. & Schult. **Alpine Hair Grass.** ¶Stems ½–1 ft, tufted; leaves short, channelled; sheath smooth; ligule long; panicle smaller; flo. often proliferous; lemma toothed. High mountains. Flo. July–Aug.

Trisetum flavescens (L.) Beauv. **Yellow Oat Grass.** ¶Stem 1–2 ft; leaves flat, pointed; ligule short; panicle yellow; spikelets about 3 flo.; lemma 2 toothed, awned. Common in England. Flo. June–July. ❉.

Koeleria cristata (L.) Pers. **Crested Hair Grass.** *K. gracilis* Pers. ¶Tufted, 1 ft; leaves mostly inrolled; sheaths hairy; panicle dense, spike-like, pale. Calcareous soils, common. Flo. June– July. ❉ on plate 97. Var. *albescens* (DC.). ¶Is a sand-dune form with whiter panicle. ❉ on plate 97.

Koeleria vallesiana (Honck.) Bertol. ¶Similar to *K. cristata*, but with the basal leaf sheaths persisting, split and fibrous, forming a dense thickened base to stems. On limestone, N. Somerset. Flo. June– July.

*Avena ludoviciana Durieu. **Winter Wild Oat.** ¶Spikelet jointed and breaking only above the glumes; lemmas awned, hairy, apex 2 toothed, without bristles. Introduced weed. Flo. July–Aug.

*Avena fatua L. **Common Wild Oat.** ¶Spikelet jointed and breaking between the lemmas; lemmas hairy, awned; apex 2 toothed without bristles. Weed of cultivation. Flo. June–Aug. ❉.

*Avena strigosa Schreb. **Bristle Oat.** ¶Spikelet not jointed; lemma hairy and awned (except 3rd lemma) with 2 fine bristles from apical teeth. Cultivated in Wales and W. Scotland. Flo. July–Aug.

The chief oat of cultivation, *A. sativa* L., has lemma without hair or apical bristles.

Arrhenatherum elatius (L.) J. & C. Presl. **Oat Grass.** *A. avenaceu* Beauv. ¶3–4 ft, often bulbous at base; spikelets 2 flo.; lower lemma long awned, 7 nerved. Waste ground and hedgerow everywhere. Flo. June–Sept. ❉.

Helictotrichon pratense (L.) Pilg. **Meadow Oat Grass.** *Avena pratensis* L. ¶1–2 ft; leaf sheaths glabrous; spikelets large, 3–6 flo.; axis short haired; lemmas long awned. Commons on chalk down. Flo. June–July. ❉.

Helictotrichon pubescens (Huds.) Pilg. **Downy Oat.** *Avena pubescens* Huds. ¶1–2 ft; leaves and lower sheaths hairy; spikelets 2–3 flo.; axis with long hairs; lemmas long awned. Damp calcareous soils. Flo. May–July. ❉.

Sesleria caerulea (L.) Ard. Subsp. *calcarea* (Čelak.) Hegi. **Blue Moor Grass.** ¶½–1 ft; leaves flat, blunt, hooded; spike bluish with scales at base; spikelets 2-flo. On limestone, N. England, Scotland, W. Ireland. Flo. April– June. ❉.

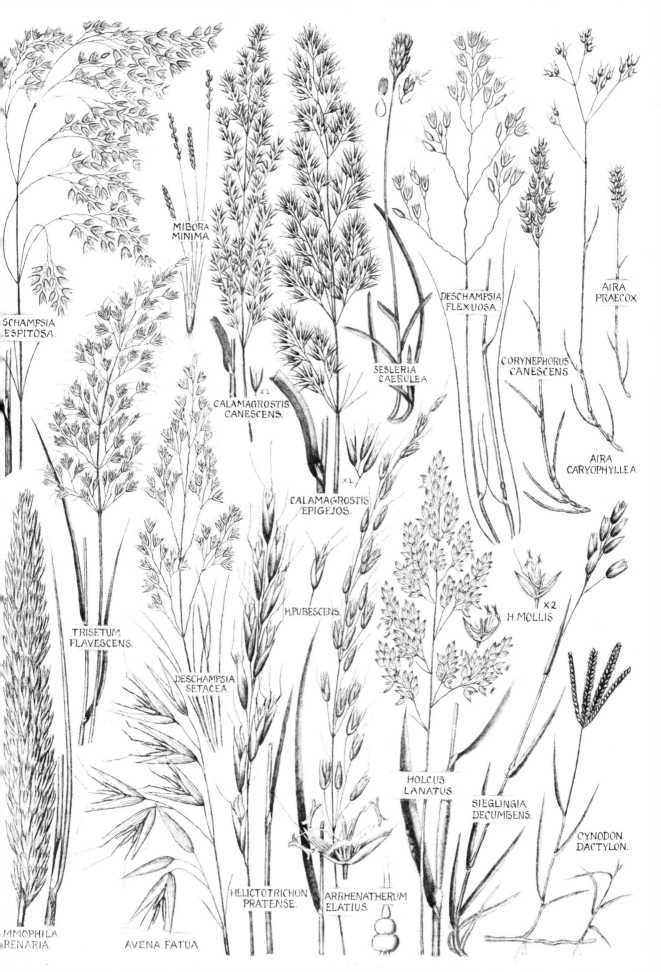

SCHAMPSIA
ESPITOSA.

MIBORA
MINIMA

CALAMAGROSTIS
CANESCENS.

×1

CALAMAGROSTIS
EPIGEJOS.

SESLERIA
CAERULEA

DESCHAMPSIA
FLEXUOSA.

AIRA
PRAECOX

CORYNEPHORUS
CANESCENS.

AIRA
CARYOPHYLLEA

TRISETUM
FLAVESCENS.

DESCHAMPSIA
SETACEA.

H.PUBESCENS.

H.MOLLIS
×2

HOLCUS
LANATUS.

SIEGLINGIA
DECUMBENS.

CYNODON
DACTYLON.

MMOPHILA
RENARIA.

AVENA FATUA

HELICTOTRICHON
PRATENSE.

ARRHENATHERUM
ELATIUS.

Plate 97   ❧ indicates plant is illustrated

GRAMINEAE (*continued*)

Melica uniflora Retz. **Wood Melick.** ¶Slender; leaf sheath with small pointed extension; panicle branched; 1 flo. fertile and sterile lemmas in each spikelet. Woods and shady banks, common. ❧

Melica nutans L. **Mountain** or **Nodding Melick.** *M. montana* Huds. ¶Leaf sheaths without pointed extension; panicle usually unbranched; 2–3 flo. in spikelet; peduncle bent. Calcareous banks, Gloucestershire northward. Flo. May–July. ❧

Glyceria maxima (Hartm.) Holmberg. **Reed Sweet Grass.** *G. aquatica* (L.) Wahlb., non J. & C. Presl. ¶Stems 3–6 ft; leaves 1–2 ft; panicle much branched; spikelets many, 4–10 flo.; lemmas oval, 3–4 mm. Ponds, fens and slow rivers. Flo. June–Aug. ❧

Glyceria fluitans (L.) R. Br. **Floating Sweet Grass.** ¶Stem 1–3 ft; leaves ½–1 ft; panicle branches few, appressed; spikelets long, 8–16 flo.; lemmas long, 6–7 mm., bluntly pointed. Ponds and streams. Flo. May–Aug. ❧

Glyceria plicata Fr. ¶Stem 1–2 ft; leaf sheaths rough; branches spreading; lemmas rounded, 3–5 mm., palea teeth included. Ponds, ditches and moorland pools. Flo. June–Aug. ❧

Glyceria × pedicellata Townsend = *G. fluitans × plicata.* Intermediate between the parents, with minutely scabrid sheaths; sterile. Widespread.

Glyceria declinata Bréb. ¶1–1½ ft; leaves grey-green; branches few, appressed; lemmas 3 lobed, 4–5 mm.; palea teeth projecting. Marshes and moors. Flo. June–Sept. ❧

Catabrosa aquatica (L.) Beauv. **Water Whorl-Grass.** ¶Stoloniferous, 1–1½ ft; leaves blunt; spikelets mostly 2 flo.; lemmas much exceeding glumes. Sides of ponds and streams, local. Flo. May–July. ❧

Cynosurus cristatus L. **Crested Dog's-tail.** ¶1–2 ft; leaves pointed; inflo. spiked; sterile spikelets of empty glumes concealing fertile spikelets of 3–4 flo. Common. Flo. June–Aug. ❧

Cynosurus echinatus L. **Rough Dog's-tail.** ¶Leaves wide; inflo. dense, oval; lemmas with long rough awns; sterile glumes short awned. Introduced, mostly in S. England. Flo. June–July.

Dactylis glomerata L. **Cocksfoot.** ¶Stout plant, 2–3 ft; leaves valuable grazing; inflo. in dense clusters; keels of glumes and lemmas rough or hairy. Meadows, abundant. Flo. June–Sept. ❧

Briza media L. **Common Quaking Grass.** ¶Perennial; leaf width about ⅛ in.; ligules short; lemmas as broad as long; anthers long. Dry calcareous pastures, common. Flo. June–Aug. ❧

Briza minor L. **Lesser Quaking Grass.** ¶Annual; leaves soft, width about ¼ in.; ligules longer; lemmas small, broader than long; anthers small. Roadsides, arable land, S.W. England. Flo. June–Sept. ❧

Briza maxima L. ¶Spikelets very large, 7–20 flo. Is naturalized in Channel Islands.

Poa infirma Kunth. **Scilly Isles Meadow Grass.** ¶Annual, 1–6 in.; inflo. lax; spikelets small, 2–4 flo.; glumes small; lemmas short and hairy; anthers small. W. Cornwall, Scilly Isles and Channel Islands. Flo. March–May.

Poa annua L. **Annual Meadow Grass.** ¶6–12 in.; leaves broad and blunt; spikelets usually about 6 flo.; lemmas longer, overlapping; anthers medium. Abundant everywhere. Flo. all the year. ❧

Poa bulbosa L. **Bulbous Meadow Grass.** ¶Shoots bulbous at base, ½–1 ft; leaves very narrow; inflo. dense; spikelets 3–6 flo. short hairs on nerves of lemmas. Sandy coasts, S. and E. England. Flo. March–April. ❧

Poa alpina L. **Alpine Meadow Grass.** ¶½–1 ft; leaves broad blunt; spikelets large, 2–5 flo.; glumes and lemmas large, oval; margins broad and white; anthers long, 2 mm. Stony places of mountains, often proliferous. Flo. July–Aug. ❧

Poa flexuosa Sm. *Poa laxa* auct. ¶Similar to *P. alpina,* but leaves narrow, tapering; inflo. narrower; spikelets fewer, smaller, not proliferous; anthers 1 mm. High mountains in Scotland. Flo. July–Aug.

Poa nemoralis L. **Woodland Meadow Grass.** ¶1–2 ft; leaves narrow, pointed; ligules short; inflo. long, slender; spikelets small, few flo. Woods and shady places. Flo. June–July. ❧

Poa balfourii Parnell. ¶Slender; leaves narrow, greyish; ligules 1–3 mm.; branches with 1–5 longer spikelets, 5–7 mm.; lower glume lanceolate. Mountains, N. Wales to N. Scotland. Flo. July–Aug.

Poa glauca Vahl. ¶Stiff stems and leaves glaucous, whitish; inflo. branches short, erect; glumes broader ovate. Highest Scottish mountains and Snowdon, rare. Flo. July–Aug.

Poa palustris L. **Marsh Meadow Grass.** ¶1–4 ft; leaves pointed; sheaths smooth; ligules long, blunt; inflo. large; lemma tip yellowish. An early introduction, by ponds, local. Flo. June–July.

Poa chaixii Vill. **Broad-leaved Meadow Grass.** ¶Large, tufted, 2–4 ft; leaves long and broad; ligules short; spikelets 5–6 mm.; lemma nerves glabrous. Naturalized in woods, local. Flo. May–July.

Poa trivialis L. **Rough Meadow Grass.** ¶Stoloniferous; leaves glossy below; sheaths keeled, rough, often purple; ligule long, pointed; lemma base long haired. Very common. Flo. June–July. ❧

Poa pratensis L. **Meadow Grass.** ¶Rhizomes slender; stems tufted; sheaths smooth; ligules short; spikelets up to ¼ in.; glumes abruptly pointed. Old pastures and roadsides, common. Flo. May–July. ❧

Poa subcaerulea Sm. **Spreading Meadow Grass.** *P. irrigata* Lindm. ¶Rhizomes long; stems scattered, solitary; lower inflo. branches in pairs; spikelets ¼ in.; glumes finely pointed. Wet meadows and sands. Flo. June–July. ❧

Poa angustifolia L. **Narrow-leaved Meadow Grass.** ¶Rhizomes slender; stems tufted; leaves stiff and narrow; ligules short; spikelets smaller, ⅛ in. Hill grassland and wall tops. Flo. May–June.

Poa compressa L. **Flat-stalked Meadow Grass.** ¶Rhizomes long; stems scattered, flattened, wiry; inflo. branches short; spikelets ⅛ in. Dry banks and old walls. Flo. June–Aug. ❧

NOSURUS CRISTATUS.

VAR. ALBESCENS.

KOELERIA CRISTATA.

MOLINIA CAERULEA.

MELICA NUTANS.

MELICA UNIFLORA.

CATABROSA AQUATICA.

GLYCERIA MAXIMA.

x2 G. DECLINATA.

DACTYLIS GLOMERATA.

x2 BRIZA MEDIA

x2 B.MINOR.

POA ALPINA

GLYCERIA PLICATA

x2

x2

POA BULBOSA

POA ANNUA

POA COMPRESSA.

POA NEMORALIS.

P. SUBCAERULEA.

x2

POA PRATENSIS

POA TRIVIALIS.

GLYCERIA FLUITANS

Plate 98 ❀ indicates plant is illustrated

GRAMINEAE (*continued*) ..

Puccinellia fasciculata (Torr.) Bicknell. **Tufted Salt-marsh Grass.** *Glyceria borrei* (Bab.) Bab. ¶Perennial; tufted; inflo. rather dense, branches short; spikelets up to $\frac{1}{4}$ in.; lemmas small, 2 mm.; anthers short. Salt marshes, S. England, Ireland. Flo. June–Sept. ❀.

Puccinellia distans (L.) Parl. **Reflexed Salt-marsh Grass.** *Glyceria distans* (L.) Wallenb. ¶Perennial; leaves narrow; inflo. branches long, deflexed; spikelets $\frac{1}{4}$ in.; lemmas small. Salt marshes and seaside banks. Flo. June–July. ❀.

Puccinellia maritima (Huds.) Parl. **Common Salt-marsh Grass.** *Glyceria maritima* (Huds.) Wahlb. ¶Stoloniferous; stems spreading; spikelets up to $\frac{1}{2}$ in.; lemmas large, 4 mm.; anthers long. Salt marshes and brackish areas, common. Flo. June–July. ❀.

*Puccinellia pseudo-distans (Crép.) Jansen & Wachter. ¶Intermediate between *P. distans* and *P. fasciculata.* Branches spreading, not reflexed; lemma with middle nerve minutely projecting. Thames estuary, rare.

Puccinellia rupestris (With.) Fernald & Weatherby, *Glyceria procumbens* (Curt.) Dumort. ¶Stems spreading or prostrate; leaves flat; spikelets $\frac{1}{4}$ in.; lemmas large; anthers short. Salt marshes and shingle banks. Flo. May–Aug. ❀.

Catapodium rigidum (L.) C. E. Hubbard. *Poa rigida* L. *Desmazeria rigida* (L.) Tutin. ¶Stems rigid, 6–10 in.; inflo. branches stiff, spreading on 1 side of axis; often purplish. On dry, mostly calcareous soils. Flo. May–July. ❀.

Catapodium marinum (L.) C. E. Hubbard. *Festuca rottboellioides* Kunth. *Desmazeria marina* (L.) Druce. ¶Stems short and stout; inflo. narrow, spike-like; branches short, appressed. Rocks and shingle by the sea, local. Flo. May–July. ❀.

Vulpia membranacea (L.) Dumort. **Dune Fescue.** *Festuca uniglumis* Ait. ¶Upper sheath inflated; spikelets large, $\frac{1}{2}$ in., and awn $\frac{1}{2}$ in.; lower glume minute or 0, upper 3 nerved. Sand dunes, S. and E. coasts, E. Ireland. Flo. June. ❀.

Vulpia ambigua (Le Gall) More. **Bearded Fescue.** *Festuca ambigua* Le Gall. ¶Sheath nearly reaching straight inflo.; spikelets $\frac{1}{4}$ in.; awn $\frac{3}{8}$ in.; lower glume very small, upper 1 nerved. Coast sand dunes, Devon to Norfolk and Breckland. Flo. May–June. ❀.

Vulpia myuros (L.) C. C. Gmel. **Rat's-tail Fescue.** *Festuca myuros* L. ¶Stem sheathed to top; inflo. long, curved; spikelets $\frac{3}{8}$ in.; awn $\frac{1}{2}$ in.; lower glume about $\frac{1}{4}$ length of upper. Cultivated and waste, sandy land. Flo. June–July. ❀.

Vulpia bromides (L.) Gray. **Squirrel-tail Fescue.** *Festuca sciuroides* Roth. ¶Stems and sheaths slender; spikelets few, $\frac{1}{2}$ in.; awn $\frac{1}{2}$ in.; lower glume $\frac{1}{2}$–$\frac{3}{4}$ length of upper. Dry banks and sandy heaths, common. Flo. May–July. ❀.

Festuca altissima All. **Wood Fescue.** *F. silvatica* Vill., non Huds. ¶Tall, 2–4 ft; leaves wide and flat; ligules long; inflo. large;

spikelets $\frac{1}{4}$ in.; lemma awnless. Woods and shady places, mainl N. and W. England. Flo. May–July. ❀.

Festuca tenuifolia Sibth. **Awnless Sheep's Fescue.** *F. capilla* auct. ¶Slender, tufted; leaves inrolled, hair-like; ligules shor sheaths open; spikelets up to $\frac{1}{4}$ in.; lemma awnless. On acid peaty soils. Flo. May–June. ❀.

Festuca ovina L. **Sheep's Fescue.** ¶Without rhizomes; leaves narrov inrolled, up to 8 in.; sheaths open; spikelets $\frac{1}{4}$–$\frac{3}{8}$ in.; lemma aw short, about 1 mm. Heaths and moors. Flo. May–July. ❀.

Festuca vivipara (L.) Sm. ¶Similar to *F. tenuifolia* but spikelets alwa producing young plants. N. Wales to Scotland.

*Festuca longifolia Thuill. **Hard Fescue.** *F. duriuscula* auct. ¶Simila to *F. ovina* but stouter; leaves up to 1 ft; inflo. often pyramida lemmas a little longer; awn up to 4 mm. Sown and local naturalized, S. England. Flo. June.

Festuca glauca Lam. **Grey Fescue.** *F. caesia* Sm. ¶Similar to *F. long folia* but with leaves very bluish white. Native but rare on Anglian heaths, also introduced to gardens.

*Festuca heterophylla Lam. ¶Tall, 2–4 ft, without rhizomes; bas leaves hair-like, 1–2 ft long, 3 angled; stem leaves short, fla $\frac{1}{8}$ in. wide. Woods, S. England, rare, introduced. Flo. June–July

Festuca rubra L.
Subsp. *rubra.* **Creeping Fescue, Red Fescue.** ¶Rhizomes long leaves narrow, basal, inrolled; sheaths tubular; spikelets $\frac{3}{8}$–$\frac{1}{2}$ in lemma 5–6 mm., awned. Very common, glaucous in salt marshe Flo. May–June. ❀.
Var. *arenaria* F. ¶Leaves very glaucous; spikelets large, hairy Sand dunes.
Subsp. *commutata* Gaudin. ¶Like *F. rubra* with sheaths tubular, bu without rhizomes. Introduced, established on dry soils, downs an roadsides.

Festuca juncifolia St-Amans. **Rush-leaved Fescue.** ¶Rhizome long; stem 1–2 ft; leaves stiff, inrolled, sharply pointed; spikele $\frac{1}{2}$ in.; lemmas 7–10 mm., hairy, short awned. Sand dunes, S. an E. coasts. Flo. June–July. ❀.

Festuca pratensis Huds. **Meadow Fescue.** ¶Tufted, 1–3 ft; leave flat; sheath auricles glabrous; shorter branch of each pair wit 1–2 spikelets; lemma awnless. In meadows, abundant. Fl June–Aug. ❀.

The hybrid *Festuca pratensis* × *Lolium perenne* = × *Festulolium loliaceu* is fairly widespread.

Festuca arundinacea Schreb. **Tall Fescue** (Huds.) P. Fourn. ¶Tufte 2–5 ft; leaves long, flat, coarse; sheath auricles hairy; shorte branch of each pair with 3–6 spikelets; lemmas 6–9 mm., ofte short awned. Grassy places. Flo. June–July. ❀.

Festuca gigantea (L.) Vill. **Giant Fescue.** *Bromus giganteus* L. ¶Tufte 2–4 ft; leaves flat, 1–2 ft, up to $\frac{1}{2}$ in. wide; sheath auricles glabrou shorter branch with several spikelets; lemma awn $\frac{1}{2}$ in. Wood common. Flo. July. ❀.

PUCCINELLIA
RUPESTRIS

CATAPODIUM
MARINUM.

×2

VULPIA
BROMOIDES

PUCCINELLIA
DISTANS

P. FASCIC-
-ULATA.

CATAPODIUM
RIGIDUM.

VULPIA
MEMBRANACEA

PUCCINELLIA
MARITIMA

VULPIA
AMBIGUA

VULPIA
MYUROS

×2
FESTUCA
OVINA.

×2
FESTUCA
TENUIFOLIA.

FESTUCA
RUBRA

FESTUCA
PRATENSIS.

×2

FESTUCA
JUNCIFOLIA

FESTUCA
ARUNDINACEA

FESTUCA
ALTISSIMA.

FESTUCA
GIGANTEA.

Plate 99 ❀ indicates plant is illustrated

GRAMINEAE (*continued*)

Lolium perenne L. **Rye Grass.** ¶Perennial; tufted, 1–2 ft; leaf width up to 6 mm.; glumes shorter than spikelets; lemmas awnless. In pastures, abundant. Flo. May–Aug. ❀.

*Lolium multiflorum Lam. **Italian Rye Grass.** *L. italicum* A. Braun. ¶Annual; 1–3 ft, soft; leaf width up to 10 mm.; glumes shorter than spikelets; lemma long awned. Cultivated and naturalized. Flo. June–Aug.

*Lolium temulentum L. **Darnel.** ¶Leaves wide; glumes equalling spikelets; lemmas broad, oval, awned or awnless. On waste places, rare.

Bromus sterilis L. **Barren Brome.** *Anisantha sterilis* (L.) Nevski. ¶Annual; leaves hairy; inflo. branches long, mostly with single wedge-shaped spikelet; lemma long awned. Roadsides and waste places, common. Flo. May–July. ❀.

Bromus madritensis L. **Madrid Brome.** *Anisantha madritensis* (L.) Nevski. ¶Annual; 1–1½ ft; lower sheaths hairy; inflo. branches erect, shorter than wedge-shaped spikelets; lemma long awned. Limestone rocks, Bristol, etc. Flo. June. ❀.

Bromus ramosus Huds. **Woodland Brome.** *Zerna ramosa* (Huds.) Lindm. ¶Perennial, 2–4 ft; leaves wide; sheaths with reflexed hairs, auricled; inflo. branches in pairs; spikelets oblong, 1 in. Woods and hedgerows. Flo. July–Aug. ❀.

Bromus erectus Huds. **Upright Brome.** *Zerna erecta* (Huds.) Gray. ¶Perennial, 2–3 ft; leaves narrow; sheaths subglabrous; branches clustered, erect; spikelets oblong. Common on calcareous soils. Flo. June–July. ❀.

Bromus mollis L. **Soft Brome.** ¶Annual, 1–2 ft; leaves and sheaths softly hairy; spikelets ½–⅞ in., hairy; lemma 8–11 mm.; palea entire. Common. Flo. May–July. ❀.

Bromus thominii Hardouin. ¶Lemma 6·5–8 mm., glabrous; grain not projecting. Common.

Bromus ferronii Mabille. ¶Lemma 6·5–7·5 mm., densely hairy; spikelets crowded. On sea cliffs, S. coasts, local.

Bromus lepidus Holmberg. **Slender Brome.** ¶Similar to *B. mollis*; leaves and lower sheaths hairy, but inflo. dense; spikelets short stalked, usually glabrous, ⅜–⅝ in., lemma 5·5–6·5 mm.; the grain projecting at the top. Hayfields, frequent. Flo. May–June.

Bromus interruptus (Hack.) Druce. **Interrupted Brome.** ¶Leaves and sheaths hairy; spikelets short, ⅜–½ in., hairy, subsessile in clusters; palea split to base. Clover fields, very rare. Flo. June–July. ❀.

Bromus racemosus L. **Smooth Brome.** ¶1–3 ft; leaves and sheaths hairy; inflo. erect; spikelets ½–⅝ in., glabrous, oblong; lemma 6·5–8 mm. In riverside meadows, England.

Bromus commutatus Schrad. **Meadow Brome.** *B. pratensis* Ehrh. ex Haffm., non Lam. ¶1–3 ft; sheaths hairy; inflo. branches longer; spikelets ¾–1 in., usually glabrous; lemma 8–11 mm. Riverside meadows and arable land. Flo. June. ❀.

The alien *B. secalinus* L. in cornfields has glabrous leaf sheaths.

This and other alien Bromes are described in Dr C. E. Hubbard Grasses.

Brachypodium sylvaticum (Huds.) Beauv. **Wood False-brome.** †Ste 1–3 ft; leaves broad, soft and flat; spikelets hairy; awn as long lemma. Hedge banks and shady places. Flo. July–Aug. ❀.

Brachypodium pinnatum (L.) Beauv. **Chalk False-brome.** ¶1–3 leaves narrow, stiff and glabrous; spikelets glabrous; awn short than lemma. On chalk and limestone, locally common. F June–Aug. ❀.

Agropyron donianum F. B. White. **Don's Twitch.** ¶Without rhizome leaves flat with slender ribs; spike rigid; lemma with short aw High mountains, Perthshire and N. Scotland, rare. Flo. Aug Sept.

Agropyron caninum (L.) Beauv. **Bearded Twitch.** ¶Without rh zomes; leaves flat with slender ribs; spike slender, curved; lemm narrowed to long awn. Hedgerows and shady places. Flo. Jun Aug. ❀.

Agropyron repens (L.) Beauv. **Creeping Twitch, Couch.** ¶Rhizom long; leaves flat with slender ribs; lemma usually awnless; ri spikelets falling entire. Weed of arable and waste land. Flo. Jun Aug. ❀.
Var. *aristatum* Baumg. ¶Has lemmas long awned.

Agropyron pungens (Pers.) Roem. & Schult. **Sea Twitch.** ¶Rhizom long; leaves with thick ribs, inrolled and pointed; sheath auricle lemmas usually awnless. Salt marshes, seaside sand and grav Flo. June–Aug. ❀.
Var. *setigerum* Dumort. ¶Lemmas awned.

Agropyron junceiforme (Á. & D. Löve) Á. & D. Löve. **Sand Twitch.** *junceum* auct. ¶Rhizomes long; leaf ribs pubescent; sheath witho auricles; spike brittle; glumes and lemmas blunt; awnless. Sai dunes. Flo. June–Aug. ❀.

The hybrid *A. junceiforme × pungens* is fairly common, also *junceiforme × repens*, chiefly in N. England.

Elymus arenarius L. **Lyme Grass.** ¶Rhizomes stout; stems 2–5 leaves glaucous, sharply pointed; spikes ½–1 ft; spikelets in pai 3–6 flo. Sand dunes on coast. Flo. June–Aug. ❀.

Hordelymus europaeus (L.) Harz. **Wood Barley.** *Hordeum europaeum* (I All. ¶Without rhizomes; 2–4 ft; sheaths mostly hairy; spikele usually in threes and 1 flo.; glumes and lemmas awned. Woods calcareous soil. Flo. June–July.

Hordeum murinum L. **Wild Barley.** ¶Annual, 1–2 ft; sheaths inflate spikelets in threes, middle 1 fertile; glumes and lemmas lo awned. Waste ground, common. Flo. May–Aug. ❀.

Hordeum marinum Huds. **Squirrel-tail Grass.** ¶Annual, 1 ft; shea inflated; spike short with long spreading awns; glume of later spikelet widened at base. Edge of salt marshes. Flo. June–July.

Hordeum secalinum Schreb. **Meadow Barley.** ¶Perennial, 1–2 sheath not inflated; spike with shorter awns; all glumes bristl like. Meadows on heavy soils. Mostly S. England. Flo. Jun July. ❀.

BROMUS
RAMOSUS.

BROMUS
COMMUTATUS.

BROMUS
ERECTUS.

AGROPYRON
PUNGENS.

AGROPYRON
JUNCEIFORME

AGROPYRON
REPENS.

AGROPYRON
CANINUM.

PARAPHOLIS
STRIGOSA

LOLIUM
PERENNE

BROMUS
MOLLIS.

BROMUS
INTERRUPTUS

BROMUS
ORITENSIS.

NARDUS
STRICTA

HORDEUM
MURINUM.

HORDEUM
MARINUM

BROMUS
STERILIS.

BRACHIPODIUM
SYLVATICUM.

BRACHIPODIUM
PINNATUM.

x 2

HORDEUM
SECALINUM

ELYMUS
ARENARIUS.

Plate 100

Gymnospermae

PINACEAE

Picea abies (L.) Karst. **Norwegian Spruce.** ¶Twigs pendulous; leaves $\frac{1}{2}-\frac{3}{4}$ in.; many on each leaf cushion. Much planted.

Larix decidua Mill. **European Larch.** ¶Leaves deciduous, $\frac{1}{2}$–1 in., bright green, many on each shoot. Much planted.

Pinus sylvestris L. **Scots Pine.** ¶Bark reddish brown, in scales; old trees flat topped; leaves 2 on each short shoot; cones about 2 in. Native, abundant in Scotland, local in England. ✿.

Pinus nigra Arnold. **Austrian Pine.** ¶Tree pyramidal; bark greyish; buds sticky; scales flat; cones about 3 in. Planted.

Pinus pinaster Ait. **Clustered Pine.** ¶Bark reddish; leaves 2; buds not sticky; scales reflexed; cones large. Planted, naturalized near Poole, Dorset.

Pinus radiata Don. *P. insignis* Dougl. ¶Has 3 leaves to each short shoot

TAXACEAE

Taxus baccata L. **Yew.** ¶Small male and female cones usually on separate plants; ovule 1, surrounded by a red fleshy cup or aril. On limestone and chalk. Flo. March–April. ✿.

CUPRESSACEAE

Juniperus communis L. **Juniper.**
Subsp. *communis*. Shrub suberect and prickly; leaves spreading, narrow, tapering to a point. Chiefly on chalk and limestone, rather local. Flo. May–June. ✿.
Subsp. *nana* Syme. *J. sibirica* Burgsd. ¶More procumbent; leaves wider and ascending, bluntly pointed. On mountains. ✿.

PINUS SYLVESTRIS.

JUNIPERUS
COMMUNIS.

YEW   TAXUS
       BACCATA.

JUNIPERUS COMMUNIS   VAR. NANA.

Index of Botanical Names

Species only are indexed. Synonyms are shown in *italics*. ✳ indicates illustration

Index of Common English Names

* indicates illustration

Ragweed see *Ambrosia artemisiifolia* pl. 45

Ragwort see *Senecio jacobaea* pl. 47 ❀

Ragwort, Broad-leaved see *Senecio fluviatilis* pl. 47

Ragwort, Great Fen see *Senecio paludosus* pl. 47 ❀

Ragwort, Hoary see *Senecio erucifolius* pl. 47 ❀

Ragwort, Marsh see *Senecio aquaticus* pl. 47

Ragwort, Oxford see *Senecio squalidus* pl. 47 ❀

Rampion, Round-headed see *Phyteuma tenerum* pl. 54 ❀

Rampion, Spiked see *Phyteuma spicatum* pl. 54 ❀

Ransoms see *Allium ursinum* pl. 85 ❀

Rape see *Brassica napus* pl. 9

Raspberry see *Rubus idaeus* pl. 28 ❀

Rat's-tail Fescue see *Vulpia myuros* pl. 98 ❀

Rattle, Red see *Pedicularis palustris* pl. 65 ❀

Ray's Knotgrass see *Polygonum oxyspermum* pl. 73 ❀

Red Bartsia see *Odontites verna* pl. 65 ❀

Red Blysmus see *Blysmus rufus* pl. 91 ❀

Red Broomrape see *Orobanche alba* pl. 66 ❀

Red Campion see *Silene dioica* pl. 14 ❀

Red Catchfly see *Lychnis viscaria* pl. 14 ❀

Red Clover see *Trifolium pratense* pl. 22 ❀

Red Currant see *Ribes rubrum* pl. 33 ❀

Red Currant, Upright see *Ribes spicatum* pl. 33 ❀

Red Fescue see *Festuca rubra* pl. 98 ❀

Red Goose-foot see *Chenopodium rubrum* pl. 72 ❀

Red Helleborine see *Cephalanthera rubra* pl. 80 ❀

Red Oak see *Quercus borealis* pl. 77

Red Poppy, Common see *Papaver rhoeas* pl. 5 ❀

Red Rattle see *Pedicularis palustris* pl. 65 ❀

Red Spurrey see *Spergularia rubra* pl. 16 ❀

Red Valerian see *Centranthus ruber* pl. 43

Red-berried Elder see *Sambucus racemosa* pl. 41

Red-veined Dock see *Rumex sanguineus* pl. 74 ❀

Reddish Pondweed see *Potamogeton alpinus* pl. 89 ❀

Reed Canary Grass see *Phalaris arundinacea* pl. 95 ❀

Reed, Common see *Phragmites australis* pl. 95

Reed Sweet Grass see *Glyceria maxima* pl. 97 ❀

Reedmace see *Typha latifolia* pl. 88 ❀

Reedmace, Narrow-leaved see *Typha angustifolia* pl. 88 ❀

Reflexed Salt-marsh Grass see *Puccinellia distans* pl. 98 ❀

Reflexed Stonecrop see *Sedum reflexum* pl. 33 ❀

Restharrow see *Ononis repens* pl. 21 ❀

Restharrow, Prickly see *Ononis spinosa* pl. 21 ❀

Restharrow, Small see *Ononis reclinata* pl. 21 ❀

Reticulate Willow see *Salix reticulata* pl. 78 ❀

Reversed Clover see *Trifolium resupinatum* pl. 23

Rhubarb, Monk's see *Rumex alpinus* pl. 74

Ribbed Melilot see *Melilotus officinalis* pl. 22 ❀

Ribwort Plantain see *Plantago lanceolata* pl. 71 ❀

Rice Grass see *Spartina × townsendii* pl. 95 ❀

River Crowfoot see *Ranunculus fluitans* pl. 2 ❀

River Water Dropwort see *Oenanthe fluviatilis* pl. 39 ❀

Rivulet Saxifrage, Alpine see *Saxifraga rivularis* pl. 32 ❀

Robert, Herb see *Geranium robertianum* pl. 19 ❀

Robert, Lesser Herb see *Geranium purpureum* pl. 19 ❀

Robin, Ragged see *Lychnis flos-cuculi* pl. 14

Rock Cinquefoil see *Potentilla rupestris* pl. 27 ❀

Rock Sea Lavender see *Limonium binervosum* pl. 56 ❀

Rock Sedge see *Carex rupestris* pl. 92 ❀

Rock Spurrey see *Spergularia rupicola* pl. 16

Rock Stonecrop see *Sedum forsteranum* pl. 33 ❀

Rock White Beam see *Sorbus rupicola* pl. 31

Rock Whitlow Grass see *Draba norvegica* pl. 8 ❀

Rock Cress, Alpine see *Arabis alpina* pl. 7 ❀

Rock-Cress, Bristol see *Arabis stricta* pl. 7 ❀

Rock-Cress, Fringed see *Arabis brownii* pl. 7

Rock-Cress, Hairy see *Arabis hirsuta* pl. 7 ❀

Rock-Cress, Mountain see *Cardaminopsis petraea* pl. 7 ❀

Rock-Cress, Tower see *Arabis turrita* pl. 7

Rocket, Annual Wall see *Diplotaxis muralis* pl. 10 ❀

Rocket, Common Yellow see *Barbarea vulgaris* pl. 7 ❀

Rocket, Dyer's see *Reseda luteola* pl. 11 ❀

Rocket, Lesser Yellow see *Barbarea stricta* pl. 7 ❀

Rocket, London see *Sisymbrium irio* pl. 8 ❀

Rocket, Sand see *Diplotaxis muralis* pl. 10

Rocket, Sea see *Cakile maritima* pl. 11 ❀

Rocket, Wall see *Diplotaxis tenuifolia* pl. 9 ❀

Rocket, White see *Diplotaxis erucoides* pl. 10

Rockrose, Common see *Helianthemum nummularium* pl. 11 ❀

Rockrose, Hoary see *Helianthemum canum* pl. 11 ❀

Rockrose, Spotted see *Tuberaria guttata* pl. 11 ❀

Rockrose, White see *Helianthemum apenninum* pl. 11 ❀

Rod, Golden see *Solidago virgaurea* pl. 44 ❀

Rod, Tall Golden see *Solidago altissima* pl. 44

Root, Coral see *Cardamine bulbifera* pl. 8 ❀

Root, Coral see *Corallorhiza trifida* pl. 80 ❀

Rose Bay see *Epilobium angustifolium* pl. 35 ❀

Rose, Burnet see *Rosa pimpinellifolia* pl. 30

Rose, Dog see *Rosa canina* pl. 30 ❀

Rose, Downy see *Rosa tomentosa* pl. 30 ❀

Rose, Guelder see *Viburnum opulus* pl. 41 ❀

Rose, Long-styled see *Rosa stylosa* pl. 30 ❀

Rose, Northern Downy see *Rosa sherardii* pl. 30 ❀

Rose of Sharon see *Hypericum calycinum* pl. 17 ❀

Rose, Short-pedicelled see *Rosa dumalis* pl. 30 ❀

Rose, Soft-leaved see *Rosa villosa* pl. 30 ❀

Rose, Trailing see *Rosa arvensis* pl. 30 ❀

Roseroot see *Rhodiola rosea* pl. 33 ❀

Rough Clover see *Trifolium scabrum* pl. 22 ❀

Rough Comfrey see *Symphytum asperum* pl. 60 ❀

Rough Dog's-tail see *Cynosurus echinatus* pl. 97

Rough Hawkbit see *Leontodon hispidus* pl. 53 ❀

Rough Hawk's-beard see *Crepis biennis* pl. 50 ❀

Rough Meadow Grass see *Poa trivialis* pl. 97 ❀

Rough-headed Poppy, Long see *Papaver argemone* pl. 5 ❀

Rough-headed Poppy, Round see *Papaver hybridum* pl. 5 ❀

Round Rough-headed Poppy see *Papaver hybridum* pl. 5 ❀

Round-fruited Rush see *Juncus compressus* pl. 86 ❀

Round-headed Club-rush see *Scirpus holoschoenus* pl. 91

Round-headed Leek see *Allium sphaerocephalon* pl. 84

Round-headed Rampion see *Phyteuma tenerum* pl. 54 ❀

Round-leaved Cranesbill see *Geranium rotundifolium* pl. 19 ❀

Round-leaved Fluellen see *Kickxia spuria* pl. 62 ❀

Round-leaved Mint see *Mentha suaveolens* pl. 67

Round-leaved Speedwell see *Veronica filiformis* pl. 63 ❀

Rowan see *Sorbus aucuparia* pl. 31 ❀

Royal, Penny see *Mentha pulegium* pl. 67 ❀

Rue, Alpine Meadow see *Thalictrum alpinum* pl. 1 ❀

Rue, Cliff Meadow see *Thalictrum minus* pl. 1 ❀

Rue, Common Meadow see *Thalictrum flavum* pl. 1 ❀

Rue, Greater Meadow see *Thalictrum majus* pl. 1 ❀

Rue-leaved Saxifrage see *Saxifraga tridactylites* pl. 32 ❀

Rue, Sand Meadow see *Thalictrum arenarium* pl. 1 ❀

Rum Cherry see *Prunus serotina* pl. 26

Rupture-wort see *Herniaria glabra* pl. 71 ❀

Rupture-wort, Ciliate see *Herniaria ciliolata* pl. 71

Rush, Alpine see *Juncus alpinoarticulatus* pl. 87

Rush, Baltic see *Juncus balticus* pl. 86 ❀

Rush, Blunt-flowered see *Juncus subnodulosus* pl. 87 ❀

Rush, Bulbous see *Juncus bulbosus* pl. 87 ❀

Rush, Capitate see *Juncus capitatus* pl. 87 ❀

Rush, Chestnut see *Juncus castaneus* pl. 87 ❀

Rush, Common see *Juncus subuliflorus* pl. 86 ❀

Rush, Flowering see *Butomus umbellatus* pl. 79 ❀